BAYBARS' SUCCESSORS

Ibn al-Furāt (d. 1405) is an understudied Mamluk historian, whose materials for the period of the later Crusades is unique. While sections of his history for the period prior to 1277 have been translated, later sections have not. His text provides both an overview and a critique of earlier historians, and supplies us with a large number of unique documents, treaties, and intimate discussions that are not to be found elsewhere. This translation provides a continuous narrative from 1277 until the assassination of al-Malik al-Ashraf in 1293, with selections from Ibn al-Furat's later entries concerning the Crusades until 1365.

David Cook is professor of religion at Rice University, U.S. His areas of specialization include early Islamic history and development, Muslim apocalyptic literature, radical Islam, historical astronomy, and Judeo-Arabic literature. His previous publications include *"The Book of Tribulations": The Syrian Muslim Apocalyptic Tradition: An Annotated Translation by Nu`aym b. Hammad al-Marwazi* (2017).

CRUSADE TEXTS IN TRANSLATION

The crusading movement, which originated in the 11th century and lasted beyond the 16th, bequeathed to its future historians a legacy of sources that are unrivalled in their range and variety. These sources document in fascinating detail the motivations and viewpoints, military efforts, and spiritual lives, of the participants in the crusades. They also narrate the internal histories of the states and societies that crusaders established or supported in the many regions where they fought. Some of these sources have been translated in the past but the vast majority have been available only in their original language. The goal of this series is to provide a wide-ranging corpus of texts, most of them translated for the first time, which will illuminate the history of the crusades and the crusader-states from every angle, including that of their principal adversaries, the Muslim powers of the Middle East.

Titles in the series include

Keagan Brewer and James H. Kane
The Conquest of the Holy Land by Ṣalāḥ al-Dīn

Graham Loud
The Chronicle of Arnold of Lübeck

Carol Sweetenham
The *Chanson des Chétifs* and *Chanson de Jérusalem*

Anne Van Arsdall and Helen Moody
The Old French Chronicle of Morea

Keagan Brewer
Prester John: The Legend and its Sources

Martin Hall and Jonathan Phillips
Caffaro, Genoa and the Twelfth-Century Crusades

BAYBARS' SUCCESSORS

Ibn al-Furāt on Qalāwūn and al-Ashraf

Translated by David Cook

Routledge
Taylor & Francis Group
LONDON AND NEW YORK

First published 2020
by Routledge
2 Park Square, Milton Park, Abingdon, Oxon OX14 4RN
605 Third Avenue, New York, NY 10017

First issued in paperback 2021

Routledge is an imprint of the Taylor & Francis Group, an informa business

Publisher's Note
The publisher has gone to great lengths to ensure the quality of this reprint but points out that some imperfections in the original copies may be apparent.

British Library Cataloguing-in-Publication Data
A catalogue record for this book is available from the British Library

Library of Congress Cataloging-in-Publication Data
Names: Ibn al-Furāt, Muḥammad ibn `Abd al-Raḥīm, 1334 or 1335-1405. | Cook, David, 1966- translator.
Title: Baybars' successors : Ibn al-Furāt on Qalāwūn and al-Ashraf / translated by David Cook.
Other titles: Tā'rīkh al-duwal wa-al-mulūk. Selections. English
Description: 1. | New York : Routledge, 2020. | Series: Crusade texts in translation | Includes bibliographical references and index. | Translated from Arabic.
Identifiers: LCCN 2019050832 (print) | LCCN 2019050833 (ebook) | ISBN 9780367223977 (hardback) | ISBN 9780429274701 (ebook)
Subjects: LCSH: Islamic Empire—History—1258-1517. | Qalāwūn, Sultan of Egypt and Syria, -1290. | Crusades—13th-15th centuries—History.
Classification: LCC D17 .I118213 2020 (print) | LCC D17 (ebook) | DDC 956/.014—dc23
LC record available at https://lccn.loc.gov/2019050832
LC ebook record available at https://lccn.loc.gov/2019050833

ISBN 13: 978-1-03-223756-5 (pbk)
ISBN 13: 978-0-367-22397-7 (hbk)

Typeset in Times New Roman
by Swales & Willis, Exeter, Devon, UK

CONTENTS

LIST OF MAPS

ACKNOWLEDGEMENTS

This translation is mostly a labor of love, as while teaching the Crusades I found I wanted to contribute to the field, even though it is not my primary study. My colleagues at Rice University, Claire Fanger and Brian Ogren, from the Religion Department, aided me with some of the medieval and Jewish connections, Maya Irish in the History Department, with the material about Aragon and Castile. Michael Decker of the University of South Florida helped me out with the Byzantine connections, and Georg Christ of the University of Manchester with the Venetian and Genoese connections. My best friend Deborah Tor of Notre Dame University read over the introduction and critiqued it. Thanks to Destiney Randolph, who also read over part of the manuscript and critiqued it, as did Jena Lopez.

My mother, Elaine Cook, read over parts of the manuscript prior to her death on January 20, 2018, and I would like to dedicate this work to her memory. She very much loved to read about the interconnections of the medieval European and Islamic worlds. May her memory be blessed.

MAPS

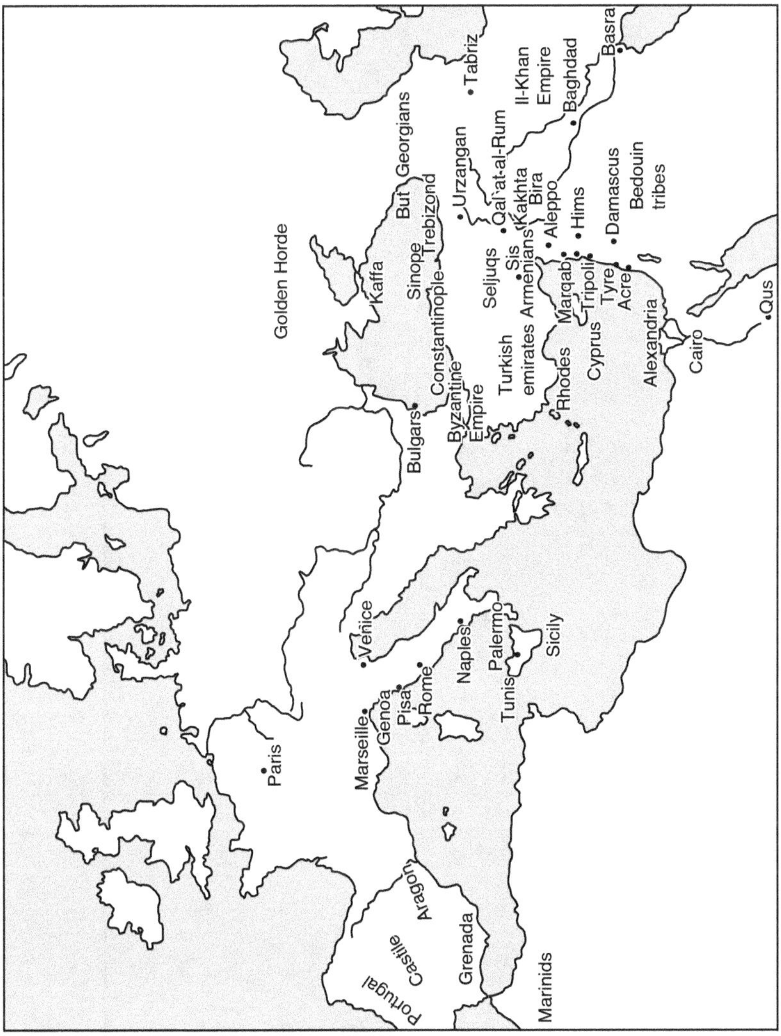

Map 1 The Mediterranean World during the time of Qalāwūn

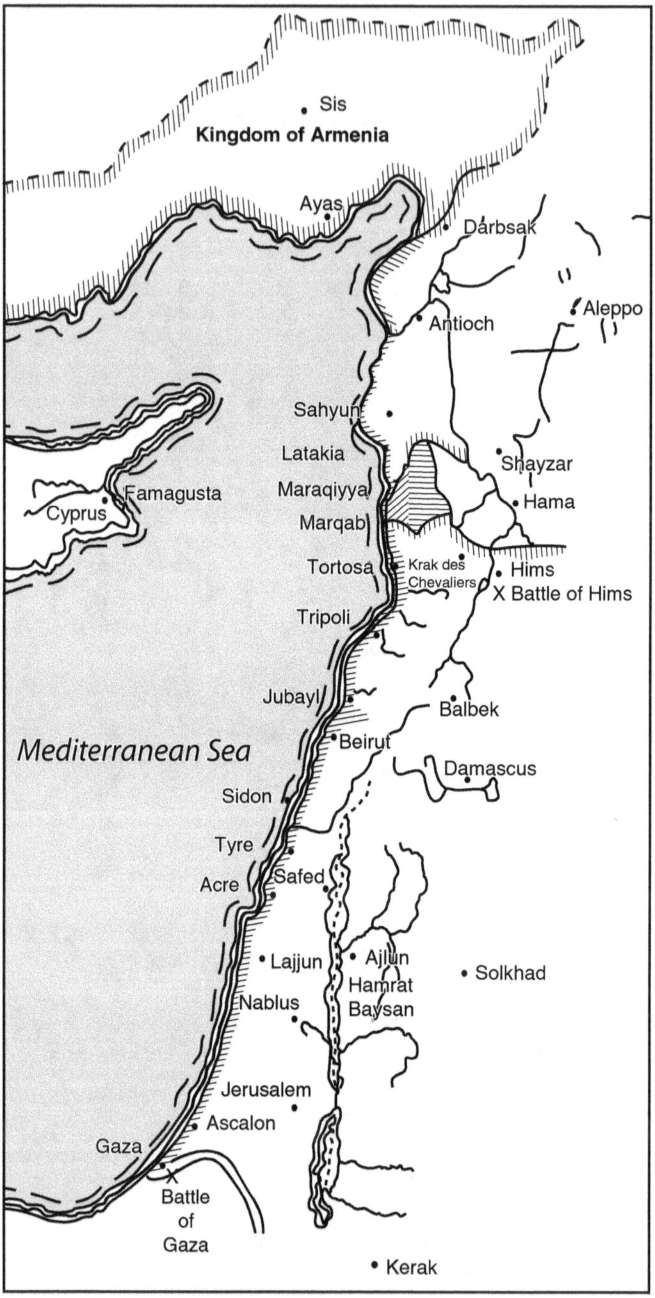

Map 2 The crusader states in the late thirteenth century

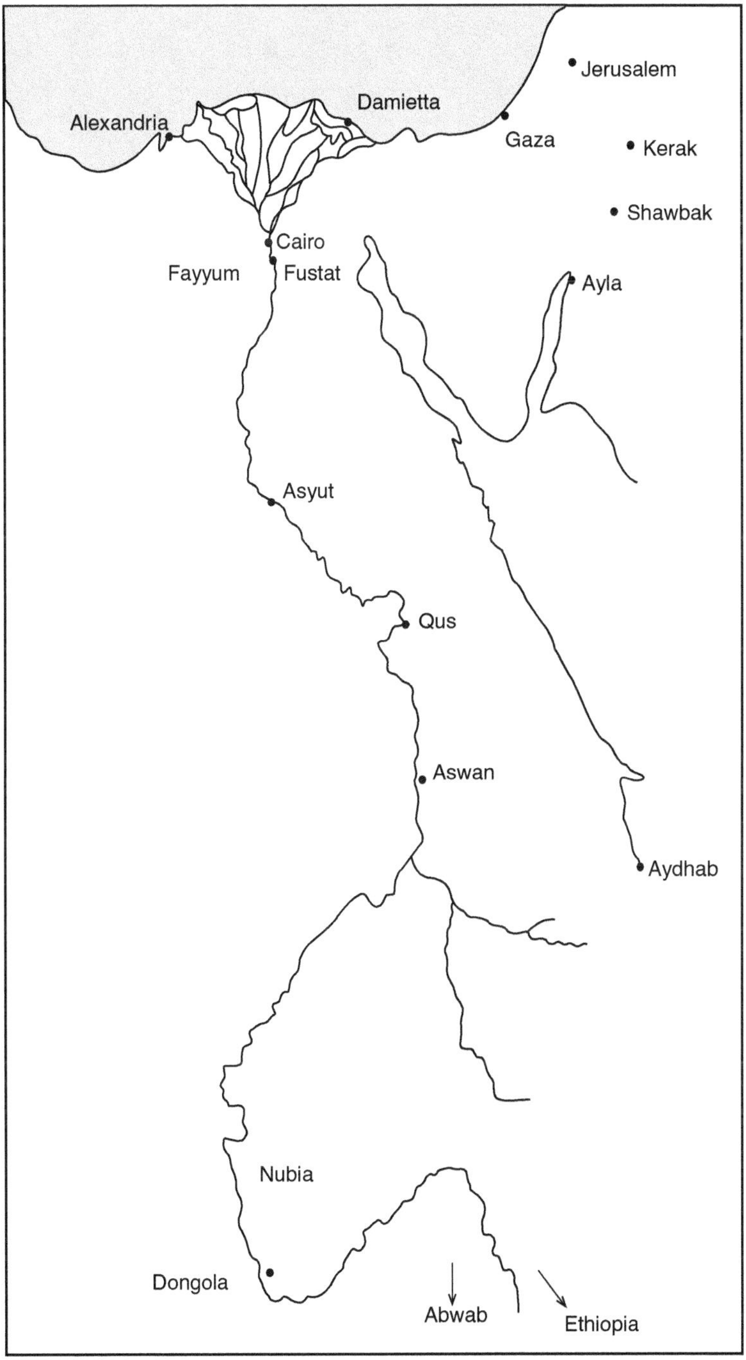

Map 3 Egypt under Qalāwūn

INTRODUCTION

Muḥammad b. `Abd al-Raḥīm Ibn al-Furāt (d. 808/1405) was one of the greatest of the Mamluk historians, but unfortunately, aside from the translation of his earlier work (till the end of Baybars' life in 676/1277),[1] he has not received the attention he so richly deserves. Biographical material about Ibn al-Furāt is sparse, but he was a secretary and a member of the Ḥanafī rite (favored by the Turkish dynasty).

Ibn al-Furāt did not even complete his major claim to fame, his *Tā'rīkh al-duwwal wa-l-mulūk*, which was intended to be a world-history. In actuality, it commences approximately with the advent of the Crusades (although some earlier sections are extant), and continues on through the reign of al-Malik al-Nāṣir (d. 742/1341). Ibn Ḥajar al-`Asqalānī states that Ibn al-Furāt completed 20 volumes of his world-history, but as he worked backwards he did not fully complete it.[2]

As this volume is a companion to *Chronicles of Qalāwūn and his son al-Ashraf Khalīl*, the general introduction to later Crusader period appearing there has not been reproduced here. Instead, this volume will focus upon later Mamluk historians covering the period of Baybars' successors: his two sons' reigns (1277–9), those of Qalāwūn (1279–90) and his second son, al-Malik al-Ashraf (1290–3).

These two rulers, Qalāwūn and al-Ashraf, were part of a succession of Mamluk sultans of Egypt and Syria (with some territories beyond) that had its roots in the failure of the Kurdish Ayyūbid dynasty in 1249–50.[3] While

[1] By M.C. Lyons and U. Lyons, *Ayyubids, Mamluks and Crusaders: Selections from the* Tā'rīkh al-duwal wa-l-mulūk *of Ibn al-Furāt* (Cambridge: Heffer, 1971), i, preface. For (limited) biographical information, see "Ibn al-Furāt" in *Encyclopedia of Islam²* (Leiden: E.J. Brill, 1960–2000) (=*EI²*) (Claude Cahen) (who merely gives the status of the manuscript without any biographical details); al-Sakhāwī, *al-Ḍaw' al-lāmi` li-ahl al-qarn al-tāsi`* (Beirut: Dār al-Jīl, 1992), viii, p. 51.

[2] Ibn Ḥajar al-`Asqalānī, *Inbā' al-ghumr fi anbā' al-`umar* (ed. Muḥammad Mu`īd Khān, Beirut: Dār al-Kutub al-`Ilmiyya, n.d. [reprint: Hyderabad ed.]), v, pp. 267–8.

[3] See R. Stephen Humphreys, *From Saladin to the Mongols* (Albany: SUNY Press, 1977), chap. 8.

there had been several strong Mamluk rulers prior to Qalāwūn who had tried to pass their ruling position on to their children—most notably the hugely successful Baybars al-Bunduqdārī (ruled 1260–77)—the former was the first to successfully found a dynasty.

Qalāwūn's success, however, was not apparent during his lifetime or even for some years after his death.[4] In general, Qalāwūn's policy was one of consolidation. Baybars, his predecessor, had conquered large swaths of territory, but the fractious nature of Mamluk succession, and the weak character of his sons who briefly succeeded him, frittered many of these conquests away. It was not until almost to the end of Qalāwūn's ten-year rule that he was finally able to rule both Egypt and Syria completely.

As Qalāwūn died suddenly in November 1290, his middle son al-Ashraf succeeded him without too much opposition. Qalāwūn had died at the height of his prestige, and while setting out to conquer the last of the Crusader cities, Acre. This latter task fell to al-Ashraf, who completed the conquest and expulsion of the Crusaders from the Syrian Levant through the summer of 1291.

Al-Ashraf, however, was nowhere near as politic as his father had been, nor had he his father's extensive military experience. Moreover, al-Ashraf tended to be a hands-off administrator, a fact of which his deputy Baydarā took advantage. Although al-Ashraf managed to conquer northwards into Anatolia, and may have been on the cusp of further conquests,[5] he alienated many of the senior emirs, who disliked his impetuousness. He was assassinated in December 1293, after a reign of only three years.

Eventually Qalāwūn's family became a dynasty through the succession of his third son, al-Malik al-Nāṣir.[6] Since the latter reigned through the first half of the fourteenth century—and Qalāwūn's further descendants continued to reign until 784/1382—the history of Qalāwūn was largely written while the family was in control. For this reason, it is useful to consider a historian such as Ibn al-Furāt who compiled his work after the family had lost its power, and was thus able to be more objective about their ancestor.

Sources

Ibn al-Furāt is interesting because he is something of an outlier with regard to the overall Mamluk historiographical tradition concerning the period of

[4] On Qalāwūn, see *EI*², s.v. "Ḳalāwūn" (Hassanein Rabie); and especially Linda Northrup, *From Slave to Sultan: The Career of al-Manṣūr Qalāwūn and the Consolidation of Mamluk Rule in Egypt and Syria 678–689 A.H./1279–1290 A.D.)* (Stuttgart: Franz Steiner, 1998).

[5] See my "Al-Ashraf Khalīl: The Uses of the Islamic-Byzantine Border in Rulership," forthcoming.

[6] See Amalia Levanoni, *A Turning Point in Mamluk History: The Third Reign of al-Nāṣir Muḥammad ibn Qalāwūn (1310–41)* (Leiden: E.J. Brill, 1995).

Qalāwūn and al-Ashraf. Other than al-Qalqashandī (d. 821/1418), whose seminal work on the art of being a Mamluk secretary contains dozens of reproduced documents, it is difficult to think of a Mamluk historian who has preserved as many documents as did Ibn al-Furāt.

Some of his sources for the period under consideration are named, the major one of whom is Ibn al-Mukarram (d. 711/1311),[7] *Dhakhīrat al-kātib* (*The Secretary's Treasure*), from which a large number of anecdotes and some documents are cited. As this work has not survived, Ibn al-Furāt's citation of it is felicitous. In general, Ibn al-Mukarram is cited anecdotally to either supplement or clarify the principal textual flow. Other named sources include `Imad al-Dīn al-Iṣbahānī (d. 597/1201), Baybars al-Manṣūrī's (d. 725/1325) major work *Zubdat al-fikra* (trans. text 4a, in *Chronicles*), with the later historians Quṭb al-Dīn al-Yūnīnī (d. 726/1326), and al-Jazarī (d. 738/1337-8).

There are a total of 31 documents in Ibn al-Furāt's history selection for this period, of which the vast majority date from the Qalāwūn's reign (28), while only three originate from al-Ashraf's reign. Of the documents cited by Ibn al-Furāt, most originate with either the Ibn `Abd al-Ẓāhir family or Ibn al-Mukarram. However, there is no evidence that Ibn al-Furāt utilized either of Ibn `Abd al-Ẓāhir's panagyrics on Qalāwūn or al-Ashraf as sources for his history on this period.

A great number of personal anecdotes are strewn throughout Ibn al-Furāt's history. Some of these are from his own teacher Zayn al-Dīn Ibn al-Bisṭāmī,[8] while others are not identified.

It is also interesting that Ibn al-Furāt does not appear himself to have been utilized by historians. Virtually none of his documents are reproduced by al-Qalqashandi, for example, nor is he cited extensively in al-Maqrīzī. We can thus speak of him as almost being an independent historian: citing from unique sources, and remaining himself largely uncited by later writers.

General content and characteristics

For the most part Ibn al-Furāt tries to give a seamless narrative that is focused heavily upon the sultan and the prominent emirs for this period. His narrative is heavily loaded with names and titles, and the material is presented in a roughly chronological form, except when there are multiple events happening at the same time.

Just as the number of documents cited in the text, the number of names in the text is impressive: a total of 320 emirs are named (although some of them may overlap), and 98 religious and bureaucratic officials are named. This

[7] Who also authored the major classical Arabic dictionary, the *Lisān al-`arab.*

[8] `Umar b. `Abd al-Raḥmān Ibn al-Bisṭāmī, d. 771/ 1369, see Ibn Ḥajar al-`Asqalānī, *Raf` al-iṣr `an quḍāt Miṣr* (ed. `Alī Muḥammad `Umar, Cairo: Khānjī, 1998), p. 292 (no. 156).

prodigious quantity of names far outstrips all of the other sources for this period, and gives us perhaps an approximation of what the Mamluk military, administrative, and religious aristocracy looked like. Of course, we should always assume that at least substantial numbers, maybe as many as half, of all the members of the elite are not named anywhere.

However, there are a number of questions concerning his history and its presentation. Although Ibn al-Furāt is a narrative history, the content of his narrative varies quite significantly. His treatment of Qalāwūn's first years is much more detailed than that of the last years, with a number of documents and treaties supplied for the former period. This plethora of documents is such that certain years, such as 684/1285, are almost nothing but a series of documents, all investitures.

One could theorize that the reason for this avalanche of documents is that Ibn al-Furāt admired Qalāwūn's administration, and sought to highlight its documents for their didactic value. One should note that, for example, the entire sequence of correspondence between Qalāwūn and the Mongol ruler Aḥmad/Tegűder is summarized without the letters being reproduced, possibly because these letters were irrelevant for Ibn al-Furāt's time.

The historical narrative for the year 686/1285 is odd. It consists of a short overview, including the capture of Marqab fortress from the Hospitallers, and then digresses into a series of six documents. Since through comparison with other historical accounts, it is possible to judge Ibn al-Furāt and assess the numerous events he chose to overlook for this year, this presentation raises questions about his priorities.

The capture of Marqab is given little prominence, which proves that Ibn al-Furāt was not using Ibn `Abd al-Ẓāhir's account of Qalāwūn. Most probably the absence of detail was because by Ibn al-Furāt's time the coastland of Syria was not of great import. But the question of why the six documents—all of them investitures: two of the Head of the Jews, one for the Head of Medicine, one for the Manṣūrī Hospital, one of the Manṣūrī College, and one of a Sufi *khanqāh* (hospice)—is a mystery. Perhaps the investitures are viewed as didactic or as examples of particularly well-written documents, but their prominence is still odd.

One aspect of Ibn al-Furāt's historical interest is his mention of the Nile inundation. This feature is quite common among Egyptian historians, both from before and after the Mamluk period. However, Ibn al-Furāt unexpectedly for the year 679/1280 gives us extensive details, on almost a daily basis, for the rise of the Nile. There does not seem to be any obvious reason for this attention to detail, reflecting from his perspective, events that occurred some 100 years in the past. The rise of the Nile does not seem to have been that significant for the attention given to it. Nor is the source for this level of detail supplied.

From the year 686/1285 there is a fairly sharp decrease in the documents Ibn al-Furāt adduces: Two letters are reproduced, and the document proclaiming

Egypt to be open to Red Sea trade (from 687/1288). Only three documents from al-Ashraf's reign are adduced.

Thus, while Ibn al-Furāt's material is extremely valuable and some of it is unique, it is surprisingly uneven for the period of Baybars' successors. Probably the inclusion of so many documents was directed at developments during his own lifetime, perhaps mismanagement at the various Manṣūrī establishments. The documents dealing with the Headship of the Jews could perhaps be seen as models for relations with religious minorities. It should be noted, however, that in all of Ibn al-Furāt's narrative there is virtually no mention of the Mamluks' relations with the largest non-Muslim minorities, the Coptic Christians (except for Ibn al-Furāt's usage of Coptic months for dating the Nile inundation).

Ibn al-Furāt and the Mamluks

Treatment of Baybars' feckless sons by Ibn al-Furāt is quite critical but abbreviated,[9] and he leaves the reader with the impression that they are unworthy of their great father. Virtually no events from the outside world, with the exception of the murder of the *pervane* (Mongol viceroy in Anatolia) in 676/1278, are noted for this two-year period.

Ibn al-Furāt's attitude towards Qalāwūn is neutral. He does not praise him excessively, and presents him—and his opponents such as Sunqur *al-ashqar*—with the titles and dignities accorded to them for the period under consideration. For example, Sunqur is referred to as al-Malik al-Kāmil, the title he took, until his defeat at Damascus in 1280, whereupon he goes back to being called Sunqur *al-ashqar*. Qalāwūn likewise during the early part of his reign is referred to as the ruler of Egypt, but then gradually receives grander titles. However, when one can compare the documents from Ibn `Abd al-Ẓāhir to those in Ibn al-Furāt it is interesting to note that the obsequiousness (such as "our master" preceding "the Sultan") usually disappears in the latter's version. The sole exception to this appears to be the circular written by Ibn `Abd al-Ẓāhir after the Battle of Ḥimṣ cited by Ibn al-Furāt.

As Ibn al-Furāt lived well past the fall of the Qalāwūn dynasty (in 784/1382), it is doubtful that he felt a strong need to present the dynasty in the most favorable light. This may be the reason why he feels free to cite a number of salacious details about the relations between Qalāwūn and al-Ashraf, as well as occasionally question the motivations behind various actions of their's, and sometimes offers interpretations of various events that are unfavorable to Qalāwūn and al-Ashraf.

Although there is a great deal of material about the religious elite in Ibn al-Furāt's text, there is little that is specifically religious about it. There are

9 Compared to al-Nuwayrī, *Nihāyat al-arab fī funūn al-adab* (eds. Najīb Muṣṭafā Fawwāz and Ḥikmat Fawwāz, Beirut: Dār al-Kutub al-`Ilmiyya, 2004), xxx, pp. 236–56.

few Qur'ānic citations, allusions, and few ritual curses of the other (such as Crusaders, although the Mongols are usually cursed), whoever they might be. Unlike either Ibn `Abd al-Ẓāhir or Baybars, Ibn al-Furāt is not given to excessive citation of poetry in his narrative (although more appears in the obituaries, which are not translated in this selection). Stylistically, Ibn al-Furāt is annalistic, but offers the reader "bridges" for long-term developments by stating that a given topic either is continued later or picks up on earlier developments.

Ibn al-Furāt on the Mongols and Crusaders

Ibn al-Furāt is primarily interested in the intricacies of Mamluk governance rather than outside affairs. He gives us little of the details appearing in earlier histories about the Mongols, the Crusaders or European kingdoms, especially those located at a distance. The one exception to this rule is the lengthy digression that Ibn al-Furāt gives about the capture of Tripoli. This digression goes into the history of the city back to the Umayyad period, but focuses upon its capture by Raymond of St. Gilles and his successors.

This digression is a bit odd, and does not appear in any of the other texts covering Qalāwūn, nor is there an analogue to this historical digression for any of the other captured Crusader cities. Perhaps this digression was to emphasize the challenge of taking Tripoli. If this is the case, it stands in marked contrast to the indifference with which Ibn al-Furāt covers Marqab—according its conquest but a paragraph.

Of the treaties detailed by Ibn `Abd al-Ẓāhir, Ibn al-Furāt cites the Treaty of Acre (for 682/1283), and the uncited treaty with the Byzantine Empire (680/1281).[10] The treaties with the Armenians, the Genoese and the Aragonese, or the correspondence with the Ethiopian emperor—all of which appear in Ibn `Abd al-Ẓāhir—are notable for their absence. Nor is there any mention of al-Ashraf's one attested treaty, that with Jaime II of Aragon (in either Jan. 1292, or Jan. 1293).

However, even the Treaty of Acre appears in an abridged form, without the place names that appear in the Ibn `Abd al-Ẓāhir version. It seems possible that the purpose for its inclusion was to demonstrate a type of treaty with the Franks/Crusaders, who were still present in Cyprus. The Armenians had vanished, and the Genoans and Aragonese were no longer, by Ibn al-Furāt's time, important factors in the eastern Mediterranean Sea. However, this interpretation does not clarify why Ibn al-Furāt nowhere mentions the Venetians or the Ethiopians, who were still very much factors for the Mamluks of the later eighth/fourteenth century.

[10] It is possible that the Byzantine treaty appeared originally in Ibn `Abd al-Ẓāhir's text, but was featured in the first section, which is lost.

Irrelevance could also explain the suppression of the correspondence between Qalāwūn and the Mongol Sultan Aḥmad/Tegűder, which appears in other chronicles, but is summarized by Ibn al-Furāt. However, if irrelevance is the key, then why the detailed treaty with the Byzantine Emperor Michael VIII Palaeologus? Surely by Ibn al-Furāt's period in the later fourteenth early fifteenth century the Byzantines were also not a major factor.

The one constant appears to have been the need for trade, whether with the Venetians, the Byzantines or the Indian Ocean states. Ibn al-Furāt in this matter does not disappoint, as he reproduces a unique safe conduct issued for commerce in the Indian Ocean, indicating the importance the Mamluks placed upon this trade. This safe conduct openly invites merchants to come to Egypt, both to trade and to settle, and offers them security. Probably Ibn al-Furāt's awareness of the grim economic realities of his time wanted to highlight such an open-door attitude.

Ibn al-Furāt is probably best seen as the last semi-independent historian for the later Crusader period. His narrative is almost independent of the other Mamluk historians, and is a very readable mixture of prose, documents, anecdotes and some poetry.

Texts and editions

Ibn al-Furāṭ, was edited by Constantine Zurayk of the American University of Beirut during the 1930s. The edition is a good one for its time, although it lacks a comparative apparatus that would be beneficial for the scholarly reader. The language is standard Arabic. In the text obituaries have been not been translated. All other materials are fully translated.

Arabic transliteration follows standard guidelines, while Mamluk and Turkish names are following either Northrup or Mazor. Common-place names are reproduced in their accepted English forms (e.g., Jerusalem, Cairo, etc.), while other names are given in their transliterated form. To facilitate comprehension I have sometimes translated the genealogies of major figures when there was interesting or useful information to be had from translation, while at other times I have left the names as is.

TEXT

Baybars al-Bunduqdārī died July 1, 1277 in Damascus. His reign had been successful, as he had expanded the Mamluk empire considerably, but his death led to a period of instability, especially in Mamluk Syria.

Mention of the sultanate of al-Malik al-Sa`īd, son of al-Malik al-Ẓāhir [=Baybars], and his ruling independently in the Egyptian homelands, while he was the fifth of the Turkish kings in the Egyptian homelands

When the decree of death befell al-Malik al-Ẓāhir Rukn al-Dīn Baybars al-Ṣāliḥī his son, al-Malik al-Sa`īd Nāṣir al-Dīn Muḥammad Berke Khān, was in the Hill Citadel in protected Cairo. The emir Badr al-Dīn Bīlīk *al-khāzindār*, the mamluk of his father, and his deputy sultan, the one who took care of his affairs, and administered his realm, was in full agreement with the emirs and the senior officials who were with him about concealing the death of al-Malik al-Ẓāhir. So they bore him to the [Damascus] Citadel, washed him, embalmed him, and then suspended him in his coffin, just as we previously explained.

Then the emir Badr al-Dīn *al-khāzindār* wrote a letter as to what had occurred, and sent it accompanied by the emir Badr al-Dīn al-Ḥamawī *al-jūkandār* to al-Malik al-Sa`īd in the Egyptian homelands. When this informative letter reached al-Malik al-Sa`īd and he understood what was in it, he demonstrated happiness, and bestowed a robe upon the one who brought the informative letter, but concealed the death of al-Malik al-Ẓāhir.

He made out that the informative letter was tidings of the Sultan's return to the Egyptian homelands, so when it was the next day, which was Saturday, the emirs rode as was their wont, to the Horse Market, while they were demonstrating grief. This was what was happening in protected Cairo.

As for what [93] was happening with the emir Badr al-Dīn *al-khāzindār*, he departed from Damascus, him and the senior emirs, the troops and the armies. Among them was a litter being borne, with a number of mamluks in its procession. They made out that the Sultan al-Ẓāhir was inside of it, but he was weak. All of that was to guard the aura [of the Sultan].

It continued like this until they arrived at the Egyptian homelands, and their arrival was in Ṣafar [July 1277] of this year. The emir Badr al-Dīn Bīlīk *al-khāzindār* entered the Hill Citadel under the Ẓāhirīd banners, while al-Malik al-Sa`īd sat in the hall of the Hill Citadel. The emir Badr al-Dīn handed over to him the treasures and the armies, and gave the investitures to him. The former waited before the latter, and continued to give him good counsel and to obey him just as he had his father (Baybars). The armies swore to him (al-Sa`īd), and the officials finished off what they had been doing.

It was said that when al-Malik al-Sa`īd sat in the hall, the rumor of his father al-Malik al-Ẓāhir's death spread, and the chamberlains cried out "O emirs! Have mercy on the Sultan al-Malik al-Ẓāhir! And pray for your Sultan al-Malik al-Sa`īd!" The uproar grew louder and the weeping, while all of them went forward and kissed the ground before al-Malik al-Sa`īd, as was usual.

They renewed their oaths to him, and the rest of the army, judges, instructors and the rest of the people swore. The emir Badr al-Dīn *al-khāzindār* was the one who swore the people, and the judges with him.

When the rule was securely in the hands of al-Malik al-Sa`īd, he continued the emir Badr al-Dīn Bīlīk *al-khāzindār* as the deputy, while the chief Bahā' al-Dīn `Alī b. Muḥammad, known as Ibn Ḥannā, was minister. Then he bestowed robes upon them, and upon the emirs, the commanders, the judges and correspondence secretaries.

The preachers in all the mosques in the Egyptian homelands delivered sermons on behalf of al-Malik al-Sa`īd on Friday 27 Ṣafar [July 30, 1277] of this year, and al-Malik al-Sa`īd prayed the prayer of the absent person[1] for his father. The post-couriers departed to Damascus with the news of al-Malik al-Ẓāhir's death, and their arrival in Damascus was on Saturday 12 Rabī` al-Awwal [August 13, 1277] of this year.

After that two emirs headed with the post to swear the emirs, army, and people in Damascus just they had sworn those in the Hill Citadel. So they were sworn, and God knows best.

Mention some of the reports about the emir Badr al-Dīn *al-khāzindār*

The emir Badr al-Dīn Bīlīk *al-khāzindār* son of `Abdallāh, known popularly as *al-khāzindār*, was a mamluk of Sultan al-Malik al-Ẓāhir, his deputy sultan, and the administrator of his realm.

He was a great emir, awe-inspiring, righteous, modest, pure of tongue, never speaking unless it was good, disliking evil people, and keeping them distant from his door, and loving good people, keeping them close, and giving

[1] Part of the standard prayer for the dead, e.g., al-Tirmidhī, *Sunan al-Tirmidhī* (Beirut: Dār al-Fikr, 1983), ii, p. 144 (no. 1029) (*bāb al-janā'iz*, 37).

charity. He had large *iqṭā`* fiefs in the Egyptian homelands and the Syrian lands, and he owned Qal`at al-Ṣubayba,[2] Bāniyās, and al-Shughr.

When al-Malik al-Ẓāhir died the emir Badr al-Dīn managed affairs deftly, and did in Syria what we have previously explained, until when he arrived in the Egyptian homelands, [94] giving command over to al-Malik al-Sa`īd.

Historians have differed as to the reason for his death. Some of them have said that when the emir Badr al-Dīn Bīlīk arrived in Egypt, he became sick shortly after his arrival, and his sickness did not last long, but he died almost immediately. It is said that he was assassinated out of envy for his position. It is said that the chief Bahā' al-Dīn Ibn Ḥannā whispered to the Sultan al-Malik al-Sa`īd that the emir Badr al-Dīn Bīlīk *al-khāzindār* desired the rule for himself, so he was believed because of his status, and because of the army's loyalty to him.

So when he passed him giving the peace greeting as usual, and sat behind a curtain, bringing out to him a *hunāb* (drink)[3] in which there was sugar and poisoned lemon, so he took the *hunāb* and drank from it, departed, lasted two days, and then died.

It is said that he drank two droughts from it, and because of their constant harassing of him because of drink, he imagine things (*takhayyala*), and threw the *hunāb* from his hand, headed towards his house, then became unwell throughout his body, the sickness became worse, and he got colic (*qūlanj*).

His doctor was `Imād al-Dīn al-Nāblusī; it is said that 3000 dinars came to him. But it is also said that this was by way of favors, on the condition that he stay quiet, and not say anything. It is said that he took the gold, and goofed off until Badr al-Dīn had died after a few days.

He died in the Hill Citadel on 6 Rabī` al-Awwal [August 7, 1277] of this year, and so there was only the space of a month and nine days between him and his master [Baybars]. The judge Muḥyī al-Dīn Ibn `Abd al-Ẓāhir, author of *Life of al-Malik al-Ẓāhir*, and the judge Nāṣir al-Dīn Shāfi` b. `Alī, grandson of Ibn `Abd al-Ẓāhir, say the following approximately:

> The first part of the bad administration was that the mamluks of al-Malik al-Sa`īd caused him to imagine wrongly about the emir Badr al-Dīn *al-khāzindār*, his father's deputy, and this suspicion spread to al-Malik al-Sa`īd's mother as well. It is said that al-Malik al-Sa`īd and his mother

[2] Now Nimrod's Castle, above Baniyas.

[3] Unidentified: al-Qalqashandī, *Ṣubḥ al-a`shā fī ṣinā`at al-inshā'* (ed. Muḥammad Ḥusayn Shams al-Dīn, Beirut: Dār al-Kutub al-`Ilmiyya, 2012), iv, p. 63 "It was usual that every emir, senior or junior, had a color specific to him, between *hunāb*, to inky, to linen color, to French (*faransīsa*) …" However, al-Nuwayrī, xxx, p. 237 says "a *hunāb* with a drink in it was brought out for him," which sounds more like a cup. Perhaps one could posit a composite word such as Arabic *inā'* + Farsi *āb*, meaning "water-contianer," but why it would add a *ha'* is a mystery.

gave Badr al-Dīn *al-khāzindār* to drink, so then he died, may God have mercy upon him, after his arrival in the Egyptian homelands by a period of days.

There were less than two months between him and his master, and God knows best which of these it was. He had a remarkable funeral procession, and was buried in his mausoleum in al-Qarāfa al-Ṣughrā (the Lesser). His death split hearts and caused eyes to weep. The people were grieved and saddened to lose him, and the mourning over him lasted three days and three nights.

When he died, the position of al-Malik al-Sa`īd became unsteady, and signs of collapse in the Ẓāhirī dynasty began to appear,[4] just as we will mention if God wishes.

Mention of the emir Sayf al-Dīn Kūndak being appointed as deputy sultan in the Egyptian homelands

When the emir Badr al-Dīn Bīlīk *al-khāzindār* died just as we previously explained, al-Malik al-Sa`īd appointed the emir Sayf al-Dīn Kūndak in his place as deputy sultan in the Egyptian homelands, in spite of his being a youth. Then al-Malik al-Sa`īd rode [95] leading the (army) groups, just as his father did, on Wednesday 16 Rabī` al-Awwal [August 17, 1277].

He was among the emirs, the commanders, and the notables, while there were robes upon them, going to under the Red Mountain (*al-jabal al-aḥmar*), which was the first of his ridings after the arrival of the army, and their swearing, but he did not transverse the city. This was a day to remember, and the people were very happy to see him. His age at that time was 19 years.

It was said that al-Malik al-Sa`īd [appointed][5] the emir Shams al-Dīn Aqsunqur al-Fāriqānī al-Ẓāhirī, majordomo, to be the deputy sultan after the death of the emir Badr al-Dīn *al-khāzindār*. He was resolute, so when the talk established him as the deputy, he bound groups to himself who al-Malik al-Ẓāhir had compelled to swear an oath of personal allegiance.

Among these was Shams al-Dīn Aqūsh, Quṭlījā al-Rūmī, Sayf al-Dīn Qilīj al-Baghdādī, Sayf al-Dīn Bījū[6] al-Baghdādī, `Izz al-Dīn Mughān *amīr shikār* (in charge of bird-hunting), Sayf al-Dīn Baktimur *al-silaḥdār* and their like.

Then the Khāṣakiyya and the mamluks of the emir Badr al-Dīn *al-khāzindār*, because of their dislike of the emir Shams al-Dīn al-Fāriqānī, conspired to

---

[4] Although it is not marked this is Ibn al-Furāt's opinion, not that of the Ibn `Abd al-Ẓāhir family.

[5] Added from the margins.

[6] Vocalized as Bījaq in al-`Aynī, *`Iqd al-jumān fī tā'rīkh ahl al-zamān* (ed. Muḥammad Muḥammad Amīn, Cairo: al-Ha'ya al-Miṣriyya, 1988), ii, p. 186.

detain him, and they made this look good to al-Malik al-Sa`īd. They sought aid from the emir Sayf al-Dīn Kūndak *al-sāqī* (cup-bearer) against him, as al-Malik al-Sa`īd had promoted him and magnified him, because he would be with him in the office, so they detained the emir Shams al-Dīn al-Fāriqānī while he was sitting at the Summit Gate (*bāb al-qulla*), and dragged him inside {the Citadel}.

They went overboard in beating him, harming him, and plucked out his beard. He was imprisoned in the Citadel, but did not last more than a few days. He then died and was given to his retainers so that they would bury him.

Al-Malik al-Sa`īd appointed Shams al-Dīn Sunqur al-Alfī al-Muẓaffarī as deputy sultan. He had a close companion (*khushdāsh*) named `Alam al-Dīn Sanjar al-Ḥamawī, who was known as Abū Khurṣ, and he appointed him to the Safedan districts, which he augmented from the Sultan's private lands (*al-khāṣṣ al-sulṭānī*) over his *iqṭā`* fief.

The Khāṣakiyya, however, were not happy with him because he was not from the Ẓāhiriyya [regiment] so they whispered to al-Malik al-Sa`īd against him, claiming that he intended to establish the Muẓaffariyya [regiment]. He did not feel safe from his machinations, so he removed him shortly thereafter.

The emir Sayf al-Dīn Kūndak *al-sāqī* was appointed to be the deputy sultan, so the emir Sayf al-Dīn Qalāwūn al-Alfī tended to his side. At that time there was a personality from the Khāṣakiyya sultanic mamluks called Lājīn al-Zaynī who came to dominate al-Malik al-Sa`īd in the rest of his circumstances, so most of the Khāṣakiyya joined together with him, and he took their [96] *iqṭā`* fiefs, contracting to them the revenues (*ṣilāt*). Every time an *iqṭā`* fief came free at the Army Chancellery, he would seize it for the one chosen, and have the deputy contend for it.

Hearts became angered between the two of them, and scorpions of evil crawled among them, as each of them planned mischief against his fellow. The emir Kūndak attached to himself a group, and the senior emirs began to support him so there developed a faction loyal to him. This division was cause for corruption and destruction.

Mention of the changing opinions of the emirs against al-Malik al-Sa`īd, and their opposition to him

On 17 Ṣafar [July 20, 1277] of this year al-Malik al-Sa`īd detained the emir Jūdī al-Qaymarī al-Kurdī, and the organization of al-Malik al-Sa`īd did not continue more than a few days after his appointment. Then al-Shabība (the youth) carried out its deeds, and whims, tended towards him, while opinions changed towards him.[7]

[7] According to al-`Aynī, *`Iqd*, ii, p. 191 Alfonso X (of Castile) sent gifts to Baybars, which were delivered to al-Malik al-Sa`īd; perhaps this is the same embassy that is mentioned in Ibn `Abd al-Ẓāhir as being received by Qalāwūn.

He was left alone with the fresh-faced mamluks, and dispersed wealth upon them, mandating that their junior mamluks be promoted, favoring them, listening to their opinions. His age was nearly 20, but he was tending towards his cronies and those of his age, so they made it seem good to him to exile the senior emirs.

This, while among them were the Ṣāliḥiyya Najmiyya emirs, who were the close coterie (*khushdāshiyya*) of his father, who had correct opinions, and penetrating resolution. Among them were the likes of the emir Sayf al-Dīn Qalāwūn al-Alfī, the emir Shams al-Dīn Sunqur *al-ashqar*, the emir `Alam al-Dīn al-Ḥalabī, the emir Badr al-Dīn Baysarā, and others among the emirs of 1000.

Because of their being embedded [in his supporters] he [Qalawun] could not achieve stability nor know who they were. A king could not do without their advice, as they were indispensable. They were those who had not particularly liked his father al-Malik Ẓāhir's rule over them, as they had been muttering, "He is king over us, while we have a better right to the rule than he!" Therefore, he began to play with their fates, causing them trials, striking close to home. He detained some of them, and then freed them the same day, and thus hatred was sown in their hearts.

On Friday 25 Rabī` al-Awwal [August 26, 1277] of this year al-Malik al-Sa`īd detained the emir Shams al-Dīn Sunqur *al-ashqar* and the emir Badr al-Dīn Baysarā al-Shamsī also, and imprisoned the both of them in the Hill Citadel for 20 days. The two of them were the two right arms of his father, so when he detained the both of them, his maternal uncle the emir Badr al-Dīn [Ibn] Berke Khān entered the presence of al-Malik al-Sa`īd's mother, and said to her

> Your son has screwed up the administration, and detained the likes of these senior emirs. It would be best (*al-maṣlaḥa*) if you return him to the straight path, because if not, his administration will fall apart, and his days will be short.

When the words of his maternal uncle reached al-Malik al-Sa`īd, he made haste to detain him as well, and imprison him, so his mother rose up against him, upbraided him, and continued to nag him until he released the aforementioned emirs, bestowed [97] robes upon them, and returned them to their previous positions.

But enmity had taken hold of their hearts, and the rest of the emirs began to worry privately about how he had treated the emir Badr al-Dīn *al-khāzindār* previously, and their imaginations went wild because they were aware of the service that Badr al-Dīn *al-khāzindār* had rendered to al-Malik al-Sa`īd. He had watched over the treasuries, and the armies, and been true in his obedience until the time when he had handed over to him. He swore to him, while the armies swore, but this did not save him, while he [al-Sa`īd] did what he did with those senior emirs.

Therefore, they gathered together, and took counsel between themselves. Some of them said, "We will depart for Syria, and leave this land for him," while others said "We will ascend to the Citadel and discuss this with him." They gathered at night, which was Thursday night, and ascended the next morning to the Citadel leading their mamluks, retainers, troops, and followers, and those emirs and armies that had joined with them.

The hall was filled with them, as well as the castle's open space, and they sent to him saying, "You have corrupted the minds, harming the senior emirs, so either you back down from that, or you will have an issue with us." He was easy with them, justifying himself to them, sending them honorary gifts, but they refused to be bought off.

Then a peace was established, and he swore to them that he intended no evil towards them. The emir Badr al-Dīn al-Aydimurī took his oath, whereupon the emirs were satisfied with that, and departed, so the matter stayed as it was.

Mention of the building of a college and a mausoleum in protected Damascus for al-Malik al-Ẓāhir's burial

During this year al-Malik al-Sa`īd wrote to the deputy sultan in protected Damascus to bury his father al-Malik al-Ẓāhir inside the walls of Damascus. So the emir `Izz al-Dīn Aydimur, the deputy of Damascus, purchased al-`Aqīqī House, inside the Gate of Release (*bāb al-faraj*) towards Damascus, opposite al-`Ādiliyya College, for 60,000 dirhams, without its outer decorations.

He built a college for the Shāfi`ites and the Ḥanafites, constructing a cupola there. Under it, he placed a tombstone. Construction began on Wednesday 5 Jumādā al-Awwal [October 4, 1277] while it was completed during Jumādā al-Ākhira [November 1277] of this year.

When the construction of the cupola was completed, al-Malik al-Sa`īd sent the emir `Alam al-Dīn Sanjar known as Abū Khurṣ and *al-ṭawāshī* Ṣafī al-Dīn Jawhar al-Hindī {the left-handed, to bury his father}.[8] The both of them arrived in Damascus on 3 Rajab [November 30, 1277] of this year. When it was Friday night 5 Rajab [December 2, 1277] of this year, which was the Night of Desires[9] in Damascus, they bore al-Malik al-Ẓāhir from the Citadel at night on men's necks, bringing him down into Damascus, while [98] they prayed over him in the Damascus Friday Mosque courtyard.

Then they brought him down into his grave, in the cupola, which had been prepared for burying him at midnight in the presence of the deputy of

8 From the margins.

9 *Laylat al-raghā'ib*, see Ibn Ḥajar al-Haytamī, *al-Iḍāḥ wa-l-bayān li-mā jā' fi laylatay al-raghā'ib wa-l-nisf min Sha`bān* (Damascus: Dār al-Hudā, 2010), p. 57f.

Damascus the emir `Izz al-Dīn Aydimur. The Chief Judge `Izz al-Dīn Ibn al-Ṣā'igh entombed him, while the Qur'ān readers were assigned from the following day.

The judge Muḥyī al-Dīn Ibn `Abd al-Ẓāhir and his grandson the judge Nāṣir al-Dīn Shāfi` both said the following approximately:

> The martyr continued to be in the Damascus Citadel until his al-Malik al-Sa`īd had purchased al-`Aqīqī House, and built a mausoleum for him in it, spending abundantly upon it.

He cried out: This is his tombstone, between my eyes, so visit from every deep ravine,
How not, when from my bitter (`aqīq) tears they buried him from it in al-`Aqīq House!

He was borne to his mausoleum on the Night of Desires during Rajab in the aforementioned year, and the emir `Izz al-Dīn, deputy sultan in Syria/Damascus and `Izz al-Dīn *al-dawādār*, and Ṣafī al-Dīn Jawhar al-Hindī were in charge of it.

They took him out upon the necks, with the light from his face guiding them as they went,
They were happy with him at night to conceal his grave, but the night and the moons do not conceal him,
They hasten voices and glances towards the earth and his graves by his being borne,
However, he is a support (rukn) they have placed upon it in order to stabilize this abode.

The judge `Izz al-Dīn al-Shāfi`ī entombed him:

He finished while he had hands by which this world was made right from the ills of time,
Therefore, he went while angels crowded around his mausoleum in lines,
Just like his clamor, since containers of musk with seals broken are within him.[10]

This renewed the sorrow for him, so it was as if the world was distressed by their disdaining compassion. This was while they fulfilled the due of commemoration, as it was the time for everyone to fulfill their dues.[11]

---

[10] Musk is a sign of being a martyr in Islam.
[11] Rhymed in Arabic.

{On 16 Dhū al-Qa`da [April 10, 1278] of this year `Izz al-Dīn Ibn Shaddād, trustee of al-Malik al-Sa`īd, established the college charitable endowment with his permission and at his direction, which he developed in Damascus. He endowed all of the village of al-Ṣarmān, from the farmlands of Bāniyās, and two portions of Bayt Rāma in the Jordan Valley, its cultivated lands, and other [lands].}[12]

Om Wednesday 18 Dhū al-Qa`da [April 12, 1278] of this year al-Malik al-Sa`īd removed the Chief Judge [99] Muḥyī al-Dīn Ibn `Ayn al-Dawla al-Iskandarī from the Cairene judiciary, and that of Upper Egypt. He added that to the Chief Judge Taqī al-Dīn Ibn Razīn, and thus amalgamated the judiciary of Cairo, Old Cairo, and Upper and Lower Egypt for him.

Some of the historians said that al-Malik al-Sa`īd appointed Chief Judge Shams al-Dīn Aḥmad Ibn Khallikān to the Damascus judiciary in place of the Chief Judge `Izz al-Dīn Ibn al-Ṣā'igh al-Shāfi`ī, and that Chief Judge Ibn Khallikān traveled from Cairo on 27 Dhū al-Ḥijja [May 21, 1278] of this year heading for Syria.

In it the Nile was plentiful over the lands of the Egyptian homelands, so prices went down until wheat was sold at five dirhams for an *ardabb* [=198 lit.], while barley was at three dirhams, and the rest of the grains at two dirhams, and God knows best.

Mention of the killing of the *pervane*, the administrator of [Seljuq] Rūm's army

When Abagha, the king of the Tatars, arrived at the Horde, he took counsel with his emirs with regard to the *pervane*.[13] A group counseled to kill him, while a group counseled to leave him alive and to return him to the lands to watch over them, to repair their disorder, and to levy their taxes.

He preferred to let him live, so let him go from supervision so that he could return to his lands. However, the Mongols' emirs' wives, such as the wives of Tūqū and Tidāwan and others, who had been killed in the battle,[14] heard that Abagha had issued the written order to let the *pervane* go. Therefore, they congregated all at the time of later afternoon, and rose weeping, crying and mourning.

Abagha heard their clamor, so he said, "What is that?" It was said to him "The ladies (*khawātīn*) heard that the Khan will let the *pervane* go free, and that he is ready to go back to his lands, so they are crying and yowling."

---

[12] Added from the margins.

[13] Mu'īn al-Dīn Sulaymān *pervane*, founder of a line of viziers that effectively ruled the Seljuq Rūm state.

[14] Referring to the *pervane*'s double allegiance during Baybars' invasion of Anatolia in 1277, when many Mongols were killed.

It is said that the ladies gathered and stood before Abagha, and cried, screamed, ripping their garments before him, and saying "This one helped kill our men! It is necessary to kill him!" He put them off for days while they were urging him every day to kill him.

When he was tired of putting them off, he ordered one of the emirs who was deployed in the lands of Sīs, whose name was Kūkjī Bahādur, to take with him 200 horsemen and to take the *pervane* to a place he specified, and then kill him there. So Kūkjī summoned the *pervane*, saying to him "Abagha wants for you to ride, and has issued an order to you that you and your followers ride with him."

So he (Kūkjī) rode, together with 32 people—but it is said 30 people—from his mamluks and retainers. He headed out with him (the *pervane*), so he took him towards the wasteland, whereupon the *pervane* knew that there was no good that was going to come of this. The Tatars then surrounded him and his followers, while his followers shielded [him]. He asked whether they could not let him off [100] until he had ritually washed himself, and prayed, so they did.

When he finished with his prayer, they killed him, and those with him, while Abagha was camped in a place of al-Aṭā`. When the *pervane*'s mamluks heard of his killing, `Alam al-Dīn Sanjar al-Barwānī and Badr al-Dīn Baktūt *amīr ākhūr* Bakbār assembled his coterie (*khushdāshiyya*) in their camp. They conspired, strung their bows, breaking out their arrows in front of them, saying, "We will only die as fighters!"

Those who had been deputized to kill them had to consult with Abagha, so when they consulted him about this, he thought well of them for this, and said "These are useful mamluks, so leave them alone, allow them to go free, and give them permission to return to their lands," so they returned.

The killing of the *pervane* was at the end of Ṣafar [August 2, 1277] of the year [6]76, and God knows best. [101]

[*Obituaries*]

Mention of events of 677 [1278–9]

On 6 Muḥarram [May 30, 1278] of this year the Chief Judge `Izz al-Dīn Ibn al-Ṣā'igh ceased rendering judgment because of the appointment of Chief Judge Shams al-Dīn Aḥmad Ibn Khallikān.

On 23 Muḥarram [June 16, 1278] the emir `Izz al-Dīn Aydimur, deputy sultan in Damascus, went out. All of the procession and the emirs went out with him to greet and the people of the town departed also to meet the Chief Judge Shams al-Dīn Ibn Khallikān. The townspeople also were going out to meet him, so then some of them arrived in Gaza.

It is said that some of them went to the first part of the sands, to Qaṭīyā, and he then entered Damascus. His day of entrance was a day to remember. People were very happy with his appointment, and his return to Damascus. He sat at al-`Ādiliyya [College] and rendered judgment. His investiture was read on 24 Muḥarram [June 17, 1278] and the Qur'ān readers recited. Every single one of the literati (*udabā'*) praised him with the best epic poems. His removal had been for seven years.

Sa`d al-Dīn al-Fāriqī declaimed:

Syria tasted seven years of barrenness; the morning of his emigration [was] a good end,
When I visited him in the land of Egypt, I extended from your two hands a Nile!

The shaykh Nūr al-Dīn Ibn Muṣ`ab declaimed:

I thought Syria's inhabitants to be united; every single one was satisfied,
Good had been had after evil, so the time was open-fisted without being closed,
They replaced grief with joy, from half of eternity in debt,
A judge coming and a judge going pleased them after lengthy gloom,
So all are thankful and complaining about the future and the past. [115]

When it had been a year since the death of al-Malik al-Ẓāhir Rukn al-Dīn Baybars al-Ṣāliḥī, there was a commemoration for him between al-Qarāfatayn in a place called al-Andalus. Repasts were made for the Qur'ān reciters, and the jurisprudents, and they were distributed among the small mosques. Tents were pitched, and the people were present according to their classes. A number of final poems were recited, so the judge Muḥyī al-Dīn Ibn `Abd al-Ẓāhir, the author of *al-Malik al-Ẓāhir's Life*, arranged on this:

O people! Listen to a word garbed in truth,
Commemoration of the Sultan will never be forgotten in neither west nor east,
Was not his funeral commemoration made in al-Andalus?

After this a number of eulogies were made for him in the Imam al-Shāfi`ī College, may God be pleased with him, and the Mosque of Aḥmad b. Ṭūlūn, the Ẓāhirī Mosque at al-Ḥusayniyya, the Ẓāhirī College, the Ṣāliḥiyya Najmiyya College, the Kāmiliyya School for *ḥadīth* [which is] *bayn al-qaṣrayn* inside protected Cairo, the Ṣalāḥiyya hospice (*khānqāh*) at the open area of the Festival Gate, and the Ḥākimī Mosque inside protected Cairo.

The *takārara* (repeaters) and the poor (Sufis) made a table (*khawān*), at which a number of the righteous attended. Concerning that it is said:

So, thanks! You have received (meal) times of piety, as good and piety have been combined,
Favors are common in it, edibles follow it; every dweller is full, then again full,

As for the passing of the Sultan, his generosity did not pass, but his piety has been left behind,
A (noble) youth living in his good (deeds) after his death, just as after a flood its course is verdant,
Our intercessory prayer on his behalf continues for the length of our lives, and God hears this prayer.

On 10 Jumādā al-Awwal [September 29, 1278] of this year al-Malik al-Sa`īd son of al-Malik al-Ẓāhir appointed Chief Judge Ṣadr al-Dīn Sulaymān al-Ḥanafī to the chief judiciary in protected Damascus in place of Chief Judge Majd al-Dīn Ibn al-`Adīm al-Ḥanafī after his death on 16 Rabī` al-Ākhir [September 6, 1278] of this year, just as is mentioned in his biography.

He had been appointed after Chief Judge Shams al-Dīn, and Chief Judge Ṣadr al-Dīn continued in the Damascus judiciary for a short while, less than three months. Then he died, and it is said that he rendered judgment for four months, and then died.

On the evening of Monday 29 Ramaḍān [February 13, 1279] of this year al-Malik al-Sa`īd [116] appointed Chief Judge Ḥusām al-Dīn al-Ḥasan b. Aḥmad b. al-Ḥasan al-Rāzī, the judge of [Seljuq] Rūm, who arrived accompanying al-Malik al-Ẓāhir Baybars from Caesarea [Qaysariyya], to be the Ḥanafī Chief Judge in protected Damascus in place of Chief Judge Ṣadr al-Dīn.

Mention of al-Malik al-Sa`īd's going to Syria

During Dhū al-Qa`da [March–April 1279] of this year the Sultan al-Malik al-Sa`īd son of al-Malik al-Ẓāhir traveled from protected Cairo to Syria to look around the realms. He arrived in Damascus on 5 Dhū al-Ḥijja [April 19, 1279] of this year and it was massively decorated for him. He was accompanied by al-Malik al-Mas`ūd Najm al-Dīn al-Khiḍr son of al-Malik al-Ẓāhir and his mother. He ascended to the Damascus Citadel, and stayed in his father's palace. The inhabitants of Damascus were overjoyed at this, and he prayed the Festival prayer in the Green Square, and performed the Festival in the Citadel.

During the first tenth of Dhū al-Ḥijja [April 14–24, 1279] the Najībiyya College opened close to the Nūriyya College in protected Damascus. Chief Judge Shams al-Dīn Aḥmad Ibn Khallikān took up the duties of instruction during this (year). The Najībiyya Hospice (*khānqāh*) also opened, which is on the southern upper overhang. The reason for the delay of the opening of the two places was the death of their endower, and the consequent watch over his inheritance and endowments. Therefore, when the time came, they were opened.

When the death of the chief Bahā' al-Dīn Ibn Ḥannā reached al-Malik al-Sa`īd, while he was in Damascus, at the end of Dhū al-Qa`da [April 13, 1279] of this year, just as is mentioned in his biography, he placed his son the chief Tāj al-Dīn Ibn Ḥannā under guard, taking his signature for 100,000 dinars. He then sent him with the post to Egypt so that the remainder of 300,000 dinars would be extracted from him, from his brother Zayn al-Dīn, and from their paternal cousin ʿIzz al-Dīn. All of that which was connected to them would be guarded.

During this year al-Malik al-Saʿīd appointed Chief Judge Burhān al-Dīn al-Sinjārī to the ministry in the Egyptian homelands in place of the chief Bahā' al-Dīn Ibn Ḥannā. [117]

On 26 Dhū al-Ḥijja [May 10, 1279] al-Malik al-Saʿīd sat in the Justice House in Damascus, and abolished the [levy] that had been levied upon the inhabitants of Damascus concerning their gardens for each year, so the people were very happy about that. Their prayers and their love for him redoubled because that (levy) had ruined the gardens' and properties' owners such that a number of them wished that someone would seize what they owned.

Al-Malik al-Saʿīd was in Damascus enjoying life to the utmost, him and his Khāṣakiyya, his mamluks, and his servants, while the inhabitants of Damascus were happy, pleased with him because of the injustices that he had removed which had built up during the time of his father.

Mention of preparing the armies for the land of Sīs

When al-Malik al-Saʿīd son of al-Malik al-Ẓāhir was established in Damascus, while the Egyptian and Syrian armies in his service, accompanied by the emir Badr al-Dīn Baysarā and the emir Sayf al-Dīn al-Alfī al-Ṣāliḥī and the al-Shabāb mamluks, listening to their opinions, and following their lead, their opinions necessitated getting rid of the senior emirs.

They then advised al-Malik al-Saʿīd to send the armies accompanied by the Ṣāliḥiyya emirs to Sīs, and the land of [Seljuq] Rūm. A detachment was sent accompanied by the emir Sayf al-Dīn Qalāwūn; another was accompanied by the emir Badr al-Dīn Baysarā. He sent the treasury with them in order to pay the armies, so they departed going on a road upon which there were no difficulties or hardships, but they were on the lookout, just as God Most High said "you (might) think them all (united) together, but their hearts are divided."[15]

The malice towards al-Malik al-Saʿīd was hidden in the depths, but the hatred had sprouted shoots from it. Obliviously, al-Malik al-Saʿīd remained in Damascus, and what happened we will mention if God Most High wishes.

Some of the historians mentioned that the entrance of that army into Sīs, its departure from it, its return to Damascus, and its dissension from al-Malik al-Saʿīd, together with its return to the region of the Egyptian homelands

[15] Q59:14. All Qur'ānic translations are from A.J. Droge, *The Qur'ān: A New Annotated Translation* (Sheffield: Equinox, 2013).

were during this year. However, it is obvious that these things all happened during [6]78, just as we will mention there, if God Most High wishes.

[*Obituaries*]

Mention of events of 678 [1279–80]

On 2 Muḥarram [May 15, 1279] of this year al-Malik al-Saʿīd son of al-Malik al-Ẓāhir Rukn al-Dīn Baybars al-Ṣāliḥī appointed the chief Fatḥ al-Dīn Ibn al-Qayṣarānī al-Ḥalabī to the Damascus ministry, while the heads rode in his formal procession, and he took up his duties that very day.

Mention of the raid by the armies against Sīs and the dissension that occurred between the Khāṣakiyya and the Ṣāliḥiyya emirs, and the return of the armies from Sīs, their being forbidden to enter Damascus, and their going to the Egyptian homelands

We had previously mentioned that al-Malik al-Saʿīd son of al-Malik al-Ẓāhir Rukn al-Dīn Baybars al-Ṣāliḥī sent the armies to Sīs. This was at the suggestion of the Khāṣakiyya emirs, and the purpose of it was to gain control of the administration to the detriment of the Ṣāliḥiyya emirs. When they were distant, the Khāṣakiyya decided together with al-Malik al-Saʿīd to detain the Ṣāliḥiyya emirs at their return from Sīs, to seize their *iqṭāʿ* fiefs, and to assign the livelihood of each of them to a single person among them.

This was when the emir Sayf al-Dīn Kūndak went up to them, while al-Malik al-Saʿīd continued in his seclusion, engrossed in his pleasures. The Khāṣakiyya had complete control over his thought-process, and he began to give them inordinate freedoms, in opposition to what his father used to do.

Then there was a contest between the Khāṣakiyya mamluks who were bound to al-Malik al-Saʿīd and the emir Sayf al-Dīn Kūndak, the senior deputy sultan. The reason for this was that al-Malik al-Saʿīd bestowed upon one of his mamluks 1000 dinars, but the emir Sayf al-Dīn Kūndak forbade this [...][16] [141] and they came to the emir Kūndak, and forced him to hear the words [...] and they entered into al-Malik al-Saʿīd, and said "Remove him," but he refused.

So this reached the emir Sayf al-Dīn Kūndak [...] *al-qaṭīfa* to expect the armies in Sīs. Al-Malik al-Saʿīd was unable to repair the relations between the Khāṣakiyya and the emir Kūndak, or to make a peace between them. This was what was happening with these.

As for what was happening with the armies that traveled to Sīs, when they entered Sīs they rushed in, and destroyed the inviolate place of the unbelievers. The emir Badr al-Dīn Baysarā went to Qalʿat al-Rūm, and the emirs

[16] Two lines marked out.

leading the armies returned. They mustered at the field to enter Damascus with the vanguard (*aṭlāb*) and the arrangement as usual.

The emir Sayf al-Dīn Kūndak greeted them, and informed them of private discussions, after having sent to them secretly, informing them of what the Khāṣakiyya had conspired against them. They kept this to themselves, but when they arrived, the emir Kūndak greeted them. He then informed them face-to-face, and swore to them, so they believed him. This was because he was the deputy sultan, and privy to the realm's secrets. They verified this so they would know of al-Malik al-Saʿīd's acting upon it. This was on top of his favoring the youth, and those of his previous actions that we have explained.

So they stayed on the field, and did not enter Damascus, but brought the codices [of the Qur'ān], and used them to swear each other. They sent to al-Malik al-Saʿīd saying that

> We will stay on the field, and that the emir Sayf al-Dīn Kūndak delivered many complaints to us from Lājīn al-Zaynī. It is necessary for us to uncover the truth, so the Sultan should send to us, so that we can hear the words of both of them. [...][17]

So they presented him to him, whereupon he presented him to the emirs, then they waited upon the letters he had with him, verifying his evil opinion of them. They then passed immediately and camped upon al-Jasūra towards the direction of Dārayā. Matters then came to light which indicated dissension, that the Sultan had [142] gone way too far in his bad opinion and administration, so he had just about used up all his chances.

He hastened to send to the emir Shams al-Dīn Sunqur *al-ashqar* and the emir Shams al-Dīn Sunqur al-Tikrītī, the majordomo, to the likes of them, seeking for them to return, begging from them all types of submission, while exerting him [al-Saʿīd] to do what would make them satisfied. They conducted negotiations with them concerning that, but nothing was accomplished other than mutual irritation.

They said, "There is no way to bring him back," so the two aforementioned emirs returned to him, and repeated the words to him. Anxiety cloaked him, and the messengers went back and forth between the two sides. They proposed to him that the Khāṣakiyya be exiled, but he was not able to do that, and in fact was incapable.

His mother said to him "I am going to betake myself to them; perhaps they will pay attention to a woman." Therefore, he gave permission to her for that, so she departed to them, while Sunqur *al-ashqar* went with her to seek to satisfy them, and to hammer out a peace between them. When she

[17] Two and a half lines marked out.

arrived, she entered into their presence, but they did not pay attention to her, or notice her presence. Therefore, she abandoned what she had been hoping.

It is said that they when the Sultan's mother met with them, and discussed the peace with them, they laid down conditions, and promised her that they would enter Damascus the very next day. Then when she returned to her son, she informed him of that, the Khāṣakiyya prevented him from fulfilling the conditions.

When this reached the emirs, they assembled the armies, and headed for the Egyptian homelands. What happened next we will mention, if God Most High wishes.

The author of *Ordering the Ways Concerning the History of Caliphs and Kings*,[18] said approximately the following:

> As for al-Malik al-Saʿīd, he delivered to the emirs what distracted them and made things unclear for them. It changed their intentions, so the courtiers of al-Malik al-Saʿīd began to correspond with the emir Sayf al-Dīn and those with him concerning al-Malik al-Saʿīd's treachery, of which they were aware, and his intention to arrest them, put them to death, and cause them to perish.
>
> Al-Malik al-Saʿīd also transmitted concerning them that which made his intentions murky, caused hidden hatreds to arise, and corrupted good intentions. The affairs of al-Malik al-Saʿīd reached the outer regions, and the emir Sayf al-Dīn Qalāwūn returned leading those armies which were with him from Sīs while al-Malik al-Saʿīd was in Damascus.
>
> The emirs demurred from entering Damascus fearing treachery, and al-Malik al-Saʿīd's mother departed to the suburbs of Damascus, and discussed with the emirs. However, they did not relent because of her words, nor did they place trust in her guidance. They were unconvinced to entrust themselves to promises. Their spirits lifted, with them preparing to prevent (Damascus) being handed over, and to defend it.

It is said that the emir Sayf [al-Dīn] [143] Kūndak, the deputy sultan, was staying in the Hill Citadel in the Egyptian homelands during the period of al-Malik al-Saʿīd's absence in Syria. What happened next we will mention, if God Most High wishes.

---

18 ʿAbd al-Raḥmān b. ʿAlī al-Bisṭāmī, *Naẓm al-sulūk fī tāʾrīkh al-khulafāʾ wa-l-mulūk.*

Al-Malik al-Sa`īd's going to the Egyptian homelands, his removal, and his being given Kerak as a realm

The judge Muḥyī al-Dīn [Ibn] `Abd al-Ẓāhir, the composer of *Life of al-Malik al-Ẓāhir*, during Muḥarram [May 1279] of that year eulogized al-Malik al-Ẓāhir Rukn al-Dīn Baybars al-Ṣāliḥī with an epic poem, and sent it to Damascus to have it declaimed over the tomb of al-Malik al-Ẓāhir at […][19] which is:

[*Ibn `Abd al-Ẓāhir's poem eulogizing Baybars*] [144]

The epic poem was declaimed in the presence of al-Malik al-Sa`īd, and when the emirs arrived from Sīs. What we previously mentioned occurred, while they went in the direction of the Egyptian homelands, al-Malik al-Sa`īd departed from Damascus […] those who stayed behind with him of […][20] and Syria, while they headed behind the armies, and followed them to the Egyptian homelands camp by camp.

He sent his mother and his treasuries to Kerak, and went, arriving at Bilbays at the middle of the month of Rabī` al-Ākhir [August 1279] of this year. He found the emir Sayf al-Dīn Qalāwūn had preceded him leading the armies to Cairo, but the army which was with him accompanying him from Syria began to plot against him.

So he returned from Bilbays to Damascus. The deputy in Damascus was the emir `Izz al-Dīn Aydimur, so when al-Malik al-Sa`īd arrived in Damascus, he found the armies surrounded in the Citadel, so [`Alam al-Dīn] al-Ḥalabī took him along, went through the vanguard, and brought him into the Citadel. Few people were killed, but the army closed it up tightly, and then rushed it. This was what was happening there.

As for what was happening with the emirs who had arrived in Cairo, the emir Sayf al-Dīn Kūndak did not allow them to enter Cairo, nor to ascend to the Citadel, as he was staying there during the absence of al-Malik al-Sa`īd in Syria according to those historians who tell of this.

Therefore, the armies pitched tents beneath the Hill Citadel, [145] and the emirs gathered, considering whom they should make Sultan. Every one of them was saying to his fellows "None but so-and-so is appropriate for the sultanate!" During the course of this, al-Malik al-Sa`īd arrived accompanied by 100 people from his mamluks, and ascended to the Citadel.

The emir Sayf al-Dīn Kūndak opened for him, and he ascended the al-Rafraf Tower over the stable, and began to shout "O emirs, return to your loyalty, and I will only do what you say." However, none of them assented to this, and they brought out letters from him which he wrote seeking a number of the Fidāwiyya [Assassins] to kill them. They surrounded the Citadel, besieging it, and climbing up to the Citadel, detaining al-Malik al-Sa`īd, and removing him from the rule.

---

[19] Unclear, the editor proposes that the missing words are "when al-Malik al-Sa`īd visited it."

[20] A line unreadable other than those words prior to the note.

They wrote concerning his removal a letter [...] on 7 Rabī' al-Ākhir [August 17, 1279] of this year, and specified Kerak for him. Additionally his brother Najm al-Dīn would be given Shawbak fortress, and then they sent al-Malik al-Sa'īd to Kerak.

The period of his reign from the time of his father al-Malik al-Ẓāhir's death until he was removed was two years, two months and some days. He arrived in Kerak and it was handed over to him on 25 Jumādā al-Awwal [October 3, 1279] of this year.

It was said that the arrival of the emirs to protected Cairo was during the month of Rabī' al-Awwal [July 1279] of this year, and they camped beneath the Red Mountain, and made contact with the emirs who were staying inside the Hill Citadel. In it there were the emir 'Izz al-Dīn Aybak *al-afram* al-Ṣāliḥī, *amīr jāndār* (guard), the emir 'Alā' al-Dīn Iqṭawān *al-sāqī*, and the emir Sayf al-Dīn Balabān al-Zarīqī, majordomo.

They approached the governor of Cairo about locking the gates, so they were locked. Lower walls had been built beyond most of them. The emirs then sent back and forth with them about the opening of the gates, so that the armies could enter going to their homes and see their children. The emirs 'Izz al-Dīn *al-afram* and 'Alā' al-Dīn Iqṭawān *al-sāqī* both descended to meet with the emirs, so the emir Sayf al-Dīn Kūndak anticipated them.

With the emirs were those who proceeded to detain the two of them, and also al-Ḥusām Lājīn al-Berke-khānī, as he had been in their company. He ordered the city gates to be opened, and the people [= soldiers] entered their homes, and the emirs bore the three detained emirs to the house of the emir Sayf al-Dīn Qalāwūn who was known as the emir Fakhr al-Dīn 'Uthmān. That was what was happening with these.

As for the emir Sayf al-Dīn Balabān al-Zarīqī, he shut and locked the Citadel gates, so the emirs proceeded to besiege it. The emirs conspiring against al-Malik al-Sa'īd who did this deed were: Baysarā al-Shamsī, Qalāwūn al-Alfī, Aytimish al-Sa'dī, Aydakīn *al-bunduqdār*, Baktāsh al-Najmī, Kushtaghdī al-Shamsī, [146] Balabān al-Hārūnī, Bajkā al-'Alā'ī, Baybars al-Rashīdī, Kundughdī al-Wazīrī, Ya'qūbā al-Shahrazūrī, Aytamish b. Aṭlas Khān, Baydghān al-Ruknī, Baktūt son of *atābak*, Kundughdī *amīr majlis* (in charge of medical issues), Baktūt Jarmak, Baybars Ṭuqṣū, Kūndak, Aybak al-Ḥamawī, Sunqur al-Alfī, Sunqur Jāh al-Ẓāhirī, Qalanjaq al-Ẓāhirī, Sāṭilmish, Qajqār al-Ḥamawī, and those others of the junior emirs, and commanders of the free-born troops (*ḥalqa*), the notables of the *mafārida*,[21] and the Baḥriyya [regiment], and they surrounded the Citadel. This was what was happening with those.

---

[21] Lit. "separate ones." An unclear category; Northrup, *Slave to Sultan* notes, p. 198, note 275 the possibility that "the *mafārida* may have been a corps of non-commissioned mamluks who perhaps received *jāmakiyya* (salaries) rather than *iqṭā*'s." Its position in this group implies, as she states, some level of status.

As for what was happening with al-Malik al-Sa`īd, when the emirs traveled from Syria, and headed towards the Egyptian homelands, just as we previously explained, he gathered the remnants of the Egyptian and Syrian armies, and summoned the Bedouins, paying them in Damascus. He then departed from it heading towards the Egyptian homelands, but when he arrived in Gaza, most of the Bedouin slipped away.

When he arrived in Bilbays the Syrian army plotted against him, and returned in the company of the emir `Izz al-Dīn Aydimur, deputy of Syria, and only a small number of his mamluks remained together with al-Malik al-Sa`īd.

Among them were Lājīn al-Zaynī, Mughulṭāy al-Dimashqī, Mughulṭāy al-Jākī, Sunqur al-Tikrītī, Aydughdī al-Ḥarrānī, Albakī *al-sāqī*, Baktūt al-Ḥimṣī, Ṣalāḥ al-Dīn Yūsuf son of Berke Khān, and similar sorts of people, while among the senior emirs, the emir Shams al-Dīn Sunqur *al-ashqar*, especially.

When al-Malik al-Sa`īd arrived close to al-Maṭariyya, the emir Shams al-Dīn Sunqur *al-ashqar* separated himself and abandoned him, but did not draw near to the emirs, but merely stayed in place until that which we will mention if God Most High wishes happened.

The Sultan's trip from Bilbays reached the emirs who were besieging the Citadel. It was said to them that he will come up from behind the Red Mountain, so they rode and headed towards the mountain, to interdict between him and the Citadel. This was a day in which the fog was piled up, and the sun's face was concealed. People could not see even their companions who were walking alongside of them.

This was a mercy from God Most High to the Muslims, so al-Malik al-Sa`īd was concealed from the eyes, and was saved from the hand of fate. He ascended the Citadel, so his mamluks opened the gate for him. When the gloom was removed, it was said to the emirs that the Sultan has ascended to the Citadel, so they tightened the siege.

Then al-Malik al-Sa`īd went through the Citadel. Lājīn al-Zaynī quarreled with Sayf al-Dīn al-Zarīqī, speaking to him rudely. So he became enraged, and descended from the Citadel to the emirs to plot against al-Malik al-Sa`īd. The mamluks one by one [147] slipped out after him.

The emir `Alam al-Dīn Sanjar al-Ḥalabī was imprisoned in the Citadel, so al-Malik al-Sa`īd brought him out, and asked his advice as to what to do. He said, "I think that you should give me those mamluks who are with you, so I can descend leading them against them, to attack them, and disperse them!" However, he did not permit him to do that, so the matter dragged on for a week, while the Citadel was under siege.

The Caliph sent to them saying, "What (*aysh*) is your goal?" They said to him "That he remove himself from the rule, so we can give him Kerak." They swore to him about this, so he assented to them about this. The Commander of the Believers, the judges and the notaries were then presented, and he descended from the Citadel, and testified for himself [...][22] he and the emir `Alā al-Dīn Aydakīn al-Fakhrī. He then handed over the wealth, treasures and stores that were in it.

His departure from the realm was during the month of Rabī` al-Awwal [July 1279] of this year, and the period of his rule had been two years, a month, and some days. Injustice [Court] continued during his days under the Chief Bahā' al-Dīn. However, the prices during his days were low, with wheat being sold six dirhams for an *ardabb* and at five, just as it was previously, while barley and beans were four dirhams and three for an *ardabb*. Praise be to the Doer of what He wills! Who judges in His dominion according to what He wishes, God suffices for us, and He is the best trustee.

Mention of the sultanate of al-Malik al-`Ādil Salāmish son of al-Malik al-Ẓāhir Rukn al-Dīn Baybars al-Ṣāliḥī, who was the sixth of the Turkish kings in the Egyptian homelands

When al-Malik al-Sa`īd was removed, and they sent him to Kerak just as we previously explained, the emirs gathered and offered the sultanate to the emir Sayf al-Dīn Qalāwūn al-Alfī, but he refused, saying "I did not overthrow al-Malik al-Sa`īd out of greediness for the dominion, nor desirous of the sultanate. The priority is that the rule should not pass from al-Malik al-Ẓāhir's progeny."

This was among the signs of Qalāwūn's good administration and his political sense, because it quieted the Ẓāhirī uprising. These regiments were most of the army in the Egyptian homelands, and also the citadels were in the hands of al-Malik [al-Sa`īd's] deputies [...][23] [148] when they had all agreed on this, they brought out Badr al-Dīn Salāmish, who was seven years old plus some months. It is said just seven years, but it is also said ten years.

They swore to him and to the *atābak* Sayf al-Dīn Qalāwūn. Badr al-Dīn Salāmish took the regnal name of al-Malik al-`Ādil, and he was the sixth of the Turkish kings in the Egyptian homelands. The mint was struck in his name, and the preachers mentioned his name and the name of the *atābak* in the sermons. This was during the month of Rabī` al-Ākhir [August 1279] but it was said during Rabī` al-Awwal [July 1279] of this year, and it is said other than that.

The *atābak* Sayf al-Dīn Qalāwūn administered the realm, and the emirs dealt with him as if he was the Sultan. The emir `Izz al-Dīn *al-afram* was established as the deputy sultan in the Egyptian homelands, while the chief Burhān al-Dīn al-Sinjārī continued in the ministry in the Egyptian homelands. This was what was happening with these in the Egyptian homelands.

[22] Four lines marked out.

[23] Six lines marked out.

As for what was happening with the army of Syria that had plotted against al-Malik al-Sa`īd, and the army that had been dispatched to Aleppo, the plotting Syrian army returned to Syria, and entered Damascus on Sunday the beginning of Jumādā al-Awwal [September. 9, 1279] of this year, accompanied by the emir `Izz al-Dīn Aydimur.

The army dispatched to Aleppo, when it heard the report of dissension that had happened between the emir and al-Malik al-Sa`īd they returned, arriving in Damascus during the month of Rabī` al-Ākhir [August 1279]. They were the emir `Izz al-Dīn Izdimur al-`Alā'ī, the emir [Shams al-Dīn] Qarāsunqur al-Mu`izzī, the emir Jamāl al-Dīn Aqūsh al-Shamsī, the emir Sayf al-Dīn Barlaghū, and others. The army was approximately 2000 horsemen.

When the plotting army arrived at [...] the aforementioned emirs conspired with the emir Jamāl al-Dīn Aqūsh al-Shamsī that they would appoint him commander over them, and that they would detain the emir `Izz al-Dīn Aydimur al-Ẓāhirī, the deputy of Damascus, because he plotted against his majordomo.

So when the emir `Izz al-Dīn and the army arrived accompanying him in Damascus as we previously explained, the emirs who were in Damascus went out to meet them. But when they arrived at the Jābiya Gate, the emir Jamāl al-Dīn Aqūsh al-Shamsī said [149] to the emir `Izz al-Dīn Aydimur [al-Ẓāhirī] "Enter with me to my house, and there will be no cause for division (*fitna*) [between the Muslims] until the written command of the Sultan arrives."

However, he only allowed him to pass, so he stayed with the emir Jamāl al-Dīn Aqūsh until after the [late afternoon] prayer. Then Izdimur al-`Alā'ī and Rukn al-Dīn *al-jāliq* came, so they took `Izz al-Dīn Aydimur al-Ẓāhirī and ascended with him to the Damascus Citadel, handing him over to its deputy the emir `Alam al-Dīn Sanjar al-Dawādārī.

During the middle tenth of Jumādā al-Ulā[24] [September 18–28, 1279] the emir Jamāl al-Dīn Bākhilī and the emir Shams al-Dīn Sunqur Jāh al-Kunjī arrived in Damascus from the Egyptian homelands. He came with a copy of the oath upon which the situation in the Egyptian homelands had been resolved with al-Malik al-Sa`īd's removal, and the emplacement of his brother Badr al-Dīn Salāmish together with the *atābak*. Therefore, the people swore in Damascus, just as they had sworn in the Egyptian homelands.

During Jumādā al-Awwal al-Malik al-`Ādil Badr al-Dīn Salāmish and the *atābak* Sayf al-Dīn Qalāwūn appointed Chief Judge Ṣadr al-Dīn `Umar son of Chief Judge Tāj al-Dīn `Abd al-Wahhāb son of the daughter of al-A`zz al-Shāfi`ī to the chief judiciary in the Egyptian homelands. This was after the removal of Chief Judge Taqī al-Dīn Ibn Razīn al-Shāfi`ī. Chief Judge Mu`izz al-Dīn al-Ḥanafī was also removed that month. Chief Judge Nafīs al-Dīn

[24] One could speculate that Ibn al-Furāt's shifting gender change between Jumādā al-Ulā and Jumādā al-Awwal reflects a change in his sources, but otherwise he gives no sign of that.

Ibn Shukr al-Mālikī was also removed, then the both of them were returned (to their positions). A Ḥanbalī justice was assigned at the time of their being returned, who was Chief Judge `Izz al-Dīn `Umar b. `Abdallāh b. `Umar b. `Iwaḍ al-Maqdisī a-Ḥanbalī.

Al-Malik al-`Ādil Badr al-Dīn Salāmish and the *atābak* Sayf al-Dīn Qalāwūn appointed Shams al-Dīn Sunqur *al-ashqar* to be deputy sultan in protected Damascus, so he went to it, arriving on Wednesday 8 Jumādā al-Ākhira [October 16, 1279] of that year. It is said the 2nd [October 10, 1279]. With him were a number of the emirs, and armies, and the people rejoiced to greet him. They interacted with him almost like one of the kings.

He stayed in the House of Felicity, and ordered [150] the emir `Alam al-Dīn al-Duwaydārī to settle in the Citadel, to take up the duties of supervision and administration of affairs. The investiture of the emir Shams al-Dīn Sunqur was read in the preaching enclosure on Friday with the notables attending, although he himself did not attend its reading.

Al-Malik al-`Ādil Badr al-Dīn Salāmish and the *atābak* Sayf al-Dīn Qalāwūn appointed the emir Jamāl al-Dīn Aqūsh al-Shamsī to be the deputy sultan in protected Aleppo, and the emir Sayf al-Dīn Qalāwūn began to detain the Ẓāhirī emirs and to requite the Ẓāhirī mamluks for their evil actions.

He detained their most notable figures, and sent them to the border regions in prisons. He did not continue punishing them, but taught them a lesson by imprisonment, then released them one by one and some of them returned to their emirship after his sultanate.

The emir Badr al-Dīn Baysarā engrossed himself in pleasure and drink, so the *atābak* Qalāwūn alone was involved in ruling the realm, so began to administer the affairs, disperse money, lead the realms, and grant favors, give, and take the hearts of the emirs. Whoever was forgotten from the Baḥriyya Ṣāliḥiyya would present himself so he would give *iqṭā`* fiefs to them, command them. He sent some of them to the Syrian lands, making them deputies in the castles, or asking concerning their progeny.

Among them there were those who were connected with manufacturing, and professions. He would order them to gather their dispersed ones, so among them were those assigned to the Baḥriyya. Among them were also those he assigned allowances and returned them to the shade of felicity.

How accurate was the one who said:

When it is difficult, the noble remember those who associate with them in hard times.

Mention of the removal of al-Malik al-`Ādil Badr al-Dīn Salāmish from the sultanate and his going to Kerak

Just as we had previously mentioned the *atābak* Sayf al-Dīn Qalāwūn, when the sultanate was offered to him, he refused and indicated instead that one of al-Malik al-Ẓāhir Rukn al-Dīn Baybars al-Ṣāliḥī's children should be nominated. Then the emirs agreed altogether upon the sultanate of al-Malik al-`Ādil Badr al-Dīn Salāmish son of al-Malik al-Ẓāhir Rukn al-Dīn Baybars al-Ṣāliḥī, and made him sultan, as we have mentioned previously.

They also made the *atābak* Sayf al-Dīn Qalāwūn the commander of the armies, so he began to prepare himself the ways, and administer the realms. When his goal was accomplished, he met together with the emirs on 20 Rajab [678] [November 26, 1279], though it is said on 21 Rajab [November 27]. They mentioned the youthful age of al-Malik al-`Ādil and that the sultanate should not devolve upon anyone other than a mature man, so they agreed to remove him, and they removed him and sent him to Kerak with his brother al-Malik al-Sa`īd.

The duration of al-Malik al-`Ādil Badr [152] al-Dīn Salāmish's rule was three months and some days. Then the emirs met together in the Egyptian homelands and took counsel about removing al-`Ādil Badr al-Dīn Salāmish, so they removed him just as we previously mentioned. Then they agreed that al-Malik al-Manṣūr Sayf al-Dīn Qalāwūn would be sultan, and appointed him.

He sat upon the sultanic throne (*takht*) in the Hill Citadel, outside of protected Cairo on Sunday 20 Rajab [November 26, 1279] in the year 678, this year. It was said [also] that he sat on Tuesday 21 Rajab [November 27, 1279].[25] The emirs and commanders rendered their oaths—all as usual with the oath-taking. He took the royal name of al-Malik al-Manṣūr, and ordered that al-Ṣāliḥī be written at the beginnings of his proclamations, rescripts and correspondence.[26] This was inscribed to the right of the *basmala* and underneath it slightly on every written record.

The post-couriers departed together with letters concerning the sultanate of al-Malik al-Manṣūr in the Egyptian homelands that had been agreed upon. He was the seventh of those Turkish rulers who had ruled the Egyptian homelands. The text of the oath of allegiance was taken to Damascus and to the other realms.

Cairo and Old Cairo, with their suburbs, were decorated, and the Citadel. The preachers mentioned him [in the sermons] in Cairo, Old Cairo, and the rest of the Egyptian homelands at the end of Rajab, the aforementioned month.

One of the first things that al-Malik al-Manṣūr took upon himself at the time of his sitting upon the sultanic throne was the cancelation of the *dawlaba* [tax] in the Egyptian homelands, as it had ruined the populace. All complaints, events and the Christians' *muqarrar* [assessment] were also cancelled This was after the assessment had been established over the Christians for a

---

25 There is some mistake with the dating here.

26 Both Northrup, pp. 67–8; and Lewicka, *Šāfi` Ibn `Alī's Biography of the Mamluk Sultan Qalāwūn* (Warsaw: Academic Publishing House, 2000) pp. 42–3 describe his relationship to al-Ṣāliḥ; additionally one should note that Qalāwūn's eldest son was named after this benefactor.

period of 12 years. Prices were reduced, and the emirs, army and populace were gladdened by this.

On 26 Rajab [December 2, 1279], and it was said on the 28th, the post-courier arrived in Damascus [and some of al-Malik al-Manṣūr's mamluks drove] the post horses from the sultanic Stable Gate outside the Hill Citadel towards protected Damascus during two days and seven hours. This [record] was never known previously. The people swore to the Sultan Sayf al-Dīn Qalāwūn in all of Syria, and he was mentioned in the sermons from the Damascene pulpits on Friday 2 Sha`bān in the year [6]78 [December 8, 1279].

Damascus was decorated beautifully, in a way never previously seen, and the decoration stayed up seven days. The Sultan al-Malik al-Manṣūr freed the emir `Izz al-Dīn Aybak *al-afram* al-Ṣāliḥī, and assigned him to the deputy sultanate in the Egyptian homelands. He confirmed the chief Burhān al-Dīn al-Sinjārī in the ministry in the Egyptian homelands, and al-Malik al-Manṣūr began to sit in the Justice Court every Monday and Thursday. [153]

On Saturday 3 Sha`bān [December 9, 1279] the Sultan al-Malik al-Manṣūr Sayf al-Dīn Qalāwūn rode with the sultanic insignia and kingly pomp, which was his first riding. He transversed Cairo, which was decorated, and it was a day worth remembering.

He wrote to the emir Shams al-Dīn Sunqur *al-ashqar* informing him of his riding, and the letter was in the handwriting of the judge Tāj al-Dīn Ibn al-Athīr. In it:

> May his days continue giving affection, seeing the victory of which you have wished, witnessing signs of triumph that will expand security for the servants, increasing praise for the dominion bestowed, which is rightfully ours.
>
> The mamluk guides from the subtleties of his information, his allowance of intercessory prayers, and the gnostic benefits God has established for him, together with the graces given to him which fill his hands, such that they take his breath away, and cause his mouth to open in praise at their beneficence. They increase the happiness of his soul, and its joyfulness, while both increase the bonds of felicity.
>
> They also adorn the bonds with pearls in this marriage consummation, strengthening thereby the powers of resolution, and making enemies consider carefully, lest they almost be dragged by the tails of defeat. Hope will be sent upon attainment by victory, and thereby manifest the affection, which were pens intending to enumerate it, they would be unable to do so.
>
> This is that the noble knowledge has encompassed in a manner that has affirmed the people's entrance into the mamluk's [Qalāwūn] obedience, and all accept him.

> When it was Saturday 3 Sha`bān year 678 [December 9, 1279] the mamluk [Qalāwūn] rode with the sultanic insignia, and the king's pomp, with the emirs, commanders, *mafārida*, and victorious armies. He arrived at the highest councils according to the customs of service, the purity of intention, and good obedience—all indicating the orderliness of the matter, and the completeness of the bond of victory.
>
> When we had completed the [public] riding, having given the supporters a promise of felicity written down, we returned to the protected Hill Citadel. This was while hands were raised to us in righteous prayers of intercession, hearts were gathered as one in love of our ruling days, hopes were pinned upon justice and its continuity, glances rose to support our lights' rising, and we mandated the circumstances of sacral warfare (*jihād*) from this point.
>
> We swore to all, if God Most High willed, to conquer the lands in the enemies' hands, and that no time would be wasted until we twisted the reins and pointed the spear-tips. We will manifest the hidden intentions in the souls, and we have commanded that protected Damascus be decorated and that the tidings be sent through the lands—encompassing both settled and nomad. May God Most High make His times open with congratulations, and thank those who hasten to aid, which will continue to be praised at every way-stop, if God Most High wills.

During Sha`bān of this year [December 1279] al-Malik al-Manṣūr ordered for the judge Taqī al-Dīn Tawba al-Tikrītī, the treasury purchaser (*bayyi` al-khizāna*) in protected Damascus, to be relieved of this office, and that extras to which he had committed himself should be forgiven him, [154] and entrusted to him the inspectorate of the Treasury in protected Damascus.

During this year, the people fasted the first part of Ramaḍān on Friday in discord and severe doubt.

On Sunday 3 Ramaḍān [January 7, 1280] the Sultan al-Malik al-Manṣūr Qalāwūn appointed the emir Jamāl al-Dīn Aqush al-Sharīfī, *amīr jāndār* (guard), to the deputy sultanate over al-Ṣalt and al-Balqā'.[27]

On Friday 8 Ramaḍān [January 12, 1280] he freed the chief Fatḥ al-Dīn Ibn al-Qaysarānī, the minister for protected Syria, and he descended to his home, after having been held under a written proclamation (*tarsīm*) in the Citadel's victorious mosque for over 30 days.

On Sunday 10 Ramaḍān [January 14, 1280] al-Malik al-Manṣūr appointed the emir Fakhr al-Dīn al-Ṭunbā al-Zaydī to the deputy sultanate of al-Quṣayr, which is close to Antioch. On that day al-Malik al-Manṣūr appointed the emir

[27] Central Jordan.

`Alam al-Dīn Sanjar al-Manṣūrī to the noble deputy sultanate of protected Balaṭinus, and the judge Fatḥ al-Dīn, son of the judge Muḥyī al-Dīn son of the judge Rashīd al-Dīn `Abd al-Ẓāhir wrote out the formal letter of appointment. Here is its text:

Afterwards, after praising God for continuously succoring blessings, the gratitude and praise for which are obligatory, sweet for those possessed of hopes, and returning prayers upon our lord Muḥammad, by whom God raised [the tribe of] Quraysh to glory, upon its ancestor, upon his family, and Companions, prayers without number or boundary.

Since so-and-so was among those who presented the gifts of his service, raising thereby to the highest, vying in his ambition, lifted by his successful governance, until the dynasty (*dawla*) magnified him, and lifted his flag, made him suffice for guarding fortresses, gifting him with penetrating good judgment. Then suppleness has begun for the offshoots, which grant him protection, so the thought should not be left behind, and it (the dynasty) has given him an investiture.

So he has been good in what was invested in him through beneficence, and his realm, of protected Balāṭinus, has been one can proudly boast against the realms, as it as ascended high, vying with Gemini in its loftiness. There is no need to guard it, because in it, are there not those who have been loyal in their attention to guarding, and have warded over it.

The session of the emir `Alam al-Dīn is the one who deserves these descriptions, the one who brings good obedience, the one who brings the lined up (for battle), who has grown up in service, now as a trainer training through his ability, and placing him in the gathering-place of respect by his right.

The noble good opinion necessitates therefore that the high command go forth that he be delegated the noble deputyship of this protected castle, and that [155] it be associated with his good descriptions. For this reason, the deputyship is delegated to him in it, according to the usual of those who have preceded him, and good obedience, returning, expending service, turning attention to every benefit gaining thereby the fruits of blessing. So let him be an equal in what is guarded, as an example, bringing the subjects to good conduct.

So when there is there is the option of either vengeance or clemency in a ruling, and the offence is less than the punishment, let him choose clemency. Let him choose justice, for it is the reins of merit, and the material for the period being judged, generosity for achieving success as a result of every good, and advancement.

(As for the) the castle, its men, its stores, its wealth, its workers, its districts, its troops, its champions, so let him pay close attention in the morning and before sunset, both in total and in part, to fortify, to gain, and to bring good things close, as well as to unite them.

He should hold fast to the tails of the pure Law (*sharī`a*), its arranged rulings, holding fast in a way that will make his praise worthy, bestowing the good (tradition) freely, to be generous in good things, with good conduct being his concern.

As for the castle, it is a trust in his care, a pearl entrusted to him to ward well, so he needs to guard it day and night, with foot (soldiers) and horse, guards and deputies: open and closed, its barking-places (for dogs). This is together with roads, guarding, watching, resting, halting, going out, entering, leveling taxes, storing, spending, turning to and turning away, holding back and compelling one following the path of corruption. All of this while accepting the one who manifests rebellion in a way that demonstrates politic, upholding the punishment of chiding, making the ways safe, renovating those places that cheer one—the instructions are many.

So let him be among those who remember this according to perspicuity, while being aided by God over what he governs and shepherds according to what he has been tasked to do, and the noble signature, may God raise it, raising it as a proof of its contents and in accord.

During the month of Ramaḍān the emir Fakhr al-Dīn Ayāz al-Malūḥī was nominated as governor over the western districts in place of the emir Nāṣir al-Dīn son of al-Muḥsinī al-Jazarī.

Mention of Ḥusām al-Dīn Ṭurunṭāy's appointment as deputy sultan over the Egyptian homelands

The emir `Izz al-Dīn Aybak *al-afram* continued as overlord deputy sultan in the Egyptian homelands promoting to al-Malik al-Manṣūr Sayf al-Dīn Qalāwūn the appointment of his mamluk, the emir Ḥusām al-Dīn Ṭurunṭāy, to the noble deputy sultanate in the Egyptian homelands in his place. This was until the sultan appointed the latter to the deputy sultanate in the Egyptian homelands in place of the emir `Izz al-Dīn Aybak *al-afram* on Thursday 14 Ramaḍān [January 18, 1280]. It is said also 23 Ramadan [January 27, 1280], and he took charge of the deputyship. God knows best which of the two it was.

On Sunday 17 Ramaḍān [January 21, 1280] the sultan al-Malik al-Manṣūr detained the emir Nūr al-Dīn `Alī son of al-Malik al-Nāṣir Ṣalāḥ al-Dīn Yūsuf, ruler of Syria, and upon [156] a number of the Nāṣiriyya [regiment].

On 26 Ramaḍān [January 30, 1280] al-Malik al-Manṣūr Sayf al-Dīn Qalāwūn removed the chief Burhān al-Dīn al-Khiḍr al-Sinjārī from his ministry over the Egyptian homelands. It was said also on Friday, 29 Ramaḍān that he detained the chief Shams al-Dīn `Īsā son of the chief Burhān al-Dīn al-Sinjārī, and their horses were taken from them, with the horses of their followers.

The chief Burhān al-Dīn and his son spent the night in the home of the emir `Alam al-Dīn al-Shujā`ī, and they stayed under house arrest for days. Their chamberlains and retainers were arrested, while they sought after the cash and revenue they had taken. This totaled 263,000 [dirhams].[28]

On Monday 2 Shawwāl [February 5, 1280] of this year al-Malik al-Manṣūr appointed the chief Fakhr al-Dīn Ibrāhīm b. Luqmān to the ministry in the Egyptian homelands, and the emir `Alā' al-Dīn Kushtghadī al-Shamsī, the majordomo of the noble house, bore the robes to him in his house in the Hill Citadel. But he strongly refused, wept, and begged off. This was ignored, so (finally) he donned the robes, taking up the office in place of the chief Burhān al-Dīn al-Sinjārī.

The chief Burhān al-Dīn stayed at the school of his brother the Chief Judge Badr al-Dīn al-Sinjārī in al-Qarāfa al-Ṣughrā (the Lesser) after he was liberated and allowed to go on his way.

On that day the judge Fatḥ al-Dīn Muḥammad son of the judge Muḥyī al-Dīn `Abdallāh son of the Shaykh Rashīd al-Dīn `Abd al-Ẓāhir took up the office of secretary, and postmaster [intelligence], and penning the noble responses in place of the chief Fakhr al-Dīn Ibn Luqmān. On that day al-Malik al-Manṣūr detained a number of the emirs and notables, among them `Alā' al-Dīn Mughulṭāy al-Dimashqī, Sayf al-Dīn Baktimur, *amīr akhūr* (shield-bearer), Sayf al-Dīn Ṭuqṣabā al-Nāṣirī, Ṣalāḥ al-Dīn Aḥmad son of Berke Tukhān, Shihāb al-Dīn Qurṭāy al-Manṣūrī, and Ṣārim al-Dīn the chamberlain, and imprisoned them.

On 5 Shawwāl [February 8, 1280] al-Malik al-Manṣūr entrusted the office of Treasury inspector in protected Damascus to the judge Taqī al-Dīn al-Tikrītī, together with the ministry in Syria, and ennobled him with the robes of the ministers, and titled him "chief." [157]

Mention of al-Malik al-Sa`īd son of al-Malik al-Ẓāhir, ruler of Kerak, taking over al-Shawbak, and then its return to al-Malik al-Manṣūr, ruler of Egypt

Al-Malik al-Sa`īd Nāṣir al-Dīn Muḥammad Berke Khān son of al-Malik al-Ẓāhir Rukn al-Dīn Baybars al-Bunduqdārī al-Ṣāliḥī al-Najmī was given Kerak when the emirs conspired to remove him from the sultanate in the Egyptian homelands, the Syrian lands, the Islamic castles, and the Ḥijāzī

[28] The editor notes the text is corrupt at this point and conjectural.

quarters, and place his brother Badr al-Dīn Salāmish in the sultanate in place of him. This was while Sayf al-Dīn Qalāwūn was his commander (*atābak*), as we previously explained.

This was conditional upon his not corresponding with the emirs, nor interfering with the armies, nor cross over to areas other than Kerak. When al-Malik al-Sa`īd set out for Kerak, and settled in it, his mamluks encouraged him and made interference in the fortresses seem good to him, taking them one by one, so he agreed with them on that.

He corresponded with the deputies, and sent the emir Ḥusām al-Dīn Lājīn, the head of the Sa`īdian *jāndār* (guard), to Shawbak. Thus, he gained control over it, and stayed in it. Sayf al-Dīn Qalāwūn wrote to him, forbidding him, but he did not desist, so he dispatched a number of the victorious army, placing the emir Badr al-Dīn Bīlīk al-Aydimurī in command.

They departed for Shawbak on Monday 9 Shawwāl [February 12, 1280], so the emir Badr al-Dīn camped up against Shawbak, and surrounded its garrison, so it was handed over on 10 Dhū al-Qa`da of that year [March 13, 1280]. He assigned a deputy to it, and returned from it.

It was said that when al-Malik al-Sa`īd was removed from the sultanate, he was given Kerak. Najm al-Dīn al-Khiḍr son of al-Malik al-Ẓāhir was given Shawbak. So when the emirs agreed to remove al-Malik al-`Ādil son of al-Malik al-Ẓāhir from the sultanate in the Egyptian homelands. They removed him, sending him to be with his brother in Kerak, just as we previously explained, who sent an army to besiege Shawbak. This was when the reign of al-Malik al-Manṣūr stabilized, just as we mentioned.

When the news of their going reached its ruler, al-Malik [...] Najm al-Dīn Khiḍr son of al-Malik al-Ẓāhir, he transferred himself to Kerak to be with his brother al-Malik al-Sa`īd. Then the army arrived at Shawbak castle, besieged it for a time, whereupon it was handed over on safe conduct. God knows best which of these happened.

The envoys of Alfonso arrived, in spite of the fact that they were actually envoys to al-Malik al-Sa`īd son of al-Malik al-Ẓāhir. Al-Malik al-Manṣūr summoned them, and they gave him the letters, and they returned having spoken face-to-face. They brought the gifts they had with them, which were very insignificant. He wrote them an answer, bestowed robes upon them, supported them, and prepared them [for their journey], so they returned during the middle of Shawwāl [mid-February 1280].

On Saturday 21 Shawwāl [February 24, 1280] al-Malik al-Manṣūr detained al-Malik al-Awḥad and his brother Shihāb al-Dīn Muḥammad, sons of al-Malik al-Nāṣir Ṣalāḥ al-Dīn Dā'ūd, ruler of Kerak, and imprisoned them both.

On that day al-Malik al-Manṣūr appointed Badr al-Dīn Bīlīk *al-ṭayyār* (the flyer) to the deputy sultanate in protected Safed castle. He transferred the emir `Alam al-Dīn Sanjar al-Kurjī to the governate. He transferred the emir Sayf al-Dīn Balabān al-Jawwādī to the protected Citadel treasury.

On Monday 23 Shawwāl [February 26, 1280] it was established that the judge Sharaf al-Dīn Abū Ṭālib son of the judge `Alā' al-Dīn Ibn al-Nābulsī would take up his duties in the Chancelleries Inspectorate in the Egyptian homelands, and he bestowed a robe upon him. He took up his duties in place of the judge Najm al-Dīn Ibn al-Uṣfūnī in Upper Egypt, and from the judge Tāj al-Dīn Ibn al-Sanhūrī in Lower Egypt.

On Tuesday 24 Shawwāl [February 27, 1280] al-Malik al-Manṣūr was enraged against the Christians, especially the secretaries of the victorious armies, and their payment, so he ordered the use of Muslim secretaries [solely]. He assigned the judge Amīn al-Dīn, the notary for the disbursement box for the secretariat of the armies in place of al-As`ad Ibrāhīm the Christian.

On that day al-Malik al-Manṣūr issued a command to demolish the Moat Monastery (*Dīr al-khandaq*)[29] outside of protected Cairo, just outside of the Conquests Gate, at the end of al-Ḥusayniyya [Shrine], and it was a day to remember. Numbers gathered which could not be counted. The writer of *The Secretary's Treasury* [Ibn al-Mukarram] said during that day the headman Tāj al-Dīn Tawba al-Tikrītī the seller was appointed as inspector of inspectors in protected Syria.

We have previously mentioned that the Sultan delegated the ministry in Syria to him, and bestowed upon him the robe of ministry, and the right to have the title of "chief," and God knows best which of them it was.

On Wednesday 25 Shawwāl [February 28, 1280] al-Malik al-Manṣūr Nāṣr al-Dīn Muḥammad son of Maḥmūd, ruler of Ḥamāh arrived at the protected Hill Citadel. Al-Malik al-Manṣūr rode out to greet him, and domiciled him in the Views of the Ram. The Sultan was very concerned with him. The author of the book *The Secretary's Treasury* said during that month a command was issued concerning the management and content of wine, open drinking and drunkenness. But there was opposition to it, so it did not last more than a few days before it was cancelled, praise to God. [159]

On Thursday 26 Shawwāl [February 29, 1280] al-Malik al-Manṣūr issued orders to remove wines, and to efface their remains, and that no one would include them [as merchandise] or drink them openly.

On Friday 27 Shawwāl [March 1, 1280] formal appointments were written for the judges of the four legal rites. It was established that the Chief Judge would be Ṣadr al-Dīn son of the Chief Judge Tāj al-Dīn son of the daughter of al-A`zz al-Shāfi`ī. He is the one who would appoint deputies throughout the lands, specifically. Then Chief Judge [...] al-Dīn al-Mālikī, Chief Judge Mu`izz al-Dīn al-Ḥanafī, and Chief Judge `Izz al-Dīn al-Ḥanbalī as justices in Cairo and Old Cairo, specifically, without deputies through the lands.

---

[29] See al-Maqrīzī, *al-Mawā`iẓ wa-l-i`tibār fi dhikr al-khiṭāṭ wa-l-āthar* (ed. Aymān Fū'ād Sayyid, London: Mu'assasat al-Furqān, 2013), iv, p. 1048 for a description.

At the end of Shawwāl [March 4, 1280] al-Malik al-Manṣūr ordered the emir `Izz al-Dīn Aydimur al-Ẓāhirī to be brought from Damascus under guard, so dispatched a number with him, and he was brought. When he arrived at the Hill Citadel, he was imprisoned in it. The crescent moon of Dhū al-Qa`da was seen the night of Tuesday [March 4, 1280].

On the day of Wednesday 2 Dhū al-Qa`da [March 5, 1280] of this year the Sultan al-Malik al-Manṣūr rode to the square at al-Būrjī, and played ball (*al-akirra*), which was the first game in it. He dispersed decorated harnesses upon some 130 horses, and robes upon the emirs as religious robes.

On Friday 5 Dhū al-Qa`da [March 8, 1280] al-Malik al-Manṣūr Sayf al-Dīn Qalāwūn sent a formal appointment to al-Malik al-Manṣūr Nāṣir al-Dīn Muḥammad, the ruler of Ḥamāh, in Ḥamāh as usual. He sent to him the sultanic standards, as well as four caskets of gold and silver, four caskets with fabrics, from other types of goods, such as waved silk (*`uttābī*), *tūrīzī*, and Alexandrine (cloths). He also sent him noble horses, sending all this with a number of the senior members of his regime. The ruler of Ḥamāh bestowed robes upon all of them, and then the Sultan allowed them to return to protected Ḥamāh.

On Tuesday 9 Dhū al-Qa`da [March 12, 1280] al-Malik al-Manṣūr, the ruler of Ḥamāh, traveled while the Sultan provided him with a noble proclamation about Bārīn,[30] and its condominium. The Sultan rode out to see him off, and stayed that day in Bahtīt, returning at the end of the day to his victorious Citadel. [160]

Mention of al-Malik al-Mas`ūd son of al-Malik al-Ẓāhir's staying after the death of his brother al-Malik al-Sa`īd in Kerak, and what was agreed from him

When the deputy of Kerak, the emir `Alā' al-Dīn al-Fakhrī left Kerak, and went to the Egyptian homelands, al-Malik al-Sa`īd was established in the sultanate in Kerak. The emir `Alā' al-Dīn Aydighudī al-Ḥarrānī al-Ẓāhirī was assigned as the deputy in it, whereupon al-Malik al-Sa`īd rode to the square in Kerak to play ball. But he was thrown from his horse, suffered a head injury, and took fever after a few days. It is said that he had consumption. It is also said that he was poisoned. He died on 18 Dhū al-Qa`da of this year [March 21, 1280]. It said also on the 13th [March 16, 1280], and it is said on Thursday the 15th.

The news of his death in Kerak castle arrived to the Sultan al-Malik al-Manṣūr on 20 Dhū al-Qa`da [March 23, 1280], and the Sultan prepared a great wake for him in the hall of the Hill Citadel. He sat wrapped in white, and the emirs, judges, learned, preachers and the whole world gathered—it was a day to remember!

---

[30] Today Birīn, located to the southwest of Ḥamāh.

The Sultan wrote to the lands and the castles that they should pray for him the prayer of the one who is absent, just as will be adduced in his biography. When al-Malik al-Sa`īd son of al-Malik al-Ẓāhir died, his deputy the emir `Alā' al-Dīn Aydighudī al-Ḥarrānī al-Ẓāhirī and those with him in Kerak took counsel, and placed his brother Najm al-Dīn Khiḍr as king in his place, giving him the title of al-Malik al-Mas`ūd.

Those mamluks around al-Malik al-Mas`ūd Najm al-Dīn Khiḍr allowed evil conduct, and dispersed the treasury money. They sought to use this [money] to bind people to them, and to add fiefs to his patrimony. Among them a group went to al-Ṣalt and took over it, sending also to Ṣarkhand, and intending to take it over as well. However, they were unable to do so.

They then sought to corrupt people, and the Bedouin and al-Tamā`a[31] got wind that they were giving money to those who would come to them. So a number of the Bedouin and others would come to them from all over the lands, and gather, attending to al-Malik al-Mas`ūd, vowing obedience to him, and being close to him with good advice. When he trusted them, and had spent wealth upon them, they got what they came for. Then they slipped away, departed, and returned to where they had come from, and so their numbers dispersed.

He and those with him did not stop spending wealth upon those who came to them until most of the treasures that were in Kerak, gathered there by al-Malik al-Ẓāhir Rukn al-Dīn Baybars al-Bunduqdārī al-Ṣāliḥī al-Najmī, the father of al-Malik al-Sa`īd and al-Malik al-Mas`ūd, were depleted. He had placed treasure in that fortress for catastrophic times, but they spent what brought them no benefit; indeed, it brought harm, and distracted people's minds.

Then they corresponded with the emir Shams al-Dīn Sunqur *al-ashqar*, the deputy sultan in protected Damascus, about a mutual agreement. This reached al-Malik al-Manṣūr Sayf al-Dīn Qalāwūn the ruler of the Egyptian homelands, so he dispatched the emir `Izz al-Dīn Aybak *al-afram* to Kerak in order to terrify [them]. Then what happened between the emir [161] Shams al-Dīn Sunqur *al-ashqar* and him what we will mention, if God Most High wishes.

On 20 Dhū al-Qa`da [March 23, 1280] of this year the judge Shihāb al-Dīn Ghāzī Ibn al-Wāsiṭī was appointed to the Chancellery Supervision in protected Aleppo, and 400 dirhams were allotted to him per month, together with six drinking-cups (*makkūks*) of wheat, and two of barley. Jalāl al-Dīn Ibn al-Khaṭīr was appointed with him in charge of the chancellery adjudication in it, and the both of them received a letter concerning that. Al-*Ṭawāshī* Iftikhār al-Dīn *al-raqīq* (the slave) the retainer was appointed to the Treasury in protected Aleppo.

[31] Unidentified, but presumably a Bedouin tribe living in the area of Kerak. Not listed in Ibn Faḍlallāh.

During this month, the emir Badr al-Dīn Baktūt al-Quṭuzī was appointed supervisor of the chancelleries in protected Aleppo and its districts. In it, al-Malik al-Manṣūr delegated the Chancelleries Inspectorate in Damascus to the headman (*al-ṣadr*) Jamāl al-Dīn Ibrāhīm Ibn Ṣaṣrā. This was after the death of the inspector there, the judge `Alam al-Dīn Muḥammad Ibn al-`Ādilī.

Al-Malik al-Manṣūr also delegated the noble deputy sultanate in Ḥiṣn al-Akrād and the conquered regions with it to his mamluk, the emir Sayf al-Dīn Balabān al-Ṭabbākhī.

The crescent moon of Dhū al-Ḥijja was seen this year on the night of Wednesday.

On Saturday 4 Dhū al-Ḥijja [April 6, 1280] the emir `Imād al-Dīn Dā'ūd Ibn Abī al-Qāsim was appointed to the governate of Nablus, and its districts, and *iqṭā`* fiefs were assigned to him and five mamluks.

On Tuesday 7 Dhū al-Ḥijja [April 9, 1280] the emir `Izz al-Dīn Aybak *al-afram*, and those with him from the victorious armies, traveled to Kerak, being dispatched, as we have mentioned the reason for that.

On Thursday 9 Dhū al-Ḥijja [April 11, 1280] the emir Ghars al-Dīn Ibn Shawār was removed from prison, given a robe, and given a command to return to his governate in Ramla and Lydda.

On Saturday 18 Dhū al-Ḥijja [April 20, 1280] the emir Badr al-Dīn Bīlīk al-Aydimurī received protected Shawbak castle under terms of safe conduct. His letters concerning that command arrived on Thursday the 23rd [April 25, 1280]. The Sultan al-Malik al-Manṣūr swore [for a safe conduct] to the emir Ḥusām al-Dīn Lājīn al-Khiṭā'ī, the head of the guard for the deputy in it, and the emir Jamāl al-Dīn al-Hamāmī, the governor of the lands in it. Robes were sent to them, and the tidings sent out from the protected Hill Citadel. Letters about that were sent to the four corners, and we have already said what was said on other matters.

In it the judge Majd al-Dīn `Īsā Ibn al-Khashshāb was appointed to the noble market inspection (*ḥisba*) in protected Cairo [162] and he took up this office. In it, the Sultan al-Malik al-Manṣūr delegated the deputy sultanate in the Damascus Citadel to his mamluk the emir Ḥusām al-Dīn Lājīn *al-silāḥdār* al-Manṣūrī, who was known as "Lājīn the Lesser." He arrived there, and inhabited it. This was on 20 Dhū al-Ḥijja [April 22, 1280]. The emir Shams al-Dīn Sunqur *al-ashqar*, the deputy sultan in protected Damascus, plotted against him, which was part of his rebellion against obeying the Sultan al-Malik al-Manṣūr, and his sultanate in Syria, just as we will mention, if God Most High wishes.

Mention of the sultanate of Shams al-Dīn Sunqur *al - ashqar* in Damascus

Al-Malik al-Manṣūr Sayf al-Dīn Qalāwūn al-Alfī al-Ṣāliḥī al-Najmī, during the period in which he was army commander, during the sultanate of al-Malik al-`Ādil Badr al-Dīn Salāmish, sent the emir Shams al-Dīn Sunqur *al-ashqar* to Syria as the noble deputy sultan in protected Damascus. This was in place of the emir Jamāl al-Dīn Aqush al-Shamsī, and he transferred the emir Jamāl al-Dīn Aqush al-Shamsī from Damascus to the deputy sultanate in the Aleppan realm.

When al-Malik al-`Ādil Badr al-Dīn Salāmish was removed, and al-Malik al-Manṣūr Sayf al-Dīn Qalāwūn reigned, and was alone as Sultan, just as we previously explained, it occurred to the emir Shams al-Dīn Sunqur *al-ashqar* to attempt to take the sultanate in Syria, so that the matter would be like it was at the end of the Ayyūbid dynasty. So he began to prepare matters for himself.

When al-Malik al-Manṣūr sent his mamluk the emir Ḥusām al-Dīn Lājīn to Damascus Citadel, he arrived there, and inhabited it, but Shams al-Dīn Sunqur plotted against him, just as we have previously explained. He gathered those emirs who were with him in Damascus, and made out to them that reports had come to him that al-Malik al-Manṣūr Sayf al-Dīn Qalāwūn had been killed, while he was drinking wine, and called them to obey him, asking them to swear an oath to him.

They assented, and swore to him, so he took the title of al-Malik al-Kāmil, and rode with the sultanic insignia and the pomp of kingliness in Damascus. That was on 24 Dhū al-Ḥijja of the year [6]78 [April 26, 1280]. At the same time he detained the emir Rukn al-Dīn Baybars al-`Ajamī *al-jāliq* al-Ṣāliḥī because of his refusal to swear the oath, and detained the emir Ḥusām al-Dīn Lājīn, deputy of Damascus Citadel, as well, who had been sent by al-Malik al-Manṣūr, and upon the chief Taqī al-Dīn Tawba al-Tikrītī. He sent forth the emir Sayf al-Dīn Balabān al-Jayshī to the rest of the Syrian realms, castles and other places to take the oaths of the deputies who were in them. He would then appoint in them who he wanted.

He tasked the headman Majd al-Dīn Abū al-Fidā' Ismā`īl son of Kusayrāt al-Mawṣilī with being the minister, and made the headman `Izz al-Dīn Aḥmad son of Muyasar al-Miṣrī the minister of interrelationships (*wazīr al-ṣuḥba*). He transferred his family from the House of Felicity in which the deputy sultans reside in Damascus, to its Citadel. At the time when his family was being transferred he ordered the Victory Gate to be locked, but to open the secret gate of the Citadel opposite [163] the House of Felicity, close to the Victory Gate, so they did that.

The people were all over the place with things, saying, "He closed the Victory Gate, moved from the House of Felicity, is dwelling in the Citadel, and appointed Ibn Kusayrāt as minister! This won't be the end of it all!" It was like that, just as we will record, if God Most High wishes.

The blessed Nile overflowed[32] on Sunday 3 Rabī` al-Ākhir [6]78 [August 13, 1279] of this year 16 cubits, and on 20 Rabī` al-Ākhir [August 30, 1279]

---

[32] Reading *gharaqa* in place of *ghaliqa*.

it was Nawrūz, which is the first day of Tūt, the first month of the Coptic calendar. The emir Jamāl al-Dīn Aqush al-Bākhilī led the Egyptian caravan for the pilgrimage with the sultanic *maḥmal*. The blessed *maḥmal* departed for the noble Ḥijāz on Tuesday 17 Shawwāl [February 20, 1280] and the caravan's judge was judge Fakhr al-Dīn `Uthmān son of the daughter of Abū Sa`d, and God knows best.

[*Obituaries*]

Mention of the events during the year 679 [1280]

On Thursday, the first day of God's month, Muḥarrram [May 3, 1280], of this year, al-Malik al-Kāmil Shams al-Dīn Sunqur *al-ashqar* rode with the sultanic insignia and the kingly pomp, entering the Green Square in protected Damascus, while the emirs, and commanders walked before him with robes on foot. He paraded through the square, then turned back and returned to the Citadel.[33]

On Friday 2 Muḥarram [May 4, 1280] al-Malik al-Kāmil Shams al-Dīn Sunqur *al-ashqar* delivered the sermon in the protected Damascus mosque.

Mention of the Egyptian and Syrian armies' meeting in battle, those emirs taken prisoner, during the first time

Just as previously, al-Malik al-Manṣūr Sayf al-Dīn Qalāwūn, the ruler of the Egyptian homelands, when it reached him about the attempts of al-Malik al-Mas`ūd Khiḍr son of al-Malik al-Ẓāhir, ruler of Kerak, to corrupt the people, and gather armies, he dispatched the emir `Izz al-Dīn *al-afram* to Kerak in order to terrify him.

When it reached al-Malik al-Kāmil Shams al-Dīn Sunqur *al-ashqar*, ruler of Damascus, that he had departed from the Egyptian homelands leading a detachment of its armies, he thought that he was the target, so wrote to him to forbid him from advancing. He said:

> I have pacified Syria, conquered the castles, and served the Sultan, so the agreement between us was that I would be the ruler over what is between the Euphrates [River] and al-`Arīsh. He deputized Aqūsh al-Shamsī in Aleppo, `Alā' al-Dīn al-Kabakī in Safed, and Sayf al-Dīn Balabān al-Ṭabbākhī in Ḥiṣn al-Akrād. Now at last he has sent someone against me to take it [168] all from me!

Sunqur *al-ashqar* dispatched an army from the Damascene armies to follow his letter, so when the letter arrived to the emir `Izz al-Dīn *al-afram*, he wrote

[33] See Nicola Ziadeh, *Damascus under the Mamluks* (Norman: University of Oklahoma Press, 1964), chap. 3 on this topography.

an appraisal to al-Malik al-Manṣūr, the ruler of Egypt, and forwarded the letter which Sunqur *al-ashqar* sent. When the appraisal arrived to al-Malik al-Manṣūr he wrote to al-Malik al-Kāmil Shams al-Dīn Sunqur *al-ashqar*, and the emirs of his coterie (*khushdāshiyya*) also wrote to him, deploring his actions, and urging him to return to obedience.

The letters were sent with the emir Sayf al-Dīn Balabān al-Karīmī al-`Alā'ī, who was part of his coterie,[34] so he arrived in Damascus on 8 Muḥarram [May 10, 1280]. Al-Malik al-Kāmil Sunqur *al-ashqar* went out to him, and met him, putting him up in the Damascus Citadel, and treating him well. However, he did not incline to what the latter said, nor did he return to what his close comrade indicated. This was what was going on with that.

As for what was happening with the emir `Izz al-Dīn *al-afram*, when the letter of al-Malik al-Kāmil Shams al-Dīn Sunqur *al-ashqar* arrived to him, and he sent its appraisal to al-Malik al-Manṣūr just as we explained, he returned to Gaza. The emir Badr al-Dīn al-Aydimurī returned from Shawbak then, after he had taken it, and assigned a deputy in it, just as we previously explained. The two of them mustered forces at Gaza.

The army that al-Malik al-Kāmil Shams al-Dīn Sunqur *al-ashqar* had sent to Gaza arrived, and at its arrival, the Egyptian army was driven back into the sand dunes. The Syrians camped, while their commander was the emir Shams al-Dīn Qarāsunqur al-Mu`izzī. When they camped at Gaza, for an hour of the day they were unwary, in spite of their small numbers, so the Egyptian army returned, and took them by surprise, overcoming them, and defeating them completely. So they returned defeated to Ramla.

Among the notables of their emirs who were taken captive were the emir Badr al-Dīn Kunjak al-Khwārizmī, Bahā' al-Dīn Yamak al-Nāṣirī, Nāṣir al-Dīn Bashqird al-Nāṣirī, Badr al-Dīn Bīlīk al-Ḥalabī, `Alam al-Dīn Sanjar al-Tikrītī, Sanjar al-Badrī, and Sābiq al-Dīn Sulaymān, lord of Ṣahyūn. They plundered their wealth, horses and their heavy armor. The post-courier arrived with the letters of the emir Badr al-Dīn al-Aydimurī at the hand of the son of the emir Badr al-Dīn Baktāsh al-Fakhrī on Thursday 15 Muḥarram [May 17, 1280].

The Sultan al-Malik al-Manṣūr bestowed robes upon Baktāsh's son and upon the post-courier. The captive emirs arrived at the sultanic gates at the Hill Citadel, whereupon the Sultan had clemency upon them, and treated them well, without confiscating from them, then set them free, bestowed robes upon them, and renewed their formal proclamations, and returned them to the victorious army. They stayed among the victorious Egyptian armies in the service of [169] the Manṣūriyya [regiment] just as we will mention, if God Most High wishes.

On Wednesday 14 Muḥarram [May 16, 1280] Shams al-Dīn Sunqur al-Ghutamī known as *al-ashqar*, the majordomo for the emir `Alam

[34] It is not clear whether this means Qalāwūn or Sunqur.

al-Dīn al-Ghutamī, presented himself, and requested from the emir `Alā' al-Dīn Kundaghdī al-Jayshī compensation for one of his *iqṭā`* fiefs. However, the emir `Alā' al-Dīn al-Jayshī refused him, and spoke to him treating him rudely. Then Sunqur al-Ghutamī stabbed him in the belly with a knife, and struck `Izz al-Dīn al-Ghazzī *al-naqīb* as well. As for al-Ghazzī, he intercepted the strike with his hand, so he was wounded, but survived. As for al-Jayshī however, his belly was torn open, and, even though one who stitched him up was brought, he died on the morning of Monday. The Sultan al-Malik al-Manṣūr commanded that Sunqur al-Ghutamī be nailed up (*summira*). Therefore, he was on Thursday, at the Zuwayla Gate, and he died on Saturday.

Mention of the dispatch of the Egyptian armies to Damascus and al-Malik al-Kāmil, ruler of Damascus, waging war against them, his defeat at Damascus and the entrance of the Egyptian army into it

When the news of the Damascene army's defeat reached its lord, al-Malik al-Kāmil Shams al-Dīn Sunqur *al-ashqar*, he was worried, and mustered his armies, writing to the emirs in Gaza loyal to al-Malik al-Manṣūr, attempting to make promises to them and suborn them. He offered each of them a castle. The emir Shihāb al-Dīn Aḥmad Ibn Ḥijjī, king of the Bedouin in the southlands, came to al-Malik al-Kāmil, together with the emir Sharaf al-Dīn `Īsā b. Muhannā, king of the Bedouin in the eastlands and northlands.

There was also aid from Aleppo and Ḥamāh, together with many men from the Ba`lbak Mountains. Al-Malik al-Kāmil took all the best into his service, paying them money, and gathering a large number. Then reports came to Damascus that al-Malik al-Manṣūr had prepared an army from Egypt, and that they were coming to Damascus. Alarming news multiplied then.

What was happening on the part of al-Malik al-Manṣūr, ruler of Egypt, was that he had dispatched the emir `Alam al-Dīn Sanjar al-Ḥalabī, from the Egyptian homelands, together with the emir Badr al-Dīn Baktāsh al-Fakhrī, the *amīr silāḥ* of the armies, with their hangers-on.

It was said that the victorious armies departed to protected Syria accompanied by the emir Badr al-Dīn Baktāsh al-Fakhrī, the *amīr silāḥ*, and Ḥusām al-Dīn Aytamish son of Aṭlas Khān. They had 4000 horsemen, and with them the emir Fakhr al-Dīn Sanjar al-Bāshqirdī. They joined with the two emirs `Izz al-Dīn *al-afram* and Badr al-Dīn al-Aydimurī, and those [troops] with them, and went forward. Their overall commander was the emir `Alam al-Dīn Sanjar [170] al-Ḥalabī.

When the report of Egyptian armies' muster at Gaza and their departure from it towards Damascus arrived at al-Malik al-Kāmil's army which was at Ramla, it drew back somewhat. As the Egyptian army advanced, the Syrian army would withdraw in front of it, because of their inferior numbers, until the first part of it reached Damascus.

When it was Wednesday 14 Ṣafar [June 15, 1280] of that year al-Malik al-Kāmil Shams al-Dīn Sunqur *al-ashqar*, the ruler of Damascus, departed from Damascus himself, leading all of the armies he had, and he pitched his vestibule at al-Jasūra, and camped there.

The Egyptian army arrived at al-Kaswa, and the vanguards were assigned, then advanced, and the two armies met [in battle] at al-Jasūra on the 15th. It was said on Monday the 17th [June 18, 1280]. It was said on Wednesday the 19th [June 20, 1280] at daybreak. They fought fiercely, and al-Malik al-Kāmil held firm, fighting fiercely. The (battle) lines continued until the 4th [hour] of the day, but few of the two sides were killed. Most of the Damascene army stayed with al-Malik al-Kāmil, but there were some which joined the army of Egypt, and there were those who retreated.

As for the armies of Ḥamāh and of Aleppo when battle was joined, they retreated, and returned to their lands. The rest of the army of Syria gave up, and most of the emirs of the Syrian army them presented themselves to the Egyptian army. Then the emir `Alam al-Dīn al-Ḥalabī charged directly at al-Malik al-Kāmil Shams al-Dīn Sunqur *al-ashqar*, whereupon he retreated immediately, accompanied by his close emirs: the emir `Izz al-Dīn Izdimur *al-ḥājj*, the emir `Alā' al-Dīn al-Kabakī, the emir Shams al-Dīn Qarāsunqur al-Mu`izzī, and the emir Sayf al-Dīn Balabān al-Jayshī.

Sunqur al-ashqar on the evening of Friday 14 Ṣafar [June 15, 1280] had sent his children, his wives, and his belongings to Ṣahyūn, so when he retreated, he took the al-Qaṭī`a road, together with the emir `Īsā b. Muhannā, the emir of the Bedouin, who was loyal to his service. They passed together next to some of his tents, so they stayed the night, with those who were with him, in the al-Raḥba Waste. He hosted them and their mounts for the duration of their stay, then went with him towards al-Raḥba. What happened we will mention, if God Most High wishes.

This was what happened to al-Malik al-Kāmil Shams al-Dīn Sunqur *al-ashqar* and those who accompanied him, who were defeated. As for the rest of the army of Syria, there were those who entered the gardens of Damascus, and concealed themselves there, those who entered the settled areas of Damascus, those who went on the Ba`lbak road. A great many arrived in al-Naṣab, one of the districts of Ḥimṣ. Among them were those who took the al-Makhraj road, `Adhrā, and the Great Path passing al-Qaṭī`a.

When [171] Sunqur *al-ashqar* was defeated, the city gates of Damascus were locked [by the Damascenes], fearing that the Egyptian army would plunder them, and the Citadel was fortified as well. The Egyptian army went immediately to Damascus, and surrounded it, settling in the camp. However, they did not try to rush the city, and the emir `Alam al-Dīn al-Ḥalabī stayed at the al-Ablaq Palace in the Green Square, and the army spent the night around him until the second day.

Then he proclaimed a safe conduct around Damascus, whereupon the emir Sayf al-Dīn *al-jūkāndār* (batman), the deputy in Citadel on behalf of Shams al-Dīn Sunqur *al-ashqar* came to the emir Rukn al-Dīn Baybars al-`Ajamī *al-jāliq* and the emir Ḥusām al-Dīn Lājīn al-Manṣūrī, who had been the deputy of Damascus Citadel, and the chief Taqī al-Dīn Tawba. This was while they were still imprisoned in the Citadel. He had them swear that they would not harm him when he took them out, nor would they harm any of those who were serving in the Citadel. So they swore, and then he took them out of imprisonment. They ordered the Citadel gate to be opened, and that the people be safe.

Then the emir Ḥusām al-Dīn Lājīn opened the Gate of Deliverance, stood at it, and forbade the Egyptian army from entering, fearing that they would run amok. Then making "people's hearts feel good" was proclaimed. He commanded the city to be decorated, and for the tidings to be sounded. So Damascus was decorated, and the tidings were sounded in the Citadel. Most of the emirs returned to Damascus, and requested safe conduct from the emir `Alam al-Dīn al-Ḥalabī, which he granted, whereupon they entered at different days. Then the emir Shihāb al-Dīn Aḥmad Ibn Ḥijjī, king of the Bedouin, presented himself in Damascus under a safe conduct.

The emir `Alam al-Dīn Sanjar al-Ḥalabī wrote to the Sultan al-Malik al-Manṣūr Sayf al-Dīn Qalāwūn telling him of the victory, and sent the emirs he had detained because of the fact that they had been loyal to Shams al-Dīn Sunqur *al-ashqar* to Egypt. He sent the emir Nāṣir al-Dīn Muḥammad son of the emir Badr al-Dīn Baktāsh al-Fakhrī, the *amīr silāḥ*, with the glad tidings to al-Malik al-Manṣūr, who was gracious to him, and gave him the command of 10 [mamluks], and treated the emirs who al-Ḥalabī had sent well, not punishing them at all. Then there happened what we will mention, if God Most High wishes it.

The deputy sultanate in protected Damascus was affirmed for the emir Badr al-Dīn Baktūt al-`Alā'ī by the commanding emirs going to Damascus, and the chief Taqī al-Dīn Tawba continued in his same office prior to his detention. The emir `Alam al-Dīn Sanjar al-Bāshqirdī was appointed to the deputy sultanate in the Aleppan realms.

In Ṣafar [June] on 25 Abīb the depth of the blessed Nile was taken, and it was 5 cubits and 20 fingers. [172]

Mention of Shams al-Dīn Sunqur *al-ashqar*'s heading towards Ṣahyūn, and his fortifying it

Shams al-Dīn Sunqur *al-ashqar*, when he took over Syria, wrote to the deputies of the castles. Among them, there were those who obeyed him, while among them there were those who did not. Among those who obeyed him were the deputies of Ṣahyūn, Burziyya, Balāṭinus, al-Shughr, Bakās, Shayzar, `Akkār,[35] and Ḥimṣ, so when he was defeated, Sunqur *al-ashqar* went in

[35] Changing from `Akkā.

the direction of al-Raḥba, when the emir `Alam al-Dīn al-Ḥalabī took over Damascus, just as we have previously explained. He [Ḥalabī] then sent a large section of the army, approximately 3000 horse, sending them accompanied by the emir Ḥusām al-Dīn Aytimish son of Aṭlas Khān, and a number of the emirs, in pursuit of Shams al-Dīn Sunqur *al-ashqar* and those with him. They departed from Damascus on Monday 24 Ṣafar [June 25, 1280] of this year.

During the beginning of Rabī` al-Awwal [July 1, 1280] of this year a section of the Egyptian army departed from Damascus, whose commander was the emir `Izz al-Dīn *al-afram*, which joined together with those in pursuit of Sunqur *al-ashqar*, so they caught up with them in Ḥimṣ and they all went together. This was what was happening with the emirs.

As for what was happening with Sunqur *al-ashqar*, when he retreated from Damascus, as noted, staying with the emir Sharaf al-Dīn `Īsā Ibn Muhannā for a time, then he headed towards al-Raḥba, where Shams al-Dīn Sunqur *al-ashqar* parted from most of those who were with him. The emir Muwaffaq al-Dīn Khiḍr al-Raḥbī, the deputy for Raḥba castle, prevented it from being handed over to him. At that point, Shams al-Dīn Sunqur corresponded with the king Abagha son of Hűlegű, the king of the Tatars, informing him of the dissension that had occurred between the Islamic armies.

He encouraged him to target the lands with his armies, and promised him that he would join up with him, aiding and supporting him in this endeavor. The emir Sharaf al-Dīn `Īsā b. Muhannā wrote to him in the same vein, so what will happen we will mention if God Most High wishes it.

When Shams al-Dīn Sunqur *al-ashqar* received the report of the armies that had departed in pursuit of him, he separated from the emir Sharaf al-Dīn `Īsā b. Muhannā. He (Sunqur) headed into the waste towards Ṣahyūn and the fortresses mentioned. He was leading those who were with him, as they were in the hands of his deputies, so he took refuge in them, at the end of Rabī` al-Awwal [July 30, 1280]. It was said that he did not separate from `Īsā b. Muhannā, but when the report of the armies reached the both of them, they both made haste to flee to Ṣahyūn, and that was in Jumādā al-Ulā [September 1280] of this year.

On the day of the battle the emir `Izz al-Dīn *al-ḥājj* Izdimur, and those with him from Aleppo, retreated to Mt. Ḥurdafīn.[36] They stayed with them (the occupants of the castle) for this period, and taking refuge with them. When it reached him that Sunqur *al-ashqar* had arrived at those castles with his number, and that he was in Ṣahyūn castle, [173] he and those Aleppans with him arrives there, so he sent them to Shayzar castle, and he stayed there. It was said that the emir `Izz al-Dīn Aybak Kurjī was in it on behalf of Shams al-Dīn Sunqur *al-ashqar*. This was happening about the emirs.

---

[36] According to vocalization in Yāqūt, *Mu`jam al-buldān* (Beirut: Dār Ṣādir, n.d.), ii, p. 240, located 3 miles from Aleppo.

As for the Egyptian army, when it reached them that Shams al-Dīn Sunqur *al-ashqar* and his supporters had entered the castles and taken refuge in them, they camped up against Shayzar, tightening around it, but not besieging it, and what happened there we will mention, if God Most High wishes it.

In [...][37] and Shams al-Dīn Sunqur *al-ashqar* when he had made himself sultan in Damascus had solicited the legal opinion of the Chief Judge Shams al-Dīn Aḥmad Ibn Khallikān, the judge of Damascus, as to the legality of fighting al-Malik al-Manṣūr, so he had rendered a legal opinion (*fatwa*) permitting it. So he had appointed him to the position of instructor at the Amīniyya [College] in Damascus in place of the judge Najm al-Dīn Ibn Sanā al-Dawla at the end of Muḥarram [June 1, 1280] of that year. He took up the duties of instruction in it on 29 Muḥarram [May 31, 1280], when the judge Najm al-Dīn Ibn Sanā al-Dawla was at that time in Aleppo.

When the Egyptian army arrived in Damascus and the fighting occurred between the army of Egypt, and the army of Syria, Shams al-Dīn Sunqur *al-ashqar* retreated, while the Egyptian army entered into Damascus. The emir `Alam al-Dīn Sanjar al-Ḥalabī stayed at the al-Ablaq Palace on the Green Square, just as we previously explained.

The emir `Alam al-Dīn Sanjar al-Ḥalabī was the one consulted with regard to appointing and removal, to granting and refusing, and when the emir Badr al-Dīn Baktūt al-`Alā'ī was renewed in the deputy sultanate in Damascus, just as previously explained, during his deputyship, he maintained cordial relations with the emir `Alam al-Dīn al-Ḥalabī.

The emir `Alam al-Dīn commanded a guard to be placed around the chief Majd al-Dīn Ismā`īl Ibn Kusayrāt, the minister for Shams al-Dīn Sunqur *al-ashqar*, and Jamāl al-Dīn Ibn Ṣaṣrā, Chancelleries Inspector in Damascus, and taking anything they wrote in its totality, then he imprisoned the both of them. Zayn al-Dīn, the trustee (*wakīl*) of the Islamic Treasury (*bayt al-māl*) and Muḥyī al-Dīn Ibn al-Naḥḥās were both beaten, and anything they wrote was taken in its totality, then he imprisoned the both of them.

The Chief Judge `Izz al-Dīn Ibn al-Ṣā'igh interceded with regard to Zayn al-Dīn, trustee of the Treasury, so he was set free, and issued a written command concerning Chief Judge Shams al-Dīn Aḥmad Ibn Khallikān and a number of the other Sufi leaders. Then the Sultan al-Malik al-Manṣūr learned that Chief Judge Shams al-Dīn Aḥmad Ibn Khallikān gave a religious opinion to Shams al-Dīn Sunqur *al-ashqar* permitting fighting him, so he issued an order to hang him.

When al-Malik al-Manṣūr's letter of a general safe conduct for the people of Damascus arrived, it was read in the presence of Chief Judge Shams al-Dīn Ibn Khallikān. The emir `Alam al-Dīn al-Ḥalabī then said "This letter

[37] A line and a half erased in the original.

is a safe conduct for those who hear it; since the judge Shams al-Dīn has heard it, he is therefore safe from [174] being killed."

Then he removed him on 21 Ṣafar [July 21, 1280] and gave the judiciary to the Chief Judge `Izz al-Dīn Ibn al-Ṣā'igh, but he refused, so he delegated it to the Chief Judge Najm al-Dīn son of the Chief Judge Ṣadr al-Dīn son of Sanā al-Dawla.

On 24 Ṣafar [July 24, 1280] the emir `Alam al-Dīn imprisoned the Chief Judge Shams al-Dīn Ibn Khallikān in the Najībiyya Hospice (*khānqāh*), and the emir `Alam al-Dīn al-Ḥalabī wrote an appraisal to the Sultan al-Malik al-Manṣūr of all the matters that had occurred. Answers returned from al-Malik al-Manṣūr, so the emir `Alam al-Dīn al-Ḥalabī sat in his vestibule on the Green Square, while the emirs and notables were gathered, and the Sultan's letter was read to them.

In it there was a general clemency for the people. The Chief Judge Najm al-Dīn Ibn Sanā al-Dawla attended this session, as well as Chief Judge Shams al-Dīn Aḥmad Ibn Khallikān, the Shaykh Shams al-Dīn al-Ḥanbalī, the preacher Ibn al-Ḥarastānī. So the emir `Alam al-Dīn freed the Chief Judge Shams al-Dīn Ibn Khallikān on 9 Rabī` al-Awwal [July 9, 1280] of this year, and he was returned to his dwelling at al-`Ādiliyya College.

The Chief Judge Najm al-Dīn Ibn Sanā al-Dawla requested from the Chief Judge Shams al-Dīn Ibn Khallikān that he vacate the dwelling at al-`Ādiliyya so that he himself could live in it. This was burdensome for him. But then the emir `Alam al-Dīn al-Ḥalabī ordered the Chief Judge Shams al-Dīn Ibn Khallikān to move from al-`Ādiliyya and to hand it over to Ibn Sanā al-Dawla, and Ibn Sanā al-Dawla renewed this demand. He had already sent to Aleppo to bring his family, and their arrival was confirmed on Wednesday 19 Rabī` al-Awwal [July 19, 1280].

He went out to meet them, and a formal order was issued so that the Chief Judge Ibn Khallikān would move from al-`Ādiliyya College. This was difficult for him, and he remained depressed because of this. Ibn Sanā al-Dawla was asked to grant a respite to Ibn Khallikān for some days until he could move to some other place, but he refused. He became more determined, but pressure was put upon him, and the Chief Judge Ibn Khallikān was under threat of breaking a formal order until the 4th hour of the day.

He collected his books, loaded up his garments for moving, and summoned porters to transport his garments to Mt. Ṣāliḥiyya. While he was in the process of moving some of it, and engrossed in moving the rest, suddenly a troop of the guard (*jāndāriyya*) riding appeared, to summon him on behalf of the emir `Alam al-Dīn al-Ḥalabī. He thought it was because the place was empty, so he showed them that he was engrossed in moving, but they said to him "You are not sought because of that. A post-courier has appeared from the Sultan's gate, so you are being sought because of that."

He thought then that this would be worse than the move, so he turned towards the deputy sultan. The Sultan al-Malik [175] al-Manṣūr's letter had suddenly come to the emir `Alam al-Dīn al-Ḥalabī, when he had rejected the appointment of Ibn Sanā al-Dawla to the judiciary, as he was deaf. He said

> We have granted clemency to both great and small, so it is not appropriate that we should single one person out with disfavor and without concealing what is connected to the rights of the judge Shams al-Dīn Ibn Khallikān, his association and service of old, as he is among the few remaining from the period of al-Ṣāliḥ [Najm the Ayyubid]. We have therefore issued a written order to return him to the judicial position in which he was.

The emir `Alam al-Dīn al-Ḥalabī bestowed a robe upon him, and he rode immediately, greeted the emirs, and then returned to the `Ādiliyya College as a judge, dismounted at the time of afternoon prayers, and took up the cases, settling in the `Ādiliyya. This was counted as one of the occurrences of release after hardship (*al-faraj ba`d al-shidda*).[38] It was said that Ibn Sanā al-Dawla gave the emir al-Ḥalabī 1000 dinars for his appointment.

The Chief Judge Najm al-Dīn Ibn Sanā al-Dawla had asked the judge Najm al-Dīn al-*s-a-?-I* to serve as a deputy for him in judgments in place of the judge Jamāl al-Dīn Ibn `Abd al-Kāfī. His taking up of affairs lasted for 20 days, then Ibn `Abd al-Kāfī was returned by the return of the Chief Judge Shams al-Dīn Ibn Khallikān.

It was said that the return of Shams al-Dīn Ibn Khallikān happened on 25 Rabī` al-Awwal [July 25, 1280] and that when the Chief Judge Shams al-Dīn Ibn Khallikān was reestablished in the judiciary, he wrote a letter to the Sultan al-Malik al-Manṣūr praying for him, and apologizing. The answer came with thanks, acceptance and apologies, but God knows best.

Mention of the delegation of the deputy sultanate in Damascus to the emir Ḥusām al-Dīn Lājīn "the Lesser" al-Manṣūrī, the Chancelleries Supervisor to the emir Badr al-Dīn Baktūt al-`Alā'ī, and the ministry to the chief Taqī al-Dīn Tawba al-Tikrītī

We have already mentioned that al-Malik al-Manṣūr Sayf al-Dīn Qalāwūn, ruler of protected Egypt, set the emir Ḥusām al-Dīn Lājīn "the Lesser," his mamluk, as deputy in the protected Damascus Citadel. He also made the chief Taqī al-Dīn Tawba al-Tikrītī the minister in Damascus, so when Shams al-Dīn Sunqur al-ashqar set himself up as sultan in Damascus he detained the both of them, and imprisoned them.

---

[38] A well-known trope in Arabic and Farsi literature.

When he was crushed and defeated, the deputy of Damascus Citadel freed them, and the emir `Alam al-Dīn al-Ḥalabī reestablished the chief Taqī al-Dīn Tawba, and set the emir Badr al-Dīn Baktūt al-`Alā'ī to be the new deputy sultan in Damascus until the Sultan al-Malik al-Manṣūr's formal proclamation would come from Egypt.

When it was the day of 11 Rabī` al-Awwal [July 11, 1280] of this year there arrived in Damascus [176] seven individuals from the post-courier horsemen from the Manṣūrī sultanic gate. With them was an investiture for the emir Ḥusām al-Dīn Lājīn "the Lesser" al-Manṣūrī for the deputy sultanate in protected Damascus, an investiture for the emir Badr al-Dīn Baktūt al-`Alā'ī as Chancelleries Supervisor, and an investiture for the chief Taqī al-Dīn Tawba al-Tikrītī as minister for Syria. For each of them there was an honorary gift, plus an honorary gift for the ruler of Ḥamāh.

When it was the 12th [July 12] the rest of the emirs gathered together in the Green Square, while the emir Ḥusām al-Dīn Lājīn donned the ennoblement of deputyship, and the emir Badr al-Dīn Baktūt the ennoblement of the supervisor. The emir `Alam al-Dīn al-Ḥalabī, the emir `Izz al-Dīn *al-afram*, the emir Badr al-Dīn Bīlīk al-Aydimurī, and the rest of the emirs, the Egyptian and Syrian armies rode, and they all went to the formal session (*khidma*) of the emir Ḥusām al-Dīn.

When they reached the Citadel Gate, they all walked on foot, and kissed the emir Ḥusām al-Dīn at the stair leading to the Secret Gate three times. Then the two emirs `Alam al-Dīn al-Ḥalabī and `Izz al-Dīn al-*afram* advanced to support him, so that he could ride, while they walked in his formal procession to the House of Felicity.

He behaved well towards the both of them, refusing to ride, continuing walking, while the emir `Alam al-Dīn al-Ḥalabī was on his right, and the emir `Izz al-Dīn *al-afram* was on his left, while the rest of the emirs and the armies were before him, as were the judges, notables and senior leaders. He continued walking until he entered the House of Felicity, and sat on the rank of deputy, while his investiture was being read.

It is said that his investiture was read on Wednesday the 11th [July 11, 1280]. The emir Lājīn at that time was a youth, good, very religious, noble, and brave, loving the learned and righteous, and treating the populace with justice and fairness, having humility with great sanctity and penetrating words.

On Thursday 12 Rabī` al-Awwal after the noon prayers, he bestowed a robe upon the chief Taqī al-Dīn Tawba al-Tikrītī, and he was given the pens of the ministry in protected Damascus, continuing on (as before).

In the month of Rabī` al-Awwal [July] a letter from `Alam al-Dīn Sanjar al-Ḥalabī arrived at the sultanic gates in the Hill Citadel interceding for the emir `Alā' al-Dīn `Alī son of Ḥusām al-Dīn *k-r-?-k* [=Lājīn] son of Berke Khan, so the Sultan al-Malik al-Manṣūr freed him. [177]

Mention of the delegation of emirate upon the Āl Faḍl, and Āl `Alī, to Fakhr al-Dīn, Shams al-Dīn and Ḥusām al-Dīn

We have already explained the disobedience of the emir Sharaf al-Dīn `Īsā b. Muhannā, and his going in the company of Shams al-Dīn Sunqur al-ashqar. When this reached the Sultan al-Malik al-Manṣūr, the ruler of Egypt, he removed his *iqṭā`* fief in favor of the emir Fakhr al-Dīn `Uthmān b. Māni` b. Hiba, the emir Shams al-Dīn Muḥammad b. Abī Bakr, and the emir Ḥusām al-Dīn Darrāj b. Ṭāhir. He established the situation that the emir Fakhr al-Dīn and the emir Shams al-Dīn would both be the joint emirs for the Āl Faḍl [tribe] and the Āl `Alī [tribe]. The grazing region for Fakhr al-Dīn `Uthmān would be from al-Rastan to al-Malūḥa, while the grazing region for Shams al-Dīn Muḥammad b. Abī Bakr would be from al-Malūḥa to al-Shaṭṭ, to the Euphrates [River]. Ḥusām al-Dīn Darrāj would be emir over the Āl `Āmir, and its grazing region would be from Rastan to al-`Aqābīyāt. Formal proclamations and investitures were written to that effect.

A copy of the investiture of the emir Fakhr al-Dīn `Uthmān written by the judge Fatḥ al-Dīn Ibn `Abd al-Ẓāhir, the chief of the noble Correspondence Chancellery, in Rabī` al-Awwal [July] of this year:

> Praise be to God who has singled out those supporting this dynasty with promotion and pride, while casting humiliation and compulsion upon those who opposed it, elongating its days until the age is completed, until its days would be described, even if they are shortened, by the happiness wherein each passes like a year, and every day like a month.
>
> We praise Him for the help and triumph He has granted to us, with victory and spreading of proclamation to those have triumphed after being wound up, and purity of proclamation towards those who stubbornly resisted it after its spreading.
>
> We testify that there is no god but God, alone, who has no associate, a testimony which if its notaries entered under the census, its benefits could never be entered into a count. In addition, that Muḥammad is His servant and His Messenger who he gave the guidance at the beginning, and the intercession at the Return, the Day of Gathering, may God pray for him, and upon his family and his companions, prayer which makes felicitous after infelicity, proud after defeat.
>
> *Afterwards*, God, praise and raise Him, when he gave us authority over the earth, and placed in our hands the right of extending and grasping, showed us how we can accomplish the good, while goodly accomplishing. He also showed how we could compel the heart to act during our days after being split, how to become stars of worth rising illuminated in the

heavens of our realm. In addition, how to encounter the good in it, for the one who seeks it, when there is something preventing him (*māni`*)[39] from the good prior to our days.

How to achieve advancement [178] for the one who when he is awkward at achieving it, it is said "This one is more deserved of it than those before" when this is the one who there has been advancement in his house since the beginning of time?" This is what has been mentioned about Āl Faḍl and Āl `Alī—they had the rank of nobility.

There was no wondering that the rank of nobility belonged to `Uthmān, so we saw fit that none should ride the saddle of glory other than its own family, just as a verse/sign does not abrogate one before it in precedence without being better than it or its like.[40] Nor should one be given its flag until the knives are fastened to him, nor should one mount a camel's hump unless one is deserved of it, first and last.

Since the august session of the emir Fakhr al-Dīn `Uthmān son of the emir Māni` son of Hiba is the one intended by this fine statement and is the spirit for the body of this praise which communicates both secretly and publicly, and is worthy of good treatment in everything, and is able to. Specifically for being the best part of the servants in that, and one that is favorably compared to all his peers, had he been measured against them.

The good noble opinion necessitates that the high command go forth continuing the one of power in his days being raised, the one of merit in his dynasty. No one will be able to overpower him in glory-seeking nor forbid him. The one of nobility, who conjoins in it the blessings that cannot be veiled from others, nor are themselves conjoined.

That he be delegated precedence over the Bedouin of protected Syria, who are those who will be mentioned following, according to the state that will establish their relative rankings. His dwellings which he must protect, far and near, settled and nomadic, built up and waste, going out and returning, from al-Rastan to al-Malūḥa, while the Bedouin are Āl Faḍl, and Āl `Alī, who can camp where they wish in these aforementioned areas, or in the camping area of the emir Shams al-Dīn Muḥammad b. Abī Bakr.

39 A pun, since the father of Fakhr al-Dīn `Uthmān was named Māni`.
40 Paraphrase of Q2:106.

Service is one, and belief is agreed on the basis of common interests, so let him be the spirit for the body of god-fearingness, not merely the spirit of its body. Let him be the first and foremost of the tribes' number, when there is need for a first,[41] be the pole for their celestial spheres, which they orbit for their administration, in reporting be their moderation and help them to stay within boundaries. In precedence, be their governor upon whom they rely in relation to his emirate in its total and parts, gathering them together in obedience, as obedience is the angel of a command in relation to the command-giver, and the foundation of goodness for both desert-dweller and settled person.

Let him know that every one of them has a dwelling (*bayt*) in it which is known, or a knowing that declares nobility among them, and a place which a child inherits from his father, and elders to whom this dwelling can return, so guard their genealogies for them, shepherd their circumstances. When they are commanded to do something according to the interests of the state, announce it to them "Enter the door and stay there."

They have fords to guard, refuges to watch, casting-places (for weapons) of which one does not speak, wintering and summering places, hunting grounds, water-passages, grazing places and pasturages, near as opposed to settled and far, raiding, charging (the enemy), lightning and flashing lightning. So let him be on the watch for all of that, and take the best and most cunning path, so as to restrain the one thirsting, to notice [179] those going out and coming back, to make this safe in a way that news of him will be pleasurable for the one who drives the camels, as well as those driven.

They have a set number for assessment, and a law (*qānūn*) which is arranged, so let him be firm in raising it, a helping hand in supporting it. Know that he is, even if he is well within his rights in that which has past, turned away from those who have died during the previous period, having been given precedence over all below him. God has returned to him the first fruits of the matter and His help, so he should not give a backbiter anything to say against him, nor enter into an affair that is dubious, but he should be above all others in service and intention, in energy and resolution, and God Most High will dispense gratitude of blessing upon him.

During this month Shams al-Dīn Sunqur al-Ghutamī and Sayf al-Dīn Balabān *al-khāṣṣ* Turkī headed as envoys to the king Mengű Teműr by sea. A

[41] Presumably this means something of a "first among equals" with regard to the egalitarian tribes.

letter for the Sultan Ghiyāth al-Dīn was written by the judge Fatḥ al-Dīn Ibn `Abd al-Ẓāhir to be delivered personally by them. Its text:

> May God glorify the victory of the honorable, lofty, sultanic, kingly, felicitous [Mas`ūd], knowledgeable, just, triumphant, victorious, Ghiyāth, pillar of Islam and the Muslims, victory [...], nobility of kings and sultans, may his position and ability be raised, his triumph and victory be realized, his enemies and their envy laid low, and may his days be marked by receiving support.
>
> The fates should continue to extend all aid to him, keeping him safe with every means of defense, paying special attention to him utilizing every means to come to his rescue. Thus we begin it with a peace greeting that is self-evident, praise whose melody adorns and fastens onto the ears, loyalty that conjoins the two best things of his lineage and kinship, and seeking to know news of him, which is coolness for the eyes, and happiness for the hearts.
>
> Thankful for the signs of him which leave a good impression in the hearts of the friends of God (*awlīyā'*), but a negative one in the hearts of the enemies, and causing him to understand that we have sent the two emirs Shams al-Dīn Sunqur al-Ghutamī and Sayf al-Dīn Balabān *al-khāṣṣ* al-Turkī as envoys in the service of the Great Khan Mengű Teműr, may his awe-inspiringness be increased.
>
> From his honorableness [we are] seeking passage for them, closeness to his service, happiness we convey face-to-face, and peace as long as they are able to return to him. Some gifts we have sent at their hands to be presented to him, so that the peace greeting would not be empty of gifts handed over, nor lacking in the sweetness of talks and discussions face-to-face, and by God, he should not lack a long life, but continue to be lofty and ascend.

In it the emir Nāṣir al-Dīn Ibn al-Ḥusnā al-Jazarī and the Patriarch *anbā* Siwus [= Yūnus] headed to the Lascarid [Palaeologan] king as envoys. [180]

On Thursday 3 Rabī` al-Ākhir [August 2, 1280] of this year Abű `Abdallāh al-Maghribī arrived at the sultantic gates at the Hill Citadel with western letters from Tūnis.

On Monday 7 Rabī` al-Ākhir [August 6, 1280] the emir `Izz al-Dīn Izdimur al-`Alā'ī arrived at the noble sultanic gates at the Hill Citadel, and the Sultan graciously gave to him the fief (*khubz*) of the emir Qayrān al-Bunduqdārī, which had passed to him from `Alam al-Dīn Sanjar al-Duwaydārī, and a proclamation was written to that effect.

On Tuesday the middle of Rabī` al-Ākhir [August 14, 1280] the emir Badr al-Dīn Baktūt son of the *atābak* arrived at the sultanic gates.

On Tuesday 22 Rabī` al-Ākhir [August 21, 1280] the Sultan ordered through the tongue of the emir Sābiq al-Dīn Lāḥ *al-dawādār* to write a rescript (*tawqī`*) that would establish a once a year grant for Shaykh Muḥammad because of piety and charity, plentiful always, and continuously useful, from the stores of the protected Damascus chancellery, of wheat ten sacks.

The writer of the book [Ibn al-Mukarram] *Treasury of the Secretary* stated: In Rabī` al-Ākhir [August 1280] a written command was issued to the emir Badr al-Dīn Baktūt al-`Alā'ī that he would be appointed to the Chancelleries Supervision in protected Damascus. We have already noted that was during Rabī` al-Awwal of this year, but God knows best which of these it was. An investiture was written for the emir Baktūt drafted by the judge Fatḥ al-Dīn Ibn `Abd al-Ẓāhir, and a copy of it was:

> Praise be to God who raises the stations of the new moons, places the supporters of this dynasty in pleasant places and beauty, eases the good things to the one of the servants whose devotion does not waver in any matter, the expert among those responsible. They are such as leave the traces of loyalty that have beautified concealing the goodness of manifestation.
>
> We praise Him a praise that chooses for it the most marvelous words in both poetry and prose. We testify that there is no god but God, alone, without any associate, a testimony of felicity of one who by its order is ordered, and due to the length of its merit fall short. We testify that Muḥammad is His servant and His Messenger who gives intercession for the community on the Day of Resurrection and Collection, may God pray for him and for his family and companions, a prayer by which its sayer acquires merchandise that will never perish.
>
> *Afterwards*, God, praise Him, when He knew of our supporters that they have pure intention, and a clear conscience, then we turn them however we wish and transfer them to affairs in accord with what pleases God Most High and pleases us, so we rear them in various ways, [181] reciting to them verses of favor in the best manner and arrangement. Thus they only increase in effort and do not desire anything other what we will.
>
> The august session considers the emir Badr al-Dīn who is the among the most distinguished of our supporters, among the first of our devotees, close to us, and whose connection to serving us is one he considers to a gift from us, and the one who we have conferred thanks upon him, forbidding him from patience.
>
> If we have promoted him, in his proceeding, he was a sword, and if we have raised him to the heavens of glory, he was a complete full moon. He

has served as Chancellery Supervisor in protected Syria, while he was the initiator of matters and followed up on them. The ropes and nets of administration were placed by him because he was the primal matter (*hayūlā*) in the obtaining of revenues, solver of problems, the refuge of hopes, the one whose order is followed, nor does fancy/whim enter into trusting him.

How could it be any other way when as it is said, money is the turner of souls which necessitates the noble good opinion that the high command go forth to delegating to him the prosperous Chancellery Supervision in protected Syria, as usual for one who is promoted there.

Let him act with fearing God, mighty and majestic, in secret and in public, to forbid and to enjoin, to take and to give, to demonstrate dissatisfaction and favor. Let him not depart from the ways of truth if he speaks, does, divides, gathers, appoints or removes, and that he should not oppress any creature on our behalf, but should remove oppression of the one who oppresses others.

He should not do what God does not praise, or the people, as there are two good outcomes for his conduct and his ways. Whenever he specifies money for us from any region, he should not leave it nor depart following his devotion without him following up on it. The instructions concerning wealth are many, and in the Chancellery affairs without number, so only by active duty can he be aware and watch over the affairs to cut off from treachery the desire of envy.

The most majestic of instructions is watchfulness, making sure that words are translated into action, and to write in a way that anyone with sense can understand. Then to order, making the order such that the one ordered does not raise his eyes to anything other than the truth, nor desire, aspire, nor pull to cut off resources. In addition, to give good advice aiming for the commonweal, and the noble signature, may God raise it, raises it as a proof in accord.

On Tuesday 22 Rabīʿ al-Ākhir [August 21, 1280] the canal of blessed mention overflowed.

On Wednesday 23 Rabīʿ al-Ākhir [August 22, 1280] the blessed unique one (*mufrad*) [= Nile inundation] arrived.

On Saturday 26 Rabīʿ al-Ākhir [August 25, 1280] which was the first of the Nasīʾ days, and there were 16 cubits in the blessed Nile. The Sultan al-Malik al-Manṣūr rode to the felicitous Nilometer, and measured the blessed column. He sailed in the victorious fireboats, and the blessed canal overflowed. [182]

This was a day to remember! It was proclaimed at daybreak that the blessed water was two fingers short of 17 cubits. Tidings were written of the surfeit of the Nile to the rest of the lands as usual, and he wrote to the emir `Alam al-Dīn al-Bāshqirdī to that effect, which this is the text:

> May God double the blessing of the high session, and specify the glad tidings in the sweetest way they can overflow, and the best they can be related, as the congratulations continue to waft towards him in that which they carry. This is as the cloth garment ties the (post) stage-stops to him, in those secrets he publishes, tying the sending forth of this correspondence. It wishes peace, having different types of tidings, guiding as praise spreads its wings, dispensing greetings that cheer, praises that exhale and permeate those witnessing them, gazing down upon the one who comes from that region, expressing copious thanks, and communicating the lovely mention of him. All this while being made happy in all people's happiness that God Most High has made easy,[42] and the inundation of the blessed Nile that He has granted.
>
> The measure of the measuring rod, its telling of the canal's breaking which God has mandated, thus guaranteeing them the sprouting of every fine pair (of plants) by the blessed overflow.
>
> We have begun this correspondence on the day of the Nile's inundation, the truth of bearing witness to it, according to what Jamīl told of Buthayna,[43] as the valleys are blossoming, and the swamps are underwater, reaching the asterix of the 17th cubit, so there is fear upon the land from that cubit's [level].[44]
>
> Therefore, we rode to the felicitous Nilometer, and then saw its blessed column where the inundation had risen to the best level, deserving the commentary of the measurement point. We hastened towards it, measuring it, and then returned to the canal's dam in the heat of our victorious certainty, so then broke it, whereupon the overflow rushed through, whereby God caused benefit and favor to arrive.
>
> By its coolness it dampened the burning heat, while because of it the salty ground became like a white pearl, as God caused hopes to be realized after a feeling that it had passed, and it revived, praise Him, the ground

---

[42] A number of puns in the Arabic.

[43] A pair of star-crossed lovers famous from early Islamic period.

[44] If the inundation of the Nile rises above a certain level then the land will be flooded rather than irrigated.

after its death.[45] Thus the earth's watering was completed, the servants (Muslims) were made secure by it, as the felicitous river (*baḥr*) was filled, the earth was covered with freshness, and there was no way left between the two mountains[46] for anything else [to pass].

God, praise be to Him, had known the beauty of our intention with regard to our subjects, so rewarded them with the bounty of His grace during the days of our dynasty (*dawla*) and the world is happy with favors, after having beseeched with righteous intercessory prayer for our days, the time of happiness and pleasure has returned.

They are trusting in God's aid, as he left them their Nile, and granted to them al-Saffāḥ and al-Manṣūr,[47] so let the council take its portion from this glad tidings, and publish it to the four corners as congratulation and tidings, of the criterion of being well-watered. If this benefit is specifically for the Egyptian homelands, then its blessing is general throughout all the rest of creation, as God, praise Him, has removed worry from the community, and reminded them by its flowing of the Flood other than it is flowing with praise, that it is a mercy. The high council continues to be focused upon (the possibility of) destruction, while guarding felicitation, with His beneficence and grace. [183]

In it, the emir Jamāl al-Dīn Aqush al-Badrī was dismissed from being the governor of protected Shawbak Castle. The emir `Alam al-Dīn Sanjar al-Ḥasūnī al-Ighānī was assigned in place of him, and in it al-Ṣafī the secretary was summoned from Shawbak to the glorious gate at the Hill Citadel.

On Sunday 27 Rabī` al-Ākhir [August 26, 1280] the emir Sayf al-Dīn Abū Bakr son of *Isfāsalār*, governor of protected Cairo, so his bequest was guarded. The emir `Izz al-Dīn Aybak al-Fakhrī was appointed after him. In it, the Nile increased one finger to complete at three fingers.

On Monday 28 Rabī` al-Ākhir [August 27, 1280] the Nile increased two fingers to complete at five fingers [total].

On Tuesday the 29th the increase was two fingers completing seven fingers [total].

On Wednesday the increase was two fingers making it nine fingers plus 17 cubits.

On Thursday first day of Jumādā al-Ulā [August 29, 1280], which was the first of Tūt, the Day of Nawrūz of the year 997, the increase in it was two fingers to complete 11 fingers plus 17 cubits.

---

45 Paraphrasing numerous Qur'ānic verses, e.g., Q30:19, 34.

46 Presumably the mountains on either side of the Nile.

47 Al-Saffāḥ and al-Manṣūr were the two first `Abbasid caliphs, whose names had messianic significance. However, the name al-Saffāḥ either originally or came to mean "bloodshedder" and was not used by any later rulers.

On Friday the 2nd, its increase was two fingers, to complete 13 fingers total.

On Tuesday the 6th just one finger to complete 18 fingers plus 17 cubits.

On Friday the 9th [September 6, 1280] the emir Sayf al-Dīn al-Jayshī arrived at the noble formal session at the Hill Citadel.

On Tuesday the 13th [September 10, 1280] the increase was one finger, to complete 20 fingers plus 17 cubits.

On Monday the 19th [September 16, 1280] the increase was one finger to complete 21 fingers plus 17 cubits. [184]

On Thursday the 22nd [September 19, 1280] the Sultan wrote a pardon for Shams al-Dīn `Uthmān al-`Ajamī for the charity and Chancellery dues he was obligated to pay. The total of that was 18,000 dirhams, gained by participating in types of commerce and goods that went forth on one journey, not more. This was through a small paper note with his signature and that of the judge Fatḥ al-Dīn Ibn `Abd al-Ẓāhir.

On Sunday the 25th [September 22, 1280] the increase was one finger to complete 23 fingers plus 17 cubits, which was the highest level of the blessed Nile inundation for this blessed year.

During this month the emir Badr al-Dīn Bīlīk al-Aydimurī was given the total of 100 horsemen, and a long proclamation was written for him concerning the 2/3s large fief, the text of which is:

> Praise be to God who has decorated the horizon of this dominating dynasty (*dawla*) with its new moon, making it to be on the step of its highpoint, aiding it, transferring it from the constellations of its radiance and the stations (of the moon) of its pride.
>
> We praise Him for His quenching grace because of its piety, radiant over its expanding tidings, every time we increase praising it and being thankful for it. We testify that there is no god but God, alone, without any associate, a testimony that the hearts speak in private and in public. In addition, we testify that Muḥammad is His servant and His Messenger sent to the peoples of the world in their entirety, may God pray for him, and for his family and companions, a prayer that will fill existence with its reward, and contains for its community salvation on the Day of its Gathering.
>
> *Afterwards*, the first one to receive the continuous graces upon him and pass them, the best of those blessings in his opinion in his establishment and the raising of the Sunna is one upon whom the pens bestow the marvels of their arrangement and prose, specifying praises exhaled by letters to diffuse them. He is also the one to whom the dominating (*al-qāhira*)[48]

[48] A double entendre as this is also the name of Cairo.

> dynasty opens its breast to ease its way, tightening its belt by carrying its ministerial load, being a trustee for carrying out the ordinances, both complete and lacking, and then brings those fortresses he conquers and constricts borne to Egypt.
>
> Since the honorable high, emir Badr Bīlīk al-Aydimurī is the full moon of these heavens, and the one who lights up its radiance, being lit by the stars of these goals, the loftiness of their pride, in the unique necklace of these pendants, the peerlessness of its pearl, the master of these riddles, and the key to its secret. The noble opinions therefore necessitate that the brides of presents be led to him in their pubic parts and virginity, spreading over him the precious gentle graces in their coupling and as a single.
>
> Gifts are bestowed upon him between yellow and red, followed successively by favors as fruits and produce. If his blessed provision is increased in its amount and magnitude, if its nine-tens is completed by a tenth, then he should know that it will be continued in its eternality and secrecy, that it will not abandon him for an hour from the felicity of remembering it. So for that reason the high order has gone forth, and the fates continue to mandate the dominating dynasty to lengthen the duration [185] of its mention, the length of its life, the properties continuing as trustees for its victory, by their swords' passing, and its spears' action, that their number be perfected to 100.

In it, a guard was set over the chief Taqī al-Dīn Tawba, the minister for protected Syria, and upon his assets. He was arrested in Syria, and removed from the ministry, as many assets were discovered. In it, a section of the Egyptian army headed out from Damascus, and joined up at Shayzar, intending to besiege it. Envoys passed back and forth between them and Shams al-Dīn Sunqur *al-ashqar* concerning handing over Shayzar.

On Monday 3 Jumādā al-Ākhira [September 30, 1280] of this year the emir `Alam al-Dīn Sanjar al-Ḥalabī arrived from protected Syria, after its situation was righted, and its affairs straightened.

On Thursday the 6th the Sultan al-Malik al-Manṣūr bestowed a robe upon the emir Sayf al-Dīn Balabān al-Rūmī, making him *dawādār* (secretary) to the learned one, not more, and upon Fatḥ al-Dīn Ibn `Abd al-Ẓāhir, according to his rank.

Mention of the Tatars' advance towards Syria and their entering into Aleppo, what they did there, and their return from it

We had mentioned that Shams al-Dīn Sunqur *al-ashqar* and the emir Sharaf al-Dīn `Īsā b. Muhannā both wrote to the king Abagha son of Hűlegű, the king of the Tatars, concerning the dissension that had occurred between the

Muslims' armies, so when what they wrote him reached him, he prepared armies, and they set out towards the Syrian lands.

These divided into three divisions: one division (headed) towards the [Seljuq] Rūm, whose commanders were Ṣamghār, Tanjī, and Ṭaranjī. One division towards the east, whose commander was Baidu son of Ṭarghāy son of Hűlegű—it was accompanied by the ruler of Mārdīn. The third division that had most of the army, and the bulk of the Mongols, accompanied by Mengű Teműr son of Hűlegű.

The reports arrived to Syria concerning that at the beginning of Jumādā al-Ākhira [September 28, 1280] of that year, so what was left of the Egyptian and Syrian armies in Damascus departed, while their commander was Rukn al-Dīn Ayājī. These joined up with the armies that were up against Shayzar, as they had pulled back from it somewhat, and camped outside of Ḥamāh when the report of the Tatars reached them.

An army from the Egyptian homelands also arrived, whose commander was the emir Badr al-Dīn Baktāsh al-Najmī, so it joined them, and all of them mustered outside of Ḥamāh. They sent reconnaissance towards the Tatars, and sent to Shams al-Dīn Sunqur *al-ashqar*: "This enemy could crush us. Only through division will that happen. It is not right that the Muslims should perish from this. Prudence (*maṣlaḥa*) [186] dictates that we assemble as one to repel it." The army of Shams al-Dīn Sunqur *al-ashqar* descended from Ṣahyūn, and *al-ḥājj* Izdimur from Shayzar. Each group camped beneath its castle, and they did not join together with the Egyptians, but joined because of their common belief, and to repel the enemy.

During the middle tenth of Jumādā al-Ākhira [October 1280] a large number of those fleeing pell-mell from Aleppo, its lands, and what was around it, from Ḥimṣ and Ḥamāh and the northern [Syrian] lands, arrived in Damascus and Ba`lbak, all fleeing from the Tatars. Only those incapable were left behind. Aleppo was emptied of troops, and they joined up with those in Ḥamāh.

Many of the inhabitants of Damascus and the Syrian lands resolved to head towards the Egyptian homelands, and the people were very perturbed. When it was 21 Jumādā al-Ākhira [October 18, 1280] a number of detachments from the Tatar armies arrived in Aleppo after they had taken possession of `Ayntāb, Baghrās and al-Darbsāk.

They found Aleppo virtually empty, as the army and its people had fled pell-mell from it. They killed those who had stayed in it in the open, plundering, taking captive, burned the Friday mosque, the exemplary schools, the Ruler's House, the houses of the emirs and the senior officials, and vandalized the city terribly. Most of those who had stayed behind concealed themselves in caves and other places. The Tatars stayed in Aleppo for two days.

On Sunday 23 Jumādā al-Ākhira [October 20, 1280] the Tatars moved from Aleppo, returning to their lands after the booty which they had acquired had gone before them. They took a great deal from the storehouses to their places. The reason for their returning from Aleppo was what they had learned about the newfound unity among the Muslims to repel them. The intention of al-Malik al-Manṣūr, the ruler of Aleppo, and his departure was also a factor, as he led the armies from the Egyptian homelands.

It is said that this was in middle tenth of Jumādā al-Ākhira [October 1280]. When they returned from Aleppo, they dispersed to their wintering quarters. This is what happened with regard to the Tatars. As for the Aleppans, the Tatars, when they returned from Aleppo, those who had concealed themselves came out, and those who had fled pell-mell from it returned, and the people became calm. God knows best.

Mention of the delegation of heir-apparency from al-Malik al-Manṣūr to his son al-Malik al-Ṣāliḥ

On Monday 17 Jumādā al-Ākhira [October 14, 1280] of this year the Sultan al-Malik al-Manṣūr [187] Sayf al-Dīn Qalāwūn al-Alfī al-Ṣāliḥī al-Najmī delegated the position of heir apparent, and the sultanate's guarantor, to his son al-Malik al-Ṣāliḥ `Alā' al-Dīn Abū al-Fatḥ `Alī. This was when he had determined to head towards Syria to meet the Tatars [in battle].

His regnal title was al-Malik al-Ṣāliḥ, and al-Malik al-Ṣāliḥ rode with the kingly pomp and the sultanic insignia, and he transversed Cairo. He was proclaimed to be sultan in the sermons, and the heir apparent. His name was mentioned in the sermons in the rest of the pulpits, after that of his father, and his formal investiture was written to that effect, which was the work of the judge Muḥyī al-Dīn Ibn `Abd al-Ẓāhir, in which he was at his most eloquent:

> In the name of God, the Merciful, the Compassionate, and in Him we trust
>
> Praise be to God who ennobled the seat of kingship with His greatness, guarded it with his legatee, strengthened His victory with delegated authority of His guidance, and made lofty the decree of His generosity with qualities combined by an early enumeration; and made the best of fathers lofty through the best of sons, by one who his father's loftiness with regard to him through his lofty nobility of character, and the fruit of his garden follows closely his pattern and hasty friendship—we praise Him for His graces which are harvested in the blossom of produce, and to the sun's light are added the moon's guidance, encompassed by the sea, blessed by the day, beautifying the beginning, prettifying the report, joining the pleasure and fragrance of times with the splendor of blades and the delicacy of daybreaks.
>
> We testify that there is no god but God, alone, without any partner—a testimony by which we clothe the tongues, every hour anew, in the lengthy shade of which we rest, by which we seek to draw near to hopes that others

besides us see as far; and we ask for prayer upon our lord Muḥammad—by whom God has purified this community (*umma*) from impurities, and made it pure in its genesis by his guidance—and prayer upon him, his family, his companions, among whom was one by whom one understands the goodness of what he left behind by his command to lead the people in prayer,[49] among whom was one by whom God constructed the bases of the religion and made him a support for the foundation,[50] among whom was one who equipped the army of destitution, and was generous with his wealth at a time of lack and hardship,[51] and among whom was one who [Muḥammad] said concerning him: "Truly, tomorrow I will give the flag to a man who God and His Messenger love, and who loves God and His Messenger" and who shone in doing this, having been further ennobled by his marriage-kinship with the People of the House,[52] and removed filth from them—a prayer that continues to reverberate through the souls, and is still the best conviviality for the times.

Afterwards, the best of one who is ennobled by occupying the ranks of the sultanate, who the garb of judgeship places him in a superior position by receiving it, one who the ascendants of dominion are resplendent by his careful attention, one who the realms hasten to acknowledge his rights, one who the dominion of his Manṣūr, may God render him aid, shines with his steadfastness, and his heir-apparent, may God render him powerful, its constructor, and the one who supervises the entry-hall of greatness, if his father is absent, in the interests of Islam.

He is his mainstay; if he is present, then he is his second, whoever beautifies themselves, the governance is missing from [188] them because of the best cub vouchsafed to a lion, who brings the weal of the community to perfection by the best downpour following spring rains, one to whom the royal ethics and the mannerisms of rule were imparted while still a boy, one who the intercessory prayers of noble parentage singled him out as its straightener—without any wretchedness in these prayers—one who was raised by the prominence of rulership until its place became higher, one who is deserved that trust be placed in him, and will succeed, one who it is worthy that it be pronounced to him: "Succeed me leading my people!", one who at every good thing advances, one who when the matters of the Muslims are delegated to him, he supervises their matters well, one who fulfills the past and the present from his father, one whose

49 Abū Bakr, the first caliph.
50 ʿUmar, the second caliph.
51 ʿUthmān, the third caliph.
52 ʿAlī b. Abī Ṭālib, the fourth caliph.

light-giving, lofty name is "there is no sword but Dhū al-Fiqār, no youth but `Alī."[53]

Since he is in the lofty, masterly, sultanic, kingly, al-Ṣāliḥī al-`Alā'ī[54] place, may God support the religion by him, and gather the submission of every muezzin necessitating obedience to him, to take care of the Muslims' affairs, until morning appears, while he is the one who makes the believers aright, he is the one hoped-for to administer these matters, and the hoped-for one with regard to the interests of the lands and the border regions, the one who treasures up victory to "heal what is in the hearts,"[55] the one for whom physiognomy (*firāsa*) testifies to the identity of his father and to him by adjudication. Is not the ruler the father of `Alī, the Victorious (al-Manṣūr)?

For these reasons mercy and compassion have been mandated for the community, that an heir-apparent be appointed for them by whom they can grasp ahold of the bond of his nobility, hasten after performing the circumambulation of the Ka`ba of his father to his sanctity (Ḥaram), plucking the flowers of justice, and the fruits of generosity from his pen and word.

The community should seek the felicity from him by al-Malik al-Ṣāliḥ, who distributes lights from his brow, and righteous deeds from his miracles (*karāmāt*) and nobility.

For this reason the highest, masterly, sultanic command of al-Malik al-Manṣūr, may God make fate to serve him, has gone forth, while the realms continue to be resplendent, from him and his heir-apparent with the sun and the moon, to delegate to him the heir-apparency and the noble deputy sultanship completely, generally, in an all-encompassing, responsible, gathering, distributing, decisive, shining, noble, eminent, loving, caring, gentle manner, with self-control in all of the noble regions and realms.

Its armies, garrisons, Bedouin, Turkmen, Kurds, deputies, governors, high and low, subjects and non-subjects, rulers, judges, hunter and game, in the Egyptian homelands, and its border regions, its regions, its lands, and all that is included in it, the Ḥijāzī realm, and all that is included in

[53] This statement is one of the foundations of the *futuwwa* guilds; al-Malik al-Ṣāliḥ's given name was `Alī.

[54] The referent is to Qalāwūn's former masters.

[55] Paraphrase of Q9:14.

it, the Nubian realm, and all that is included in it, the Ṣafadan conquests, and the coastal Islamic conquests, and all that is included in them, the Syrian realms, its fortresses, castles, cities, regions and lands, the Ḥimṣan realm, the Ḥiṣn al-Akrādian realm, and the mountainous region and their conquests, the Aleppan realm, its border fortresses, lands, and all that is included in them, the Euphrates realm, and what is included in it, and all the rest of the Islamic castles both on land and at sea, on level and rugged ground, Syrian and Egyptian, Yemenite and Ḥijāzī, east and west, far and near.

That the keys of the affairs [189] in those noble realms would be cast upon him, that the sultanate of his father, may God immortalize his reign, would be entrusted to him in order for the community to witness with their own eyes at one time a sultan and caliph, heirship and entrustment, upon which the narrators can rely, which the camel-drivers can hum, while ears are cognizant of them, and tongues speaking about them.

An entrustment proclaimed to all the peoples and to every possessor of sword and pen, to every possessor of knowledge and a flag, of what [Muḥammad], may God's prayers and peace be upon him said, to the one he named, may God be pleased with him, when he appointed him master because of the glory of that to which he appointed him: "To whomever I am master, `Alī will be his master."[56] Every king of a region will receive and acknowledge this statement; every army leader is covered and encompassed by this entrustment; every region must deputize someone who will accept and kiss it, that there be a copy in front of him, for him to follow; every pulpit must proclaim it in its sermon, declaiming the *furqān* [the Qur'ān] of this advancement and reciting it.

As for testaments, we have made our son and heir-apparent aware of these in a way that will be impressed upon his pure mind, and its nourishment has begun to develop his branch. It is necessary for the glimmers to illuminate testaments being blessed by this noble formal investiture, for Friday mosques to make the good happen wherever it happens, while trusts of which we tell you, O our son, may God make us glorious with your length (of life), so that the like of an informer will not tell you.

So "fear God as if you see Him, for as you do not see Him, he sees you."[57] Aid the Divine Law (*al-shar`*), for when you aid it, God will aid you against the enemies of the religion and your enemies. Let justice overflow

[56] The tradition of Ghadīr Khumm, used commonly by Shi`ites. Here "`Alī" is al-Malik al-Ṣāliḥ.

[57] A common Sufi saying.

in speech and in writing until your tongue and your two hands hasten to enunciate it.

Command the right and forbid the wrong,[58] knowing that tomorrow you will have to give an account of this before God. Forbid your soul from whims, so that you do not see yourself when you forbid yourself. Protect the subjects, and command the deputies to bear them through difficulties, and uphold [God's] limits (*al-ḥudūd*), organize the armies, sending out raids on land and at sea to every place is praiseworthy, guard the border regions, pay close attention to matters, secure the servants, God's pure and beloved ones, redoubling for them their sanctity and good treatment.

Know that God has chosen us over the worlds,[59] but the people are brothers, especially those possessed of successful initiative and preponderant opinion. Whoever, when they boast of being related via the Ṣāliḥiyya [regiment] it should be said to them: "How good are the pious (*ṣāliḥ*) predecessors!" so seek counsel from them concerning the issue, confer with them about the important matters of the lands, concerning every secret and open [matter]; also those senior emirs, who are left over from previous rulers, and the treasures of the earlier kings—treat them this way, explaining to them with good treatment.

As for the armies, they are the builder and the building, so act with forbearance towards them, and make sure that they love you because of your good treatment towards them, acting well, and have obedience towards you as part of their creed, so that love for it (obedience) will engulf them, then they will become obedient as a result of your looking fondly upon them.

Ensure that every ethnicity, land and people from among them has the right to approach you with good counsel of any type, for this and they are a precious gift to you, so make your commands with penetrating wisdom, while listening to them.

As for other injunctions, we will give them to you freely as guidance in our own time, and will drill you in them according to clear verses. God Most High will increase your crescent moon until He takes you to the level of the full moons, and will nourish your branch until we consider it to be ripened in the best possible blooming, and flowering. [190] He will supply you with the felicity of our sultanate, by which you have been titled, in blessing, and will inspire you to shoulder His party (*shīʿatihi*)

---

58 The important basis for Islamic social justice.

59 Paraphrase of Q3:42 directed at Mary.

by following His way (*sunna*) until you are able to grasp hold of it in the same manner as us, and will make the subjects be at peace, safety, justice and good treatment with you until you fear no evil nor dread any reverse.

The post-courier arrived in Damascus with the letter of al-Malik al-Manṣūr, in which he informed them of the appointment of his son as heir apparent.

On Friday 28 Jumādā al-Ākhira [October 25, 1280] the Sultan's letter was read in the Friday Mosque of Damascus a little after the Friday prayers, guaranteeing that he had made his son al-Malik al-Ṣāliḥ `Alā' al-Dīn `Alī his heir apparent, and that he was coming to repel the Tatars.

A short while after finishing off from reading that, the tidings of the Tatars' retreat from Aleppo to their lands arrived, so this gave the people great happiness and peace. So they took glad tidings from the appointment of al-Malik al-Ṣāliḥ's appointment as heir. It was said that al-Malik al-Manṣūr Sayf al-Dīn Qalāwūn's delegation of the heir apparency to his son al-Malik al-Ṣāliḥ happened in Rajab [November 1280] of this year, so God knows best which of them it was.

During the end of Jumādā al-Ākhira [October 26, 1280] al-Malik [al-Manṣūr] removed the chief Fakhr al-Dīn Ibrāhīm b. Luqmān from the ministry in the Egyptian homelands, so he returned to the Correspondence Chancellery. He was listed among the total number of secretaries, and removed from being the Chancellery Chief. The Sultan appointed the chief Burhān al-Dīn al-Khiḍr b. al-Ḥasan al-Sinjārī to his ministry after the chief Ibn Luqmān was removed, which was his second appointment, but God knows best.

Mention of al-Malik al-Manṣūr's heading towards Syria to meet the Tatars [in battle], his arrival in Gaza, and his return to the Egyptian homelands

When it reached al-Malik al-Manṣūr Sayf al-Dīn Qalāwūn al-Alfī al-Ṣāliḥī al-Najmī, ruler of the Egyptian homelands and the Syrian lands,[60] the Tatars' movement and their entrance into the Syrian lands, he issued orders to the armies. They then prepared and he departed from Egypt heading towards Syria, accompanied by the Islamic armies in the Egyptian homelands, with the purpose of repelling the Tatars from the Syrian lands. He arrived at protected Gaza. This was what happened with regard to al-Malik al-Manṣūr.

As for what was happening with regard to the Tatars and the Islamic armies already dispatched, the Tatars, when it reached them that the Islamic armies were unified in order to repel them, the Sultan's movement, and his departure to meet them, they retreated to their lands from Aleppo.

When it reached those armies dispatched in Syria that the Tatars had retreated from Aleppo, they dispersed to pursue them, then they returned,

[60] The first time Ibn al-Furāt has accorded him this title.

and the Syrian army stayed in its lands, while the Egyptian army headed towards the service of al-Malik al-Manṣūr in Gaza.

This was because when he arrived there, he received the news of the Tatars' retreat, so he hesitated to proceed towards Damascus [191] because there was no need for him to be there, in addition to the burden of going to Syria.

During these days a number of Sunqur *al-ashqar*'s emirs fled, and entered into the obedience of al-Malik al-Manṣūr, serving him.

On Thursday 10 Sha`bān [December 5, 1280] of this year al-Malik traveled from Gaza, returning to the Egyptian homelands, and God knows best.

During the month of Rajab [November 1280], one of the months this year, the emir Badr al-Dīn Durbās was appointed governor of Jīnīn and Marj Banī `Āmir.[61] The judge Fatḥ al-Dīn son of Muḥyī al-Dīn wrote the investiture for that, of which the following is the text:

> *Afterwards*, praise God for his raising of the full moon of his supporters after a hard-won race, removing to the one he has chosen, plucking him from the distress of his error, and the error of his distress. This is putting into action the one who he knows from his obedience is the best choice and the most informed, the best extemporizer, and the fleetest.
>
> Prayers upon our lord Muḥammad who God guided this community by his light and his traditions, and upon his family and companions who did not turn from his path, nor departed from his preference, a prayer which is the equivalent of a proclamation of sincerity in its secrets.
>
> Since the session of the emir Badr al-Dīn is among those with pure originality and disdainful soul, coupled with the service association to the Ṣāliḥī dynasty (*dawla*), the meritoriousness by which his sword and pen were ennobled, by which his knowledge and flag are lifted up, the intuitive knowledge which went forth becoming knowledge,[62] describing types of praiseful actions while speaking: It is our opinion to delegate to him the governates which will be made greater by his appointment to them. Since a governor is proud of his appointment, these are boasting of the one who is appointed to them.
>
> For this reason the high order has gone forth to delegate to him this governate, so let him take it up know that he has from this dynasty's good will that which will raise him to that which is higher and loftier. The word of these governates is less than his ability in the meaning, and so this delegation is according to the one who hopes.

[61] Jīnīn = present-day Jenin in the northern West Bank; Marj Banī `Āmir is the Jezreel Valley in Israel.

[62] Playing on the difference between *ma`rifa* (experiential or intuitive knowledge) versus *`ilm* (revealed knowledge).

These governates will not know healing in their long-term without one who knows the best kind treatment and (medical) treatment, and it is necessary for less than one drop to fall from a torrent, and from a drop, then a drop can form into rivers, flowing seas. So let him act according to fear of God, in his secret and public (conduct), in his forbidding and enjoining, in his dividing and judgments, vengeance and forbearance.

Let him build up these lands which whims have divided, and diseases have disordered, for it is the time to set them aright, and to alter their prosperity, especially as their harvest time is near, as their governor governs and manages them, so they (camels) walk briskly, tinkling, it (plants) are moist then turn green, and are grassy.

Let him bring its family to it from all quarters and places, count them with all strength, and might, until its fourth becomes a grazing area after being sown, and a pasture filled with springs, its water-source licit for those coming and going. Let him keep corrupters and mischief-makers far away, and let him guard it from being suddenly attacked with the energy of one who attacks like a lion.

Let him be among those good-opinioned of him in all matters, whenever these pits are filled with sugar-cane, [192] which is a support of realms and kings, and whenever cash is prepared for the border fortresses, its dinar should be struck, and paid towards it with care in dispatching it, making it plentiful, doubling it, and increasing it, urging it to be raised, building up its valley, and establishing the conditions of its charities.

He should hold fast to the Muḥammadan Law (*sharīʿa*), in word and deed, in binding and loosening, in many injunctions, but to others he should be most knowledgeable in it, and should treasure up obedience to this noble dynasty.

During this year a fellow appeared known as al-Jāmūs (water buffalo), pretending to be a trickster and a bawdy fellow. He would wield a sword, a scimitar (*simanṭāra*), alone,[63] and try to duel with those who opposed him outside of protected Cairo, then take whatever he wanted from them. People were afraid of

[63] This may be one of the earliest attested notices of the scimitar using this name, which is usually seen as derived from the Farsi *shamshīr*. However, it is not clear whether Ibn al-Furāt is imposing this word from his fifteenth-century context (when the word begins to be attested in Italian) upon the thirteenth-century event. In any case, the novelty of this rogue, wielding a curved blade, appears to be the point of the story. Presumably he either stole it or found it on a battlefield, since it was usually a blade used by horsemen.

him, and he stayed with a number of people in their homes, as he overawed them and they gave him what he wanted. People were afraid of him, used him as a by-word, and began to talk about him a lot. Proverbs were even made about him. He killed a number, so the authorities lay in wait for him in a number of places. Most said that he was in the area of al-Lawq and al-Bawrjī, and those areas.

Another fellow appeared together with him called al-Maḥwajab, and the both of them were active for a while. Finally, the Sultan al-Malik al-Manṣūr summoned the governors of Old Cairo and Cairo, so they were threatened if they did not bring the both of them, speaking to them coarsely.

It happened that one of the mamluks of the emir `Alam al-Dīn Sanjar al-Masrūrī *al-khayyāṭ*'s, governor of Cairo, who was present close to one of the villages outside of protected Cairo, then saw a fellow, who he didn't like, but then became aware that he was al-Jāmūs. So he shot him with an arrow, whereupon the latter fled, entering one of the orchards where he was detained.

He was brought before the governor, and al-Maḥwajab was brought with him, so the Sultan ordered them to be nailed up, so they were, at Zuwayla Gate, one of the gates of protected Cairo. There they stayed for days until they both died.

During it the emir Najm al-Dīn Ibrāhīm son of Nūr al-Dīn Ibn al-Sadīd was appointed as governor of protected Old Cairo in place of the emir `Izz al-Dīn Aybak al-Fakhrī.

During it, the emir Sayf al-Dīn Bāsiṭī was confirmed as the deputy in protected Ṣarkhand castle, while the emir `Izz al-Dīn became the governor in that castle. They both headed from protected Egypt to it.

The judge Abū `Abdallāh Muḥammad b. al-Mukarram b. Abī al-Ḥasan b. Aḥmad al-Anṣārī the secretary said: I wrote before them a memorandum dictated to him by our master Fatḥ al-Dīn Ibn `Abd al-Ẓāhir, chief of the noble Correspondence Chancellery, the text of which was:[64]

> A blessed memorandum, beneficial for many of the interests upon which the two emirs Sayf [193] al-Dīn and `Izz al-Dīn at the time of their heading to the protected Ṣarkhand fortress.
>
> They should uphold justice with regard to the subjects, treading the way of truth in each issue, upholding the favor of God Most High, which will cause our favor as well. Let justice be for the both of them a creed, god-fearingness a religion, without either one being aware of the wealth or property that is in the hand of the other, [without] either of them opposing the other without reason, so let them fear and be in awe of God, avoiding and shunning falsehood, nor let either of them think for a moment that they are far from us lest they desire or raise their eyes

[64] Compare version in al-Qalqashandī, *Ṣubḥ*, xiii, p. 106f.

towards injustice. We are a mirror and an ear for them, so they should be careful about interests, grasping onto the tails of the truth, and concerned for the subjects.

1. They should proceed to carefully check the walls of the victorious castle, its towers, curtain walls (*badanāt*), and gates, seeing what needs to be repaired, mended or constructed, guarding this diligently, making every effort to repair what can be repaired, mend what is necessary, and keeping abreast of what they discover and intend to do.
2. They should proceed to do an inventory of the victorious castle's resources, and the constructed treasury, verifying the wealth, stores, treasures and revenues that are inside of it, writing all of them down on sheets, and sending a copy of them to the noble gate.
3. They should proceed to do a review of the commanders of the castle's men, those receiving allowances and stipends in it, auditing their declared allowances and salaries, being vigilant that payment to them is regular and on a fixed timetable.
4. They should clarify from the outgoing emirs `Izz al-Dīn and `Alam al-Dīn what are the special interests of this castle, what its matters are, significant and insignificant. This is because they were noticeably good at administration, had good influence, and took the best possible way, so they both should learn from the [former] as to the interests and important issues they can make clear, so that they can take charge intelligently.
5. The matter of the deputyship and general governance in the victorious castle, settling and employment of the men, including firing those who need to be fired, belongs to the emir Sayf al-Dīn Bāsiṭī, with the participation of the emir `Izz al-Dīn concerning the matter of men, firing and employment.

   The matter of deputyship will ultimately belong to the emir Sayf al-Dīn Bāsiṭī, as well as the governance in it, but the matter of the governorship of the castle belongs to the emir `Izz al-Dīn, and both of them should take part in it according to the usual with regard to deputyship and governorship.

   The emir Sayf al-Dīn should be in the house in which the emir `Izz al-Dīn al-`Alamī lived, and his governance during the deputyship should be like his, while the emir `Izz al-Dīn should live in the house in which the emir `Alam al-Dīn formerly lived, and his governance for the governate should be like his. Let no one go beyond his limit, nor depart from what has been decided. Each one of them should behave towards his fellow according to his due, in what has been assigned to him, and watch over all the interests, being as two spirits in one body.
6. They should proceed to assign [194] men to their centers and their houses as usual night and day, especially if there are breaches,

dispersal or neglect, then some will need to pick up the slack. The matter should be arranged in the best possible way.

7. They should be stationed during the usual times at the castle gate to search out injustices for the subjects in the castle and the area, and should seek for justice, for their caller to call out, hearing their word, stopping the one acting unjustly, and aiding the one wronged. Seeking out the justice that is necessary, and spreading it among the subjects, stopping the harmful hands.
8. When the castle doors are locked each night, the keys should stay the night with the deputy in a specified place, after the governor has put his seal upon it as usual. When he hands them over, he hands them over with his seal as usual.
9. The treasures, the stores, and the wealth—there should be an effort to gather them within the castle; rather than to store them in a new place, the old should be used. Every granary in which there are stores should be checked. Cash should be lifted out into a purse, placed into the treasury, and a seal placed upon it. Not even one grain new should be given out until the old has been exhausted; indeed the old should be completely gone. The same applies to the rest of the resources.
10. Whenever there is an appraisal of those receiving allowances and living stipends, this should be as usual without partiality. Let him enter the chancellery, while they are engrossed in the appraisal lest the appraisal not take place properly with regard to the incapacitated men with their paucity of means, while the chancellery bureaucrats take a lot with their plethora of means. The latter should be the first to be appraised, not the one who has no wherewithal, such as a man incapacitated or one possessed of little means. So one should accompany him during this in order to watch over the dues belonging to the weak.
11. They should have a good deal of firewood, coal, and salt in the storerooms, and also a selection of everything needed. Both of them should expend effort to gather wealth, to store it up in the treasury so that they will not be a distraction, but be able to turn themselves to the mind during most times towards thinking about wealth to be gathered or property to be stored away without this being neglected.
12. They should inform the upper gates most times for the concessions that need to be renewed, and the transportation of treasuries' wealth that needs to be completed, as well as the granaries of the storehouses. In the same way, they should inform the deputy sultan in protected Damascus as usual, and let their informing be complete in nature, in both of their writing. Whoever has a change in interest at a given time, he should choose to submit a separate report.
13. They should not enable any one of the men assigned to the protected castle [195] or the guard to slack off on their watch or to leave it. Nor should any of the men depart from the castle without permission, and such should return immediately. God is the one who grants success.

On Saturday 26 Ramaḍān [January 19, 1281] al-Malik al-Manṣūr removed the chief of the Egyptian homelands, the Chief Judge Ṣadr al-Dīn `Umar son of the Chief Judge Tāj al-Dīn `Abd al-Wahhāb son of the daughter of al-A`zz al-Shāfi`ī, Chief Judge in the Egyptian homelands. He had acted well during his governate, taking the path of righteousness and firmness, choosing right and justice in his rulings. The Sultan appointed the Chief Judge Taqī al-Dīn Muḥammad b. al-Ḥusayn b. Razīn al-Shāfi`ī after he removed Chief Judge Ibn bint (son of the daughter of) al-A`zz, and returned him to being the Chief Judge in the Egyptian homelands.

In this year, the Sultan al-Malik al-Manṣūr dispatched the emir Badr al-Dīn Baktāsh al-Najmī to Ḥimṣ, and dispatched the emir `Alā' a-Dīn Aydakīn *al-bunduqdār* al-Ṣāliḥī to the coastlands to guard them against the Franks.

During it the emir Sayf al-Dīn Balabān al-Ṭabbākhī, deputy sultan in Ḥiṣn al-Akrād, wrote to the Sultan al-Malik al-Manṣūr asking his permission to raid the Franks in Marqab because when they had learned of the Tatars' advance they had been emboldened, and desired to expand. The Sultan gave him permission in that, so he mustered the fortresses' armies, the Turkmen emirs, and the foot soldiers, having mangonels and siege implements along with him.

He headed towards Marqab fortress, and camped close by it, so its inhabitants hid from him, and made no movements during the first part of the siege. The army began very strongly wanting to give battle, so it advanced to the fortress' side, whereupon the Franks showered them with arrows, and crossbows[65] from the highest sections of the fortress. At the same time, the Muslims' arrows were unable to reach them, so the army was disturbed.

Al-Ṭabbākhī then ordered them to fall back a bit from the fortress, but they thought that it was a rout, so they turned (around completely). He was unable to do anything other than to follow them, and the Franks sortied out on their heels, catching the Muslims. A number were wounded, robbed, and especially the foot soldiers were taken prisoner. This reached the Sultan al-Malik al-Manṣūr. He disapproved of it, and it got on him, so he resolved to journey to Syria. What happened then we will mention, if God Most High wishes.

Mention of the Sultan al-Malik al-Manṣūr heading towards Syria

During 1 Dhū al-Ḥijja [March 24, 1281] of this year, and it is said on the 3rd, the Sultan al-Malik al-Manṣūr Sayf al-Dīn Qalāwūn departed from the Hill Citadel in protected Egypt heading towards protected Syria leading all of his armies. He camped in the Straw Mosque, having left his son, his heir apparent, al-Malik al-Ṣāliḥ `Alā' al-Dīn `Alī in the citadel. He assigned the emir `Alam al-Dīn Sanjar al-Shujā`ī al-Manṣūrī to serve him, disbursing moneys, and

---

[65] Reading *jurūḥ* instead of the editor's *khurūj*.

administering the affairs of the noble realm, together with the minister, who at that time was the chief Burhān al-Dīn al-Khiḍr son of [196] al-Ḥasan al-Sinjārī.

The judge Muḥyī al-Dīn Ibn `Abd al-Ẓāhir sat in protected Cairo to read the post, and to execute the business of the realm, while the emir Zayn al-Dīn Kitbughā al-Manṣūrī was confirmed as the deputy sultan in the Egyptian homelands. The judge Abū `Abdallāh Muḥammad b. al-Mukarram b. Abī al-Ḥasan b. Aḥmad al-Anṣarī the secretary wrote for the emir Zayn al-Dīn Kitbughā al-Manṣūrī a blessed memorandum, the duplicate of which is for Dhū al-Ḥijja, year 678 [April 1280]:

> A memorandum, beneficial for the collected good deeds which the high, emirate, Zaynī session of Kitbughā al-Manṣūrī, deputy of the noble sultanate, may God lengthen its glory, should carry out important matters of the Egyptian homelands, its situations, interests, and that which is assigned to it, what is decided and divided in protected Cairo and old Cairo, and all of the rest of the districts of the Egyptian homelands, may God Most High defend them. This is together with the high, Ṣāliḥī, kingly, sultanic, lordly, noble decrees that proceed from it, may God Most High cause them to be executed in their matters, issues, governates, governors, bearing (of responsibility), escorting, guarding, and renovating it according to what will be explained in it.

1. The noble Law is binding upon its rulers and judges in executing its problems, and carrying out its rulings, so hold to it in breaking and sealing it.
2. Justice, fairness and truth should be the basis for this noble realm, its cities, its villages, its districts, its governates, wherever all of the subjects are, whether elite or commoners, far or near, absent or present, going or coming. Take up the righteous complaints from all of the people during these radiant days, letting the tongues speak on this, so that justice is God's proof, and the way of the good, so let him repel every harm and harmer.
3. Blood [vengeance]: he should rely upon the noble Law's ruling for it. The one who has to receive retaliation should be handed over to his antagonist to receive retaliation according to the noble Law, and whoever has to be cut, should be cut according to the noble Law.
4. Matters specific to protected Cairo and old Cairo, may God Most High guard both of them, and one should not lord it over another nor should the strong act strong over the weak, nor should any demonstrate aggression against another at any time.
5. A major priority is that none should walk in the city, nor in the suburbs in the Ḥusayniyya [shrine area] or the plots (*aḥkār*) during the night, except in cases of absolute necessity, nor should anyone depart from their house, except in cases of absolute necessity. Women should not go out during the night, nor should they depart, or walk at all.

6. The prison (*ḥubūs*) should be watched and guarded night and day, and the Frankish, Antiochean[66] and other prisoners should all have their beards shaven. As long as it grows, one should rely [197] upon them to do that.

   One should keep a close eye upon the prison from inside, keeping an eye on the prisoners who are employed, and the men who take them outside. Guarantees should be taken from the *jāndāriyya* (guard) who are with them. No strangers or anyone doubtful should be utilized, nor should the prisoners who are being employed night in any place other than the prison, nor should one depart for some special matter, neither to the baths, to church, or for recreation without their fetters. These should be tightened at all times, and guard should be doubled at night on the weapons storeroom (*khizānat al-bunūd*), inside and outside, on top and around it, as well as the cloakroom (*khizānat al-shamā'il*), and elsewhere in the prison.
7. A number of the troops should be assigned to patrol the city, to search out alleyways, to lock up pathways, to seek out camel-men (*aṣḥāb al-arbā`*), and to teach those camel-men who loiter in the center a lesson. The pathways should be locked up. Likewise, a number should be dispatched to the Ḥusayniyya [shrine] area, and the plots, all of the centers, and this should be depended upon. Whoever is caught during the night in opposition to the written command, walking without a good excuse, should be detained and punished.
8. The gates must be very closely watched, searching outside and inside doing the night, and at their opening and closing times.
9. The places where youths congregate, with those lewd and loose people, and the mob (*al-zanṭara*)[67]: it is not permitted for anyone to congregate in those places either night or day, and this should be stopped completely so that there is mortal fear and respect. Those malcontents, loose fellows and loiterers should be reproved.
10. Dispatched (troops) should be assigned around the twin cities, protected Cairo and old Cairo, as usual, and likewise the region of al-Qarāfa, behind the Citadel, towards the [Nile] River, and outside of al-Ḥusayniyya. Not a single night should receive a reprieve, nor should the dispatched leave their posts other than for movement or when it is completely light.

---

[66] This appears to be the only reference to Antiochean prisoners, presumably those remaining from the conquest of Antioch in 1268. It is not clear why they are categorized separately from the other Frankish prisoners, perhaps because they had no treaty to protect them.

[67] Not listed in dictionaries, comp. Ibn Iyyās, *Badā'i` al-zuhūr fī waqā'i` al-duhūr* (ed. Muḥammad Muṣṭafā, Beirut: Franz Steiner, 1960–74), i:2, p. 211 for this trans.

11. It should be a priority that men and women should not congregate together at the two Qarāfas on Friday nights, and the women should be forbidden this.
12. The issues of those missing in the victorious register (*paykār*), needing to be for those who govern them in their affairs and interests, to free their dues to their deputies, youths (*ghilmān*) and their trustees. Whoever has a region from which a due is exclusive, but does not apply themselves to their established regions, in what they owe, their hands will be strengthened, and testimony will be taken against their trustees as to what they have confiscated such that those trustees will not be able to say to in the register (*paykār*) that "our trustees wrote it, and answered that they did not confiscate anything for us," so that would be a reason for refusing their complaints.
13. The canal for protected Cairo and old Cairo must be maintained: digging it, keeping it up, on time, in a way that it works well and smoothly without bothering anyone. On the contrary, everyone should work on the section that is adjacent to him.
14. The bridges of the Cairene outskirts need to be maintained and widened, and effort should be expended in their being set well, keeping their drains open and guarding the passers-by from them. They need to be well maintained, completed according to the blessed Nile's season, and not depart from our mandate more than usual, or not guard [198] anyone from the work that is obligatory for them. The order applies to its dredging (*jarārīf*) and its instability (*muqalqalāt*), according to the previous noble written commands with regard to bridges, both near and far.
15. A section on districts and governates: the noble, sultanic, lordly, Malikī al-Ṣāliḥī al-`Alā'ī examples, may God Most High ennoble them, in maintaining the work on the bridges, making them well, and widening them, expending upon the smaller bridges (*qanāṭir*), and the flood-gates (*tirā`*). Including working on what from it has been destroyed, mending what is dilapidated, repairing those gates that have become decrepit, and acquiring different types according to the need during the Nile season.

    The noble written commands rely upon that for protection, and the order with regard to them as well as the dredging and the instabilities according to the previous noble written commands. Those are that no one should work according to rank, and whoever is obligated to work there, should work according to usual during the Ṣāliḥī days. All of the administrators (*wulāt*) need to be personally present, and not to rely upon supervisors.

    Anything that is achieved there, whether it is deficient or there are gaps, is guaranteed by the life (*rūḥ*) and wealth of that administrator. One should put the maximum amount of pressure upon the administrators, they should be cautioned heavily, and the signatures of the administrators should be taken that the bridges' work will be maintained according to the level of the written command concerning them, and that they be maintained. No ruptures should remain, nor anything where people fear the outcome, nor where there is fear of the result, when they are worked according to the written order.

16. One should proceed to the governors, and extract the noble sultanic amounts in assigning the local watch (*khufarā'*) in accord with the situation that it was during the Ẓāhirī days. From town to town there should be a watch that should dwell in tents (lit. houses of hair) upon the roads among the lands to watch over those going forth and those returning back. Anyone who is missing something, he should be obligated for its return. It should be proclaimed in the lands that no one should journey during the night nor halt, and the people should not journey other than between the sun's rising and its setting. This should be affirmed completely.

17. The protected border cities (*thughūr*), their matters and issues must have attention paid to them, and extracting the noble sultanic amounts for their issues, their circumstances, guarding them, watching over the prisoners in them, and making sure that guarding them is well-known, being alert to the issues of the border, enticing the merchants' hearts and winning their minds and their good treatment by amity and justice, such that the merchants will arrive, and settle in the border cities. It should be affirmed to them that which is extracted (taxes): obtaining wealth, types of stores, types for the permanent stores (*khazā'in al-ma`mūra*), and the Needs Hospice.

    They should be commanded that this is the time of the sea's opening, merchants being present, wealth accumulation, repairing various matters, and many cargoes coming, so their arrival in them (the border cities) should be affirmed for them, and that the cargoes will be many. But also that there will be no excessive extraction of dues for the boats arriving, nor will the one profiting be squeezed (*fadhlika*), nor will its cargo be diminished, but will arrive in its totality to the permanent Islamic Treasury, as usual.

    It should be affirmed to them that the business transactions and obtaining fabrics, and goods, according to their various types, and removal of blame concerning them in that the matter of business transactions will not be ceased, nor its importance delayed from its set time. Whatever mamluks, slave girls, silk, cash (*`ayn*), satin, silver, stone, [199] and spun gold sticks will be subject to obtaining (dues) as usual.

18. It should be affirmed for the governors of the districts that the appropriation of Chancellery dues from their regions, and causing them to arrive in cargoes on time, and attending personally to the circumstances of its threading (gold) and its pressing on time, and reliance of the benefit of each action upon what is compatible with it, and

the benefit of extracting, storing, transporting, sowing, working, and spending necessitates it. They should be cautioned against obtaining harm or the manifestation of incapacity, or breaks in resolution, inability of good judgment, or what will necessitate disapproval, or make censure necessary. They should be firm in this—especially with regard to those chance times when it is best to seize an opportunity, in accord with what one observes.

19. The Chancellery land-tax (*kharāj*) should be watched over, and made to grow, nor should anything be disbursed from it without a noble written order from us. One should check as to whether the written order comes with this and that it is answered in accord.
20. Dues for the emirs, the navy (*al-baḥriyya*), the victorious free-born troops, the troops, and their regions should be gathered for their deputies, and trustees, and notary-witnessing should be taken for that against them, in kind, in dirhams and other things. The trustees should not need to have any complaints concerning them that would come to the level of those in the register (*paykār*). In the case of such their livelihoods should be terminated and this time-wasting should be ceased.
21. One should deliver to the governors, the supervisors and the bureaucrats the paperwork of what has been obtained for those given original *iqṭā`* fiefs in every land, and for such a one in the region, and those who have separate estates (*ṭīn*) in a region, for the one whose region is according to a written order, let him validate the situation of those having *iqṭā`* fiefs during this military and regional year, what each of them is obtaining. Nothing should be obtained from any of the bankrupt nor neglectful governors, nor should one go after the trustees because of the emirs or *iqṭā`* fief owners being missing from the register. None of the *iqṭā`* fief owners should need to complain because of being late, property being destroyed, or being harmed.
22. The Bedouin in the lands, their subsidies should be terminated, sureties should be taken, and one should guard against them, writing to the deputies and governors in the districts sounding the alarm if even one of them bears a sword, a spear or weapons of any sort. It is not permitted for any one of them to purchase these from Cairo, and whoever disobeys this, and carries (weaponry) on a journey from land to land, this will be taken from him and destroyed, and he will be punished.
23. The trustees, it has reached us that they participate in commerce with the moneys of those given *iqṭā`* fiefs, and spend from them in the same way a property-owner would. Every trustee participating in commerce using the wealth of his employer or spending it should be investigated, and a report sent to the noble gate.
24. Dues owed to the Permanent Chancellery on behalf of each property, every land, and village, must be resolved, and the elders of those lands should be questioned, and testimony taken against them that the Chancellery is owed such-and-such dirhams, such-and-such *ardabb*s,

which they will undertake to pay [200] in agreed-upon installments, and usual set times. There should be no necessity for envoys going back and forth or for supervisors to go out to extract this amount from the subjects to relieve them, or to go easy on them lest the burden be doubled, and the dirham becomes two. The point in that should be only to go easy with the heavy-handedness upon the subjects, and that the due arrives at the Permanent Chancellery without harm being caused.

25. When the *jāndār* (guard) departs from Cairo to the districts, it should not be given more than two dirhams (weight) ingot for work. The due which comes from it should be given to its rightful possessor. If gossip or injustice occur because of that or harsh treatment, then this should be written down against him, so (the offender) will go but the due will go with its owner together with him, and it should be reported that so-and-so of the *jāndār* was present, and this-and-that occurred from him, explaining the whole picture, in order that these livelihoods be terminated.
26. When one of the governors sends an envoy in order to collect a due from one of the villages in his district, let what is given to the *jāndār* for the duration of a day's journey be half an ingot, and for two days be a dirham, not more. Any *jāndār* that goes beyond this, and takes more, will be punished, and will be removed from that governate.
27. Proofs should be written up against every trustee who takes for his employer something from his action, his region from the Chancellery, or the peasants. Nothing should be handed over to him without the testimony of proofs from his register. A copy of this proof should be made for the Permanent Chancellery of what he has taken from his region of complaints made against him because of his using the due for commerce, and the matter of his trustee should be brought to our attention, together with the due he took, and the testimony against him should be sent bound with the report.

   The matter of the testimonies should be arranged according to what has arrived from each *iqṭā`* fief owner so that we can know the contents of the proofs and the testimonies of the aggregate *iqṭā`* fief owners from the lands and regions separately, together with everything that was obtained from each of them: cash, stores, what was late payment from and thus we will know the picture of *iqṭā`* fief owners' and lands' matters, and their circumstances, and remove complaints from those whose complaints need to be removed, and know their situation clearly.
28. You should read this memorandum from the pulpits, paragraph by paragraph, so that near and far will hear it, and it will reach both present and absent, and each one act on its contents. Anyone who deviates from it or acts in opposition to it, he will be notified of our severity and the intensity of our anger which he will encounter, and peace.

During Dhū al-Ḥijja [March 1281] of this year the emir Sharaf al-Dīn ʿĪsā b. Muhannā arrived from Iraq in the service of al-Malik al-Manṣūr Sayf al-Dīn Qalāwūn, ruler of the Egyptian homelands and the Syrian lands. He sought to return to service, and asked for forgiveness for his excessive crimes in aiding Shams al-Dīn Sunqur *al-ashqar*, and that he had resolved to join up with the Tatars. His meeting with al-Malik al-Manṣūr was in al-Rawḥā campsite. When he arrived to render service, the Sultan rode up to him, welcomed him, honored him, and was magnanimous in honoring him, treating him well.

[*Obituaries*]

Mention of the events during the year 680 [1281]

The crescent moon of Muḥarram, first of this year's months, was seen on the night of Tuesday [April 22, 1281].

Mention of the truces confirmed with the Franks

While al-Malik al-Manṣūr was at al-Rawḥā campsite, Frankish envoys came to him asking to renew the truce, and to extend that of al-Ẓāhir Rukn [al-Dīn] Baybars al-Bunduqdārī al-Ṣāliḥī al-Najmī. They continued to press for this until the truce between al-Malik al-Manṣūr, and his son al-Malik al-Ṣāliḥ ʿAlā' al-Dīn ʿAlī, was concluded with the commander of the Hospitallers' House, and all the Hospitaller brethren in Acre[68]

> for a period of ten complete and consecutive years, ten months, ten days and ten hours. The first of that was on Saturday, 12 Muḥarram [May 3, 1281] which corresponds to two, and it is said three, of Ayyar, years 1592 of Alexander son of Philip the Greek. This is 7 Bashnus, year 997 of Diocletian covering all of the lands of the Sultan al-Malik al-Manṣūr Sayf al-Dīn Qalāwūn and his son al-Malik al-Ṣāliḥ ʿAlā' al-Dīn ʿAlī, including all of the regions, realms, castles, fortresses, cities, lands, villages, agricultural lands, lands, ports, seas, harbors, border fortresses, and other lands from the Euphrates [River] to Nubia.
>
> It covers the traveling merchants on dry land and at sea, on flat land and mountains, during night and day, and including the castle of Marqab [205] together with the Marqab (animal) pens in its rights and boundaries.
>
> Truce is established between the would-be king of Syrian Tripoli Bohemond son of Bohemond, king of the Franks, for a period of ten years,

[68] It is difficult to know where the text of this truce begins. Compare P.M. Holt, *Early Mamluk Diplomacy (1260–1290): Treaties of Baybars and Qalawun with Christian Rulers* (Leiden: E.J. Brill, 1995) pp. 62–5.

complete and consecutive, the first of which is 27 Rabī` al-Awwal of the year [6]80 [July 16, 1281] which corresponds to the month of Tammūz in the year 1592 of Alexander the Greek.

This covers the lands of al-Malik al-Manṣūr and al-Malik al-Ṣāliḥ his son, near and far, flat land and mountainous, deep valley and plateau land, old and newly constructed, what is adjacent to Tripoli, and the Ba`lbakan realm which borders it, its mountains, its wayfaring and mountainous villages, the mountains of al-Ḍanniyīn and al-Qaṣabīn, together with all of their dues, the newest conquests, which are Ḥiṣn al-Akrād, Aflīs, al-Qulay`āt, Ṣāfītā, Mī`ār, Aṭlī`ā, `Akkār fortress, Marqiyya, its city, its lands, and its condominia.

These are royal lands,[69] and all of the lands in these regions which we have mentioned, together with Marqab's condominia, which are included in the peace with the Hospitaller's House, its town, and city, what is considered to be part of it, and known as it, namely, fortresses, villages, the lands of the Lady, Balāṭinus, Qurfayṣ, and its lands, Jabala, Latakia, Antioch, al-Suwayda, and those lands, Baghrās fortress, Dīrkūsh fortress, Ṣahyūn, Birziyya, the Ismaili fortresses (*ḥuṣūn al-da`wa*), and others from the rest of the Islamic realms, and what God Most High will conquer at the hand of al-Malik al-Manṣūr and his son.

Also covering the ports, the coastal lands, the towers, and the lands of the Prince, Tripoli, what is included in it, Anafa, al-Batrūn, Jubayl, and those lands, `Arqā, its lands which are specified in the truce, numbering 51 districts, what belongs to the knights and to the churches, numbering 21 lands, including what belongs to the knight Roger de la Valée to the south of Tripoli which is a condominium.

On the condition that the tower of Latakia and its port shall be established for levying of its dues, taxes, stores and other items as a condominium, and their place is established [206] in Latakia according to the guidelines of the Rukn al-Ẓāhir's [Baybars'] truce's stipulations.

On the condition that the Bridge of Artūsiyya there would be 16 people from the Sultan's youths (*ghilmān*) to guard for dues, who will be the supervisor, the notary, the secretary, with three youths to attend them, and ten foot soldiers in the service of the supervisor. They would have dwellings at the bridge in which they will live. No harm to the Prince's subjects will come from them; they will only forbid those forbidden items that it is necessary to forbid.

---

69 Holt reads al-Lakma.

They will not forbid the summer and winter stores that are coming from `Arqā and its lands, and other places, nor will the supervisor there harass them. Beyond that, those who cross from the lands of the Sultan, dues will be taken from them. No stores shall enter Tripoli under the protection of the Prince nor anyone else without the necessary [dues] being taken from them.

In the same way, the Sultan will not renew the building of a castle he has begun from scratch in the lands upon which the truce is applicable.

On the condition that the galleys from both parties are safe, each from the other. This will not be abrogated by the death of one of the two, nor shall it change. He will not treat any of the Sultan's enemies well, nor make an agreement with him either by sign, by writing, by sending of envoys, by correspondence, or by speaking face-to-face.

The situation was established thus, and the envoys returned, so the emir Fakhr al-Dīn Ayyāz al-Muqrī the chamberlain was sent to take the Franks' oath, together with the commander of the Hospitallers, according to the peace that had been agreed, so he swore them.

Mention of the conspiracy of the emir Kūndak and a number of emirs to kill al-Malik al-Manṣūr, his learning of this, and detaining them

The emir Sayf al-Dīn Kūndak was one of the mamluks of al-Malik al-Ẓāhir Rukn al-Dīn Baybars al-Ṣāliḥī al-Najmī. Circumstances moved him around until he achieved the deputy sultanate in the Egyptian homelands during the sultanate of al-Malik al-Sa`īd son of al-Malik al-Ẓāhir.

Then there occurred some conflicts between him and the personal guards (*khāṣakiyya*) of al-Malik al-Sa`īd which turned him against the latter. Then there were differences between him [al-Sa`īd] and the senior emirs which necessitated them agreeing to remove him, so they placed al-Malik al-`Ādil Badr al-Dīn Salāmish son of al-Malik al-Ẓāhir after him. Then they removed him (as well) because of his youth and inexperience, and placed Sultan al-Malik al-Manṣūr Sayf al-Dīn Qalāwūn al-Alfī al-Ṣāliḥī al-Najmī just as we have previously detailed.

The emir Sayf al-Dīn Kūndak was removed from the deputy sultanate in the Egyptian homelands, but continued to be an emir. When the Sultan al-Malik al-Manṣūr headed towards Syria as we explained, arrived at Rawḥā campground, and settled in there, it reached the emir Badr al-Dīn Baysarā al-Shamsī during the first part of Muḥarram [May 1281] of that year that the emir Sayf al-Dīn Kūndak al-Ẓāhirī al-Sa`īdī together with a number of the other Ẓāhirī Sa`īdī emirs conspired that they would [207] upon their arrival at Ḥamrā' Baysān and the ford would kill al-Malik al-Manṣūr.

So the emir Baysarā went to al-Malik al-Manṣūr to make him aware of what he had learned. Then letters from well-wishers (*munāṣiḥīn*) from Acre arrived to the Sultan telling him "Protect yourself. There are a number of emirs around you who have conspired to kill you, and they have corresponded with the Franks, saying to them: Do not conclude a peace with him, for the matter is imminent."

The Sultan protected himself, and Kūndak and those with him resolved to attack the Sultan violently at night while he was in his royal tent (*dihlīz*) and assassinate him. A number of the Ẓāhirī Jawānīs agreed with them on this, but they found the Sultan had already protected himself and rode from Rawḥā. Then he advanced, treating the matter lightly, until all of the emirs had gathered around him at Ḥamrā' Baysān.

Then he reproved Kūndak, and those with him, reminding them of the correspondence that they had maintained with the Franks, so they confessed to that, and admitted it, begging for clemency. The Sultan ordered for them to be detained, so Kūndak, Aydughmish al-Ḥakīmī, Baybars al-Rashīdī and Sāṭilmish *al-silāḥdār* were detained in the royal tent, and then sent to the camp.

Those Barānī emirs and the Jawānī mamluks who had conspired with them [in the plot] were detained—they totaled 33 individuals. A number feared, so they fled, while part of the army followed them. Some of them were brought from the Ba`lbak Mountains, while some of them from Ṣarkhand district. This was what was happening with regard to those.

As for what happened with regard to the emir Kūndak, and the other emirs: Aydughmish, Baybars and Sāṭilmish, the Sultan ordered them to be put to death. The emir Kūndak handed over the deputy sultanate in the Egyptian homelands to Ḥusām al-Dīn Ṭurunṭāy al-Manṣūrī. They took him to the Sea of Galilee, and drowned him in it, although it is said that they cut off his head first, and then drowned him afterwards because of arguments between them they had along the road. As for Aydughmish, Baybars and Sāṭilmish that was the end of them.

When the emir Sayf al-Dīn Aytāmish al-Sa`dī, the emir Sayf al-Dīn Balabān al-Hārūnī, and a number of the emirs learned—and it was said that from the Baḥriyya [regiment] and the Tatars there were around 300 horsemen detaining the emir Sayf al-Dīn Kūndak and his supporters—they rode and drove towards Ḥamiyya, heading towards Ṣahyūn and joined up with Shams al-Dīn Sunqur *al-ashqar*, when he was still going by the royal title of al-Malik al-Kāmil, and stayed with him.

When they departed the Manṣūrī camp, al-Malik al-Manṣūr dispatched the emir Badr al-Dīn Baktāsh al-Fakhrī and the emir Rukn al-Dīn Baybars Ṭaqṣū al-Nāṣirī, with their troops, after them, but they did not catch up with them, and they returned. Al-Malik al-Manṣūr ordered the placement of a guard around all of the rest of the emirs who wanted to defect to Shams al-Dīn Sunqur *al-ashqar*, and their livelihoods were confiscated in their entirety. [208]

Mention of the Sultan al-Malik al-Manṣūr's entering Damascus

When al-Malik al-Manṣūr detained the emir Sayf al-Dīn Kūndak, the emir Sayf al-Dīn Aydughmish, and those with the two of them, the emir Sayf [al-Dīn] Aytimish al-Sa`dī and Sayf al-Dīn Balabān al-Hārūnī and those with the two of them fled to Shams al-Dīn Sunqur *al-ashqar*, just as we have previously explained. The Sultan traveled and went to Damascus, arriving there on 19 Muḥarram [May 10, 1281], and it is said that his arrival was on the 20th. This was the first time he had entered it, and the people came out to greet him. It was a day to remember! He stayed in the Citadel, so what happened then we will mention if God Most High wishes.

On 22 Muḥarram [May 13, 1281] while al-Malik al-Manṣūr was in Damascus, he removed the Chief Judge Shams al-Dīn Aḥmad Ibn Khallikān al-Shāfi`ī from the Shāfi`ī chief judiciary in protected Damascus. He delegated the Shāfi`ī chief judiciary in Damascus to Chief Judge `Izz al-Dīn Ibn al-Ṣā'igh al-Shāfi`ī, after having given stipulations to which he assented.

He also delegated the Ḥanbalī chief judiciary in Damascus to the Chief Judge Najm al-Dīn Aḥmad son of the Chief Judge Shams al-Dīn `Abd al-Raḥmān al-Ḥanbalī. The judiciary according to the rite of Aḥmad b. Ḥanbal, may God be pleased with him, had been vacant since the time when Chief Judge Shams al-Dīn had withdrawn from it, heading towards the Ḥijāz in the year 678 [1279], so the Sultan now delegated it to his son Najm al-Dīn at the suggestion of his father. Robes were bestowed upon both of the judges.

During Muḥarram [May 1281] of this year after the death of Chief Judge Ṣadr al-Dīn `Umar son of Chief Judge Ṭāj al-Dīn `Abd al-Wahhāb b. Khalaf al-Shāfi`ī known as Ibn bint (son of the daughter of) al-A`zz, in protected Egypt, the judges Burhān al-Dīn Ibn al-Ṭarā'ifī, noble correspondence secretary, was appointed to the inspectorate of the Ṣāliḥiyya mausoleum which is on the line of *bayn al-qaṣrayn* inside protected Cairo.

Then after this noble command concerning his appointment was received from the Sultan al-Malik al-Manṣūr from the victorious army in Syria, the appointment of the emir `Alā' al-Dīn Kushtghadī al-Shamsī, the majordomo, to the inspectorate of the Ḥusaynī shrine. Another noble command arrived which appointed the judge Taqī al-Dīn `Abd al-Raḥmān brother of the judge Ṣadr al-Dīn to the Ṣāliḥiyya mausoleum and school, as an inspectorate, in place of his brother Ṣadr al-Dīn, in addition to the inspectorate of the Permanent Treasuries which he already had. He then should suffice himself with teaching at the school and the mausoleum, and the positions that were in the hands of his brother, and he should turn his attention from the inspectorate of the Permanent Treasuries to the Permanent Chancellery. [209]

During Rabī` al-Awwal [July 1281] of this year the Sultan removed the chief Burhān al-Dīn Khiḍr al-Sinjārī from the ministry in the Egyptian homelands, and detained him, his son, and dependents. He and his son were imprisoned in the protected Citadel.

Mention of the peace arrangement between al-Malik al-Manṣūr and Shams al-Dīn Sunqur *al-ashqar*, and what was settled between the two of them

During the first part of Ṣafar [June 1281] of this year al-Malik al-Manṣūr dispatched a good portion of the Egyptian and Syrian armies under the command of the emir `Izz al-Dīn Aybak *al-afram*, accompanied by the emir `Alā' al-Dīn Kushtghadī al-Shamsī, to Shayzar. They departed from Damascus, going to Shayzar, whereupon missives passed back and forth between al-Malik al-Manṣūr and Shams al-Dīn Sunqur *al-ashqar* concerning a peace during the first tenth of Ṣafar [late May 1281].

The peace's provisions were that Shams al-Dīn Sunqur *al-ashqar* would hand over Shayzar to al-Malik al-Manṣūr's deputies, while he would be compensated by al-Shaghar and Bakās, which had both been taken from him, together with Fāmiya, Kafarṭāb, Antioch, and a number of different properties.

Shams al-Dīn Sunqur *al-ashqar* would raise from these [territories], together with what was already in his possession—which was Ṣahyūn, Balāṭinus, Birziyya, and Latakia—600 horsemen to aid Islam. The emirs who were with him, if they stayed with him, would be among his emirs. If, however, they presented themselves to al-Malik al-Manṣūr they would be safe, and not be punished.

When it was Sunday 4 Rabī` al-Awwal [June 23, 1281] of that year the emir `Alam al-Dīn Sanjar al-Dawādārī, who was Shams al-Dīn Sunqur *al-ashqar*'s *khazindār* (treasurer), presented himself on behalf of Shams al-Din Sunqur *al-ashqar*, with a copy of the oath confirming what had been agreed. Al-Malik al-Manṣūr swore upon that, and wrote an investiture for the lands. Sunqur *al-ashqar* asked that he be described by the word "king," but al-Malik al-Manṣūr did not assent to that, so he was described as an "emir." He was addressed in the correspondence as "the high, masterly, lordly, knowledgeable, just, Shamsī."

In protected Damascus, the newfound unity was proclaimed, and those who had presented themselves on behalf of Shams al-Dīn Sunqur *al-ashqar* returned to him. Al-Malik al-Manṣūr sent alongside them on his behalf the emir Fakhr al-Dīn Ayyāz al-Muqrī the chamberlain and the emir Shams al-Dīn Qarāsunqur *al-jūkandār* al-Manṣūrī, so the two of them took Shams al-Dīn Sunqur *al-ashqar*'s oath upon that also. They returned to Damascus on Monday 12 Rabī` al-Awwal [July 1, 1281].

Tidings were sent out from Damascus Citadel, and the people were happy because of that. Al-Malik al-Manṣūr sent a great many fabrics, vessels and cattle to Shams al-Dīn Sunqur *al-ashqar*, and the peace and agreement was arranged. [210] The Syrian and Egyptian armies returned from Shayzar to protected Damascus, as there was no need of them because of the peace, and God knows best.

On Thursday 1 Rabīʿ al-Awwal [June 20, 1281] which was 25 Ba'ūna year 677 [?] the blessed [Nile] level stood at six cubits and 18 fingers.

Mention of the peace arrangement between al-Malik al-Manṣūr and al-Malik al-Masʿūd son of al-Malik al-Ẓāhir, ruler of Kerak, and what was established between the two of them

Envoys from al-Malik al-Masʿūd al-Khiḍr son of al-Malik al-Ẓāhir Rukn al-Dīn Baybars al-Bunduqdārī al-Ṣāliḥī al-Najmī came to al-Malik al-Manṣūr Sayf al-Dīn Qalāwūn, ruler of the Egyptian homelands and the Syrian lands, seeing a peace, and to expand beyond Kerak—to have that which al-Malik al-Nāṣir Ṣalāḥ al-Dīn Dā'ūd al-Ayyūbī, former ruler of Kerak, had possessed. Al-Malik al-Manṣūr did not assent to this nor to his staying in Kerak as a base.

His missives passed back and forth to the Sultan, and he asked that Kerak and its districts from the Mawjab line to al-Ḥasā be confirmed in his possession. He sought conditions, among them sending the male and female siblings, children of al-Malik al-Ẓāhir to Kerak, and the return of the Ẓāhirī properties to them. Al-Malik al-Manṣūr assented to that, and peace was concluded, with the Sultan swearing upon it. The emir Badr al-Dīn Bīlīk al-Muḥsinī *al-silaḥdār* (sword-bearer) and the judge Tāj al-Dīn Ibn al-Athīr headed to Kerak, and the two of them swore al-Malik al-Masʿūd. He was addressed by the Correspondence Chancellery in the same way as was the ruler of Ḥamāh. The peace between them took effect during the first tenth of Rabīʿ al-Awwal [late June 1281], and it was proclaimed in protected Damascus, and God knows best. [211]

On Wednesday 19 Rabīʿ al-Ākhir [August 7, 1281] of this year the wife of al-Malik al-Ẓāhir Rukn al-Dīn Baybars al-Bunduqdārī al-Ṣāliḥī al-Najmī came to the outskirts of Damascus from Kerak. With her she had her son al-Malik al-Saʿīd Nāṣir al-Dīn Muḥammad Berke Khān son of al-Malik al-Ẓāhir dead in a coffin (*tābūt*).

When it was Thursday night the 20th they lifted the coffin with ropes over the tops of the walls. They then lowered it on the other side, without it going through the city gate. They took it to the mausoleum of his father al-Malik al-Ẓāhir at night, placing it in his tomb with his father in his grave. Chief Judge ʿIzz al-Dīn Ibn al-Ṣā'igh entombed him just as he had his father, while al-Malik al-Manṣūr at that time was in protected Damascus.

When it was the morn of his burial, al-Malik al-Manṣūr was present at the Ẓāhirī mausoleum. With him were the senior emirs, the senior bureaucrats, the judges, the learned, the Qur'ān readers, and the preachers (*wuʿāẓ*), so the Qur'ān readers read, the preachers preached in his presence, and he manifested sadness for him [al-Saʿīd].

It was said that al-Malik al-Sa`īd's mother arrived with him dead to Damascus on 28 Rabī` al-Ākhir [August 16, 1281] and that the Sultan was present at the mausoleum of al-Malik al-Ẓāhir on the following morning, the penultimate day of Rabī` al-Ākhir, and God knows best which of these dates it was. The mother of al-Malik al-Sa`īd stayed in the house of the ruler of Ḥimṣ, and she was honored to the maximum, given sustenance, and God knows best.

On Thursday 20 Rabī` al-Ākhir [August 8, 1281] the blessed Nile overflowed 16 cubits and three fingers, which was 14 Masrā, and the Nilometer was measured as the blessed dike broke. Tidings of the blessed Nile's surfeit were written to al-Malik al-Manṣūr Sayf al-Dīn Qalāwūn, while he was in protected Damascus, and to all the other lands.

During Rabī` al-Ākhir [August 1281] after the death of Rashīd al-Dīn Ibn Buṣāqa [?] al-Iskandarī, the inspector of Alexandria, the judge Kamāl al-Dīn Ibn Salāma was appointed to the inspectorate of Alexandria.

During Jumādā al-Ulā [August–September 1281] of this year one of the water-sellers in protected Cairo passed by a fellow, crowding up on him with his beast of burden, which excreted upon him. The two of them had words, grabbed each other, whereupon that fellow stabbed the water-seller with a knife and killed him. This was [212] the story, so he was ordered to be hanged.

During it one of those troops under arms in Cairo passed by a tailor who asked from him if he would hand over something to be tailored by him, so the two of them had words, whereupon the soldier struck him, then killed him. He was ordered to be hung.

During it the Frankish envoy from Marseille (*marsīliyya*) died, so his livelihood was protected. During it, a fellow known as al-Kuraydī in protected Old Cairo was detained. It was said about him that he would strip [his victims], and that he was known for his thievery and bawdiness. An order was given to nail him up, so he was nailed upon a camel. He lingered for days, being paraded around through Old Cairo and Cairo.

One of the most amazing things told about him was that the trustee responsible for him deprived him of food and drink, not in order to increase his suffering, but to shorten his life. However he said, "Don't do it, because bad life is better than death," so he fed him and gave him drink. Then some interceded for him, so they let him go, and he was let go while still alive, but put in prison, where he died after a few short days.

During Jumādā al-Ākhira [September–October 1281] of this year al-Malik al-Manṣūr's written command arrived in protected Cairo offering clemency to `Alā' al-Dīn son of the judge Tāj al-Dīn from being sought. He appeared, after having concealed himself for a lengthy time because of the intercession of his mother. She wrote a page to the Sultan, who accepted her intercession, so he was freed.

In it the judge `Alam al-Dīn Ibn al-Qammāḥ was appointed to teach at the Zayn al-Tujjār College in Old Cairo, close to the Great Mosque in place of the judge Shams al-Dīn son of the chief Burhān al-Dīn.

On the 10th [September 26, 1281] which was 29 Thoth, the first Coptic month, the blessed Nile's increase came to 18 cubits and four fingers, through which God gave benefits.

Mention of the Tatars' returning to Syria, the battle which occurred between them and the Islamic armies at Ḥimṣ, and the Tatars' defeat

During this year reports reached the Sultan al-Malik al-Manṣūr Sayf al-Dīn Qalāwūn, ruler of the Egyptian homelands and the Syrian lands, of Mengű Teműr, the brother of Abagha son of Hűlegű, king of the Tatars, entering the lands of the Rūm [Seljuqs] leading the Mongol armies. He camped between Caesarea [Keysari] and Iblastayn, so al-Malik [213] al-Manṣūr sent reconnaissance.

They headed from `Ayntāb, and ran across a detachment of Tatars close to the Hūtī [Hūnī] waste, where al-Malik al-Ẓāhir had crushed the Tatars. They were victorious over them and took a man called Julnār Bahādur, *amīr akhūr* to Abagha son of Hűlegű, king of the Tatars, who had been heading himself to scout out the fields. They took him prisoner, and sent him to al-Malik al-Manṣūr in Damascus. He was presented to him while the latter was in the Green Square outside of Damascus on 20 Jumādā al-Awwal [September 6, 1281] of this year.

Al-Malik al-Manṣūr befriended him, asking him about the reports, so he mentioned that the Tatars were a great number, more than 80,000 horsemen of the Mongols, and that they were determined to proceed through the lands in one fell swoop,[70] and would be riding from their campsite at the beginning of Rajab [October 16, 1281].

Al-Malik al-Manṣūr's order to prepare the troops, and to call for sacral warfare (*jihād*), and meeting the Tatars [in battle] went out, and he sent to the rest of the lands to muster [troops] to Damascus because of the Tatars' proximity to the lands. When it was the day of 18 Jumādā al-Ākhira [October 4, 1281] a large number accompanied by the emir Aḥmad Ibn al-Ḥijjī arrived in Damascus from Iraq, and support from al-Malik al-Mas`ūd Najm al-Dīn Khiḍr son of al-Malik al-Ẓāhir Rukn al-Dīn Baybars al-Bunduqdārī, ruler of Karak, entered together with them.

During this month the laggards from the Egyptian homelands' armies presented themselves, but none of the Bedouin or Turkmen or those from other regions were dilatory. Reports during Jumādā al-Ākhira [September–October 1281] arrived that they [the Mongols] had ridden from their campsite, and that they were traveling in parties, that one of them accompanied by King Abagha son of Hűlegű, king of the Tatars, had headed towards al-Raḥba, with the lord of Mārdīn, so al-Malik al-Manṣūr sent reconnaissance to al-Raḥba accompanied by Bujkā al-`Alā'ī.

---

[70] The editor notes difficulty here, so the translation is conjectural.

Alarming news multiplied, and Aleppo emptied out of people and troops, who absented themselves towards Ḥamāh and Ḥimṣ, abandoning stores, crops and goods. Dispatch riders departed towards them, and the Islamic armies themselves set out during Jumādā al-Ākhira [September–October 1281] following on the heels of their departure.

On Sunday 26 Jumādā al-Ākhira [October 12, 1281] al-Malik al-Manṣūr himself departed from Damascus, and camped on the field. None of the armies lagged behind, and it is said he departed from Damascus leading the victorious armies and camped at al-Zanbaqiyya.

On the penultimate day of Jumādā al-Ākhira [October 14, 1281] al-Malik al-Manṣūr traveled from the field to join up with the armies advancing towards Ḥimṣ. [214]

On 11 Rajab [October 26, 1281] of this year al-Malik al-Manṣūr and the rest of the armies and groups camped at Ḥimṣ, and sent to Sunqur *al-ashqar* a number of missives requesting his presence with his emirs and armies, until finally it was confirmed that he was coming down from Ṣahyūn with his fighters on the condition that he be allowed to return to it when the battle was finished.

So he descended, and came towards the Sultan at Ḥimṣ, going to meet with him, but asking the emir Sayf al-Dīn Aytimish al-Sa`dī to have him swear another oath so as to increase his feeling of security. Then he was presented, together with the emirs who were with him, who were Aytimish al-Sa`dī, Izdimur *al-ḥājj*, Sanjar al-Dawādārī, Bayjaq al-Baghdādī, Girāy, Shams al-Dīn al-Ṭunṭāsh and his son,[71] plus the Ẓāhiri emirs who were with him.[72] The Muslims were overjoyed at their presence, and this was before the battle by two days. Their ingathering was completed on Tuesday 12 Rajab [October 27, 1281], achieving unity and agreement in the face of the enemy. The emir Shams al-Dīn Sunqur *al-ashqar* and all of those with him were treated with the utmost respect, given hospitality, assigned quarters, and a royal tent (*dihlīz*) was pitched for him to the right of the Manṣūrī royal tent. The reports of the abandoned enemy entering the lands reached a fever pitch. This was what was happening with those.

As for what was happening with the Damascenes, the people went terrified on the morning of Wednesday [presumably October 28, 1281] to the Great Mosque of Damascus: the weak, the children and the elders. They all supplicated to God, mighty and majestic, to aid the people of Islam and to destroy their enemy. They brought out the `Uthmānic codex,[73] and others upon their

[71] In Baybars' text there is no "and."

[72] Presumably those who had fled after the failed assassination attempt upon Qalāwūn previously.

[73] According to David James (ed.), *Manuscripts of the Holy Qur'ān from the Mamlūk Era* (Riyāḍ: King Feisal Center for Research and Islamic Studies, n.d.), pp. 31, 34 the earliest surviving Mamluk Qur'ānic manuscript dates to 704/1304.

heads. The preacher, the Qur'ān readers, and the callers to prayer all came out onto the oratory outside of Damascus,[74] beseeching God Most High for aid and victory. This was what was happening with the Muslims.

As for what was happening with the Tatars, they during the middle tenth of Jumādā al-Ākhira [September–October 1281] advanced alongside the edges of the Aleppan lands, while during the final tenth of Jumādā al-Ākhira [mid-October1281] Mengű Teműr arrived in `Ayntāb and the field around it. This was what was happening with Mengű Teműr and those with him.

As for what was happening with King Abagha son of Hűlegű, king of the Tatars, he went secretly with a group of the Tatars, of around 3000 horsemen, to al-Raḥba, and they camped up against Raḥba castle on 26 Jumādā al-Ākhira [October 12, 1281]. King Abagha continued with that group concealing himself in the districts of Raḥba on the shores of the Euphrates [River], expecting the battle that was to occur, until what we will mention, if God Most High wishes.

Mengű Teműr and those armies with him continued to advance slowly, slowly, in opposition to their usual method [215] so when they arrived at Ḥamāh they vandalized its districts, destroying al-Malik al-Manṣūr's, the ruler of Ḥamāh, garden and his villa (*jawsaq*), with all of the buildings in it.

All this time the Muslims' army was at the ready outside of Ḥimṣ, and the report came that Mengű Teműr was at Ḥamāh leading the Tatars' armies of 80,000, among them 50,000 Mongols. The rest were apostates (*murtadda*), Georgians,[75] Rūm [Seljuqs], Armenians and Franks. One of the mamluks of the emir Rukn al-Dīn Baybars al-`Ajamī al-Ṣāliḥī *al-jāliq* defected to them, and guided them to the Muslims' weak points, telling them of their numbers. They moved on Thursday from Ḥamāh and arranged their troops, driving forward, seeking battle, with their commander being Mengű Teműr son of Hűlegű, brother of Abagha son of Hűlegű, king of the Tatars.

A fellow from the Tatar army entered Ḥamāh, and said to the deputy in it

> Write this very hour to the Sultan, on a bird's wing, and make him aware that the group is 80,000 fighters in the center, among them 44,000 Mongols. They will advance to the center, while their right flank is very strong, so strengthen the left flanks of the Muslims, and guard the standards.

So the deputy wrote that to al-Malik al-Manṣūr, who when he read the message, arranged his armies, and put them in the van.

The Muslims spent the night on the backs of their horses, and at daybreak on Thursday 14 Rajab [October 29, 1281] which was the battle day, al-Malik al-Manṣūr rode and arranged the victorious Islamic armies in accord with

---

[74] An interesting manifestation of popular religion.

[75] According to *Kartlis Tskhovreba: History of Georgia* (ed. Metroveli, trans. Jones, Tbilisi: Artanuji, 2014), pp. 373–4 the Georgian king fought in the battle.

what we will describe citing what the emir Rukn al-Dīn Baybars *al-dawādār* al-Manṣūrī from his work *Zubdat al-fikra fi tā'rīkh al-hijra*.[76]

This was that the victorious right flank contained al-Malik al-Manṣūr, ruler of Ḥamāh, the emir Badr al-Dīn Baysarā al-Shamsī, the emir `Alā' al-Dīn Kushtghadī al-Shamsī, and their auxiliaries. In the right flank vanguard there was the emir Sharaf al-Dīn `Īsā b. Muhannā, [the tribes of] Āl Faḍl, Āl Murrā, the Bedouin of Syria, and those who were attached to them.

The blessed left flank contained the emir Shams al-Dīn Sunqur *al-ashqar*, and those emirs with him, the emir Badr al-Dīn Bīlīk al-Aydimurī, the emir Badr al-Dīn Baktāsh, *amīr silāḥ* (armorer), the emir `Alam al-Dīn Sanjar al-Ḥalabī, the emir [Badr][77] al-Dīn Bajkā al-`Alā'ī, the emir Badr al-Dīn Baktūt al-`Alā'ī, the emir Sayf al-Dīn Jabrak al-Tatarī, and those auxiliaries with them. In left flank vanguard were the Turkmen massed, the army of Ḥiṣn [216] al-Akrād and al-Jālīsh.

The center contained the emir Ḥusām al-Dīn Ṭurunṭāy, the deputy sultan in the Egyptian homelands, with his auxiliaries, the emir Rukn al-Dīn Ayājī the chamberlain, the emir Badr al-Dīn Baktāsh son of Karmūn, together with the royal mamluks with them. The Sultan al-Malik al-Manṣūr waited underneath the victorious standards, while surrounded by his mamluks, dependents, and officials.

The Tatars' squadrons appeared, and it was said that the number of the Tatars was 100,000 horsemen, or more, while the Muslims' army was half of that or less.[78] Battle was joined between Rastan and the Orontes [River] and the intersection of fields there, and those districts. It is said that the battle was on the Ḥimṣ Depression close to the shrine of Khālid b. al-Walīd, may God be pleased with him.

They fought from the daybreak until its end, and it was a huge battle, the like of which had not been witnessed before. It was said that the two sides met at 4th hour of the day on Thursday. The enemy's left flank came at the Islamic right, and this was the first clash. The Muslims held firm, and the Tatars' left was completely defeated, ending up in the Tatar center. In it was Mengű Teműr, the Tatar commander.

As for the Islamic left flank, the Tatars' right clashed with it, but the former did not hold firm because of their squadrons following one after another, so it was defeated and those in it retreated. The same with the left wing of the center, so the Tatars followed behind the retreating Muslims until they came under Ḥimṣ, whose gates were locked.

---

[76] Text 4 (a).

[77] The editor notes a blank in the text.

[78] The editor notes in the right margin under this statement in the same hand there was written: "The emir Shams al-Dīn Aqsunqur *al-silaḥdār* al-Manṣūrī said: I was among the Tatars for over 20 years, but I never knew of them having gathered or mustered this number the like of this time."

There they fell upon the camp-followers, the common people, the foot fighters (*mujāhidīn*) and the youths[79] outside of Ḥimṣ, killing a great many of them. Islam was on the verge of a difficult point, as the Muslims from the left flank did not know of the victory the right had achieved, nor did the Tatars who followed behind them know what had happened to their left.

Some of those who were retreating from the left flank snuck away to Damascus, some of them to Safed, while some of them arrived in Gaza. When the Tatars who had pursued those retreating from the left flank saw that they were victorious they dismounted from their horses on the field near Ḥimṣ Dam, ate food, plundering the armor, pavilions and treasuries, all the while expecting that their fellows would appear.

When they were taking their time, the former sent to scout out the news of them, so the reconnaissance returned, informing them that Mengű Teműr, their commander, had fled, so they mounted their horses and went back, returning. This was what happened with the Tatars' right flank and the left flank of the people of Islam.

As for what happened to the rest of the armies, we have mentioned that the right flank of the people of Islam held firm, and [217] the Tatars' left retreated—a complete victory, which ended up in the Tatar center, in which Mengű Teműr, their commander, was. The right flank then pursued the enemy, while al-Malik al-Manṣūr stood firm in his place under the standards, while the kettledrums were beaten.

Then the senior and famous emirs, and their bravest ones, like Sunqur *al-ashqar*, Baysarā, Ṭīburs al-Wazīrī, *amīr silāḥ* (armorer), Aytimish al-Sa`dī, Ḥusām al-Dīn Lājīn deputy of Damascus, Ḥusām al-Dīn Ṭurunṭāy, deputy of the Egyptian homelands, al-Dawādārī, and the likes of them, when they saw the steadfastness of the al-Malik al-Manṣūr, they returned to fighting the Tatars. `Īsā b. Muhannā advanced towards them, leading his (Bedouin) followers on a broad line, which completed their crisis point. They killed a huge slaughter of Tatars.

Al-Jazarī in his *History* tells that an *amīr jāndār* (guard) known as Ibn Jamaqdār told me that "when our left flank was defeated, but our right flank was victorious, I studied those who stayed with al-Malik al-Manṣūr under the standards, so they were approximately 300 horsemen. Then Mengű Teműr, the Tatars' commander, stayed visible among his army. But then God foreordained that he would dismount from his horse, looking at the horses' feet, where he saw the armor and the mounts. He believed that they were armies, so he rose up to ride, but his steed threw him, casting him to the ground. At that the Tatars all alighted because of him, taking him, and bearing him, so

[79] Amitai trans. "grooms" in "Foot-Soldiers, Militiamen and Volnteers," in Robinson (ed.), *Texts, Documents and Artefacts* (Leiden: E.J. Brill, 2003), pp. 233–49, at p. 240.

when the Muslims saw them doing this, they attacked as one man, and victory happened during that attack."

It was said that the emir `Izz al-Dīn Izdimur *al-ḥājj* attacked among the Tatar army, pretending that he was one of those retreating, going towards their commander, and called among them for them to bring him to their commander Mengű Teműr. When he was close to him, he attacked him, casting him to the ground. At that all of the Tatars dismounted because he had fallen, so when the Muslims saw that they had dismounted, they attacked them as one man. There was the victory for the Muslims, and Mengű Teműr fled wounded, while the army followed him.

It divided up into several sections: one took the Salamiyya and the desert direction, while one took the direction of Aleppo and the Euphrates [River]. This was what was happening with those.

As for what was happening with the Tatar right flank which had defeated the left flank of the people of Islam, when it returned looking for their commander, Mengű Teműr. This was while the army and al-Malik al-Manṣūr stood firm in their places with only a small number of mamluks around him, approximately 1000 horsemen, as the rest of the army had dispersed in pursuit of the Tatars who were retreating. Some from the right flank continued fleeing, while al-Malik al-Manṣūr ordered that the standards be furled up, and the kettledrums cease while the Tatars passed them by.

However, they [Mongols] did not advance towards him, while he was very steadfast against them. When they advanced slightly towards him, he came at them, so they retreated, not waiting for anything. [218] This was a complete victory! The last of them retreated before the sun set, and went towards al-Jabal in the footsteps of their retreating fellows to catch up with them.

This was one of God's, praise Him and be raised, hidden graces: the fact that the retreating Tatars went towards al-Jabal. If not, had they returned towards the Muslims, there was no one in the Muslim army who could resist them or fight them. However, God Most High aided the Muslims against the unbelievers, so the Tatars turned tail and fled, by the grace of God and His mercy. This encounter revealed the mass killing of Tatars, who could not be counted.

The Sultan al-Malik al-Manṣūr returned that day to his campsite after the war broke off. Previously he had distributed the gold in the treasury among his mamluks, having given it all over. The short missives (*baṭā'iq*) were written announcing victory, and the Sultan spent the night, the night of Friday, on the campsite.

At dawn there was shouting in the pavilions, so the people thought that the abandoned enemy, the Tatars, had returned. Al-Malik al-Manṣūr rode together with those who had been in the pavilions with him, but after a short time the report was revealed to be false. It turned out that it was a number of the army that had been pursuing the Tatars after defeat had returned. More Tatars were killed during the retreat than were killed during the battle. A number [of Mongols] concealed themselves from them [the pursuit] by the side of the Euphrates [River], so the Sultan ordered that fire be lit from jars located beside the Euphrates, so most of those who were concealed there were burned. Thus, that group of them who took the Salamiyya path perished.

On the morning of Friday 15 Rajab [October 30, 1281] the day after the battle, al-Malik al-Manṣūr prepared a number of the army and the Bedouin, the commander of whom was the emir Badr al-Dīn Bīlīk al-Aydimurī, to follow after the Tatars. Then al-Malik al-Manṣūr transferred his campsite from the outside of Ḥimṣ to the lake in order to distance himself from the stench [of corpses]. Ibn Mukarram said in his composition *The Secretary's Treasury*, the upshot of which was: when the two groups had met in battle, the left flank had been defeated, as they did not stand more than a short while in battle, but retreated at the sight of the abandoned enemy.

When the abandoned enemy saw that, they were enthused, and their goals increased. However, the Sultan and his close coterie, his emirs and those in the center held firm to the utmost, so God caused His victory to descend upon His religion, aiding the Muslims with His angels, and the Tatars were completely defeated. Swords took them; most of them were killed, and the rest turned tail.

One who was present at the battle informed that God Most High sent black birds against them that slapped their faces.[80] Among the most amazing things is that they had fed their horses with wheat during these days, so when they led them to battle, they burst open, so the abandoned ones were left foot soldiers. Hands took them, and the peasants and [Mamluk] foot-soldiers went out against them.

Among the most amazing stories told is that those retreating ran across Georgians hiding, approximately 5000 horsemen, so they said to them "Give us your horses so we can save ourselves on them, for they are fresh!" However, they said to them "You don't have more right to our horses than we do, so you would be saved, while we get killed." They fought, and a large number of them were killed.

Among [219] the most felicitous things that happened was the killing of Ṣamghār, who was their senior commander, their greatest and bravest one. He had raided many times into Syria. Mengű Teműr was very badly wounded, and had to go tied up to his saddle after he had fallen to the ground, as we have previously explained. A number of the Mongols were killed.

Of the Muslims, over 200 were martyred during this blessed battle. Among them, of the emirs, ʿIzz al-Dīn Izdimur *al-ḥājj*, who was the one who wounded Mengű Teműr, and cast him off his horse. This was the reason for the Tatars' defeat, and the Muslims' victory. He was, may God have mercy upon him, one of the best emirs, and his soul told him that he would rule.

80 Compare Q105:3 (story of Abraha and the elephant).

Also Sayf al-Dīn Balabān al-Rūmī *al-dawādār* al-Ẓāhirī, ʿAlam al-Dīn Sanjar al-Irbilī, Badr al-Dīn Baktūt al-Khazindārī, Shams al-Dīn Sunqur al-ʿUrsī [?],[81] Shihāb al-Dīn Tūtil al-Shahrazūrī, Sayf al-Dīn Balabān al-Ḥimṣī, Nāṣir al-Dīn Muḥammad son of Jamāl al-Dīn Ṣayram al-Kāmilī, ʿAlāʾ al-Dīn ʿAlī son of the emir Sayf al-Dīn Baktimur *al-sāqī* (the cupbearer) al-ʿAzīzī, Nāṣir al-Dīn Muḥammad son of Aybak al-Fakhrī, Badr al-Dīn Bīlīk al-Sharafī al-Shaybānī, Sharaf al-Dīn Ibn ʿAlkān [?], the ruler of Mosul, al-Ba's al-Shadid, and others, may God envelope them in His mercy, and the judge Shams al-Dīn Ibn Quraysh, secretary of the noble roll, who went missing, and no report was known of him. This is what happened with regard to Mengű Teműr and al-Malik al-Manṣūr, and the matter of the blessed battle.

As for what was happening with the Damascenes, a note came to them after Friday prayer on 15 Rajab, the day after the battle, containing the news of the victory and triumph, and the Tatars' retreat. Tidings were announced from Damascus Citadel, and the people were very happy with that. The Citadel and the city were decorated, candles were lit. When it was after half the night on the night of Saturday 16 Rajab, the second day after the battle, a great number of the Muslims' army arrived outside of Damascus. Among them were a number of the defeated emirs from the left flank, so they told of what they had witnessed from the first, and that they had been defeated, but they did not know what transpired after that.

Therefore, the Damascenes had terrible anxiety and fear [220] and their happiness turned to grief. A large number of them prepared for defeat, and opened the city gates. Nothing was left other than for them to actually leave them their homes, but then at that very moment a post-courier came from al-Malik al-Manṣūr, and informed them of the victory. He arrived at almost the same time as the morning call to prayer, and then delivered a letter to the emir Nāṣir al-Dīn Ibn al-Ḥarrānī, which was read that very hour in the Damascus Friday Mosque. This letter contained the tidings of victory, so happiness was made complete, and the people returned to the decoration process, while the post-courier headed towards protected Egypt with that news. That is with relation to those.

As for the inhabitants of Egypt, on Thursday 21 Rajab [November 5, 1281] the small missives from Qāqūn arrived at the protected Hill Citadel informing that a number of the victorious army's left flank arrived retreating from the abandoned enemy, and some of the emirs arrived in Qaṭīyā. Among them was Ibn al-Aydimurī.

The Muslims had already begun entreating God Most High, and performing the *qunūt* (supplication) prayers, plus reading the book of al-Bukhārī in both Egypt and Syria. They began to recite the Qurʾān in the al-Ḥusayn b. ʿAlī b. Abī Ṭālib Mosque, may God be satisfied with the both of them, in

[81] Vocalization uncertain.

protected Cairo, and in the Friday mosques, the smaller mosques, and the (Sufi) hospices. They begged for His clemency and sought shelter in His forbearance.

The Sultan al-Malik al-Ṣāliḥ son of al-Malik al-Manṣūr dispatched an army immediately whose commander was the emir Ṣārim al-Dīn Uzbak al-Fakhrī, and the other Bedouin with him, to Qaṭīyā to repel the retreaters, and to have them return to al-Malik al-Manṣūr. He forbade those who wanted to enter protected Cairo. Thus, none of them were able to do so, and all of them returned to the service of Sultan al-Malik al-Manṣūr.

Then after this shocking small note had been received, the spread of alarm, and hearts' (feeling) anxiety during the midst of the day, God Most High favored them with His grace. The birds arrived with small missives tied to their necks, giving the aroma of awe-inspiring glad tidings of the abandoned Tatars' defeat.

Then the post-courier of Sayf al-Dīn al-Zu`ārī and `Izz al-Dīn al-Maghribī arrived with letters heralding good tidings, so the glad tidings were publicized, and Old Cairo and Cairo with their suburbs were decorated, together with the Citadel. He [al-Ṣāliḥ?] wrote to the rest of the lands with this news, and they ordered the tidings and the decorations, and the tidings and decorations stayed in place for a number of days—may God make it the first victory for the religion and the opening for the Muslims' happiness!

Al-Malik al-Ṣāliḥ son of al-Malik al-Manṣūr wrote a letter to his father, commending him, and asking for clemency for the retreaters, interceding from his pleasure on their behalf. He sent the tied-up letter to him via the emir Badr al-Dīn Baysarā al-Shamsī, to hand it to him personally. This was to affirm the intercession about them, and the restoration of favor. This was what was happening with them.

As for what was happening with al-Malik al-Manṣūr, when he finished off with this blessed battle, he resolved [221] to return to protected Damascus. Then Shams al-Dīn Sunqur *al-ashqar* took leave of him, and returned from Ḥimṣ to Ṣayhūn, his fortresses, and his castles that were granted to him.

The Sultan al-Malik al-Manṣūr returned to protected Damascus, while in his service there were a number of emirs who had been with the emir Shams al-Dīn Sunqur *al-ashqar*. They were Sayf al-Dīn Aytimish al-Sa`dī, Sanjar al-Dawādārī, Giray al-Tatarī, and his children, Tamājī and a number of the emirs who had been with him.

His arrival in protected Damascus was on Friday 22 Rajab [November 6, 1281] before prayers, and the people came out to greet him. He entered, while before him were a number of the emirs, and it was a day to remember. The people rejoiced greatly at his coming, with the poets praising him, and there were many poems of praise and congratulation about this tremendous victory.

On 27 Rajab [November 11, 1281] the reports arrived in Cairo and Old Cairo, and the noble gates at the Hill Citadel that the Sultan had returned from Ḥimṣ, and entered protected Damascus as a victor (*manṣūr*) on Friday the 5th [hour] of the day 22 Rajab. When al-Malik al-Manṣūr had settled in Damascus, he dispatched an army to al-Raḥba to defend those in it from the Tatars. This was what was happening with those.

As for what was happening with King Abagha, the king of the Tatars, he, just as we have previously explained, went leading a group of the Tatars to al-Raḥba, and besieged it. However, when the small notes of al-Malik al-Manṣūr reached the deputy of al-Raḥba informing him of the victory, and the defeat of the Tatars, he ordered the glad tidings to be proclaimed in al-Raḥba, and the people publicized the victory. This reached Abagha, king of the Tatars, so he left al-Raḥba heading for Baghdad. This was what was happening with Abagha.

As for what was happening with the Tatar who had retreated during the blessed battle, the Sultan, when he dispatched the emir Badr al-Dīn al-Aydimurī, just as we previously explained, he proceeded until he reached Aleppo, and stayed in it. However, he sent most of those who were with him to pursue the Tatars until the Euphrates [River] so that a huge number of them perished, drowning at the crossing of the Euphrates.

A number of those retreating crossed at protected al-Bīra castle, so its army descended upon them, killing 500 of them, taking 150 people prisoners, and crushing a large number of them. It is said that the inhabitants of al-Ma`rra also went out against them at their crossing, taking vengeance upon them, so that they were dispersed. The total (number) of retreaters was 1500 horsemen, who headed towards Baghrās. Among them were the senior commanders of the ruler of Sīs, his relatives and courtiers, so [222] the emir Shujā` al-Dīn al-Shaybānī, and a number of the army came out against them, so he killed them, and took them all prisoner. Only 20 of them were saved. He further described how the ruler of Sīs headed on a weak mixed-breed horse (*akdīsh*), while the Turkmen pursued him.

Among the totality of the retreaters were 4000 horsemen who headed along to Salamiyya. When the deputies in al-Raḥba heard of them, they guarded the fords and crossings against them. Thus, they stayed in the dry land, then died of thirst and hunger. 600 of them gave themselves up, but they attacked them from al-Raḥba, killing most of them, and taking a large number prisoner. They were brought to al-Raḥba where their heads were cut off.

Tatar prisoners continued to straggle and stream into Damascus, while there were repeated reports about their weakness, division, their horses perishing, and the local inhabitants taking them hostage. They were scattered among the wastelands and the mountains, dying of thirst and hunger.

King Abagha, king of the Tatars, when he left al-Raḥba, as they were proclaiming the glad tidings, just as we explained previously, stayed opposite al-Raḥba awaiting the reports of the army that would come to him, so when the first of the retreaters arrived, together with his brother Mengű Teműr who was wounded. He was angered at Mengű Teműr, and said to him "Why (*lesh*) didn't you die, together with the army, so that you weren't retreating, you and those with you?" He was angered at the commanders as well for that reason.

Then Abagha went to Baghdad, then to Hamadan, while Mengű Teműr went to the lands of al-Jazīra, settling on the island of Ibn `Amr. This island belonged to his mother, who had been given it by his father Hűlegű when it was conquered.

On Monday 25 Rajab [November 9, 1281] the emir Badr al-Dīn al-Aydimurī arrived in Damascus, with those of the army returning from pursuing the Tatars, and having exacted the maximum vengeance upon them. It was commanded that the tidings would be announced by those mentioned in it: for protected Cairo and Old Cairo the emir Ḥusām al-Dīn Lājīn *al-silaḥdār* al-Rūmī, for Qūṣ and Upper Egypt, other than al-Fayyūm, the emir Badr al-Dīn Baydarā al-Manṣūrī, the emir of the council, for al-Fayyūm, the emir `Alam al-Dīn Sanjar, *amīr akhūr* al-Manṣūrī, for Alexandria the emir `Alam al-Dīn Sanjar, *amīr jāndār*, for Damietta, the emir Badr al-Dīn Bīlīk Abū Shāma al-Muḥsinī, for the west, the emir `Izz al-Dīn Aybak *al-silaḥdār* al-Manṣūrī, and for Ashmūm, the emir Shams al-Dīn Ibn al-Jamaqdār, the deputy for the *amīr jāndār.*

A letter from the Sultan al-Malik al-Manṣūr to al-Malik al-Muẓaffar, ruler of Yemen, arrived at the noble gates at the Hill Citadel. He commanded [223] for it to be sent with the tidings of the abandoned enemy's defeat. Thus, al-Malik al-Ṣāliḥ son of al-Malik al-Manṣūr commanded that a letter be written from it, which was penned by the judge Muḥyī al-Dīn Ibn `Abd al-Ẓāhir. A duplicate of it:

> May God make aid of the Shamsī Muẓaffarī's standing-place glorious, and so the glad tidings continue to arrive of his fame, firing up his abode, guiding to its happiness, aiming for his way of acting, sending to the pulpits of his protected realm, finishing of the inkstands of precious history-writers accounts. However, it continues to generate new noble codices, piling up organized contracts, immortalizing thereby every memory lest the previous apocalyptic battles be forgotten, and building up the foundations of guidance, without which the supports of the straightened spears would have been destroyed.
>
> The owned-one (*mamlūk*) serves in the same service as his father, following the path, and continues in the praiseworthy actions in which his father took part, other than the servant learned this art, and described the loyal following by which both of them are given patronymics and to the peak of which both are glued.
>
> Therefore, he will open with mention of my blessings, through which God has blessed every believer at the furthest corners of the earth, which is the

blessing by which Islam was returned to being a youth, the (moving) star of its felicity shown forth, the day of its victory as a full moon (*badr*).[82] The people of love and mutual aid have begun congratulating because of it, while the angels of the heavens are grateful to the Sultan of Islam, and performing intercessory prayer on his behalf.

Prior to it the mountains' hearts were almost split asunder, while the clouds' tears were being waded through, with livers perishing about to be cut. This was because the abandoned Tatars gathered all those who believed in their (incorrect) belief (*ẓann*) that it would defeat the number singly, and so every brave man elected to join with the backs of his fleet horses from the day of his birth, and they flocked in, seeking to accompany what they had treasured, and defended.

They granted by the might of their great ones, and the commanders of the *tumān*s (10,000s), who never have ever heard that they were fearing or cringing in a battle. Our master the Sultan heard their reports, and their fire burned the brighter at his touch, and changing their usual methods of attacking, coming deliberately, as if they intended mutual friendship and then mutual collision, but the four corners filled with fear, and the lands with pillage.

They came to the campsites just as earthquakes come, rising against the lands of Islam like the rising of judgment descending, stretching out binding them, taking over the realms and garrison cities, taking kings and helpers lightly, sure that the desert and villages would not be saved from them, nor those shielded by walls and seas.

Our master the Sultan and his troops waited to ambush them, alighting, grasping their swords, seeking to drag them, to have their association (with other deities) fall in the midst of the Islamic lands, to bring them down, to throw them into the lowest fire of death by overtaking.

When they came close to protected Ḥamāh [224] and their buildings became clear from their villages, as Ḥimṣ lured them in, our master the Sultan pounced upon them making their young old, coming towards them, driving towards them, arranged like Khālid b. al-Walīd. Angels followed him from behind with their aid, while kings bolstered his numbers and provisions. The Muslims in the rest of the lands at that hour had beaten on heaven's gates, unsheathing the prophets' weapons through intercessory prayer.

[82] A pun with the Battle of Badr (624).

Every shrine and mosque in Cairo, old Cairo, Damascus, and the regions was filled at that hour with lines of beseeching prayers at that time, standing, jostling shoulder-to-shoulder, just as ranks of fighters (*mujāhidīn*) were firm, side-by-side, in those processions.

God Most High gazed upon His creation with blessing of those prostrating foreheads, and those who brought suckling infants to intercede with God, so God sent His eagles of victory to cast, and unsheathe swords of conquest to cut necks, and shed blood. Our master the Sultan stood firm longer than any other sultan, and God caused victory of the religion to rise as a result of his intention, receiving him well, and made him blossom.

The enemy had 100,000 opposing, fighting, fixing arrows, aggressive, sword-in-hand, confronting, slavering, causing wounds, but they [Muslims] were patient in the heat of bitterness, seeing that death is better than defeat. None turned to flee other than those who the sword asked for a delay of an hour during the day. Some of them fled, while death said to them "Say: Flight will not benefit you."[83]

This was on Thursday 14 Rajab [October 29, 1281]. Those ones who turned [Mongols] were those whose horses' birds snatched at them while at river-crossings and mountain-passes, the ones who the wind blew at them from a remote place. Everything attacked them, even the ravens, vultures and eagles, while the armies pursued them to the banks of the Euphrates, to the flags of al-Raḥba, and to the twisty passes of Sīs. The inhabitants of al-Bīra came out against them leading armies taking rest, while all of the fortresses' inhabitants leading their slaughtering troops.

Every sword was placed upon those resting, while the ring of captivity was fastened around those permitted (to live). Their kings were killed, the descendants of Hűlegű, and others, so God hastened their spirits to the Fire, while the earth refused to conceal any of their bodies, but cast them into the waste and abandoned villages.

This apocalyptic battle was revealed to be from overarching grace, complete victory and conquest. Senior Mongols declaimed in Transoxiana:

If your year astonished you, then return to Ḥimṣ during the next (year).

Our master the Sultan twisted the reins, while the captive Mongol kings were driven before him as if they were drunk, when they were not.

[83] Q33:16.

Spear-heads bore the fruit for every champion in how he did well [225] cutting off heads, and how he placed the name of God upon the padlocks of his armies, so as to move them forward, as they had repelled aggression and been sufficient against hopelessness.

The traveling reports arrived with that (news), and creation's congratulations were general, the glad tidings sounded in every direction, while the angels soared until the horizon burst with lightning-bolts and the heavens crashed their tidings with thunder. When this awesome news was welcomed, of which the inhabitants of the realms had been ignorant, our master the Sultan was not neglectful in cheering the lord[84] with these greetings in the same manner. So let everyone get to work!

He hastily sent a post-courier to us, with a noble proclamation to the lord, so we sent it in the same manner, having it accompanied by some servants who would be deputies (dual) to explain these apocalyptic wars in which Islam was born anew, to bring the noble hearing close to these events from afar.

God knows, and the Muslims, that seeing the battle personally is not like a report, so by God's life, this aid is memory to humanity, because it sufficed for the Islamic religion in a great manner. God took by it a deep vengeance (*thā'r*) for the imams and the community (*umma*), and our master is most deserved of being happy because of it from every pulpit, and to be given precedence because of it by writing it, for it is the most noble of what could be written in ink, and the most majestic of what can be told.

The lord should continue to be happy for the believers because of God's victory, and give thanks for the stances of the Sultan, who is not neglectful of aiding God's religion, and making it bright, and God grants success.

During Rajab [October–November 1281] a letter from the emir `Alā' al-Dīn Aydakīn al-Fakhrī arrived at the noble sultanic gates at the Hill Citadel in protected Egypt, informing that the royal command had arrived that Ghars al-Dīn Ibn Shāwar should continue in the governate of Lydda and Ramla. However, Sa`d al-Dīn Ibn Qillīj should be transferred from it to the governate of Hebron (*al-khalīl*), upon him [Abraham] and our lord and prophet Muḥammad, the Messenger of God, be the best of prayer and peace.

Taqī al-Dīn Tawba al-Tikrītī was assigned to be supreme inspector in Syria, and the judge Tāj al-Dīn Ibn al-Sanhūrī continued to be an inspector with

84 Presumably the Rasulid king of Yemen.

him. The emir `Alam al-Dīn Sanjar al-Dawādārī was assigned as supervisor and administrator (*mudabbir*) in the Gazan lands in the Euphrates realm.

Ibn al-Mukarram said in his composition *The Secretary's Treasure*, and others [did] as well, during Sha`bān [November–December 1281] al-Malik al-Manṣūr delegated the Chancelleries Supervision in Syria to the emir `Alam al-Dīn Sanjar al-Dawādārī. He delegated the supreme inspectorate in Syria to the judge Tāj al-Dīn `Abd al-Raḥmān Ibn al-Shīrāzī, and God knows best which of these two versions it was.

During the month of Rajab [October–November 1281] al-`Ushrān revolted,[85] and looted Nablus, killing a great number. `Alā' al-Dīn Aydakīn al-Fakhrī rode to them from Gaza, and detained a number of them, hanging 32 of them. He also detained `Imād al-Dīn Ḥijjī Ibn Shāwar, and a number of the vandals, and imprisoning them [226] in protected Safed.

In it the emir `Alā' al-Dīn Aydughdī al-Ṣarkhandī was assigned as deputy in all the Gazan and coastal lands in order to straighten the lands, and to cut off al-`Ushrān's supplies. In it an accident happened to Shaykh Taqī al-Dīn Muḥammad b. Daqīq al-`Īd while he was teaching at the Imam al-Shāfi`ī College, may God be pleased with him, in al-Qarāfa al-Ṣughrā, usually taught by the judge Taqī al-Dīn Ibn Razīn after his death.

During it the Shaykh `Alam al-Dīn son of the daughter of Isḥāq al-`Irāqī was appointed to teach in Imam al-Ḥusayn College, may God be pleased with him. During it the emir Shihāb al-Dīn son of the Citadel governor the emir *shikār* arrived from protected Syria to release the mares, to train them, and break them, and then to hand the mares over. During it, the emir Sayf al-Dīn Bāzī al-Manṣūrī was assigned as the noble deputy sultan in Ḥimṣ. The emir Ṣārim al-Dīn al-Ḥimṣī was made an assistant to him over the affairs, as a warning to him about his obligation. During it, the emir Jamāl al-Dīn Aqush al-Ḥimṣī was appointed over the city of Nablus and that which is with it, in place of Zayn al-Dīn Qarājā al-Badrī.

The crescent moon of Sha`bān [December 13, 1281] this year was seen on Saturday night.

During it, the emir Sayf al-Dīn Quṭuz al-Manṣūrī was freed. During it the emir `Alam al-Dīn Sanjar al-Ḥamawī Abū Khurṣ was freed and made to go to Syria. During it letters from the governor of Qūṣ arrived that the Bedouin of the Juhayna and Rafā`a [tribes] fought together in the Aydhāb Waste, having a number killed between them. They had taken refuge with the ruler of Suakin,[86] even though he was probably helping one against the other. He wrote to the noble `Alam al-Dīn al-Sam`ānī, ruler of Suakin, that he was not to interfere with them. On the contrary, he should try to make peace, and not

[85] See Irwin, "Tribal Feuding and Mamluk Factions in Medieval Syria," in Robinson (ed.), *Texts, Documents and Artefacts*, pp. 251–64, at pp. 255–6.

[86] Port on the Red Sea, in present-day Sudan.

help one (tribe) against the other, to try to improve the road and guarantee the safety of travelers.

Zayn al-Dīn Ibn al-Qammāḥ was appointed to the inspectorate of al-Buḥayra in place of Muwaffaq al-Dīn Ibn al-Shammā`. Shams al-Dīn Muḥammad son of the judge `Alam al-Dīn Ibn al-Qammāḥ was appointed to return to the Imam al-Shāfi`ī College in al-Qarāfa al-Ṣughrā with a noble rescript.

On 11 Sha`bān [November 25, 1281] the letter of the emir Jamāl al-Dīn, governor of al-Manūfiyya, arrived informing that the Banū Ṣūra [tribe] had divided into two groups, and had mobilized a number [of troops]. He had ridden to them, making them fear the outcome of this, and then sent righteous elders to them, but they did not repent. Their banding together in groups with swords, spears, provisions, and horses happened, so he dispatched a number of victorious freeborn troops (*ḥalqa*) against them.

He was commanded to ride, detain the vandals, and take their horses, weapons and provisions, and then his letter arrived saying that they had reconciled, and had dispersed, and God knows best. [227]

Mention of al-Malik al-Manṣūr's going to Damascus, and his return to the Egyptian homelands, and his safe arrival in his Citadel

On Sunday 2 Sha`bān [November 16, 1281] of this year the Sultan al-Malik al-Manṣūr Sayf al-Dīn Qalāwūn al-Alfī al-Ṣāliḥī al-Najmī departed from protected Damascus, returning to the Egyptian homelands, and the people came out to wish him farewell, supplicating with prayers on his behalf. The blessed post arrived at the noble gates of the Hill Citadel in protected Egypt, and informed of the Sultan's departure from Damascus, towards the Egyptian homelands.

Preparation of decoration was commanded, and for the castles to be readied. The emirs' deputies were ordered to go out to their castles' places, and to work on decorating them. Provisions were set aside on 10 Sha`bān under the auspices of the emir `Alam al-Dīn Sanjar al-Shujā`ī al-Manṣūrī. There were various types[87] in every dwelling: of flour 60 "pieces," of barley 400 *ardabb*s, of sheep 100 "head," of chickens 200 birds, of pigeons 50 birds, of straw 100 loads, and of acacia (*sanṭ*) firewood, 100 *qinṭār* (4493 kg).

The Sultan departed from Gaza on the morning of Thursday 13 Sha`bān [November 27, 1281] and arrived Monday 17 Sha`bān [December 1, 1281] in Qaṭiyā, but the victorious armies were delayed somewhat behind him.

On Thursday the 25th the Sultan stopped at Ghayfā, and camped there. The emir Sharaf al-Dīn al-Jākī *al-mihmandār* (in charge of hospitality) arrived at the noble royal tent to arrange for the kings' envoys who were in Cairo, and their going out to greet the noble entourage.

---

[87] Following the editor's suggestion of how to interpret *inṣāf.*

Al-Malik al-Ṣāliḥ ʿAlāʾ al-Dīn ʿAlī son of al-Malik al-Manṣūr departed to greet his father—he together with the emir Zayn al-Dīn Kitbughā, the deputy of the noble sultanate, while the emir ʿAlam al-Dīn Sanjar al-Manṣūrī stayed in the Citadel. The Sultan al-Malik al-Manṣūr rose from outside protected Cairo to the victorious Hill Citadel on Saturday 22 Shaʿbān [December 6, 1281] under his standards, while the Tatar prisoners went before him. Some of them were carrying their broken standards and their drums (*ṭubūl*), and they did not go through protected Cairo. However, it is said that the prisoners, their drums, and the *jeter* (royal umbrella) of Mengű Teműr went and did go through the city, which was a day to remember.

On Sunday 23 Shaʿbān [December 7, 1281] the Sultan freed the emir Rukn al-Dīn Mankūrus al-Nāṣirī al-Fāriqānī, and during it the Sultan entered the noble Treasury [228] and assigned the robes to the rest of the emirs and courtiers, bestowing robes especially upon the traveling secretaries of the roll in the noble service.

On Thursday 27 Shaʿbān [December 11, 1281] the Sultan al-Malik al-Manṣūr sat, and requested the Yemeni envoys, so they were presented before him with gifts. They were Majd al-Dīn Ibn Abī al-Qāsim, Tāj al-Dīn, and Muḥyī al-Dīn Ibn al-Bīlqānī.

On Saturday 29 Shaʿbān [December 13, 1281] the *iqṭāʿ* fiefs of the emir Sayf al-Dīn Aytimish al-Saʿdī were returned to him, which were Nāy and Ṭunān, and the command of 100 horsemen. At the time of his going out to Shams al-Dīn Sunqur *al-ashqar* his fiefs were given to the emir ʿIzz al-Dīn Aybak *al-afram*. These were now taken back from him, and returned to their rightful owner. The emir ʿIzz al-Dīn Aybak *al-afram* had his old fief returned to him from the one who had taken it.

During it, the Sultan gave a command to the emir Sayf al-Dīn Quṭuz al-Manṣūrī. During it after the death of the Chief Judge Taqī al-Dīn Ibn Razīn al-Shāfiʿī, al-Malik al-Manṣūr delegated the Shāfiʿī chief judgeship in the Egyptian homelands to the Chief Judge Wajīh al-Dīn ʿAbd al-Wahhāb son of the jurisprudent Ḥusayn al-Bahnasī al-Muhallabī. He rose at the hour of his appointment, with the notary witnesses in his service before him, on the Night of Doubt to see the Ramaḍān crescent moon as usual. An investiture was written for him.

During it the emir Rukn al-Dīn Baybars al-Ḥalabī the chamberlain Ayājī was detained. Among the reasons for which he was punished were his retreat at the Battle of Ḥimṣ.

On Saturday 6 Ramaḍān [December 19, 1281] of this year the Yemeni envoys were presented before the Sultan, and they asked him for a shirt (*qamīṣ*) of safe conduct, and that a copy of the safe conduct be written upon the front of it. He assented to that, and gave them a shirt. A copy of the safe conduct was written on the front of it for both him and his children. The Sultan al-Malik al-Manṣūr and his son al-Malik al-Ṣāliḥ made a mark on it, but the Sultan told them that this was not a usual activity, but that he had assented to it in order to bestow honor upon their master, and to fulfill his honor (*`irḍ*) and importunate request. He prepared gifts and valuables for him, a piece of emerald, some of the half-breed (*akdīsh*) Mongol horses, and something of their provisions.[88]

During the month of Ramaḍān, a copy was made of the Sultan al-Malik al-Manṣūr's oath to [229] the Lascarid [Palaeologan] King, ruler of Constantinople. A copy of an oath had arrived via his envoys, which was translated into Arabic, so the date of his oath was the date corresponding to the end of Muḥarram year 680 [May 20, 1281]. This is a duplicate of the text:[89]

> Since the Sultan, great in genealogy, high, glorious, the great of the ethnicity, al-Malik al-Manṣūr Sayf al-Dīn Qalāwūn, ruler of the Egyptian homelands, Damascus and Aleppo, desires that there should be affection between him and my realm, so my realm also favors this, and choses that there should be affection between it and his mighty sultanate, so for this purpose it is incumbent to place this matter on an even basis as an oath and agreement that will continue the affection in this manner between my realm and his mighty sultanate firmly without any disturbance from this day.
>
> Which is Thursday, 8 Ayyar of the 9th indiction (*tā'rīkh*) of the year 6789 from Adam, which is the last part of Muḥarram 680 [mid-May 1281], swearing an oath upon the holy Gospels of God, the noble Cross which gives life, that my realm will be guarding the Sultan, great in genealogy, high, glorious, the great of the ethnicity, al-Malik al-Manṣūr Sayf al-Dīn Qalāwūn, ruler of the Egyptian homelands, Damascus and Aleppo, and his sons, the inheritors of rule of his mighty sultanate's continuous affection, complete and pure friendship, and my kingdom will never make a move, ever, against his mighty sultanate in war, nor against his lands, his castles, or his armies.
>
> My kingdom will never move to make a way against him in such a way that this Sultan, great in genealogy, high, glorious, great of the ethnicity, al-Malik al-Manṣūr Sayf al-Dīn Qalāwūn, ruler of the Egyptian homelands, Damascus and Aleppo, should guard similarly over my realm, and the beloved child of our realm, the Komnenus, Angelus, Dukas,

---

[88] See Éric Vallet, "Diplomatic Networks of Rasulid Yemen in Egypt (Seventh/Thirteenth to early Ninth/Fifteenth Centuries)," in Frédéric Bauden and Malika Dekkiche (eds.), *Mamluk Cairo, a Crossroads for Embassies* (Leiden: E.J. Brill, 2019), pp. 581–603, at p. 585.

[89] Holt, *Early Mamluk Diplomacy*, pp. 122–8 (trans.), and a number of sources for previous translations.

Palaeologus, the king Andronicus, and the heirs of our realm, continuous affection, and pure complete friendship.

His mighty sultanate will never move against our realm in war, ever, nor against our lands, our castles, nor against the armies of our realm, nor move (with) another in warring against our realm either. Envoys traveling from his mighty sultanate will have the absolute right to pass through the lands of my realm, without anyone forbidding them, or hindering them, and they can head to where they are going on behalf of his mighty sultanate. In the same way, they can return to his mighty sultanate.

No wrong or oppression shall occur to the merchants coming from the lands of his mighty sultanate to the lands of our realm; on the contrary, they are permitted to conduct their merchandising affairs, and the same pertains to those merchants coming to the lands of his mighty sultanate from [230] the lands of our realm. None shall find wrong or oppression, but on the contrary, they shall be permitted to conduct their merchandising affairs.

Just as the merchants intending to go to the lands of his mighty sultanate from the inhabitants of my realm's lands to uphold the necessary due for their goods. Let this also be levied upon those coming from the lands of his mighty sultanate to my kingdom's lands according to the necessary due upon their goods.

If merchants from the lands of Sūdāq[90] are present, and want to journey to the lands of his mighty sultanate, no hindrance will come to those people in my kingdom's lands; on the contrary, in their passing and their return they will be without one forbidding them or hindrance after they pay the necessary due on their goods in the lands of my kingdom.

Likewise, if merchants from the inhabitants of his mighty sultanate's lands arrive and desire to pass to the lands of Sūdāq, they can pass through the lands of my realm without hindrance or anyone forbidding them, and in the same way when they return. All of this is after they pay the necessary due.

Those merchants who from the lands of his mighty sultanate, and those from the inhabitants of Sūdāq, if they are present accompanied by mamluks or slave girls, then they should be returned the lands of his mighty sultanate without hindrance or anyone forbidding them, other than those

[90] Soldaia, in the Crimea.

who are Christians because our law and the form of our religion does not grant us this with regard to Christians.

If there are in the lands of his mighty sultanate Christian Roman (*rūm*) mamluks or others from the different Christian ethnicities, who hold fast to the Christian religion, and the people manumit them, and then let those with them, freedmen, have permission and absolute rights from his mighty sultanate to return via the sea to the lands of my realm.

Likewise, if one of the inhabitants of his mighty sultanate's lands wishes to sell a Christian mamluk, then this same should apply to any of my realm's envoys, merchants, or people from my realm without hindrance; on the contrary, they should purchase the aforementioned and return him visa the sea to the lands of my realm with hindrance.

In addition, if this Sultan, great in genealogy, wishes to send to the lands of my kingdom goods for sale, or my realm wishes to send goods for sale to the lands of his mighty sultanate, then let this happen. If his mighty sultanate wishes for the goods of his merchandising to be safely in the lands of my kingdom like that free from all dues, and if he wishes for the merchandising of my kingdom in his lands pay the necessary dues, then let his mighty sultanate pay all the necessary dues in my kingdom in the same way.

If his mighty sultanate allows sending people from the lands of my realm to his glory the sultanate's lands, then they should send me good horses, and bear them to the lands of my kingdom. Likewise, if his mighty sultanate wishes something of the good products of my kingdom's lands, then my realm also will allow to his mighty sultanate to send people to bring and to bear those to his mighty sultanate.

Since there are corsairs in the sea [231] from the western lands, who have conspired at various times to carry out harmful actions in the lands of my kingdom,[91] likewise these corsairs have found a group of the lands of his mighty sultanate, and have carried out harmful actions against them, then if these corsairs do these things by conspiring in my kingdom's lands' region, for this when a group from my realm's lands is present in the lands of his mighty sultanate for the purpose of trade, they should be detained by the inhabitants of his mighty sultanate's lands, and should be fined.

---

[91] Compare the list of Genoese complaints against the Byzantines from 1290–4 written by Nicola Spinola, in Robert Lopez and Irving Raymond, *Medieval Trade in the Mediterranean World: Illustrative Documents Translated with Introductions and Notes* (New York: Columbia University Press, 1955), pp. 305–14.

For this reason a written decree should go out from his mighty sultanate to all of his lands, that any one from the lands of my realm should not be fined for this reason nor be detained, and if one of the inhabitants of his mighty sultanate's lands demonstrates that he has been fined or oppressed by any one of the inhabitants of my kingdom's lands, then let him notify my kingdom of that.

If the one who has carried out the fining is from the inhabitants of my kingdom's lands, then my kingdom will order and have that loss returned to the lands of his mighty sultanate, and likewise if one from the inhabitants of my realm's lands said that he has been treated unjustly or fined by one of the people of his mighty sultanate's lands then his mighty sultanate should order for that fine to be returned to the lands of my kingdom.

And also if the affection is proceeding in this manner, and the friendship between my kingdom and his mighty sultanate is pure, such that he sends to my kingdom asking for help and aid to my kingdom at sea, to the detriment of a mutual enemy, then my realm will delegate this order to the choice of his mighty sultanate to assign how inside the text of the oath together with the rest of the specific paragraphs in it, and in which form he will help and aid my realm at sea.

But if he does not wish aid and assistance of my realm, then my realm will grant that this paragraph not be placed in the text of his mighty sultanate's oath, and this oath, then, my kingdom will guard it firmly for his mighty sultanate, without wavering in the least, if he, the great Sultan, will swear to me an oath just like it. Then he will keep affection for our realm firm, without wavering in the least, and peace.

When I translated this oath into Arabic, I wrote a copy of an oath for the Sultan al-Malik al-Manṣūr, and here is a duplicate of it:

I say, and I am so-and-so, that when his majesty the majestic Lord Michael Dukas Angelus Komnenus Palaeologus, the one who holds the Roman realm, and Constantinople the awesome, greatest of the Christian (*masīḥiyya*) kings, may God give him long life, desired that there be affection, friendship and love that will never end with the changing days, nor disappear with the disappearance of years and spans, between his realm and that of my mighty sultanate.

This will be affirmed by the swearing of an oath upon it, whose date is Thursday 8 Ayyār year 6789 to Adam, may the prayers of God be upon him, in the presence of the envoy of my mighty sultanate the emir Nāṣir al-Dīn Ibn al-Jazarī, and the glorious Patriarch Anba Yūnus, Patriarch of Alexandria.[92]

The two envoys, so-and-so, and so-and-so, brought the text of the oath to my mighty sultanate, seeking to facilitate an oath and agreement for this matter also between my mighty sultanate, to continue the affection in that which is [232] between his realm and my mighty sultanate, that it should be firm and continuous, continually and always.

For my mighty sultanate from this day, which is Monday the beginning of the month of Ramaḍān year 680 [December 14, 1281] of the Prophet Muḥammad's *hijra*, upon whom be the best prayer and peace, to swear by the great God, merciful and compassionate, knower of the unseen and the seen, the secret and the public, and what breasts conceal. And upon the great Qur'ān, upon the One who revealed it, the one to whom it was revealed, who is the noble Prophet Muḥammad, may the prayer and peace of God be upon him.

Upon the continuation of friendship, the establishment of pure love towards the majestic Lord Michael, the one who holds the Roman realm, and Constantinople the awesome, and to the beloved son of his realm the Komnenus Angelus Dukas Palaeologus, the king Andronicus, and to the heirs of his kingdom's realm.

My mighty sultanate will never, ever move against his realm in war, nor against his lands, his castles, or his armies, on land or at sea, and my mighty sultanate will never cause another to move against him in war, such that the majestic king Lord Michael will ensure this similarly for my mighty sultanate, to my kingdom, my lands, my castles, my armies, my son al-Malik al-Ṣāliḥ `Alā' al-Dīn `Alī, and the heirs of my kingdom from my children.

This friendship and pure love will continue, and his kingdom will never move against my mighty sultan, nor against my land, my castles, my armies, nor against my realm. Nor will he cause anyone else to move waging war against my mighty sultanate's realm, on land or at sea, nor aid anyone in opposition to my mighty sultan or my enemies from along the other religions and ethnicities.

Nor will he concur with this or make way for them to cross to my mighty sultanate's realm to do harm in any way to it with his effort or ability. The

[92] Following Holt, and Canard. Anba Yūnus served (for a second time) during the period 1271–93.

envoys passing from my mighty sultanate's realm to Ber Berke and his sons, and their lands, these regions, and the Sūdāq Sea [Black Sea] and its land will be safe, tranquil, having the right to pass on land and sea.

They will have the absolute right to pass through the lands of the majestic king Lord Michael from their beginning to their end, without anyone forbidding them, or any hindrance, whether sent on land or sea according to the necessity of that time's interest for my mighty sultanate's realm.

They will have the right to head where my mighty sultanate sends them in these lands, and likewise can return to my mighty sultanate's realm safe, tranquil, without being forbidden with regard to any of the envoys they might go to from those regions or a westerner (*gharīb*).

Everything with them such as mamluks, slave girls, and other things—never should there be any form of wrong or oppression for the merchants coming from the realm of the majestic king Lord Michael to the lands of my mighty sultanate. They should pass back and forth safe, tranquil, carrying out their commerce. They should have oversight for the going forth and returning, for staying and for journeying, so that [233] the merchants of my mighty sultanate's realm will have in the lands of the majestic king Lord Michael's realm the same. They should be overseen, and should not encounter any wrong or injustice in the lands of the majestic king Lord Michael's realm. Whoever is there is subject to the necessary due to pay from both parties according to what has been established, without inequity or oppression.

If those merchants from Sūdāq or westerners bring mamluks or slave girls the realm of the majestic king Lord Michael will allow them to pass with them to the realm of my mighty sultanate, without forbidding them.

If corsairs, when they attempt to take one of the Muslim merchants at sea, as the corsairs are considered subjects of the realm of the majestic king Lord Michael, my mighty sultanate will go to him to search after them. None of the deputies of my mighty sultanate's realm shall interfere with this ethnicity because of them until it can be verified that they are taking (booty), or the precise money is revealed being in their possession.

This is in accord with the text of the majestic king Lord Michael's oath, and what belongs to the majestic king Lord Michael from the lands of my mighty sultanate like that.

On the condition that the envoys passing back and forth between the two parties from my mighty sultanate and from the realm of the majestic king

> Lord Michael will be safe, tranquil in their journey, and their staying on land and sea, and the subjects of my mighty sultanate and the subjects of the realm of the majestic king Lord Michael among both parties from the Muslims and others are safe, tranquil, both going forth and coming back, honored, safeguarded, and this oath will continue to be kept, vocalized, continuous, established in perpetuity and continuity.[93]

During Ramaḍān [December 1281–January 1282] also the emir Bahā' al-Dīn Qarāqūsh was appointed to Qūṣ and Akhmīm after the emir Rukn al-Dīn Baybars, mamluk of `Alā' al-Dīn *al-ḥarbdār* (in charge of spears).

During Shawwāl [January–February 1282] of this year the sultanic *maḥmal* traveled as usual.

On Thursday 1 Dhū al-Qa`da [February 11, 1282] al-Malik al-Manṣūr detained the emir Sayf al-Dīn Aytimish al-Sa`dī, and a number of the emirs, and imprisoned them. In Damascus the emir Sayf al-Dīn Balabān al-Hārūnī, Sunqrān al-Kurdī and others were also detained. Aytimish and al-Hārūnī had returned from being with Shams al-Dīn Sunqur *al-ashqar* to the service of al-Malik al-Manṣūr after [234] the conflict with the Tatars, just as we previously explained.

During it, the emir Nāṣir al-Dīn Ibn al-Muḥsinī al-Jazarī and the judge Sharaf al-Dīn Ibrāhīm b. Faraj, a secretary of the noble roll, headed towards Yemen as envoys, and they traveled via `Aydhāb. The son of Sharaf al-Dīn Ibn Faraj headed with him to Yemen.

Mention of the kingship of Aḥmad Aghā son of Hűlegű over the Tatars after the death of his brother Abagha son of Hűlegű, king of the Tatars

We had mentioned that the King Abagha son of Hűlegű, king of the Tatars when he learned of his armies' defeat, he stayed opposite al-Raḥba in order to see who would bring him news of the army. The first of the retreaters arrived to him, with his wounded brother Mengű Teműr. He was angry with him and with the commanders, so he separated from them, going to Baghdad and then to Hamadan.

When he came close to Hamadan, he died, out of grief and sadness over his armies, in the sub-districts of Hamadan, between the two Feasts [February–April 1282] of this year. He was approximately 50 years old, and he was a king of high ambition, courageous, brave, trained in battle, and experienced in affairs. After his father, there was never the like of him again. His realm

[93] According to Pachymeres, *Relations Historiques I–II* (ed. Albert Failler, Paris: Institut Français d'Études Byzantines, 1984), p. 658f. Michael worked with the Mongols in Asia Minor almost immediately following this treaty (which does not appear to be mentioned in Byzantine sources).

was wide, his wealth was plentiful, his armies most numerous, and his word among the troops, in spite of their number, was obeyed. He had good judgment, resolve, and ability to manage.

When his brother Mengű Teműr headed towards Syria leading the armies, it was not at his instigation, but he was advised to do it, then agreed. He settled opposite al-Raḥba, and then stayed opposite it anticipating what would happen. When he verified his army's defeat, he returned back, then sickened and died.

His brother Aḥmad son of Hűlegű was king after him, and he was a Muslim, who did not believe in fighting the people of Islam. Mengű Teműr son of Hűlegű had been wounded the day of the conflict, just as we previously explained. A deep grief took him because of the defeat that had happened to him and his army after he was on the verge of achieving his goal with regard to the Muslims' army, just as we previously explained.

So he was sad about that, and told himself that he would return and gather the armies of his father Hűlegű, go to Syria, and take revenge. Then God Most High brought his brother Abagha's death close to him, and hastened his spirit to the Fire. When he learned of his death, and the kingship of Aḥmad Aghā, his back was broken, his will to live shattered, and a recurring epilepsy killed him on Ibn `Umar Island. God, mighty and majestic, gave the lands and the servants [Muslims] peace from him, and that was at the end of this year [April 10, 1282], and it was said at the beginning of the year 681 during the first tenth of Muḥarram [April 1282].

This King Mengű Teműr had courage, initiative and boldness, but was much given to spilling blood. He was a Christian, as some of the historians have related, among them al-Jazarī, and he had a crooked neck. He died when he was approximately 30 years old.

It is said that judge [235] Jamāl al-Dīn Abū `Abdallāh known as Ibn al-`Ajamiyya poisoned him because he knew he was going to head to the Syrian lands. After Mengű Teműr's death a fellow called al-Qarqūbī, who was the guarantor (*ḍāmin*) of Ibn `Umar Island for the Tatars, went and summoned the judge Jamāl al-Dīn Ibn al-`Ajamiyya saying that he had poisoned Mengű Teműr. Mengű Teműr's mother took the judge Jamāl al-Dīn and all of his children, and slaughtered them, may God's mercy be upon them. She confiscated all of their wealth, then after that then the Tatars took al-Qarqūbī, the one who hastened to Jamāl al-Dīn, raised him up, and then killed him in the worst possible way, him and his children.

Some of the historians said in it after the death of Chief Judge Nafīs al-Dīn Muḥammad, known as Ibn Shukr, the jurisprudent of the Mālikī rite on Friday 1 Dhū al-Ḥijja [March 13, 1282] of this year, al-Malik al-Manṣūr delegated the Mālikī chief judiciary in the Egyptian homelands to the Chief Judge Taqī al-Dīn Abū `Alī al-Ḥusayn son of the jurisprudent Sharaf al-Dīn Abū al-Faḍl `Abd al-Raḥīm son of the jurisprudent imam, *mufti* (adjudicator) of the sects Jalāl al-Dīn Abū Muḥammad `Abdallāh b. Shās al-Judhāmī al-Sa`dī, the jurisprudent of the Mālikī rite. It was said that his appointment was in the 681 [1282], as we will mention, if God Most High wishes.

[*Obituaries*]

Mention of the events during the year 681 [1282]

During Ṣafar [May–June 1282] of this year the Sultan al-Malik al-Manṣūr Qalāwūn al-Alfī al-Ṣāliḥī al-Najmī, the ruler of the Egyptian homelands and the Syrian lands, detained the emir Badr al-Dīn Baysarā al-Shamsī and the emir Kushtghadī al-Shamsī, and surrounded their *iqṭā`* fiefs. It was said that he detained the both of them, and others. The emir Badr al-Dīn Baysarā continued to be imprisoned until the Ashrafi period, when he was freed, as we will mention at the proper place, if God Most High wills.

During it, the reports of the deaths of the Tatars' king Abagha son of Hűlegű and Mengű Teműr were confirmed, and dissension among the abandoned Tatars. The land was free from them, may God Most High destroy them!

During the month of Rabī` al-Awwal [June 1282] of this year the envoys of Būghā, who were the emir Stawarus, the emir Nūrghās, and Sayf al-Dīn Abū Bakr arrived at the sultanic gates. The Lascarid [Palaeologan] envoy Kyros (*kūrīs*) al-Adurnali [of Adrianople] arrived together with them.[94]

During it Alfonso's envoys, who were *mayor* Felipe the Spaniard and his companion the priest *pere* Estéban arrived in Alexandria. With them were 63 people, horses, mules for a gift, of 15 "head," after seven "head" of them had died. Among the arrivals were 35 women [247] pilgrims.

On 11 Rabī` al-Ākhir [July 19, 1282] of this year al-Malik al-Manṣūr delegated his ministry in the Egyptian homelands to Najm al-Dīn Ḥamza b. Muḥammad al-Uṣfūnī, who received the title of "chief." The beginning of his career and rise was that he governed half of Mushārafat al-aṣl[95] in the districts of Qūṣ. Then he governed the inspectorate of the districts of Qūṣ during the period of al-Malik al-Ẓāhir Rukn al-Dīn Baybars al-Bunduqdārī al-Ṣāliḥī al-Najmī. Then he was placed in the inspectorate of the districts of Akhmīm. After that, he was transferred to among the retainers until he was appointed to the chief inspectorate in the Egyptian homelands.

Then al-Malik al-Manṣūr appointed him to his ministry in the Egyptian homelands. He was knowledgeable concerning the accounts, so the state was straightened during his ministry. However, the period of his ministry did not last long, because he died almost exactly a year to the day after his ministry began.

---

[94] Possibly Kyrsites, leader of the Thracians, documented for 1305 in Erich Trapp, *Prosopographisches Lexikon der Paleioologen Zeit* (Vienna: Verlag der Ősterreichischen Akademie der Wissenschaften, 1976–96) (CD-Rom version, no. 14077).

[95] Presumably a place name.

The shaykh Jamāl al-Dīn Muḥammad Ibn al-Mukarram said in it the judge Taqī al-Dīn Ibn Shās was appointed to the Mālikī chief judiciary in the Egyptian homelands after the death of the judge Nafīs al-Dīn Ibn Shukr, but we have mentioned that at the end of the previous year, and God knows best which of them it was.

During the end of Jumādā al-Ākhira [October 4, 1282] of this year the Chief Judge Wajīh al-Dīn `Abd al-Wahhāb b. Ḥusayn al-Bahnasī al-Muhallabī asked to be relieved of the Cairo judiciary and the eastern side. He mentioned that he was too weak to combine the (administration of) two cities and their suburbs, so he was relieved of the Cairo judiciary and the eastern side.

The Sultan al-Malik al-Manṣūr delegated to the judge Shihāb al-Dīn al-Khū'ī the chief judiciary in Cairo, and the eastern side. He had been in charge of the judiciary on the western [side], but then was transferred to the chief judiciary on Cairo and the eastern side. He continued there until he was transferred to Syria, just as we will mention in its proper place.

When Chief Judge Shihāb al-Dīn was appointed to Cairo and its districts, the judge Wajīh al-Dīn was given the judiciary of Old Cairo, and Upper Egypt, which was split off for him. Ibn al-Mukarram said that the appointment of Chief Judge al-Khū'ī was in Rajab [October 1282].

Mention of swearing the noble ruler of ennobled Mecca

During Sha`bān [November 1282] of this year the noble Abū Numay, ruler of ennobled Mecca, swore using this oath:[96] [248]

> I have purified my intention, made pure my conscience, made sure that inwards and outwards are the same in the obedience of our master the Sultan al-Malik al-Manṣūr, and his son al-Malik al-Ṣāliḥ, and the obedience of their children, the heirs of their dominion, and I am not concealing any form of evil or treachery either in soul, in dominion or in sultanate.
>
> I am an enemy to those who have enmity towards them, a friend to those who befriend them, at war towards those at war with them, at peace with those at peace with them. Obedience towards a third party will never cause me to leave obedience towards them, nor will I turn towards any direction other than theirs. I will not do anything that is in opposition to what has been agreed, nor will I or anyone else (*zayd wa-lā `amr*) in their governance over me, nor over ennobled Mecca or its sanctum (*ḥaram*), or the standing place of its mountain [`Arafāt].

[96] Compare version in al-Qalqashandī, *Ṣubḥ*, xiii, p. 318–9.

I will keep to what I stipulated to our master the Sultan and to his son with regard to the victorious noble covering (*kiswa*) which comes from protected Egypt, and will hang it on the noble Ka`ba at the time of every pilgrimage. No other covering will be above it. I will accord precedence to his victorious flag over every flag during the pilgrimage, nor will I give precedence to any other flag.

I will facilitate the visitation of the holy sanctuary (*ḥarām*) during the pilgrimage days, and at other times, to visitors, to those circumambulating, to those appearing, to those secluding themselves in prayer (*`ākifīn*), those taking refuge because of its sanctity, the pilgrims, and those standing. I will endeavor to protect them from every enemy in deed and word, from those who kidnap people from around it. I will give them safety in the road hither, making their watering places sweet for them.

By God, I will continue to make the sermon with their name alone, and to have coins struck with the victorious noble name. In obeisance I will be devoted to my lord, and I, by God, by God, will follow his written commands just as a deputy does to the one who appointed him deputy. I will be ready at his command, the first one who hears to assent, and I will keep the stipulations of this oath from its first to its last [part], and not forswear.

Mention of the King of the Tatars' envoys' arrival at the noble gates of the Hill Citadel in protected Egypt

During Sha`bān [November 1282] of this year envoys of King Aḥmad Aghā Sultan son of Hűlegű, king of the Tatars, arrived, who were shaykh Quṭb al-Dīn Maḥmūd, and it was said `Abd al-Raḥmān, al-Shīrāzī, the judge of Sivas, the emir Bahā' al-Dīn, *atābak* of Sultan Mas`ūd, ruler of [Seljuq] Rūm, the chief Shams al-Dīn Muḥammad Ibn al-Ṣāḥib, who was among the followers of the ruler of Mārdīn, who was Ibn Sharaf al-Dīn al-Tītī.

At the news of their arrival to al-Bīra, al-Malik al-Manṣūr ordered them to be guarded so that absolutely no one would see them. So they had them (Mongols) travel by night until they were presented before al-Malik al-Manṣūr at the Hill Citadel in protected Egypt. They brought a letter from Aḥmad Aghā Sultan son of Hűlegű who was king of the Tatars, after Abagha [249] son of Hűlegű. This letter contained that he had been made king of the Tatars, and that he was a Muslim, had ordered the construction of mosques, schools and charitable endowments, and ordered the resumption of the hajj. Then the letter went on to various other subjects, such as types of piety, sacrifices, seeking common ground, tamping down the flames of dissension (*fitan*) and wars.

He mentioned that his soldiers had found a spy in the garb of poor (Sufis), so they had detained him, and that usually the sentence for this is death, but he sent him to the sultanic gates. He said that he has no need of spies or anyone else after an agreement is reached, or anything that would attract the Sultan's attention. He made his desire for a peace clear, and that he wrote it in the middle of Jumādā al-Ulā [mid-August, 1282].

Al-Malik al-Manṣūr answered him pleasantly with a congratulations on his conversion to Islam, and answered him on his seeking a peace, he said to his envoys

> I only rely upon the words of Shaykh `Abd al-Raḥmān because of what I know of his religion and his influence over King Aḥmad Aghā Sultan, and upon his minister, the ruler of Mārdīn, and a great number of approximately 200,000 horse and foot, plus camp followers and others.

His envoys returned having been honored, so they entered secretly, met with the Sultan secretly, and he returned them secretly. None but those emirs dispatched to bring them saw them—those were the emir Ḥusām al-Dīn Lājīn al-Rūmī and the emir Sayf al-Dīn Kabak al-Manṣūrī, both of them chamberlains.

During the night of Saturday 2 Ramaḍān [December 4, 1282] after the fast-breaking (*ifṭār*) they went accompanied by the emir Sayf al-Dīn Kabak al-Manṣūrī the chamberlain, and arrived in Aleppo on 6 Shawwāl [January 7, 1283] of this year. Then they headed towards their lands.

During the month of Ramaḍān [December 1282] of this year the emir Shams al-Dīn Sunqur al-Ghutamī arrived at the sultanic gates in the border port of Damietta. He was accompanied by the envoys of the Sultan al-Malik al-Manṣūr to Berke, and with them there were envoys from King Okajī[97] and others.

During it Baktūt al-Shamsī, `Alā' al-Dīn Iqṭawān *al-sāqī* (the cup-bearer), and Shihāb al-Dīn Qurtāy were detained, and imprisoned.

The judge […][98] Muḥammad b. al-Mukarram said and on Sunday 18 Ramaḍān [December 20, 1282] [250] year [6]81 our master Fatḥ al-Dīn son of the master Muḥyī al-Dīn Ibn `Abd al-Ẓāhir called us witness himself as he manumitted his concubine, mother of his two children, `Alā' al-Dīn `Alī and Ruqayya, paying her marriage price for 100 dinars cash at the time. The marriage-contract was written for that date.[99]

The judge Badr al-Dīn Muḥammad son of the Shaykh Burhān al-Dīn Ibn Jamā`a al-Kinānī, the Shāfi`ī jurisprudent, was appointed to teach at

[97] Perhaps the Chaghatai prince Bőgei.

[98] The editor proposes that this blank would have given Ibn al-Mukarram's honorific, Jamāl al-Dīn.

[99] al-Bayhaqī, *Faḍā'il al-awqāt* (Beirut: Dār al-Kutub al-`Ilmiyya, 1997), p. 52 on the auspiciousness of this date.

al-Qaymariyya College in protected Damascus, and he described the instruction in it. On 19 Shawwāl [January 20, 1283] of this year the judges and the learned were present at his instruction, and it was a day to remember.

During this year al-Malik al-Manṣūr delegated the Aleppan realm to the emir Shams al-Dīn Qarāsunqur *al-jūkandār* al-Manṣūrī. He asked the Sultan for permission to rebuilt the Friday mosque of Aleppo and its citadel, as the Tatars had destroyed the both of them. It was granted him, and he rebuilt them better than they had been previously.

During it a fellow from the younger Oirats named Shaykh `Alī came on delegation to the service of the Sultan al-Malik al-Manṣūr in protected Egypt. He had entered into the religion of Islam, and served the (Sufi) shaykhs, focusing upon spiritual exercises and separation [from society], so one of the poor (Sufi) miracles had appeared around him.

A number of the younger Mongols followed him, so he led them out of those lands to Syria, then to the Egyptian homelands. They stood before al-Malik al-Manṣūr, so he treated them well: among them were al-Aqūsh, Timur and `Umar, three brothers, and Jūbān, and a number who al-Malik al-Manṣūr assigned to the personal guards (*khāṣakiyya*), and then transferred to become emirs. Then some disreputable matters with regard to the Shaykh became known, so he was imprisoned. Al-Aqūsh was then also imprisoned, but Timur and `Umar died in service (to the Sultan).

On 21 Ramaḍān [December 23, 1282] of this year the Wool Market (*sūq al-labbādīn*) and the Jayrūn Market in protected Damascus burned reaching the walls of the Friday mosque, and the fire spread to the Basin Bath (*ḥamām al-ṣaḥn*), and the Wood House. The fire began at the time of sundown, and continued for three days. As a result of it, the deputy sultan in Damascus, the emir Ḥusām al-Dīn Lājīn al-Manṣūrī, and the other emirs, the army, the miners (*ḥajjārīn*) and the woodworkers rode so as to destroy that which was in front of the fire [as a firebreak].

It died down, but the Booksellers' Market was burned. Among that which was burned there were 15,000 volumes belonging to Shams al-Dīn Ibrāhīm al-Jazarī al-Kutubī, not counting notebooks and loose leaves. The cause of the fire was that one of the goldsmiths washed his garb, spread it, and put a coal from the fire underneath it, then left it, going out to eat. The fire caught on the garb, and then spread to some woven cloth that was hanging, then from that to the roof. Only four shops from the Wool-makers Alley quarter were saved. [251]

On the Day of `Arafāt [March 10, 1283] of this year in Damascus the emir `Izz al-Dīn Aybak Kurjī was detained, with the emir `Alam al-Dīn al-Rūbāsī, and the emir Nāṣir al-Dīn Muḥammad son of the emir `Izz al-Dīn Aydimur al-Ḍāhirī, the past deputy sultan, his father, in Damascus, and Zayn al-Dīn son of Shaykh `Adī, and were imprisoned.

The emir Suktāy son of Qarājīn Nayīn arrived, him and Qarmashī, to the Egyptian homelands during 674 [1275] accompanied by the emir Bāyanjār al-Rūmī during the period of al-Malik al-Ẓāhir Rukn al-Dīn Baybars al-Bunduqdārī al-Ṣāliḥī al-Najmī. When it was the year [6]81 al-Malik al-Manṣūr Sayf al-Dīn Qalāwūn married the lady Ashlūn Khātūn daughter of Suktāy, and he bedded her. She became the mother of al-Malik al-Nāṣir Nāṣir al-Dīn Muḥammad son of al-Malik al-Manṣūr Sayf al-Dīn Qalāwūn.

During it al-Malik al-Ṣāliḥ `Alā' al-Dīn `Alī son of al-Malik al-Manṣūr Sayf al-Dīn Qalāwūn married the lady Mankubak, daughter of the emir Sayf al-Dīn Nogai son of *khān* Qit`ān. Nogai at that time was imprisoned in the border port of Alexandria. Al-Malik al-Manṣūr gave a written command that he was to be freed, and he was brought to the high gates, favors were showered upon him, and the marriage price was set at 5000 dinars cash. 2000 of that was paid up immediately, and God knows best.

During it, al-Malik al-Manṣūr learned that one of the Georgian kings departed from his lands to visit noble Jerusalem, and return clandestinely. His name was Touta Souta son of Kaliari, and his description was given. He had a companion whose name was Ṭībghā son of Ankwār, and they sailed from the coastlands of Būṭ, so the roads were watched [252] for him from every direction. Every place he arrived a report was sent to al-Malik al-Manṣūr. When he arrived in noble Jerusalem, he was detained together with his interpreter. They were both brought to the Egyptian homelands, and imprisoned there.

One of the historians said and during it a truce was established between al-Malik al-Manṣūr and the Commander, Brother William of Beaujeu, Commander of the Templars' House in Acre and the coastlands, and the Templars in Tortosa, for a period of ten years, the first of which was 5 Muḥarram year [6]81 [April 15, 1282].

The blessed Nile's flooding during this year finished off at 17 cubits and 18 fingers. The emir of the Egyptian *maḥmal*, Nāṣir al-Dīn Alṭinbughā al-Khwarizmī led the people in pilgrimage this year, and Ḥusām al-Dīn Muẓaffar the majordomo al-Fāriqānī brought the noble Ka`ba's covering with him, and the emir `Alā' al-Dīn *al-bunduqdār* headed as a pilgrim among a large caravan, and God knows best.

[*Obituaries*]

Mention of the events during the year 682 [1283]

The crescent moon of Muḥarram on this year was seen on Thursday night [April 1, 1283].

During it a rescript (*tawqī`*) was written in the name of the emir Shams al-Dīn Sunqur al-`Asā'ī al-Manṣūrī from the revenues collected from the Syrian lands, of which the total would be 100 sacks (*gharāra*) to be divided into two halves, being given to him. He was sent to Syria to stay with the emir Ḥusām al-Dīn [Lājīn], the deputy of Syria, until he could specify an *iqṭā`* fief for him.

During it al-Malik al-Manṣūr, the ruler of Ḥamāh, arrived at the noble gates at the Hill Citadel in protected Egypt, submissively, and as a visitor. The Sultan al-Malik al-Manṣūr Sayf al-Dīn Qalāwūn rode out to greet him leading a procession. The ruler of Ḥamāh stayed in the sultanic Views of the Ram, and hospitality and board were assigned to him as usual.

During it [April 1283] the tributes (*jawālī*) were levied upon the protected peoples [Jews and Christians] in the Egyptian homelands. The usual practice was to levy them during the month of Ramaḍān of the previous year, but this had been delayed to go easy on them. Most of them were levied during that day in the noble Justice House under the Citadel in the presence of the chief Najm al-Dīn al-Uṣfūnī.

The tributes for the land of Hebron were set aside for our lord and prophet Muḥammad, upon him be the best of prayer and peace, with its districts, noble Jerusalem, with its districts, and the tribute of Bethlehem and Beit Jālā because of the construction of a pool in the land of Hebron for the pilgrims who were coming and visitors.[100] A command was issued that this sum would be set aside under the control of the judge, the governor and those serving. This would be until the emir `Alā' al-Dīn Aydughdī al-Ruknī could come and initiate its construction.

On the 4th [April 4, 1283] he wrote to the emir Jamāl al-Dīn Aqush al-Sharīfī that he was returning to the emir Sharaf al-Dīn Rāshid b. Bashīr's council, and that there was a rescript in his hand to carry forward his emirate as usual over his fellows who were known by his name, which was half of an emirate over Banū Mahdī [tribe] as usual. Thus, there was a strong bond between him and the session of [260] the emir Nāṣir al-Dīn Ibn Ḥasan on this benefit, and they were both in agreement. "We commanded that 20 sacks with the Ṣalt weight, 15 of wheat, and five of barley," be released to him under another rescript by his hand.

On the 6th the Sultan al-Malik al-Manṣūr headed to the Giza bank [of the Nile] and began heading towards al-Buḥayra to dig the canal known as al-Ṭīriyya. The armies were headed and the ruler of Ḥamāh, in his service upon this occasion, while the emir `Alam al-Dīn Sanjar al-Shujā`ī al-Manṣūrī sat in the protected Citadel. With him was the emir Shams al-Dīn Qarāsunqur *al-jūkandār*, the emir `Alā' al-Dīn Aydughdī *al-silaḥdār*, and `Izz al-Dīn Aybak *al-khazindār*, and others.

From every emir 12 horsemen were dispatched every night after the evening prayers with the emir `Alam al-Dīn, governor of Cairo. The number of those dispatched was 60 horsemen, assigned around the Citadel on the outskirts of Cairo, the Ḥusayniyya [Mosque], and other places.

[100] Mujīr al-Dīn al-`Ulaymī, *Uns al-jalīl fī tā'rīkh al-Quds wa-l-Khalīl* (`Ammān: Muḥtaṣib, 1973), ii, pp. 79, 88–9 records a number of building projects in Hebron completed by Qalāwūn and al-Ashraf, including a guardhouse (*ribāṭ*) and a hospital, but no pool.

It was proclaimed to the army that they would depart to dig, join the victorious royal tent, and dig the canal. Its length was 6500 *qaṣaba*, its breadth was three *qaṣaba*, and its depth was four *qaṣaba*, using the Ḥākimī [measurement] *qaṣaba*. It was completed in ten days, and the districts of al-Buḥayra overflowed because of it, whereas previously they had not for many years.

A number of delegates arrived, the number of whom was 19 at least, and their story was revealed. They mentioned that they were close relatives of Bashīr and Mūsā who had come as a delegation during Sha`bān year [6]81 [November 1282]. Among them was an elderly shaykh, who was the father of one of the three previously mentioned. He mentioned that he had something to say to the Sultan, so he was taken in the company of Sayf al-Dīn Baktūt al-Qaymarī from the victorious freeborn troops to the victorious royal tent.

From Qūṣ horsemen arrived from Mawjūd al-Sābiq, governor of Armanat, and of the herds sold in Qūṣ 447 "head" arrived, whose value was 7080 [dirhams].

On the 14th [April 14, 1283] a noble note (*mithāl*) arrived at the Hill Citadel, whose date was 13 Muḥarram, whose contents were that the sultan al-Malik al-Manṣūr, ruler of Ḥamāh had interceded on behalf of Ibrāhīm b. [...] and he commanded for him to be freed. "He should be sought in the Citadel prison or the Cairo prison; wherever he is, he should be freed."

Ayyāz al-Muḥammadī al-Manṣūrī brought a special letter, but when he arrived at the Egyptian coastlands, he died.

During it Muqbil b. Ṣāliḥ al-`Uqbī arrived from the noble Ḥijāz, and told that the prices were low, that the pilgrims had stood on Wednesday and Thursday, that the ruler of Yemen had sent neither a covering [for the Ka`ba] nor pilgrims [261] but that he had guarded himself, and had transferred stuffs valuable to him to Ta`izz.[101] He also told that of the `Irāqī caravan not even one had made it [to Mecca]. Reports differed concerning it. It was said that it got lost in the desert, and that the Bedouin took them, or that it turned back, vanished in the desert, and that none of them arrived. However, the Syrian caravan was safe.

The town crier of Cairo, Mu'min b. `Ajam al-`Aṭṭār, came to blows with his mother after the last night prayers when his spirit was choked. And on the 14th also Amīn al-Dawla Abū `Uthmān and his traveling companion Shaykh `Alī Lūkantī, envoys of India, and their youths, arrived at the noble gates in the Citadel in protected Egypt, so provisions were assigned to them. Their king's name was Abū Bakhba, who is the ruler of Ceylon.

On the 26th [April 26, 1283] those who could translate the letters brought by the envoys arriving from India were sought, but not one was found. The letters that were brought at their hands had the form of a page of delicate gold, breadth about three fingers, in length about half a cubit, while around

[101] A pun in Arabic.

it was a rounded ring. Inside of it there was something like a green palm papyrus, with writing on it that was similar to the Greek (*rūmī*) or Coptic script.[102]

The envoys were asked concerning what was written in their letter, so they brought a page in which was written that he had caused his envoy [...][103] and his traveling companion, and intended to send gifts with them to the noble gate. Somebody said to them, "There is no way," but he said to them "Travel by way of Hurmuz [Straits]," so they presented it.

They mentioned that the contents of the letter were wishes of peace, a prayer for the Sultan—that the lands of Ceylon are Egyptian, and that the lands of Egypt are Ceylonian. He had abandoned the company of the ruler of Yemen for a time, and was attached to loving the Sultan, may God make his dominion eternal, and requested that an envoy of our master the Sultan present himself to him, accompanied by the envoys which are with him, and another envoy to Aden. He will expect them to present themselves through this way [the Red Sea].

> Jewels I have, pearls, and rubies I have,[104] ships I have, female elephants I have, many fabrics of silk and other types I have, red dye, and cloves (*qirafā*)—everything that a noble could want, I have, and many spears I have. If our master the Sultan each year requests 20 boats from me, I will send them to him. So let our master the Sultan send forth the merchants to these lands.

The ruler of Yemen's envoy came this year, and requested gifts, and a female elephant to ride upon to Yemen, but the ruler of Ceylon returned him without giving him anything. This was out of love for the Sultan that he had prepared gifts and a female elephant for the gates of our master the Sultan. He mentioned that in this realm of Ceylon there were 27 [262] castles, there were mines for jewels and rubies, diving-places [for pearls?] night and day, and that he was lacking in nothing. This was the form of the letter according to the envoys, and they mentioned that it was not right for any other than the king to read it.

On Monday 4 Ṣafar [May 4, 1283] of this year al-Malik al-Manṣūr, ruler of protected Ḥamāh, journeyed and al-Malik al-Manṣūr, the ruler of Egypt, rode to see him off, and he went to his land.

On Thursday 5 Rabī` al-Awwal [June 3, 1283] of this year a truce between al-Malik al-Manṣūr and the rulers in Acre came into force, according to

---

102 Presumably a variant on the Sanskrit script.

103 The editor notes *wa-r-m-ā-y/t/n/b-h* which he could not vocalize.

104 Kāshānī (*ca.* 700/1300), *`Arā'is al-javāhir va-nafā'is al-aṭāyib* (Tehran: Mā'ī, 2007), pp. 30–1, 39, 46 lists many jewels coming from Sri Lanka, including rubies

what had been established between them both in its explanation, and a duplicate of it is:[105]

> Truce between our master the Sultan al-Malik al-Manṣūr Sayf al-Dīn Abū al-Fatḥ Qalāwūn al-Malikī al-Ṣāliḥī and his son Sultan al-Malik al-Ṣāliḥ, `Alā' al-Dunyā wa-l-Dīn, `Alī, may God immortalize their sultanate, and the rulers in the realm of Acre, Sidon, `Athlīth, and the lands which concluded this truce.
>
> These are: the Seneschal Odo, *bailli* of the realm in Acre, in the presence of the majestic Commander Brother William of Beaujeu, Master of the Templars' House, in the presence of the majestic Commander Brother Nicholas Lorgne, Master of the Hospitallers' House, the most majestic Marshal Brother Conrad [of Feuchtwangen?], the deputy master of the Teutonic Knights.[106] [263]
>
> Peace, for a period of 10 complete years, 10 months, 10 days and 10 hours, the first of which will be Thursday 5 Rabī` al-Awwal 682 from the Prophet [Muḥammad's] *hijra* [June 10, 1283], which corresponds to 3 Ḥazīrān 1594 from the conquest of Alexander, son of Philip the Greek [sic].
>
> Upon all the lands of the Sultan and his son, which are those they rule, are under their governance, obedient to them, and are contained by their hands on this day, from all the regions, realms, castles, fortresses, districts, cities, villages, farmlands, and land, which is the realm of the Egyptian homelands, may God Most High protect it. Including the coastal borders, castles, and Islamic fortresses in it, the coastal border of Dimyāṭ [Damietta], the coastal border of Alexandria, both of which are protected, Nastarawa, Santariyya, and the ports, coastlands and dry lands that are ascribed to it, the coastal border of Fuwwa, the coastal border of Rosetta, the lands of [36] the Ḥijāz;
>
> The coastal border of protected Gaza, the ports and lands that are in it, the realms of Kerak and Shawbak, and their districts, al-Ṣalt and its districts, Buṣrā and its districts, the realm of al-Khalīl [Hebron], may the prayers and peace of God be on it, the realm of noble Jerusalem (*al-Quds*) and its districts, al-Urdunn, Bethlehem, and its districts, and the lands of both of them, Ashkelon, and its districts, ports and coastlands, the

[105] As the text of this truce is different from the version given in *Chronicles*, text 1 (a) it is retranslated here. Compare Holt, pp. 73–91, who offers a composite text.

[106] Literally the German Hospitaller's House.

realm of Jaffa, and al-Ramla, its port, and its districts, Caesarea, and its port, coastlands and districts, Arsūf, and its districts, the castle of Qāqūn, and its districts and lands, Lydda, and its districts, the districts of al-`Awjā and its salt-pans, the lands conquered during the time of [al-Malik] al-Sa`īd, its districts and farmlands.

He mentioned all the rest of the lands of Islam that are the realm of al-Malik al-Manṣūr and his son, and then mentioned after that this citation:

And all of what belongs to our master the Sultan and his son which is specified in this blessed truce or not specified, upon all the armies, all of the subjects from the rest of the people, in their totality, according to their differences, their types of people and ethnicities, the religions of which they are a part, those who go back and forth to and fro from the rest of the Muslims' lands, and from all of the different merchants, travelers and those going back and forth over land and sea, over plain and mountain, during night and day, they would be safe, tranquil in their process of going forth and coming back, in their selves, their wealth, their children, their wives, their goods, their male slaves, their followers, their quadrupeds, their riding beasts, and all of that which is connected to them, and everything their hands contain of different [264] other types.

From the rulers of the realm of Acre …

In addition, it mentioned all the names we have previously mentioned.[107]

… from all the Franks, the brethren, the knights who are under their command, encompassing all their coastal realm, from all the various Franks, who have taken residence in Acre and the coastal lands who fall under this truce, and those who arrive by either land or sea, from their various ethnicities, and types.

None will attack the lands of our master the Sultan, or his son, nor their fortresses, their castles, their lands, their properties, their armies, their troops, their Arabs [Bedouin], Turkmen, Kurds, subjects, according to their various ethnicities, and types, encompassing quadrupeds, wealth, stores, and other things with treachery, evil, nor should they fear anything despicable, neither raiding, harassment, harm or so forth.

In the same way, any lands, fortresses, castles, property, provinces either on land or at sea, on flat land or mountainous, that our master Sultan

[107] Listed in *Chronicles*, text 1 (a).

al-Malik al-Manṣūr and his son al-Malik al-Ṣāliḥ should seek to conquer or to surround, either themselves, their deputies or their armies.

In the same way all the lands of the Franks upon which this truce is established now in the coastal lands, which are the city of Acre, its gardens, its lands, and its mills, and those vineyards that are specified for it, and the different concessions it has around it, these are continued by this truce.

It mentioned the names of the lands upon which this truce was established, then after that, in the following form:

All of these Acran lands and what is specified in this truce are safe from our master the Sultan al-Malik al-Manṣūr, from his son al-Malik al-Ṣāliḥ, and from their armies and troops, from their servants, and these lands are delineated inside this blessed truce. Whatever is specific and whatever is worked jointly is tranquil. Those are their subjects, the rest of the ethnicities of the people, those who are long-term there, and those passing back and forth, according to their varied ethnicities, and religions.

Those passing back and forth to it from all the Frankish lands, the merchants, the travelers, those passing back and forth to and fro, on land and sea, during night and day, on plain and mountain are safe in themselves, wealth, children, [265] boats, riding beasts, and all that is connected with them, and everything that is included in their hands whatever it might be from the Sultan and his son and from everyone who is under obedience to them. None of these will attack them nor attack these aforementioned lands that have concluded the truce with evil, injury, nor raiding.

Neither of the two aforementioned parties, the Islamic and the Frankish will attack the other with injury or harm. This is decided specifically for the Franks, according to the above belongs to them, and what has been agreed that belongs to the Sultan and to his son will be specifically for them. The condominia will be as explained, and the Franks will not have any other lands or condominia other than those that have been explained in this truce, and the lands that have been specified in it.

On the condition that the Franks do not renovate anything outside of the walls of Acre, ʿAthlīth, or Sidon, of that which is outside the walls in these three regions, nor castle, tower, or fortress, old or new.

On the condition that if someone flees from the lands of the Sultan or his son to Acre or the coastal lands specified in this treaty, and tries to convert to Christianity, then converts of his own free will, everything that he took with him will be returned, and so he would be left naked. If he is not trying to convert to Christianity, nor converts, then he will be returned to their high gates with everything that he took with him, together with intercession on his behalf after having been given a safe conduct.

In the same way for one who is from Acre and the coastal lands that are included in this truce, and tries to convert to Islam, and then converts of his own free will, everything that he took with him will be returned, so that he will be left naked. If he is not trying to convert to Islam, nor converts, then he will be returned to the rulers of Acre, the *bailli* of the realm, and the commanders, with everything that he took with him, together with intercession on his behalf, after having been given a safe conduct.

On the condition that those forbidden things, which are known of old, are established on the basis of their being forbidden from both parties. Whenever one of these forbidden items is found among the Muslim merchants of the Sultan and his son's lands, or those others according to their different religions and ethnicities, in Acre or the coastal lands that are included in this truce, such as weaponry, and other items, they will be returned to one from whom they were purchased, and the price will be returned to the purchaser. However, his wealth should not be confiscated from him in order to ruin him, nor should he be harmed for that reason—neither he nor his wealth.

In the same way if the Frankish merchants come up from Acre or the coastal lands included in this truce to the Islamic lands that are included in this truce according to their different ethnicities and religions, and some of the forbidden items are found with them, such as weaponry, and other items, they will be returned to the one from whom they were purchased, and the price will be returned to the purchaser. However, his wealth should not be confiscated from him in order to ruin him, nor should hc be harmed.

The Sultan and his son have the right to seize[108] from those [266] subjects who depart from their lands according to their different religions and ethnicities when something is among the forbidden items, and in the same way the *bailli* of the realm of Acre and the commanders have the right to seize from those of their subjects who are departing with forbidden items from their lands which are included in this truce.

Whenever an item is taken from either of the two parties, or someone is killed from one of the two parties—taking refuge in God—the taken

[108] Reading *yaqtaṣilū* in place of *yaftaṣilū*. Holt translates "have jurisdiction over" but does not state on what basis he reads this.

item should be returned in its entirety if it can be found, or its value if it is lost. For the one killed, compensation for him at the level of his equal from his social status: a knight for a knight, turcopole (*ba/urkīl*)[109] for a turcopole, a merchant for a merchant, a foot soldier for a foot soldier, a peasant for a peasant.

If the matter of the slain person or the stolen item is concealed, the leeway given to investigate is 40 days. If the stolen item is found, or the slain person is resolved, then the stolen item should be returned in its entirety, and the compensation for the slain person should be at the level of his equal. If it is not found, then there will be an oath upon the responsible person of that place in which the accused is located, and three persons from that area will be chosen.

However, if the responsible person refuses the oath, then three people that the other party shall choose will be sworn on behalf of the accusing party, and he shall take its value.

If the responsible person is unfair, and the money is not returned, then the accuser has the right to submit this issue to the governing authorities of both parties, and the leeway after that submission will be 40 days. The responsible ones from both parties agree to bind themselves to be loyal to this stipulation. Whenever they have concealed a slain person or a stolen item, or attempted to take a due, but do not do it, then it will be upon everyone in his area of authority to nominate one who the kings of the two parties appoint to carry out this policy: whether it is taking of life, money, hanging or complete ostracism of those who are specified, if they do this in his area or land.

If someone flees with money, and confesses part of it, but denies part of what he is accused of, then it is obligatory for him to swear that he did not take other than what he has returned. If the accuser is not convinced by the oath of the fleeing one, then the responsible one of that territory should swear that he did not find anything other than what he returned. If he denies that anything came with him at all, then he should place the one who fled under oath that he did not arrive with anything belonging to the accuser, and the responsible one from those regions should swear that he did not arrive with anything.

On the condition that if a boat from among the Sultan and his son's merchants' boats, who have concluded this truce, should break apart, or (one)

[109] Following Holt.

belonging to one of his Muslim subjects or others according to their different ethnicities and religions, in the port of Acre, its coastlands, or the coastal lands which have concluded this truce, then everyone inside of them are safe for their persons, wealth, goods, and trading goods. If the passengers of these boats which have broken apart [= crashed] are found, then their boats and their wealth are to be handed over to them. If they have disappeared through death, drowning or [267] merely going missing, their livelihoods should be guarded, and then handed over to the Sultan and his son's deputies.

In the same way, boats that are headed from these coastal lands that have concluded the truce belonging to the Franks, the same is applicable in the lands of the Sultan and his son. Their livelihood should be guarded, if its possessor is not present until it can be handed over to the *bailli* of the realm in Acre and the commanders.

Whenever one of the merchants who go back and forth, departing and returning according to their different ethnicities and religions from the lands of the Sultan and his son dies in Acre, Sidon, `Athlīth, and the coastal lands included in this truce, his money shall be guarded until it can be given to their deputies.

In the same way, the merchants departing and returning, going back and forth from Acre, Sidon, `Athlīth and the coastal lands which are included in this truth according to their different ethnicities and religions, if one of them dies in the Islamic lands which are included in this truce, his money will be guarded until a time when it can be handed over to the *bailli* of the realm in Acre and the commanders.

On the condition that the Sultan, and his son's the galleys, wherever they are constructed and depart will not be harassed harmfully by the coastal lands that have concluded this truce. Whenever these aforementioned go in a different direction the ruler of that region if he is allied with the rulers in the realm of Acre then they will not enter the lands that have concluded the truce, nor take provisions from them.

If the ruler of that region to which the victorious galleys go is not allied with the rulers in the realm of Acre, and the lands which have concluded this truce, then they can enter into those lands and take provision from them, and if anything of these galleys should break apart—taking refuge in God—in one of the ports that has concluded the truce or its coastlands. If it is going towards someone who is allied with the realm of Acre, or with the commanders of its stores, but they do not have an alliance with them, then the *bailli* of the realm in Acre, and commanders of the

[Templars and Hospitallers] Houses will guard it, and ensure that its men have provision, the ability to repair what has fallen apart in it, and safe return to the Islamic lands.

It is null and void to move what has broken from it, or—taking refuge in God—to throw it into the sea. If it is headed towards lands which are allied with the realm of Acre and its commanders, or if it does not have an alliance with the one to whom it is destined, then it has the right to provisions, and for its men to be domiciled in a land that has concluded the truce, and then to be sent to the region commanded. This provision shall be applicable to both sides.

On the condition that if one of the Frankish sea-kings[110] or others were to move through the sea intending to harm our master the Sultan or his son in their lands which have concluded this truce, the deputy of the realm, and the commanders in Acre will notify (*taʿrīf*) our master the Sultan and his son [268] of their movement prior to their arrival to the Islamic lands included in this truce by the period of two months. If they arrive after the lapse of two months then the *bailli* of the realm in Acre and the commanders will be not held accountable under their oath for this section.

If an enemy from the Tatars or others moves from the land direction, whichever of the two sides receives [the news] first should notify the other. On the condition that an enemy from the Tatars or others target the Syrian lands—taking refuge in God—on land, and the Islamic armies' successes precede them, and the enemy arrives close to the coastal lands included in this truce, and intends harm to them, then *bailli* of the realm in Acre and the commanders should defend themselves, their subjects and lands by any means available to them.

If a pell-mell stampede occurs—taking refuge in God—from the Islamic lands to the coastal lands included in this truce, then the *bailli* of the realm in Acre and the commanders are obligated to guard them, defend them, and stop those who are attacking them harmfully, so that they will be safe, tranquil with those who are with them.

On the condition that the deputy in realm of Acre and the commanders instruct the rest of the coastal lands upon which this truce is applicable that sea-piracy to take provisions is not acceptable, nor upon one who is carrying water. If they capture one of them [pirates] they should arrest him, if they sell goods among them, the *bailli* of the realm in Acre and

110 Probably the reference was to Charles of Anjou.

the commanders should hold them until their [rightful] owner appears and they be handed over to him. In the same way, this is applicable to the Sultan and his son concerning the matter of sea-piracy from both parties.

On the condition that the sureties in Acre and the coastal lands included in this truce, every one of them receive a sum or stores. Let the responsible one for that place in which the surety is kept swear, together with the one on duty, and the secretary, at the same time, that this person is a surety, and that he is obligated for such-and-such dirhams or stores, cattle or something else.

When the responsible one, the one on duty, and the secretary swear in the presence of the Sultan and his son's deputy on that basis, then the surety's family will uphold his debt to the Franks, and discharge it. As for the sureties that are taken with regard to those fleeing pell-mell, or about whom it is feared that they would flee to the lands of Islam, the responsible ones and the ones on duty should refuse to take an oath on them, and they should be discharged.

On the condition that no new due be levied upon the traveling merchants going forth and coming back from either of the parties that is outside of the usual. They should continue with the usual dues until the end of the time (period), and dues should be collected from them according to the usual. No new written order or due should be levied which is outside of the usual, and known in every place in levying dues. This shall be levied at that place without additions [269] from either of the two parties.

The merchants and travelers going back and forth shall be safe, tranquil, protected by both parties during their journey, their staying, their going forth and their return with the types and goods accompanying them—those which are not forbidden.

On the condition that it be proclaimed in the Islamic lands and the Frankish lands which are included in this truce that whoever is among the peasants of the lands of Islam should return to the land of the Muslims, whether he is Muslim or Christian, and likewise for those who are among the peasants of the Frankish lands should return to the Frankish lands, whether he is Muslim or Christian, known to be living there by both parties.

Whoever does not return after this proclamation will be expelled by both parties, and it will not be possible for the peasants of the Muslim lands to stay in the Frankish lands that have concluded this truce, nor for the peasants of the Frankish lands to stay in the Muslim lands that have concluded this truce. The return of the peasants from one party to the other will be under safe conduct.

On the condition that the Church of Nazareth, and the four closest hospices (*buyūt*) are for the visitation of pilgrims and others, from the Religion of the Cross [Christianity], great and small, according to their various ethnicities and peoples, from Acre and the coastal lands that are included in this truce.

Priests and monks shall pray in the church and dwell in the hospices for the visitors to the Church of Nazareth specifically. They will be safe, tranquil in their setting out, and their presenting themselves at the borders of the lands included in this truce. If the stones in the aforementioned church are crumbling, then they should be thrown outside. No stone should be placed upon another for the purpose of building. None shall harass the priests and monks in this with an illicit gift, because of the Religion of the Cross' visitors without right.

The Sultan and his son commit themselves to protect these lands delineated which have concluded this truce with themselves, their armies, their troops, and from all would-be thieves, robbers, vandals of those who come under their rule and are obedient to them.

The *bailli* of the realm in Acre and the commanders in it commit themselves to guard the Islamic lands delineated which have concluded this truce with themselves, their armies, their troops, and [from][111] would-be thieves, robbers and vandals of those who come under their rule and are obedient to them in their coastal realm which is covered by this truce.

The *bailli* of the realm in Acre and the Houses' commander in it, the rulers in Acre, and the coastal lands included in this truce commit themselves to uphold what is included in this truce, all of its stipulations, stipulation by stipulation, [270] paragraph by paragraph, and work according to its rules and reservations attached to its stipulations until the end of the period. Each of them should be loyal to the oaths they have sworn affirming that they will be loyal to all of what is in this truce to which they have sworn.

This blessed truce will continue between the Sultan, his son, their children, and their children's children, and the rulers in the realm of Acre,

---

[111] The text apparently is missing a *min* which would be the equivalent of the previous clause.

Sidon, and `Athlīth, who are the Seneschal Odo, the aforementioned commanders, so-and-so, and so-and-so, until the end of it.

It will not be changed by the death of one of the kings of the two parties, nor by the change in commander and the appointment of another, but rather it will continue in the same manner until the end of it, and its finale with its arranged stipulations, its established bases, complete, perfect. Whenever this blessed truce comes to an end or—taking refuge in God—some abrogation occurs, there will be a grace period of 40 days for the two parties.

The return of everyone to his homeland will be proclaimed after months, that the people should return to their homelands safe, tranquil, not being prevented from journeying between the two parties. This will not be nullified by the removal of one of the two parties, and its rules will be enforced continuously and consecutively for years, months and days until its finale. The one who is removed and the one who is appointed in his place commit themselves to keeping it, and acting according to its stipulations until the end of its specified period.

This truce will continue with its stipulations, paragraphs, asides and bases, and the situation will go according to the best possible manner until the end of it. Upon all of that, there is favor, concord, agreement, and the two sides have sworn to it, and God grants success.

Text of the oath that the Sultan al-Malik al-Manṣūr swore for this blessed truce:

I say, and I am [...] by (*wa)* God, by God, by God, in God, in God, in God, BY (*ta*) God, BY God, BY God, by the awe-inspiring God, who seeks, dominates, harms and benefits, apprehends and causes to perish, knows what is clear and what is concealed, knows the secret and the public, the Merciful, the Compassionate, and by the Qur'ān, and what it revealed, and by whom it was revealed to, who was Muḥammad son of `Abdallāh, may God pray for him and wish him peace, and what it says *sūra* by *sūra*, verse by verse.

By the month of Ramaḍān, I will be loyal to keeping this blessed truce, which has been established between myself and the Acran realm, and the commanders in it, over Acre, `Athlīth, Sidon, and its lands, which are contained within this truce, whose duration is ten years, ten months, ten days and ten hours, the first of which is 5 Rabī` al-Awwal the year 682 according to the *hijra* from the first of it to the last of it, and I will keep and hold myself to all of its explained stipulations which are in it, and carry out affairs according to its guidelines [271] until the finale of its period.

> I will not seek to reinterpret it, nor make up things that are not in it, nor seek a religious opinion in order to break it as long as the rulers in the city of Acre, Sidon and `Athlīth, who are the guarantors for the realm in Acre, the commander of the Templars' House, the commander of the Hospitallers' House, and the deputy commander of the Teutonic Knights House now, and those who will be appointed after them as trustees for the realm or as commanders for a house in this aforementioned realm will be loyal to their oath which they have sworn to me and my son al-Malik al-Ṣāliḥ, and my children, to establish this truce which has been arranged now, as long as they act according to it, and its explained stipulations, until the end of the period, holding fast to its guidelines.
>
> If I break this oath, then I bind myself to make the pilgrimage to sacred House of God in ennobled Mecca barefoot without wearing any armor 30 times, and I bind myself to fast permanently, other than those days upon which it is forbidden.

Then he mentioned the rest of the oath's stipulations, and God is the guarantor of what we say.

The text of the Franks' oath upon which they swore for this truce:

> By God, by God, by God, in God, in God, in God, BY God, BY God, BY God, by the truth of the Messiah, by the truth of the Messiah, by the truth of the Messiah, by the truth of the Cross, by the truth of the Cross, by the truth of the Cross, by the truth of the three hypostases, from one essence, by which it is named, from the Father, the Son and the Holy Spirit, one God, and by the truth of the noble divinity (*lāhūt*) made flesh in awe-inspiring humanity. By the truth of the pure Gospel, and by the truth of the four Gospels that Matthew, Mark, Luke and John transmitted, by the truth of their prayers and their invocations, by the truth of the Twelve Apostles, the Seventy, and the 318 gathered in the church [council]. By the truth of the voice which descended from heaven upon the Jordan River, then rebuked it, by the truth of God, who revealed the Gospel upon Jesus [`Īsā] son of Mary, the Spirit of God and His Word,[112] by the truth of the Lady Maria, the mother of light, St. Mary and John, the twice baptized, St. Thomas and St. Matthew.[113] By the truth of the great fast, by the truth of my religion and the one I worship, and what Christians believe, what was bestowed down from the baptized Fathers and priests:

---

112 This line appears to be a Muslim interpolation, perhaps covering over a more Christian description of Jesus. For these Qur'ānic descriptions of Jesus, see Q3:45, 4:171.

113 Following Holt.

I, from this time and hour, I have purified my intention, have made my conscience clear in loyalty to the Sultan al-Manṣūr and his son al-Malik al-Ṣāliḥ, and their children, in everything that is contained in this blessed truce on the basis of which the peace is concluded for the realm of Acre, Sidon and ʿAthlīth, and their lands which are included in this truce which are named inside of it.

Its period is ten years, complete, ten months, ten days, and ten hours, the first of it is Thursday 3 Ḥazīrān, year 1594 of Alexander son of Philip the Greek. I will act upon all of its stipulations, stipulation by stipulation, and I will bind myself to be loyal to every paragraph in this aforementioned truce until the end of its period.

I, by God, by God, and the truth of [272] the Messiah, by the truth of the Cross, by the truth of my religion, will not cause harm to the lands of the Sultan or his son or to one contained in it, or the rest of the people in their totality that it contains, nor to one who passes back and forth from it to the lands that are included in this truce, neither in harm, or injury, to person, or wealth.

I, by God, and by the truth of my religion, and the One I worship, will continue in covenant, mutual truce, being mutually open, and friendly, guarding the Islamic subjects, and those who pass back and forth from the sultan's lands, and those who proceed from them and to them, acting in the manner of those who have covenant and who have established binding mutual friendship.

Holding back harm and aggression from people, and wealth, I will bind myself to loyalty to all of the stipulations of this truce until it is completed, as long as al-Malik al-Manṣūr is loyal to the oath by which he swore to the truce. I will not break this oath nor anything of it, nor take exception to it, nor anything in it, seeking to break it.

Whenever I oppose it or break it, I will be excommunicated from my religion, my belief, and the One I worship, and I will be in opposition to the Church. I will have to make a pilgrimage to noble Jerusalem 30 times barefoot and without any armor, and I will have to redeem 1000 Muslim prisoners from the Franks' captives and liberate them. I will be excommunicated from the divinity that is made flesh in the humanity.

The oath is my oath, and I am so-and-so; the intention in it is completely the intention of the Sultan al-Malik al-Manṣūr, and the intention of his son al-Malik al-Ṣāliḥ, together with the intention of the one who is taking my oath to the both of them upon it, upon the noble Gospel. I have no other intention, by God, and the Messiah is the guarantor of what we say.

The truce and oaths are complete, and God knows best.

On 10 Rabī al-Awwal [June 8, 1283] of this year al-Malik al-Manṣūr delegated to the chief Burhān al-Dīn al-Khiḍr al-Sinjārī the inspectorate and instruction in the Imam al-Shāfi`ī College, may God be pleased with him, in al-Qarāfa with an allowance (*jāmakiyya*) a stipend, and a written command testifying to the charitable endowment document of al-Ṣalāḥī Yūsuf b. Ayyūb b. Shādī b. Marwān, may God Most High have mercy upon him. This was for a salary for instruction each month of 40 dinars transacted by a disbursement each dinar of 13 1/3 dirhams, for the inspectorate 10 dinars, plus the stipend, and the fees. For each day 60 *raṭl*s [= approx. 30 kg] of bread, using the Egyptian *raṭl*, and two draughts of sweet water.

This school was lacking in a lecturer for 30 years, and had to get by using assistants, who were ten. This situation continued until the year 678 [1279] when the Chief Judge Taqī al-Dīn Ibn Razīn was appointed to lecture there after he was removed from the Shāfi`ī chief judiciary in the Egyptian homelands. He was established at half salary, and then it was transferred after his death to another at a quarter salary. The matter stayed like that until the present, then it was delegated to the chief Burhān al-Dīn al-Khiḍr al-Sinjārī through a noble sultanic Manṣūrī rescript, and God knows best.

During this year it reached al-Malik al-Manṣūr that al-Malik al-Mas`ūd, ruler [273] of Kerak, and those emirs who were with him, had broken the peace that was established between al-Malik al-Manṣūr and al-Malik al-Mas`ūd. The emir `Alā' al-Dīn Aydughdī al-Ḥarrānī, the deputy of al-Malik al-Mas`ūd in Kerak, presented himself at the noble gates, transmitting to al-Malik al-Manṣūr that they intended to muddy things up.

So al-Malik al-Manṣūr wrote to al-Malik al-Mas`ūd and those with him, warning them from that, but they did not heed the warning. Then al-Malik al-Manṣūr sent a dispatch to Kerak during this year—and it is said during the following year [68]3, just as we will mention—via the emir Badr al-Dīn Baktāsh al-Fakhrī, *amīr silāḥ* (armorer), and ordered to deliver the message to them. What happened we will mention, if God Most High wishes.

After the death of the chief Najm al-Dīn Ḥamza b. Muḥammad al-Uṣfūnī, the minister for the Egyptian homelands, during the month of Rabī` al-Ākhir [July 1283] of this year, just as is mentioned in his biography, the Sultan al-Malik al-Manṣūr delegated the inspectorate of Upper Egypt to the judge Sharaf al-Dīn Abū Ṭālib son of `Alā' al-Dīn Ibn al-Nābulsī. He also transferred the judge `Izz al-Dīn Ibn Shukr from the victorious Army Chancellery Inspectorate to the inspectorate of the eastern side, giving both of them robes. They took up their duties while the emir `Alam al-Dīn Sanjar al-Shujā`ī was the administrator of the noble realms, and they worked closely with him.

Mention of the conquest of Qaṭīnā castle

This fortress was once considered to have been numbered among the castles of Āmad. Then it passed into the hands of the king of the Rūm [Seljuqs], and then into the hand of the abandoned enemy, the Tatars, whose deputies were in it. It harmed Karkar castle, and the border regions that adjoined it, but it was not possible to take it via siege.

So the [Mongol] deputies were treated kindly, and they [the Mamluks] sought to turn the allegiance of those in it, so when it was the year [6]82 [1283] this year, the castle was lacking in stores, so al-Malik al-Manṣūr dispatched the men of Karkar to it, who tightened the noose around it. Then its inhabitants begged for the Sultan's mercies, to which he assented, whereupon the deputies handed it over to al-Malik al-Manṣūr. They then brought a number of men from al-Bīra castle, `Ayntāb and al-Rawandān, and placed the stores, weapons and provisions that they would need inside of it, and so it became one of the strong fortresses of Islam.

Mention of the conquest of the border fortress of al-Kakhtā

Al-Kakhtā castle is one of the strongest, highest and most perfect fortresses ever built. Al-Malik [274] al-Manṣūr expended considerable effort to gain it, and add it to the Islamic fortresses. He promised those inside fair promises, so they assented to hearing and obeying, killing the deputy who was in it, who was al-Shujā` Mūsā.

They corresponded with the deputy of the noble sultanate in the Aleppan realm, giving over the castle. He sent the emir Jamāl al-Dīn al-Ṣarṣarī, the emir Rukn al-Dīn al-Ṣarṣarī, the emir Rukn al-Dīn Baybars *al-silaḥdār*, and the emir Shams al-Dīn Aqush al-Shamsī al-`Ayntābī, and those with them. They received the fortress, and swore those inside to al-Malik al-Manṣūr and his son al-Malik al-Ṣāliḥ `Alā' al-Dīn `Alī, clothing them with noble gifts.

Then he sent them one group after another to the noble sultanic gates, so al-Malik al-Manṣūr treated them well, giving *iqṭā`* fiefs to those who were deserving, and sending an armory-factory (*zardkhānāh*) to it, with siege implements, and it was established among the number of Islamic fortresses during this year. This castle became a cleavage in the Armenians' gullet, and a means by which to carry out raids.

Mention of the Sultan's going from Egypt to Syria

During the middle of Jumādā al-Ulā [August 1283] of this year the Sultan al-Malik al-Manṣūr Sayf al-Dīn Qalāwūn al-Ṣāliḥī headed from protected Egypt to Syria, and arrived in Gaza on 7 Jumādā al-Ākhira [August 3, 1283] of this year, and stayed there for days.

Ibn al-Mukarram said in his composition *Treasury of the Secretary* in summary: on 10 Ṣafar [May 10, 1283] of this year Mūsā al-Ḥusaynī's dissension happened,[114] and the correspondence with the ruler of Kerak that brought him to naught. God repelled his evil by His clemency and nobility, so that we were delayed in the castle in the mosque of the king's brother for 30 plus days, but praise to God for the outcome. On 7 Jumādā al-Ulā [August 3, 1283] God Most High granted us release and liberation from the dissension of Mūsā al-Ḥusaynī and we returned to the secretaryship in the noble roll where we had been previously.

On Saturday the 19th [August 15, 1283] the noble sultanic caravan traveled to protected Damascus, while the army was accompanying him, and I was among the number of the secretaries who departed with the noble presence. Then an inspector for land-ownership (*ṣuḥba*) and the surveyor of Syria[115] was summoned along the road. He wrote about that to the emir ʿAlam al-Dīn, the administrator of the noble realms.

His answer arrived that he had departed in the noble service of ʿIzz al-Dīn Ibn Shaddād, and proposed appointing him, but was answered that the master ʿIzz al-Dīn was worthy of better than that. The judge Shihāb al-Dīn Ghāzī Ibn al-Wāsiṭī was sent for, and appointed to the inspectorate of ownership and the surveyor of Syria. A rescript was commanded for him [275] so I wrote him down for the fourth *iqṭā*ʿ fief, and for his allowance, it was established at 500 dirhams for a month, with 10 *ardabb*s of wheat, and barley. He took up his duties, and headed to Damascus, where a robe was bestowed upon him.

The emir Badr al-Dīn al-Quṭuzī took up the duties of supervision with him, and al-Asʿad b. al-Sadīd as collector (*mustawfī*). The Sultan detained Ghars [al-Dīn][116] Ibn Shawār, and appointed in his place the emir ʿAlam al-Dīn Sanjar al-Ṣāliḥī in Ramla. ʿImād al-Dīn Ibn Abī al-Qāsim was removed from noble Jerusalem, and he appointed in his place Najm al-Dīn Ayyūb al-Sawnajī.

On Friday 8 Rajab [October 2, 1283] of this year al-Malik al-Manṣūr entered protected Damascus and stayed at the Citadel. When the noble caravan had settled into protected Damascus, he issued a command that all allowances would be returned back to what they were during the Ẓāhirī period, and should be returned, and cancelled. A number of the Syrians were investigated concerning this, and an amount of money was extracted. Among those investigated was the judge Taqī al-Dīn Tawba, the judge Tāj al-Dīn Ibn al-Sanhūrī, who produced the money, and forgiven the rest of what they were assessed.

---

[114] Which does not seem to be mentioned by other sources, nor are there any details about it.

[115] Northrup, p. 226 notes that the function of this office is obscure; see al-Qalqashandī, *Ṣubḥ*, iv, p. 525.

[116] Correcting from *al-gh-r-z*, as he has been mentioned previously.

Tāj al-Dīn Ibn al-Sinjārī, the Chief Judge for protected Aleppo, confirmed upon being brought into the presence, that *al-ṭawāshī* Rayān al-Khalīfatī entrusted 8000 dinars to Sharaf al-Dīn Ibn al-Iskāf, and that the sum had been willed into the hand of `Izz al-Dīn Ibn al-Ṣā'igh, Chief Judge of protected Damascus.

Chief Judge `Izz al-Dīn was investigated on Friday 22 Rajab [October 16, 1283], and he had already presented himself at the Umayyad Mosque in order to listen to the judge Jamāl al-Dīn Ibn `Abd al-Kāfī's sermon. The latter had been appointed to do the sermon and to be the imam at the Friday Mosque in Damascus. Then the former headed from the Mosque to the Citadel, and was brought into the presence of the emir Badr al-Dīn al-Aqra`ī, the supervisor of interrelationships (*al-ṣuḥba*), and to the judge Shihāb al-Dīn Ibn al-Wāsiṭī, the inspector of interrelationships.

The supervisor issued a command to the Chief Judge `Izz al-Dīn to lead the prayers at the Ḥabāla Mosque,[117] but he did not pray Friday prayers there, so then the matter got worse for him, and he was removed from the Shāfi`ī chief judiciary in Damascus on 23 Rajab [October 17, 1283]. People were forbidden from entering into his presence, or meeting with him, other than what was strictly necessary.

He was charged with having a waist-belt and a turban whose value was estimated to be 25,000 dinars, and that they had both been in the possession of `Imād al-Dīn son of Shaykh Muḥyī al-Dīn Ibn al-`Arabī.[118] However, it belonged to al-Malik al-Ṣāliḥ Isma`īl son of Asad al-Dīn Shīrkūh, and then had passed to `Imād al-Dīn Ibn al-Ṣā'igh, then from him to his brother, the judge `Izz al-Dīn Ibn al-Ṣā'igh.

He was also charged that the emir Nāṣir al-Dīn, son of the emir `Izz al-Dīn Aydimur, the deputy sultan, his father, had entrusted to him a large amount, and the matter got worse, and al-Malik al-Ẓāhir had had someone investigate him. However, the matter turned out to be the complete opposite of all of this. It was that the judge `Izz al-Dīn was able to prove the enmity of the judge Tāj al-Dīn al-Sinjārī, who was ruling in Aleppo. Prosecutors were unable to establish the provenance of [276] the turban and the waist-belt, or the pearls and hyacinths (*balkhash*) which were supposedly on it. Thus, he was completely exonerated from wrongdoing in the trust in ways that would be too lengthy to mention here, and in which there is no benefit.

The emir Ḥusām al-Dīn Lājīn, deputy sultan in protected Damascus, was victorious for him, and brought over the emir Ḥusām al-Dīn Ṭurunṭāy, deputy sultan in the Egyptian homelands, to aid him. The both of them addressed al-Malik al-Manṣūr concerning him, so he was released on 28

[117] Ibn al-Mibrad, *Thimār al-maqāṣid fī dhikr al-masājid* (ed. As`ad Talas, Damascus: Institut Français de Damas, 1943), pp. 65 (#37) or 69 (#70).

[118] The famous Sufi mystic who had died in Damascus in 637/1240.

Sha`bān [November 21, 1283] of this year, but he continued to be unemployed until he died.

When the Sultan removed Chief Judge `Izz al-Dīn Ibn al-Ṣā'igh from the Shāfi`ī chief judiciary in protected Damascus, he delegated the chief judiciary to Chief Judge Bahā' al-Dīn Yūsuf son of Chief Judge Muḥyī al-Dīn al-Zakī. It was said that the removal of Chief Judge Ibn al-Ṣā'igh and the appointment of Chief Judge Ibn Muḥyī[119] al-Dīn al-Zakī were during Sha`bān [November 1283] of this year, and robes were bestowed upon them.

During Sha`bān the judge Sharaf al-Dīn Ibn Muzmir was commanded to take up the duties of the Syrian inspectorate for the third time, and an allowance of 450 dirhams was established for him. During it, the emir Shams al-Dīn Qarāsunqur *al-jūkandār* al-Manṣūrī was appointed as deputy sultan in protected Aleppo in place of the emir `Alam al-Dīn al-Bāshqirdī. He came to the followers of al-Bāshqirdī, and he gifted them with the *iqṭā`* fiefs of the emir Badr al-Dīn al-Izdimurī in protected Egypt.

Ibn al-Mukarram said in it our master the Sultan, may his victory bring glory, gifted us and a number of junior secretaries of the noble roll, with the usual benefices that happened every time he traveled. These were allowances (*jāmakiyya*) of two months as a gift, without any deduction.

Al-Malik al-Manṣūr stayed in protected Damascus until he had ordered its affairs, and established its interests, then departed from protected Damascus on 2 Ramaḍān [November 24, 1283] of this year, returning to the Egyptian homelands. He arrived there and entered the Hill Citadel on Thursday 24 Ramaḍān [December 16, 1283], although it is said 25 Ramaḍān.

During Shawwāl [December 1283–January 1284] of this year the sultanic *maḥmal* departed from protected Egypt to the noble Ḥijāz as usual. Ibn Mukarram said that the master `Imād al-Dīn son of the master Tāj al-Dīn led it, together with the master Shams al-Dīn son of the master `Alam al-Dīn Ibn al-Qammāḥ.

Mention of the raiding on the Sīs lands

The Armenians, when they came together with the Tatars, they intentionally burned the Friday Mosque in protected Aleppo. So when the Tatars retreated, and matters went back [to what they had been previously], and this year started up, al-Malik al-Manṣūr wrote to the deputy sultan [277] in the Aleppan realm to send out a raid against the Sīs lands because of the Armenians' intentional burning of the Aleppan Friday Mosque.

Al-Malik al-Manṣūr also dispatched an army from the Egyptian homelands and from the Syrian army for that purpose, so they headed off, raided, and reached the city of Ayas. They killed a number of its people, plundered

[119] Correcting the mistake of naming him Zakī al-Dīn.

and destroyed. When they returned, and arrived at the Iskandarūna Gate, the Armenian army caught up with them, so they fought, but the Armenians were defeated, and the Islamic army pursued them to Tel Ḥamdūn, while making off with a number of their horses. The Islamic army returned with victory and booty.

During this year, a nobleman[120] was detained in al-Ḥadath, among the mountains of Syrian Tripoli. His aspiration had risen, and a numb large number of the people of those mountains had joined with him. They fortified al-Ḥadath, so the Turkmen went after him, and surrounded him until they overpowered him, took him prisoner, and brought him to the sultanic gates, whereupon God sufficed to take care of his evil for the Muslims.

During it the king of the Franks in Cyprus departed to go to the coastlands to fight (*ghāzī*), but the wind blew him to the direction of Beirut, so then he departed from it, and went to raid in those parts. The inhabitants of Carob Mountain concealed themselves, taking him by ambush, killing his followers, and taking 80 men prisoner. They took a great deal of money, horses, and mules from him, so he sailed the sea, heading towards Tyre. It was not long before he perished, and his spirit went to Hell, "and it is an evil destination!"[121]

During it two men from the Qipchaq jurisprudents arrived, who were Majd al-Dīn Aṭā and Nūr al-Dīn, from Taman-Mänggű, who was upon the royal chair (*kursī*) of Berke's house. They brought a letter at their hands from him in the Mongol script, so it was read.

Its contents were that he had entered into the religion of Islam, and that he upheld the laws of the Muḥammadan religion. He entrusted his letter to the jurisprudents who were coming, and requested that they receive aid for a righteous pilgrimage. They mentioned straight from their lips that the king asked the Sultan for his description, a description by which he could receive Muslim names, and that he sent them a caliphal flag, and a sultanic flag, by which they could fight the religion's enemies. So al-Malik al-Manṣūr provisioned the jurisprudents for the noble Ḥijāz, and when they returned he provisioned them to their destination.

During it the construction of the mausoleum that al-Malik al-Manṣūr had commanded from the emir `Alam al-Dīn Sanjar al-Shujā`ī, the administrator of the realm, was completed by its construction for the mother of his son al-Malik al-Ṣāliḥ `Alā' al-Dīn `Alī close to the shrine of the Lady Nafīsa, may God be pleased with her, and al-Malik al-Manṣūr and his son al-Malik al-Ṣāliḥ descended to the mausoleum, giving a great deal of charity, and assigning to it copious religious endowments. [278]

---

[120] Reading as *biṭrīk* as in *Chronicles*, text 1 (a).

[121] This phrase appears many times in the Qur'ān, e.g. Q9:73.

Mention of the construction of the Manṣūriyya College *bayn al-qaṣrayn* inside protected Cairo, together with its mausoleum, hospital and Qur'ān school

When al-Malik al-Manṣūr saw the Ṣāliḥiyya Mausoleum, which he had initiated for the mother of his son al-Malik al-Ṣāliḥ, close by the Lady Nafīsa Shrine, may God be pleased with her, it amazed him, and he ordered the emir `Alam al-Dīn Sanjar al-Shujā`ī, the administrator of the noble dynasty (*dawla*) to initiate building a mausoleum for him, a college, a hospital and a Qur'ān school *bayn al-qaṣrayn* inside protected Cairo.

The agent (*mutaḥaddith*) selected the house known as al-Quṭbiyya, and the area adjacent to it, which is *bayn al-qaṣrayn*, then bought the aforementioned house, and that are adjacent to it, (purchasing it) with the Sultan al-Malik al-Manṣūr's own money, and then compensated those inhabitants of the Quṭbiyya House with the palace known as the Emerald Palace. This is a palace that is on the Festival Gate open space in protected Cairo.

Purchase of the Quṭbiyya House, and transfer of the dwellers from it to the Emerald Palace happened on 28 Rabī` al-Awwal [June 26, 1283] of this year. Al-Malik al-Manṣūr assigned the emir `Alam al-Dīn al-Shujā`ī, the state administrator, to be the supervisor over the construction. The latter demonstrated involvement and care that was previously unheard of, and it was constructed in the quickest possible time.

Mention of some reports concerning Shaykh `Abd al-Raḥmān, his arrival, and those Tatar envoys with him to protected Damascus

The origin of shaykh `Abd al-Raḥmān was as a pupil of shaykh Muwaffaq al-Dīn al-Kawāshī who educated him, worked with him, employed him, and taught him the Greatest Name of God. It is said that shaykh Muwaffaq al-Dīn gave him a book on the science of enchantment (*al-sīmīyā'*)[122] and told him "Head to the river with this, and wash it" so `Abd al-Raḥmān took it from the shaykh Muwaffaq al-Dīn, went, parted from him, and disappeared, but then returned to the shaykh and informed him that he had washed it, but then the shaykh `Abd al-Raḥmān involved himself in this knowledge from that book.

He headed to the land of the Tatars and met with the wives, showing them some of that knowledge to the degree that they were able to grasp, and he paid special attention to the mother of King Aḥmad Aghā Sultan during Aḥmad Aghā's youth. Thus he formed a special bond with him, so when Aḥmad Aghā grew up, he asked him to convert to Islam, and to become an example.

When Aḥmad Aghā ruled the sultanate of the Tatars, shaykh `Abd al-Raḥmān managed the rest of his realms, and came to have very high status in his eyes, until he could actually stand before him. Things that he did caused

122 From the Greek σημεία "signs," popularized by al-Būnī (d. 622/1225).

them to favor him, and he was in charge of all of the charitable endowments. His fame was great in all the eastlands and Aḥmad Aghā Sultan issued a command that he ride with the *jeter* (royal umbrella). Therefore, he rode with the *jeter* and the armor-bearers and the *jāndāriyya* (guard) just like kings, throughout the rest of the Persian and Iraqi lands.

Then King Aḥmad Aghā Sultan, son of Hűlegű, king of the Tatars, sent the judge Quṭb al-Dīn Maḥmūd al-Shīrāzī, [279] the judge of Sivas, and the emir Bahā' al-Dīn *atābak* to Sultan Mas`ūd, ruler of [Seljuq] Rūm, together with a number of others to al-Malik al-Manṣūr, ruler of the Egyptian homelands, to negotiate a peace. No peace was achieved between the two of them, so he returned them politely. He said to them "I only trust in the words of shaykh `Abd al-Raḥmān because of what I know of his religion, and his influence over King Aḥmad Aghā Sultan, over his minister the ruler of Mārdīn, and a great number of approximately 200,000 horsemen and foot-soldiers and their followers," just as we previously explained.

When the envoys of King Aḥmad Aghā Sultan, king of the Tatars, returned to him after having been with al-Malik al-Manṣūr and informed him of what he said, he prepared shaykh `Abd al-Raḥmān, accompanied by Ṣamadāghū, the emir Shams al-Dīn Muḥammad Ibn al-Tītī, known as "chief," Zayn al-Dīn, ruler of Mārdīn, and a number to accompany them, approximately 150 in number, and sent them to al-Malik al-Manṣūr.

This was to establish for shaykh `Abd al-Raḥmān the basis for a peace between Aḥmad Aghā Sultan, king of the Tatars and al-Malik al-Manṣūr, ruler of Egypt. Shaykh `Abd al-Raḥmān thought that once he entered into the presence of al-Malik al-Manṣūr he would have power over him, and that he would be able to perfect in that realm what he had perfected in Iraq.[123] When he arrived in al-Bīra, the emir Jamāl al-Dīn Aqush al-Fārisī, one of the emirs in protected Aleppo, met him, and forbade him from carrying the *jeter* and weapons. He also turned (Shaykh `Abd al-Raḥmān) aside from the road commonly traveled until he brought him to Aleppo, and then to protected Damascus.

His arrival to Damascus was on the night of Tuesday 12 Dhū al-Ḥijja [March 2, 1284] of this year. None of the people were able to see him, nor speak to him, and when he arrived in Damascus he was domiciled at the Hall of Satisfaction, and 1000 dirhams was assigned to him and those with him every day as spending money, while the food, sweets, fruits, and other things came from another 1000. He stayed in the Citadel until al-Malik al-Manṣūr arrived in Damascus, and the Sultan resolved to travel to protected Syria, then delayed it until he headed there during the year [6]83 as we will mention, if God Most High wishes.

During Dhū al-Ḥijja [March 1284] the Sultan summoned the judge Tāj al-Dīn Ibn Sanhūrī from Syria, and appointed him to the Chancelleries

[123] That he would be able to use his magical powers over Qalāwūn.

Inspectorate in the Egyptian homelands in place of the judge `Izz al-Dīn Ibn Shukr. He performed his duties in tandem with the judge Sharaf al-Dīn Ibn al-Nāblusī.

During it, the judge Shihāb al-Dīn Ibn al-Wāsiṭī was commanded to write as one of the noble roll, in addition being assigned to the inspectorate of Inter-relations (*ṣuḥba*) which he already had. He wrote and specifically shadowed the emir `Alam al-Dīn Sanjar al-Shujā`ī, the administrator of the noble realm, and God knows best.

During this year al-Malik al-Ashraf Ṣalāḥ al-Dīn Khalīl, son of al-Malik al-Manṣūr [280] was married to Bārdakīn, daughter of the emir Sayf al-Dīn Nogai son of *nuwīn* Qaṭ`ān. She was the sister of his brother al-Malik al-Ṣāliḥ `Alā' al-Dīn `Alī's wife. **[End of vol. VII]**

Mention of the events during the year 683 [1284]

In Muḥarram of this year [March–June 1284] Qaidu's envoys returned, and al-Malik al-Manṣūr Sayf al-Din Qalāwūn al-Alfī al-Ṣāliḥī al-Najmī sent the emir Sayf al-Din Balabān al-Ḥalabī and Muẓaffar al-Dīn Mūsā as envoys to the king Qaidu, and others. With them were many gifts and awe-inspiring valuables. He sent with them the emir Sharaf al-Dīn al-Jākī to protected Alexandria so that they could travel from it.

During it, the victorious army headed to Kerak accompanied by the emir Badr al-Dīn Baktāsh al-Fakhrī and the emir Rukn al-Dīn Ṭaqṣū. The Sultan ordered the emir Badr al-Dīn Baktāsh *amīr silāh* (armorer) to correspond with the inhabitants of Kerak, so that they would have the opportunity to repent from their breaking of the agreement that they had done deliberately.

Therefore, he corresponded with them, but they did not repent from their intention, so he surrounded Kerak. Horses from that army grazed upon their fields, then he returned from Kerak, and the matter was allowed to slide. Then what happened we will mention in another place, if God Most High wishes.

After the death of Shaykh `Izz al-Dīn al-Mārdīnī al-Ḥanafī, the lecturer at al-Ṣāliḥiyya College which is *bayn al-qaṣrayn* inside protected Cairo on 12 Muḥarram [March 31, 1284] his teaching appointment was given to Shaykh Mu`izz al-Dīn al-Nu`mān the jurisprudent belonging to the Ḥanafī rite.

During it the emir Sayf al-Dīn *al-m-?-d-?-ī* [?][124] was appointed to the governate of Qūṣ in the place of the emir Bahā' al-Dīn Qarāqūsh. In it the emir Majd al-Dīn `Umar b. `Īsā al-Ḥarāmī was appointed to the governate of Suyūṭ in place of the emir *al-m-?-d-?-ī* [?]. In it the emir `Izz al-Dīn Aydimur al-Kawjī (or Kurjī) was appointed to the governate of Akhmīm in place of the emir Sayf al-Dīn Balabān al-Fārisī. During it the emir Shihāb al-Dīn Qurṭāy

124 Probably the emir Sayf al-Dīn Mihranī/Mihwanī who was governor of Bahnasā in 683/1284.

al-Jākī was appointed to Qalīyūb in place of Ḥusām al-Dīn Lū'lū' al-Kārī (or Hakkāī). [2]

On the 22nd of it [April 10, 1284] the emir Shams al-Dīn Ibrāhīm b. Khalīl al-Ṭūrī was appointed to the governate of al-Rawḥā, and the roads leading to the Franks: al-Harāmīs, and al-Rawḥa towards `Athlīth, Haifa, and Acre in the place of the emir Nūr al-Dīn. He was given an *iqṭā`* fief for his retinue and ten mamluks (*ṭawāshī*). A memorandum was written for him delineating the benefits that were expected to be reaped from it.

> From it: A memorandum concerning that which the session of the emir Shams al-Dīn Ibrāhīm b. Khalīl al-Ṭūrī intends with regard to his fulfilling the duties the emir Nūr al-Dīn used to fulfill, concerning which he has been commanded. These duties include the border fortresses that adjoin the Franks, which are al-Harāsmis to al-Rūḥā to Caesarea to Arsūf to the `Awjā River.
>
> All of these regions are under the inspectorate of the emir Shams al-Dīn, just as the lands of al-Rūḥā, the districts that are in condominium with it, and those not in condominium. They are under his inspectorate, and under his hand, as was usual with the emir Nūr al-Dīn al-Ṭūrī. Its basis is that his word is executed; his sanctity is entirely inviolate in that region.
>
> Section: Relying upon the condominia of the lands, and the joint courts connected to `Athlīth, Haifa, and Acre in what the truce's conditions contain. What is forbidden will continue completely, such as horse, mules, and implements of weaponry in their various types. All of these forbidden things will continue to be so in their totality until the end of the Ẓāhirī period. On whoever is found with any of the above, the truce's conditions will be applicable to him.

Then there are sections that we have suppressed because of their length.

On Wednesday 1 Ṣafar [April 19, 1284] of this year the emir Sayf al-Dīn al-Mihrānī (or al-Mihwānī) headed to the governate of al-Bahnasā and al-Ashmūnīn in place of the emir Badr al-Dīn Kaykaldī, governor of al-Bahnasā, also the emir Fakhr al-Dīn Ibn al-Turkmānī, governor of al-Ashmūnīn. In it the pilgrims came (joined up with) to `Imād al-Dīn Ibn al-Athīr and Shams al-Dīn Ibn al-Qammāḥ, and the rest of the pilgrims.

On Friday the 24th [May 12, 1284] the Friday prayers were held in the Great Mosque, which the judge Muḥyī al-Dīn son of the Shaykh Rashīd al-Dīn `Abd al-Ẓāhir constructed in al-Qarāfa on a path close to the tomb of his father Shaykh Rashīd al-Dīn `Abd al-Ẓāhir. Judges, learned, and senior figures gathered in it, and it was a day to remember.

1 Rabī` al-Awwal [May 18, 1284] of that year, on Thursday, in open view, the emir Ḥusām al-Dīn Ṭuruntāy, the noble sultanate deputy, circumcised his children, and the emirs gathered altogether in the hall, where they were sprinkled with gold, and many dirhams. It was quite excessive, and it was a day to remember.

During it the judge Fatḥ al-Dīn Ibn `Abd al-Ẓāhir circumcised his son `Alā' al-Dīn `Alī in the home of the emir Badr al-Dīn Ibn *al-naqīb*. [3]

Mention of what was agreed upon between Arghun son of Abagha son of Hűlegű and his paternal uncle Aḥmad Aghā Sultan, and his killing [the latter] and taking over as king of the Tatars

When the Tatars' kingship past after the death of King Abagha son of Hűlegű, king of the Tatars, to King Aḥmad Aghā Sultan, son of Hűlegű, just as we previously explained, Arghun son of King Abagha son of Hűlegű was staying in Khurāsān. With him were a number of the Tatars' army, and so King Aḥmad Aghā Sultan sent to his nephew Arghun to have him swear an oath.

However, he refused to enter into obedience to him, so Aḥmad Aghā sent an army to him, which defeated Arghun's army, taking him prisoner. They brought him to his paternal uncle Aḥmad Aghā Sultan, and some of his courtiers whispered to him that he should have him killed. He said "He is a devil (*shayṭān*) who does not believe."

Aḥmad Aghā was very inattentive, so when they advised him to kill his nephew Arghun, he wanted to kill him. However, some of his ladies entered into his presence, saying, "If your nephew is killed, then bone will be removed from the Khan's bone. There is no benefit in it." Therefore, he did not kill him, but handed him over to one of the Mongol emirs, a commander of 10,000, among which there were 10,000 horsemen. He made him as if he was proscribed. Aḥmad Aghā then stayed in Tūrīz [Tabriz?] and Khurāsān and those lands, while Arghun was with the horse.

Al-Jazarī tells in his *History*: one of the reliable merchants told me concerning this Arghun that he would line up seven "head" of horse, then say to his companions "On which of them do you want me to ride?" So they would point out a horse from this line-up, so then he would jump from the ground, straight on to the horse's back that had been specified.

Together with his amazing grasp of horsemanship, when his paternal uncle handed him to that commander, he began to laugh with him, and to win him over. He [Arghun] said to him

> This King Aḥmad Aghā Sultan has converted to Islam, and changed the *yāsā* of Genghis Khan, corresponding with Muslims so as to make peace with them. If he keeps on going then there will be almost nothing

> left of the Mongols. Now he has sent after the *akrād* (thieves), intending to bestow *iqṭā`* fiefs upon them, and give them all the Tatars' lands. He wants to destroy Hűlegű's and the Khan's[125] bone.

He continued to goad him, to amaze him, to promise things to him, and to make him wish for things until he became aware of everything negative about his paternal uncle Aḥmad Aghā Sultan. So the commander said to Arghun "If I let you go, aided you, and helped you sit upon the throne of kingship, what would you do for me?" He said, "You would become the supreme arbiter of the entire realm as long as I rule."

When it was one of the nights, this commander requested a number of Mongol emirs who wanted to get rid of Aḥmad Aghā Sultan, and had not converted to the religion of Islam with him, telling them secretly what Arghun had said to him, so they said "Everything that Arghun said was correct. If you rise with him, we are with you!" So they promised this to each other on the second night, rose in the night against Aḥmad Aghā Sultan's army and his supporters.

They did not know what was happening, other than their throats were being cut, and a sword was upon them, so they retreated, and the supporters of Arghun entered into the presence of King Aḥmad Aghā [4] Sultan, while he was among the Horde. They removed him from the throne (*takht*), broke his back, killed him, and threw him on the road, may God Most High have mercy upon him.

It is said that the former name of Aḥmad Aghā was Tegűder, but when he converted to Islam, then he was called Aḥmad, and began to compel the senior Mongols to convert to Islam willingly or unwillingly, so they took revenge upon him for that. When Arghun refused to enter into obedience to him, he detained him, imprisoning him together with a number of the other senior Mongols, ignoring the dangers.

They then conspired to kill him, coming to Arghun, setting him free, taking `Alī Nāq, King Aḥmad's deputy, by surprise, then killing him, and going to the Horde. King Aḥmad Aghā perceived them, so he rode a horse, and fled from them, but they caught up with him, killed him, and made Arghun king. This was during this year.

It is said that the killing of Aḥmad was during the previous year, [6]82, but God knows best which of these two it was. When Arghun sat upon the throne of kingship, and it was morning, he mustered the army, dispersed and fragmented, so that everyone hastened to obey King Arghun, and wish him long life. Everyone who opposed or fled, they killed.

The minister Shams al-Dīn Ibn al-Juwaynī, the chief of the chancellery, minister to Abagha, fled to the mountains, but the supporters of King Arghun

125 Presumably Abagha.

expropriated all his wealth and properties in all the Persian, Iraqi, [Anatolian] Rūm lands, in Mosul and the east, and God knows best.

al-Malik al-Manṣūr heads to Damascus

On Sunday 8 Jumādā al-Ulā [July 23, 1284] of this year the Sultan al-Malik al-Manṣūr departed from the Hill Citadel traveling to protected Syria. His heading towards Syria was made illustrious by meeting with Shaykh ʿAbd al-Raḥmān and the Tatars who were with him as envoys of King Aḥmad Aghā, Sultan, son of Hűlegű, king of the Tatars.

On Wednesday 11 Jumādā al-Ulā [July 26, 1284] al-Muwaffaq b. al-Rashīd b. Abī Khalīfa presented himself at the royal tent of al-Manṣūr. He converted to Islam, and the Sultan ennobled him, so that he was named Aḥmad. He issued a written command the same allowances (*jāmakiyya*), salaries (*jarā'iyya*) and rank as his two brothers did when they converted to Islam, and this was written for him.

On the 14th [July 29, 1284] the Sultan wrote to his son al-Malik al-Ṣāliḥ to appoint the emir ʿImād al-Dīn Aḥmad b. Bākhil to the governate of al-Buḥayra, and its districts, so he did that. Ibn al-Mukarram said in his composition *The Secretary's Treasury* during it al-Kakhtā castle was conquered, and the emir Iftikhār al-Dīn Yāqūt al-Mughīthī was sent there as deputy, together with Rukn al-Dīn Baybars al-Dimashqī as governor, and a memorandum was written for the both of them. A copy of it: [5]

> A blessed memorandum in the hand of the emir Iftikhār al-Dīn Yāqūt al-Mughīthī's session, the deputy in al-Kakhtā, and Rukn al-Dīn Baybars al-Dimashqī, the governor in it, relying upon it, and looking to the noble important matters for precedent, waiting at its boundaries, and relying upon good intention for the best interests of the border fortress.
>
> These are: when the two of them arrive from protected Aleppo, they should seek to inform the high, emirate, Shamsī session, who is the deputy for the magnificent sultanate in the Aleppan realms, together with what has been added to them, concerning the stores that have been transferred to this border fortress, and assign men to them.
>
> Establish this among the best interests and circumstances, and the two of them should take a roll (of paper) on which there is an audit of the revenues (*maṣāliḥ*) upon which he relies. He is, may God glorify him, our deputy in the lands, and after God, he is the support in these lands. He is the initiator in the conquest of this protected border fortress, energetic in his command in a way that what is planted will grow.

> Whenever he establishes what the revenues and issues are, clarifying to the both of them upon which means they need base themselves for this border fortress, just as it is in the other border fortresses. Then they both will rely upon his sign, and wait for the command to be issued for all of these revenues, whose benefit accrues to the dominating state (*dawla*).
>
> They will then head forth with the peace of God Most High to the border fortress of al-Kakhtā on the road the companions who will travel it with them will show to them, to take them both there, to defend them, to show them the way. The both of them would then take a letter to the emir Ḥusām al-Dīn Ṭurunṭāy al-Majallī and those dispatched with him that they are to hand over the protected border fortress to the both of them, and he is to return to Aleppo—he and those dispatched with him who the emir Shams al-Dīn indicates[126] should be presented.
>
> Those dispatched who the emir Shams al-Dīn indicates should stay with the both of them from among the victorious Aleppan freeborn troops as reinforcements. This is just as we informed him in the correspondence delivered by the both of them to him, and we have already issued a command that a number of them should be dispatched as reinforcements at the beginning of their term. Until matters stabilize at this border fortress, and its circumstances are set in order, its affairs should go according to the best means. Accordingly its men will be settled, while the determination of those in it will be strengthened, and then, if God wishes, it will come to the point where those lands behind it will feel secure because of it.

Then it mentioned paragraphs which we have suppressed due to unnecessary length, then after the mention of these paragraphs, which their transcription is in the handwriting of the both of them, and where they have more than enough ability, sufficiency, expertise and knowledge upon which to rely, for which one should be grateful for their going out and returning.

We have previously mentioned the conquest of the border-fortress al-Kakhtā for the year [6]82 that has passed, and God knows best which of these it was.

On Saturday 12 Jumādā al-Ākhira [August 26, 1284] of that years al-Malik al-Manṣūr arrived in protected Damascus, staying at its Citadel. At the time of the Sultan's arrival in Damascus Muslim spies from the Tatars' lands arrived as well, informing (him) that King Aḥmad Aghā, king of the Tatars, was killed and that Arghun son of [6] his brother Abagha son of Hűlegű had taken the kingship of the Tatars.

They had left him, after he had already sat upon the throne (*takht*) of kingship in the Horde. So when al-Malik al-Manṣūr verified these spies' words,

[126] Reading *yushīru* in place of *yasīru* in accord with the next sentence.

he was patient until nightfall, then wrote a command that 1500 of his mamluks should cover the gray-red siege machines (*aqbīya*) with embroidery, filmy embroidered scarves (*kulūtāt al-zarkash*) and straps of gold. Before them would be 1500 candles—a candle with each mamluk.

When the mamluks wore what they were ordered to wear, and lit those candles the Sultan al-Malik al-Manṣūr ordered the shaykh `Abd al-Raḥmān and his companion the emir Ṣamadāghū the Tatar, and the chief Shams al-Dīn Muḥammad son of the chief Sharaf al-Dīn al-Tītī,[127] known as Ibn al-Ṣāḥib, the minister to the ruler of Mārdīn. These were the envoys of King Aḥmad Aghā Sultan, son of Hűlegű, king of the Tatars, who had been brought during Dhū al-Ḥijja of the year [6]82, the previous year, as we explained then.

When they presented themselves before the Sultan al-Malik al-Manṣūr they delivered the letter that they had brought from Aḥmad Aghā, and he heard it from them. They returned to their place, and then he asked to bring them in a second time and hear what they had to say, so he would respond to it on the spot. They were brought in a second time, he heard their words, until he had heard everything they had, and the mission on which they were.

Then al-Malik al-Manṣūr informed them on their third time that the one who sent them, King Aḥmad Aghā Sultan, had already been killed. Arghun son of Abagha was now reigning in his place, and sat on the throne of the realm. Then they sultan ordered them to be transferred from the Hall of Satisfaction to one of the citadel halls that very night, and to assign for them just enough [provisions].

They were transferred and their assigned provisions which they were assigned previously were reduced, but they were given just barely enough. It was said to them: "Whatever gold you have from King Aḥmad Aghā Sultan, give it to al-Malik al-Manṣūr," but they did not admit to anything.

Al-Malik al-Manṣūr sent to them the emir Shams al-Dīn Sunqur *al-a`sar* the majordomo, and he said, "The Sultan has issued a command to transfer you to another place, so each of you should gather your clothes." Each one of them rose, carrying their clothes, so when they all went to the entryway of the house they were searched. A great deal of gold, pearls and other items were taken from them then.

It was said that on the shaykh `Abd al-Raḥmān's hand there was a prayer-bead chain of pearls whose value exceeded 100,000 dirhams, and it was taken from him together with all that was taken. They were imprisoned and the shaykh `Abd al-Raḥmān died during that year, just as we will mention in his biography if God Most High wishes. His companions stayed imprisoned for

[127] Correcting from al-Bītī.

a period, and it was difficult for them. Then the emir Ḥusām al-Dīn Lājīn, deputy sultan in protected Damascus, wrote to al-Malik al-Manṣūr because of them [7] so he issued a command to liberate them.

The emir Shams al-Dīn Muḥammad Ibn al-Ṣāḥib stayed imprisoned, and was transferred to the Hill Citadel in protected Cairo, and imprisoned there for a lengthy time. Then he was released, and appointed to the Justice House in the Egyptian homelands.

He then entered the service of the Sultan Nāṣir al-Dīn Muḥammad son of al-Malik al-Afḍal Nūr al-Dīn ʿAlī, brother of al-Malik al-Manṣūr, the ruler of Ḥamāh, but he returned and died along the road between Damascus and Ḥamāh. The Sultan wrote a letter in which he consoled the ruler of Ḥamāh because of his nephew's death that was written by the judge Fatḥ al-Dīn Ibn ʿAbd al-Ẓāhir.

The Sultan removed the emir ʿAlam al-Dīn Sanjar al-Duwaydārī from the Chancelleries Supervision in protected Damascus, and added it to the responsibilities of the emir Shams al-Dīn Sunqur *al-aʿsar*, the sultanic majordomo in Damascus. Thus, the Chancelleries Supervision and the majordomo were combined.

The Sultan transferred also the emir Nāṣir al-Dīn al-Ḥarrānī from the governate of the protected city of Damascus to the deputy sultanate in Ḥimṣ. He added the governate of the city of protected Damascus to the emir Sayf al-Dīn Ṭūghān, the would-be governor of the flatlands. Then al-Malik al-Manṣūr determined to travel and return to the seat of his realm in the Egyptian homelands, so the emirs got their armor outside of Damascus citadel, but then the disaster of the flood happened which we will mention.

Mention of the disastrous flood in protected Damascus

On Wednesday 20, and some say 21, Shaʿbān [November 1 or 2, 1284] of this year, which corresponds to 1 Tishrīn al-Thānī [November], which is [the Coptic] 5 Hatūr the heavens rained during the first part of the night. Then heavier rain followed the rain, and it grew, as the sound of thunder intensified. Lightning followed the entire night until the first part of the morning, and then a flood came.

It rose until it reached the level of the flood we described for the year 609 [1212], taking all of the heavy armor belonging to those Egyptian emirs who had left their armor out, and of the army. It carried away horses, camels, standards, and other things.

It is said that the emir Badr al-Dīn Baktāsh al-Najmī lost what was valued at over 450,000 dirhams. The flood crashed into Paradise Gate, breaking its locks, and the bulwarks that were behind the gate. The water entered into the Muqaddimyya College, and stayed there until midday. Gradually the water dried out during Wednesday and Thursday.

Then more rain came, which was separate from the first rain, and it destroyed a number of houses on Mt. Qāsīyūn, outside of Damascus, and its suburbs. Then the waters abated.

Muḥammad b. al-Mukarram said in his composition *The Secretary's Treasury* to the effect that when it was Wednesday the 21st a great flood came to the Horse Market that is outside of protected Damascus until it filled the Barada [River]. The water rose until it overtopped the houses, and the hostels (*fanādiq*). It entered in through the Wellness (*salāma*) Gate, and went through the gates drowning master, horse and camel in numbers that cannot be [8] counted.

Fabrics, implements and other items were destroyed in unknown quantities. Most of the fabrics of the emir Badr al-Dīn Baktāsh al-Najmī were under water, as were his horses. The emir 'Alam al-Dīn Bāshqirdī had more than 60 camels drowned, while others lost many camels. Another flood similar to this one came on Friday the 23rd [November 4, 1284].

Mention of the Sultan's return to the Egyptian homelands

When the Sultan al-Malik al-Manṣūr Sayf al-Dīn Qalāwūn had stayed in protected Damascus long enough to arrange its affairs, he resolved to travel, and return to the seat of his realm in the Egyptian homelands. The emirs put their armor outside of Damascus Citadel, and then the flood came, just as we previously explained.

He headed towards the Egyptian homelands on Saturday the 23rd, and it is said, the 24th of Sha'bān [November 5, 1284] of this year, and arrived in protected Egypt, and entered the Hill Citadel on Tuesday 18 Ramaḍān [November 28, 1284] of this year.

Mention of the ascension to kingship of the king of Ḥamāh after the death of his father al-Malik al-Manṣūr

After the death of al-Malik al-Manṣūr Nāṣir al-Dīn Muḥammad al-Ayyūbī, ruler of Ḥamāh in Shawwāl [December 1284] of this year, as was mentioned in his biography after he had ruled his realm for 41 years, five months and four days, the report of his death came to the noble gates at the Hill Citadel.

When the Sultan al-Malik al-Manṣūr, ruler of protected Egypt, learned of it, he delegated the realm of Ḥamāh to al-Malik al-Muẓaffar Taqī al-Dīn Maḥmūd son of al-Malik al-Manṣūr, ruler of Ḥamāh, treating him the way his father was treated with honorary gifts and correspondence. He sent an ennoblement and a formal proclamation accompanied by the emir Jamāl al-Dīn Aqush al-Mawṣilī the chamberlain, sending with him a number of honorary gifts to his uncle al-Malik al- Afḍal and his cousin the emir 'Imād al-Dīn, and a number of his close relatives and emirs, and God knows best.

During Dhū a-Qa`da [January 1285] of this year the Sultan al-Malik al-Manṣūr ordered the emir `Alam al-Dīn Sanjar al-Ḥalabī to be detained, so he was imprisoned in the Hill Citadel in the Egyptian homelands.

Mention of Muhannā's emirate over the Bedouin after the death of his father, the emir `Īsā

After the death of the emir Sharaf al-Dīn `Īsā b. Muhannā b. Māni` b. Ḥudhayfa, the emir of the Bedouin, during the [6]83 [1284] which is mentioned in his biography, al-Malik al-Manṣūr, the ruler of protected Egypt, delegated the emirate over the Bedouin to his son the emir Ḥusām al-Dīn Muhannā.

The Sultan increased his *iqṭā`* fiefs, and gave him more authority, so he acted similarly to his father in doing good, generosity, good treatment, and making sure that all of the Bedouin obeyed him. He became well known among the kings and others. [9]

Mention of the quick construction of the Manṣūriyya College, its mausoleum, Hospital and Qur'ān school

During this year the construction of the Manṣūriyya College, which is *bayn al-qaṣrayn* inside of protected Cairo, together with its mausoleum, the Manṣūrī Hospital, and the Manṣūrī Qur'ānic school. When the spectator eyes this magnificent construction, the breadth of its courtyard, the height of its walls, the strength of its building, and then hears that it was constructed in this short period, he might very well not believe it.

When the construction which we mentioned was finished, al-Malik al-Manṣūr Sayf al-Dīn Qalāwūn endowed it as a charity from his Caesarean properties, the grazing grounds, shops, baths, hostels, plots of land (*aḥkār*) and other properties in Syria. All of this would earn a great amount from rent, surplus and harvest. Most of this was at the disposal of the hospital, then for the mausoleum with its cupola. He also assigned a charity for the College but it did not suffice, but the charity from Syria he assigned to the Qur'ān school did suffice.

As for the hospital, the Sultan al-Manṣūr when he endowed it, and arranged its affairs, he called for a goblet of drink (*sharāb*), and then drank it. He said, "I have endowed this according to my means; now others should endow it—master, mamluk, soldier, emir, minister, great and small, free and slave, male and female." He made sure that anyone who was sick was discharged from it after becoming well, and went on their way. Prior to departure, they would receive a garment. Whoever died would be prepared, wrapped, and buried. He assigned natural physicians, ophthalmologists, surgeons, and those restorers, who could treat ophthalmia, the sick, the wounded, and those broken, both men and women.

He assigned furnishers to it [...][128] which is the charitable endowment and other things that pertain to their profession. They also transfer the price of types of things from the lock-box, just as is done in administration, and deposit the renters' rents into the lock-box. They also write up each month the work that is deserving of what price, the renters. They count what has been transferred to the lock-box, the moneys that have been deposited with them, and then direct those to a benefactor or a merchant. Each community would bring of that part of it from their accounts, daily, monthly, and yearly to the inspector and the collector. That is what is connected to the hospital.

As for the mausoleum under the cupola, the Sultan al-Manṣūr assigned to it 50 readers of the Qur'ān, who would read God's Book night and day in shifts. He authorized payment of 20 dirhams to each of them every month.

He assigned an imam from the rite of Imam Abū Ḥanīfa, may God be pleased with him, and that he would receive 80 dirhams every month from the charitable endowment. Each year on the night in which the prayers for the month of [10] Ramaḍān would be completed there would be a complete ermine (*musinjab*) beaver (*muqandaz*)[129] robe from the Sultan's treasury.

He assigned a head (*rīs*) and six people for the call to prayer; for the head each month 40 dirhams, for the six callers to prayer, each one of them 30 dirhams a month. This was on the condition that they announce from the highest minaret standing now, and perform the prayers, staying behind the imam.

He assigned for the study of Qur'ān exegesis a lecturer, conferring upon him the stipend of 133 and 1/3 dirhams every month, plus an assistant for him for 40 dirhams a month, and for the students, their provisions would be for 30 people and totaling 300 dirhams each month.

He assigned for the study of the tradition (*ḥadīth*) in which the tradition of the Messenger of God would be recited, a lecturer, an assistant, and students, who would get each month the equivalent of what the lecturer in Qur'ān exegesis, his assistant and students got. Additionally, there would be a reciter who would recite the tradition in front of the lecturer during the lesson times. He would recite aiding the general populace in front of him as well every Wednesday morning. For this, he would be assigned 30 dirhams.

He assigned for the librarian 40 dirhams each month, and for the library storehouse, its books will come from the noble seals and the fourth part designated for the sultan (*al-rub`āt al-mansūba al-khaṭṭ*), the books of exegesis,

[128] The editor notes that there appears to have been a page skipped in the manuscript as this sentence beginning does not cohere with the one following, even though there is no space break. He speculates that a scribe accidentally skipped over an entire page by mistake.

[129] Reading *muqandaz* (from Farsi *qunduz* "beaver") in place of *muqandar*.

tradition, jurisprudence, [Arabic] language, medicine, fine literature, and chancellery [documents]—a great many.[130]

He assigned to it servant bound to it: six people, for each of them 50 dirhams, who would stay in the aforementioned cupola to protect its revenues, and to prevent any from entering it beyond the prayer times, and other than the *ṭawāshīs* of the night-watch, those carpet-makers, and gate-keepers, who receive an allowance that is specifically for them.

He assigned for it an imam from the Shāfiʿī rite, who would receive 30 dirhams each month, and a head, and four callers to prayer, each one of them equivalent to the four [sic!][131] callers to prayer in the cupola. The head, just as its (other) head, was to announce the prayer from the highest minaret that was previously mentioned, and those are the substitute callers to prayer.

He assigned for it one who would supervise the recitation of the Book of God Most High, and assigned for him 40 dirhams each month. He assigned for it lessons from the four [legal] rites: the Shāfiʿiyya, the Ḥanafiyya, the Mālikiyya and the Ḥanbalites. Each sect would have a lecturer for it, who would receive 200 dirhams, and three assistants, which each of them would receive 75 dirhams a month, plus 50 students for all of them in total, who would receive 750 dirhams each month. Other than those from the night watch, the carpet-makers and those deputized for allowances specifically for them.

As for the Qur'ān school, al-Malik al-Manṣūr assigned for it two jurisprudents who would teach the Book of God Most High to 60 young pupils who were taken from the Muslims' orphans, and he assigned for them an allowance each month, and salary each day. For the both of them each month 30 dirhams, and each day three *raṭl*s [= 1.35 kg] of bread, clothing for the winter, and clothing for the summer.

He assigned for the orphans, that each one of them would receive each day two *raṭl*s of bread, and clothing for the winter, and clothing for the summer. Al-Malik al-Manṣūr [11] may God make his reward generous, and have mercy upon him, specified different types of piety, and good deeds, and these blessed initiatives and the righteous charitable endowments have continued, thriving as their endowment has been increased, and have developed with the good intention of their endower, and the careful oversight of the overseers, but sometimes decrease with bad oversight or mismanagement. Every time has a period and [types of] men.

When the Manṣūrī Cupola, the school, the hospital and the Qur'ān school were all completed, and all of the arrangements were made, the endowments completed, the Sultan al-Manṣūr set it into motion in these places, rode, saw

[130] See Doris Behrens-Abouseif, *The Book in Mamluk Egypt and Syria* (Leiden: E.J. Brill, 2018), pp. 71–2.

[131] Six above.

it with his own eyes, sitting in the hospital together with the emirs, the judges, and the learned ones, and it was a day to remember.

Mention of the Sultan's going from Egypt to Syria

On 15 Dhū al-Ḥijja [February 22, 1285] of this year the Sultan al-Malik al-Manṣūr Sayf al-Dīn Qalāwūn headed from protected Egypt to protected Syria, and God knows best

[*Obituaries*]

Mention of the events during the year 684 [1285]

During the 7th hour of Saturday, 16, but some say 15, of Muḥarram [March 24 or 23, 1285] of this year which corresponds to 28 Bramhāt of the Coptic months, year 1001 of the Coptic years, while the ascendant was in Cancer, al-Malik al-Nāṣir Muḥammad son of al-Malik al-Manṣūr Sayf al-Dīn Qalāwūn al-Alfī al-Ṣāliḥī al-Najmī was born in the Hill Citadel.

The tidings of his birth came to his father al-Malik al-Manṣūr while he was in his camp at Thieves Ruin (*khirbat al-luṣūṣ*) just before he entered protected Damascus, so al-Malik al-Manṣūr was gladdened by his birth, and saw a good omen in it. Then he attained his goal of conquering Marqab, as we will mention if God Most High wishes. Al-Malik al-Manṣūr arrived in Damascus on Saturday 22 Muḥarram [March 30, 1285] of this year.

Mention of the conquest of Marqab fortress

During this year the Sultan al-Malik al-Manṣūr Sayf al-Dīn Qalāwūn al-Alfī al-Ṣāliḥī al-Najmī headed from protected Damascus to Marqab fortress to rescue it from the Franks, may God Most High abandon them, because its inhabitants had committed actions that violated the truce which had been achieved between them and the Sultan, just as we have previously explained, and did not abide by their conditions.

This fortress belonged to the Hospitallers' House, and it was among the impregnable fortresses, known for its impregnability. It was a watch point (*marqab*) over a small village close to the sea, which was also close to this fortress. Its ruler had built a great tower, which none could hope to attain, unreached by arrows, or even by mangonels' stones.

This caused harm to the Muslims which was only known to God Most High, and the martyr Sultan Ṣalāḥ al-Dīn Yūsuf al-Ayyūbī was not able to take it, nor was al-Malik al-Ẓāhir Rukn al-Dīn Baybars al-Bunduqdārī [18] al-Ṣāliḥī al-Najmī, may God Most High have mercy upon the both of them. But God Most High made it a storehouse for al-Malik al-Manṣūr Sayf al-Dīn Qalāwūn al-Alfī. God, mighty and majestic, conquered by conquering Marqab fortress after he (Qalāwūn) had stayed at Marqab for a period of 38 days.

It is said that he camped at Marqab during the first part of Rabīʿ al-Awwal [May 7, 1285], besieged the fortress, and constructed tunnels. When the Franks saw that he was on the verge of taking it by force, they requested safe conduct, and they handed the fortress over, so al-Malik al-Manṣūr received it at the 8th hour of the day, Friday, 19 Rabīʿ al-Awwal [May 25, 1285] of this year.

When the fortress, its districts, and its watch point were taken over, and God Most High had graciously allowed its conquest, and relieved the Muslims from it, al-Malik al-Manṣūr sent its inhabitants to Tripoli, and the fortress because one of the Muslims' fortresses. Al-Malik al-Manṣūr then returned back to protected Damascus.[132]

During 8 Rabīʿ al-Ākhir [June 13, 1285] of this year the upright shaykh Abū al-Ḥasan son of al-Muwaffaq son of al-Najm son of the upright Abū al-Ḥasan son of Samuel the doctor, was appointed as the Head of the Jews. Ibn al-Mukarram, the secretary of the noble roll, wrote him an investiture:

> Since God, may He be praised, cast upon us the keys to affairs, and placed the commonweal in our hands, giving us glorious victory—and whoever He grants victory is the victorious one (al-Manṣūr), we manage the populaces' affairs, necessitating our observing the creatures so as to protect ourselves from the rest of the nations. We guard the wealth of each community because of protecting it, so we, praising God, are concerned with the benefit of the populace.
>
> If their religions and opinions differ, their rites and tendencies have separated a noble people from us, a blessed disposition related to us, overflowing from us, we constrain every community according to its own law, treading the paths of its base and boughs, relying upon guarding their protected status, continuing their laws (*nāmūs*), respecting its leadership and those following the leadership, treating all the same among their strong and weak, and their women, in the truth, among their nobles and those looking up to the nobles. Praise be to God for that grace which is above all graces, inspiring us to look favorably into the interests of other communities.
>
> Since the shaykh, the high, the head, the sufficient, the one brought close, the wise, the upright, crown of doctors, trusty one for kings and sultans, Abū al-Ḥasan son of the Shaykh al-Muwaffaq son of Abū al-Najm son of the upright Abū al-Ḥasan the doctor, may God open his breast,[133] may

[132] This abbreviated account of the conquest of Marqab suggests that Ibn al-Furāt did not have access to Ibn ʿAbd al-Ẓāhir (*Chronicles*, text 1 (a)).

[133] Cf. Q94:1, presumably to convert to Islam.

God make his matter easy, rest his secret from those who preceded him as Head of his ethnicity. May a witness to his nobility arise from his predecessors, and from himself, and may he be a headman for his co-religionists, a Head in his rite and law. This is because his family has already attained fame with their religiosity, is known among his people for sufficiency, and trust which breaks down the noble opinions that we discourse for him among his co-religionists, and the headship over his people and community.

Thus the high command has gone forth that he continue to be judge (*ḥākim*) over the communities, a king for the Arabs and non-Arabs, that the Headship of the Jews be delegated to him over the rest of their sects, the Rabbanites, the Karaites, and the Samaritans who are in protected Cairo, Old Cairo [19] and the rest of the Egyptian homelands.

This grants him precedence with his speech over any speaker, that he would be an exemplar in his action, and the knowledge that he is protected in matters in which he has our support [?],[134] of which notice interests us, and he is trusted in what he does to guard its circumstances, which necessitate having and keeping a pact.

Our order is that those we have appointed should be relied upon to right the wrong one, to straighten the waverer, to bear them according to the manner of their religion, by which they are judged, to lead them in the ways of their belief, which they believe, to do well by them. By this he will bring them to straightened circumstances, bring them to their ordering, harmonizing their actions and words in order for their obedience to us be sincere, and that their counsel to us would be correct.

So let all of the Jewish and Samaritan[135] groups take heed of his authority, be satisfied with his judgment, and his reproof, nor let anyone from among them oppose his judgment on the basis of the law's text, either for or against him. Nor obstruct him with regard to what is behind him, or before him, nor open a prayer session without his order and judgment, nor leave the assembly without him being first, or at his command, nor should anyone seek to go over his head, or go against his will.

He has the right to appoint deputies who he chooses, and others who he wills, he can place over every group one from that particular group who will satisfy them, to judge among them according to their rite and

[134] Editor notes that this is probably corrupt.
[135] Reading *s-m-r-a* as *al-sāmira*.

opinion. Whoever disagrees or stands against him, is stubborn or opposes him, he has the right to punished them, to mandate punishment upon him, to excommunicate him in accord with his law that is binding upon his religion.

So let him hold fast to the religion, not departing from its clear ways (*sunan*), and to cast this good treatment that will necessitate thanking him, and cognizance of his righteousness, and let both him and his people glory in gratefulness to our grace, and pray for the glory of our victory, and the continuance of our days.

Whoever read this noble written command or has it read to them, among all the deputies, supervisors, the governors and officials, let him act in accord, and stand in fulfillment of it, enjoining respect to the aforementioned Head, to take care of him, and know the worth of what we have invested in him, aiding him in doing what we have appointed him to do, and the noble signature, may it be raised in accord.

The writing of the judge Muḥyī al-Dīn Ibn ʿAbd al-Ẓāhir wrote another investiture in the same vein, of which this is its text:

Afterwards, praise to God who made the kindness of this dominating dynasty purify its protection towards the Jews one Head after another, choosing this (protection) for its people just as He chose Moses from its his people, who made their souls merry, as long as he was over them, as a precious one from among them, and prayers upon our lord Muḥammad the *ummī* (unlettered) prophet, the Messenger who completed the testament upon those part of the community and those protected, may God pray for him, and for his family and his companions as long as a supporter rains (blessings).

Justice of this realm which guards over religions and sects, and includes them in general fairness and aid by the most generous portions, the most loyal [20] justice, to pick them up from time's disaster when it threatens, from its turning it away while raging, to clutch them just as prophecy was clutched to the descendants of the (Twelve) Tribes, continuing to watch over the family (*al-āl*) and protection for the Muslims, together with protection (for the Jews), which necessitates the best of expertise and care for that which is sacred, allowing them the affairs of their own religion according to which they are sworn, and granting[136] them what they have agreed to.

[136] Reading with al-Qalqashandī according to the editor's suggestion.

They keep their laws (*nawāmīs*) by their rabbis, may their intention be beautified,[137] when they are spoken to face-to-face, and their countenances are well when every Israelite is seen studying the totality of the Torah, when memorizing the books of their prophets well, in the most complete manner.

Whomever they heed, they heed because of precedence; his exertion (in study) has only to last for a day, until he has become an authority among his people, and even the Head of the headship. Then he has become without peer, numbered as many among them, and described as one who can interpret the Hebrew of their books in the best exegesis, deserved among his people (*sha`b*) to be Chief Priest. Hearts have become bound to him in the best binding completely, and their ignorant ones shield their beliefs by his cultivated learning behind his party lest they return to being as servants.

Since the Head so-and-so was eulogized by these good qualities, was the lifeblood to the body of this delegation, was the language for praises of this broad acclaim, the center of this appointment, may these hands in their reaching forth and grasping envelope this newborn. May the best thoughts necessitate these descriptions, rendering them hard, and whoever draws the first fruits of blessings near to the hand of his precedence in a garden choked with them, let him pluck its tender (fruits).

The good noble command necessitates distinguishing him from the sons of his ethnicity in the truest manner, and to permit him to bestow and to raise the most majestic of that which is permitted. The high command continues to choose, so let it beautify the choice, and go forth with the rain that gives general benefit through increasing wealth, creating channels (*wihād*), digging water-holes, and rivers, to delegate to him the Headship of the Jews, according to their differences—namely Rabbanites, Karaites and Samaritans, in the Egyptian homelands, my God protect and keep it safe.

Let him make their circumstances strong through god-fearingness, planting them in self-reflection, without withering, while their aims are not marred by doubt or complaints, as favor descends upon them from us, removing any rancor from them until both the manna and the quail will never part from them.[138] So let him fear God in that which he leaves, come to Him, and do well in enticing and captivating hearts to bring to Him.

[137] According to the editor's suggestion.

[138] See Exodus 16:13, 31; and Q2:57, 7:160.

Stay away from haughtiness, so it would not be said, "It is like he is distant, as if he never left the desert."[139] The Rabbanites, who are the most numerous people and the most sizable party, treat them with advantageous companionship, and worthy piety, especially as you are one of them. Do not, however, tend towards them against others according to what the "self [= soul] indeed the instigator of evil"[140] commands.

The [21] Karaites, who are known among this religion as those who adhere to the proofs, and keep the matter of the lunar months strictly, place over them someone who will not rule them harshly when they are bereaved—someone who is trusted by them. Do not deviate from this, nor do wrong, or bridle them with the bridle of one who lights up, denying those who hold to this on the night of the Sabbath, or saddle up.[141]

As for the Samaritans, they are the people who allowed hardship (*shaẓaf*) in their wars, and not one of them will eat with you, nor drink with his eating, or drinking. Anyone from your sect (*madhhab*) who is capable of responding to this by hook or by crook, let him do so by a method he utilizes, and escape from it. However, if not, then say to him

> O Samaritan, you have looked into what you (all) did not previously look into, so let your judgment with regard to them be final, and then accompany them, for the growing place is not land pieces nor a shoot that says forever, so do not be that growing place.

Order them to keep their ordinances (*qawānīn*) so that not one of them will transgress the Sabbath, and make the matters of their compacts fair, treating selection and arrangement for them with balance, in accord with his books.

Only select notables for every *ḥazan* (cantor) and *dayyān* (religious judge), those who are blood descendants of David, and have the sanctity of connection, then give him his due, accompany him honorably, and honor his accompaniment.

As for the poll-tax (*jizya*) it is for your blood relations and your children, and it is for defending them, not as a payment for them, or on behalf of

[139] *Tīh* means both "haughtiness" and "desert."

[140] Q12:53.

[141] Karaites were known to not be willing to light fires prior to the Sabbath which would continue to burn during its duration. See L. Nemoy, *Karaite Anthology* (New Haven: Yale University Press, 1952), pp. 209f. on holidays from the legal collection of Samuel al-Maghribi (d. 1434).

them, and it repels harm as a protection from disputes. It rescues you from the sword, and constitutes a fee for the House of Islam, just as it is a protection for the realization of benefit, so pay it, as by it your souls are redeemed. If you count it has one of God's unnumbered blessings, then count the graces of God through it, and do not be hostile to it.

Continuously in gentle reproof of the one who abandons a sign (*ʿalāma*),[142] and the one who looks to free himself of it, say to him in public and in private, "Silence!" and whoever depends upon perpetuating or forsaking what we have commanded, dwelling upon neglecting (it), as he is not satisfied that the yellow flag of the dynasty is raised over his head, then let him widen his disapproval and commit himself to it as insignia.

If a group rises to aid him from among them, show them the sign which is bran (*khushkār*) for their milled wheat of disapproval, and teach them to avoid fraud which would change the covenant (of the *dhimmi*) and make it disappear, and restrain the one who weighing that which would nullify it. As for the one who is open to that (rebellion) he will go for what he wants, transfer their characteristics from that. If you refuse to do that, then our vengeance will follow. "Say: The good and the bad are not equal."[143]

It is known that the one to whom the blowing in the *shofar* (*būq*) is assigned he is only as you have said for the sake of remembrance (*tidhkār*), so exert yourselves that it not be for remembrance of the (golden) calf, "an image of it, (having) a mooing sound."[144]

This is Our instruction to you and to them: so say to them this is the gift of the dynasty, its treating you well, its grace upon you, its caring for you, and your view, each time our good treatment is recited to them should be: "Sons of Israel! Remember My blessing which I bestowed upon you."[145] [22]

On 7 Jumādā al-Awwal [July 11, 1285] of this year al-Malik al-Manṣūr Sayf al-Dīn Qalāwūn entered the Sultanic Treasury in protected Damascus, and bestowed upon the judge Muḥyī al-Dīn Ibn al-Naḥḥās, the inspector of the aforementioned treasury, the robe of ministry, which was a robe, a red waved

---

[142] Presumably the discriminatory signs that Jews and Christians had to wear during the Mamluk period.

[143] Q5:100.

[144] Q7:148, also Q20:88.

[145] Q2:44.

silk (*`uttābī*) cloak, having above it a flowing (*farjiyya*)[146] blue robe above it, trimmed with ermine and beaver. He delegated the ministry in Damascus to him in place of the chief Taqī al-Dīn Tawba al-Tikrītī,

On Friday 15 Jumādā al-Awwal [July 19, 1285], al-Malik al-Manṣūr removed the emir Sayf al-Dīn Ṭūghān from the governate of the city of Damascus, and set him over the governate of the lowlands specially.

He appointed the governate of Damascus to the emir `Izz al-Dīn Muḥammad Ibn Abī al-Hayjā'. Al-Malik al-Manṣūr then headed from Damascus to the Egyptian homelands on the morning of the day of Monday 18 Jumādā al-Awwal [sic! July 22, 1285]. He arrived at the Hill Citadel in protected Egypt on Tuesday 29 Sha`bān [October 30, 1285] of this year, as he had spent some time in Tell al-`Ajūl.

On Tuesday 7 Ramaḍān [November 6, 1285] envoys from the Frankish kings arrived, and presented themselves before the Sultan al-Malik al-Manṣūr, and they presented those gifts they had brought. As for what was from the Emperor, there were 32 porters carrying gray squirrel pelts (*sinjāb*), 14 brown slaves (*sumūr*), five with scarlet cloth (*saqallāṭ*), and 13 with Venetian satin. As for what was from the Genoans, a "head" (or tall) galley (*sārsīnā*)[147] with two loads bearing six hunting falcons (*sanāqir*) and a piebald dog, which one of the historians said was bigger than a lion.

As for what was from the Lascarid [Palaeologan], there was a load of satin, and four of carpets. Their gifts were received and they were recompensed as usual in good treatment and kindness, and God knows best.

On 11 Ramaḍān [November 10, 1285] was the appointment of the judges Muhadhdhab al-Dīn, `Alam al-Dīn[148] and Muwaffaq al-Dīn, the children of Abū Khalīfa, to the position of head of medicine. The judge Muḥammad Ibn al-Mukarram wrote their investiture for that, and this is a copy of it:

> Praise be to God, the one who benefits by grace, guiding the truly-guided to the community, and giving of great good in wisdom, we praise Him in that He has generously bestowed a portion of the dominion upon us, and supplied us with our victory over our enemies in every breath, and turned our conquering resolution to aiding His religion and the interests of His creation, so there is nothing left for us other than this resolution, so we testify that there is no God but God alone, having no associate, a testimony which raises the belief and makes the intention high, preserving

[146] Discussion in Dozy, *Dictionnaire détaille des Noms des Vêtements chez les Arabes* (Beirut: Libraire du Liban, n.d. [reprint]), pp. 327–34.

[147] Reading as *sār shīnā*, but otherwise unattested.

[148] Presumably `Alam al-Dīn Jīrjīs [=Ibrāhīm after his conversion to Islam] b. Mikhā'il b. al-Fāris, said to have been confirmed as the head of doctors for Egypt in 684/1285 (al-Maqrīzī, *al-Muqaffā al-kabīr* [ed. Muḥammad `Uthmān, Beirut: Dār al-Kutub al-`Ilmiyya, 2010], ii, p. 491 [no. 1057]).

family and protected [people], and we testify that Muḥammad is His servant and Messenger, prophet of mercy, revealer of dark night, enlightener of darkness, may God pray for him in a way that lifts his memory high, and raises his name, and upon his pure family and his most noble companions who built up his religion, and inherited [23] his knowledge, and wish him peace, which will continue their nobility throughout time, and cause his forbearance to remain.

Afterwards, the most majestic benefits encountered, and the best of professions the one who has a family can perform, the most beautiful is that who says to a position "welcome" as he is appointed to it, especially when he is deserved of it, and by it he returns the sword to its scabbard, returning the function to its owner who is most worthy of it.

Since knowledge is, as is related, "Knowledge is of two types,"[149] the knowledge of religions and the knowledge of bodies, it is incumbent upon us that we perfect both of these types of knowledge, devoting to the both of them what remains of our victorious days to leave the best legacy, so we have upheld their insignia as to make those who are absent from our noble realms, as well as those who are present, so that everyone will gain from that, whether they are absent by hearing (about it) or present by seeing it.

We desire to guard our subjects in that to which they are in need of guarding: health of religion and body, so we know that it is not possible to undertake the ordinances without being health in body outwardly, and healthy in religion inwardly.

So we have instituted for these two noble knowledges blessed buildings which were founded upon god-fearingness and perfected in accord, so that its essence nor its rules will disappear, but continue satisfactorily, and with benefit for all during our days for everybody, and that the good will arrive at all of our subjects. We have given a position for that reason to the learned and doctors who we have selected, and we are satisfied with this selection.

Since the head doctor is the position to which appointment is a trust for the spirits and free action for the (departed) shadows, as well as being an expenditure for those making right, and for taking up the duties of doctoring with regard to surgery, healing and so forth, the one who is set for treatment and the need for dispensing of medicine must be selected

[149] Al-Dārimī, *Sunan* (Damascus: Dār al-Qalam, 1996), i, p. 108 (no. 370).

from those who are suited for this, and assigned, that the most proficient man be picked.

At the high council the judge Muhadhdhab al-Dīn is among the servants of the kings, him and his father, and grew up among them, him and his brother, with his (other) brother, and they were cognizant of his good advice, and devotion, so they preferred him, honored him, and bore witness to his merit, so they made him Head before then, and advanced him. This position he has already filled, so it has become a regular one for him, in which his superior qualities are manifest, and his influence is noted, as the full moons are added to the light-giving lights of his carrying out its duties. Examples of his overseeing his duties are superfluous.

Noble opinions therefore necessitate that this position be safeguarded in its value, even it would be best to delegate it to one whose moon has dimmed, so for that reason the high command has gone forth to delegate the headship of the doctors to him, and to his brothers augustly sitting, the judge `Alam al-Dīn Ibrāhīm and the judge Muwaffaq al-Dīn Aḥmad, may God Most High make them glorious, according to the usual in promotion and headship.

So let him take up his duties, fearing God in regard to his affair, vigilant about his secret, open, knowing about the recompense of a believer equally, following the Truth, depending upon truthfulness, walking the paths of those who are riding making his way clear, and let him receive this appointment in the best manner, and carry it out with a happy face, to govern in its affairs with justice, and to treat fairly in detention and beating. Let him look into the affairs of those who receive disbursements among the doctors and the natural healers, so as to discover [24] the affairs of the ophthalmologists and the surgeons, to establish them in their principles to which they have ascended, and to keep them within norms, other than when a grave sin has from him is manifest, and he persists in it.

Let him approach them with firmness and conciliation according to the way they conduct operations with a knife, so let not one of them perform an operation without experienced doctors witnessing it. Let him uncover the affairs of those who die on the roads, and rely in actions regarding terminal cases, among those who operate with a knife and other (instruments). He should not associate with such a person's evil, nor even hope for any good from them, but let him forbid them from sitting (to operate), thus turning that one away from harming bodies, and destroying souls. Whoever hears that he is in the outskirts or the countryside should not quarrel with him as long as he does not, but then he should not expend in seeking such a person out in order to protect himself.

Let him instead write to forbid that person, then exert himself to restrain such a person, and inform everyone who is open or hidden of this practice, then verify what goods he has obtained. Whoever one finds out that he is one who is acting freely (*ahl al-taṣarruf*), then he should be turned out with the masses. One who it is not established that he is worthy, then it is not possible for him to loosen his tongue, nor extend his arm (to be able), so let him enjoy gazing upon the matters of potions or drugs (*`aqāqīr*) or medicines, so let him see to gathering them or dispensing them one-by-one, or constituting them, or making them from ingredients, in accord with his level of intelligence.

Let him put watchfulness into that, so that nothing is sold other than what is certain as to its contents, and his selection. Let him take the one who desires to work with this knowledge in composition, and knowledge of nutrition, difficult questions, memorizing *al-Fuṣūl*,[150] or researching *al-Qānūn*[151] or *al-Kulliyyāt*.[152] Whoever reaches this level of purity, let him receive him well, and whoever deserves permission and to be entrusted let him refer back to the words of the just wise ones, and give the position its due, without denying anyone who has the right to something. Denial of someone who has a right stops others. No one will want to learn knowledge if its student has no hope of anything good coming from it, nor should he give the wisdom to one who is not appropriate for it, lest he be wronged, nor forbid it from the one who is appropriate for it, lest he be guilty.

As for his two brothers, the judge `Alam al-Dīn and the judge Muwaffaq al-Dīn, let them know that the judge Muhadhdhab al-Dīn has the right of precedence, age and merit, upon which the soul relies, and is calm, so they should both render to him the sanctity of brotherhood, and know that the brother's strong arm is a grace on the level of prophecy, so they should humble themselves to venerate him at the level of brotherhood, and to raise him from the guidance (level) of brotherhood to the manners of fatherhood, that he would be their reference-point (*marja`*) when hearing improvements, no matter who is in the position or who he has placed, and their reliance upon him in the rest of their doings.

---

[150] Probably referring to Hippocrates' *Fuṣūl*; Ibn al-Nafīs (d. 687/1288) wrote *Sharḥ fuṣūl Ibqraṭ* during this time.

[151] Written by Ibn Sīnā (d. 428/1036–7).

[152] Probably Ibn Rushd's (d. 520/1126), *Kitāb al-kulliyyāt fī al-ṭibb.*

When this is problematic for them, let them turn to him for clarification, and let him solve it. They should not deal with a matter nor parse it without him being present or before him, as he, may God Most High make him glorious, when he is alone, is sufficient, but especially when there is mutual agreement, and conjunction of opinions. If something good happens when they are separate, let him be grateful for this grace, and let him intercede for the ordinance of praising it by the way (*sunna*).

Let him dwell in Cairo, in proximity to the plethora of books and registers (*bayākīr*)[153] aiding in his specialization for the Manṣūrī Hospital lectureship. This position should confer upon the two assignees their due in good administration and giving good influence.

For we have not appointed him to this valuable position, nor conjoined between the headship and the lectureship, for any other reason than we have placed him in our state (*dawla*) [25] in Ibn Sīnā's place. How could it be otherwise, when he is the Head shaykh? Every single deputy who stands before this rescript must strengthen his hand to support his interests that are known because of this noble letter, and aid him in his right path, stand at attention for his orders and prohibitions, his perfect rendering of judgments, and act according to them.

For he is the root from which his clear proofs shine forth, and his structures stand. Anything prior to him is abrogated, and its signs are no longer in force, so let his judgment descend, let his knowledge be firm, and let his written command be executed through the ages. The noble signature, may it be lifted, stands as a proof in accord.

Muhadhdhab al-Dīn was appointed to teach at the newly built Manṣūrī Hospital, and Ibn al-Mukarram, secretary of the noble roll, wrote his investiture for that. A copy of it:

Praise be to God who administrates the cosmos by His wisdom, covering over all existence with His mercy, through the benefit of healing is a barrier against the harm of illness, just as His gifts have intervened without promises. We praise and thank Him, as He is the thanked and praised one, redoubling praise standing and sitting, on the side, and in prostration,, asking Him to increase his grace, for it is the people of grace and generosity.

We testify that there is no god but God, unique, without any associate, the testimony of God, the angels, and those possessed of knowledge as

[153] Probably from the Farsi *paykar*.

witnesses, and we testify that Muḥammad is His servant and Messenger, the proclaimer of gardens and eternity to his community, may God pray for him and for his family and companions, a prayer that is continuous until the promised day.

Afterwards, we, since God bestowed upon us the insignia of belief, His religion, praise be to God, has been victorious through us over all the rest of the religions, and "we have struggled for God with the struggling due Him,"[154] by the hand, by the heart and by the tongue, and we have constructed by His knowledge and Laws every marvelous perfection, and assigned notable learned ones to every lofty matter in it, choosing for him the best of the people of knowledge in medicine, jurisprudence, tradition, and the Qur'ān, and we have seen all the kings who have come to us, even if they have specialized in the best policy for the subjects are interested in the knowledge of religions but neglect the knowledge of bodies.

All of them create schools, but do not apply themselves to a hospital, heedless of his word [Muḥammad]: "Knowledge is of two types." Do not learn one from its subjects by immersion into medicine which harms him, nor should he hesitate to seek that knowledge which is handed down to him. One should not prepare for himself a place to just be immersed in this art, nor place upon a pedestal a man who exemplifies this ideal.

Our knowledge, praise be to God, is of that of which they were ignorant, and we remembered this close connection as long as they neglected it, so we have arrived in such a religious and worldly situation as they have not, so we have built a hospital, by which eyes are overcome at its splendor, and it exceeds the other buildings by sign and proof, guarding health and weal of every life.

If one is there to be healed, he will be treated, or if one comes distressed [26] by sickness, he can seek healing, or the moon can look over him without any healing for returning him with healing. We have endowed righteous charitable endowments that fill the eyes, and their number fills the ears, returning him from it with his hands filled. We have permitted all types of medicines to both noble and ignoble, to the commanded and the commander (*amīr*), and we have made equal benefit from it to small and great, rich and poor.

We know that there is no equal to it in our realm, nor in its perfection, nor have we made any equal to it in endowment or stipulation, but made

[154] Q22:78 (paraphrase).

it a place for working with medical knowledge, which had almost become unknown, mandating to the people to come to its sea, the sweetest of watering-stops, as we have made it easy for them as long as forbearance is easier than awakening, and have gowned it with medical learned ones, who can deliver lessons, by which both the head of this field and a beginner can benefit, being certain of bodily health, and protection of souls, so thus we find the head of this group the most appropriate for this appointment, and cannot be satisfied with one who does not have this distinction—and we know that when we have appointed it, it will become a marvel, and turn into a wonder.

Since according to the high session Muhadhdhab al-Dīn is the indicated head, the one to whom the fingers have entered agreement, it is as if he was the doctor Hippocratus, nay, the august Socrates, nay, the meritorious Galen, nay, the greatest Dioscorides. The noble opinions have necessitated that his majesty be augmented by his appointment to this august position, that he be led to it, while they drag their tails,[155] and that it be said to him "No other is worthy of it! And you alone are right for it."

For this reason a high command has gone forth that he will continue to be an aid to the religion, a dispenser for knowledge, to delegate the teaching of medicine to him in the newly constructed Manṣūrī blessed hospital in protected Cairo, knowing that he is distinguished in this field, and that with physiognomy and diagnosis, he is the Socrates of this region—if there be another Socrates—and trusting that we have picked up a jewel, and we are happy with the good, having fallen upon an expert.

So let this grace be received with majestic thanks, and a plethora of praise, redoubling that which has been and building upon it, so positioning this blessed knowledge in the place of one who fulfills an obligation, and way (*sunna*) [of the Prophet]. Let him know that he has merit, and to gird it with blessing, and to redouble its beautiful traces upon him, and to redouble the reins upon him, to nullify by his practice of health that which Ibn Buṭlān composed, to demonstrate for us the device of secrecy in his administration, for he is the Galen of the age, so let him expend everything to save from sicknesses and to heal from illnesses, for he is the Ibn Sīnā of the times.

Let the sum total of students congregate around him, and let every student among them give him what he asks, so that every seeker would attain the highest in practice, opening for them his breast, expending his life

[155] Repetition of this phrase immediately after has been deleted.

for them, to reveal to them this knowledge of which the secret is hidden, to show to them what is concealed from them, making it open, so making them into a naturalistic number, and a group of ophthalmologists (*kaḥḥālīn*), surgeons, and a group compelled, working with iron (surgeons), and others with the names of herbs (*ḥashā'ish*), potency of drugs, and knowledgeable about their attributes.

Let each of them be ordered to guard that which needs guarding, and to know [27] above and beyond, to take that which is appropriate for his tongue and speech, and not to absent himself in practice, to specialize in each branch of medicine, and all of its fields, so as to better a talent, to apply every talent to the different types of merit, to uncover for them what is difficult for them, so that there is nothing left that is unclear.

To ease in this blessed place the masters of the knowledge, group after group, and to demonstrate each morning, if God Most High wishes, double what was demonstrated today, so that it will be said to all of the students when he mandates their diploma and certificate, His shaykh has done well, who taught him, and that the one who graduates from this will be skilled, ad worker in all of this according to the stipulations of the endower, may God make his aid glorious, standing at His service, may God execute his order.

During the middle tenth of Ramaḍān [mid. November 1285] of this year, the judge Taqī al-Dīn Ibn Shās al-Mālikī was appointed to lecture at the blessed Manṣūrī College, and the judge Ibn al-Mukarram, secretary of the noble roll, wrote an investiture for that. A duplicate of it:

Praise be to God who made the learned the heirs of the prophets, and ordered us to follow their example, and to take heed of their lead, made paradise an inheritance for His god-fearing servants, we praise Him according to those gracious gifts he has filled (the earth), the dominion and rule He has given us, while adding capacity in knowledge and body, choosing us specifically.

We testify that there is no god but God, unique, without any associate, a testimony which magnifies beyond the level of doubt and skepticism, and we testify that Muḥammad is His servant and Messenger, given intercession and secrets specifically, may God pray for him and for his family and companions, a prayer that fills the earth and heavens.

Afterwards, for we continue, grace and bounty be to God upholding the obligation of those who have the insignia of this religion and way (of the Prophet), acting to construct its thought, sending to aid its reins, directing the establishment of its followers' (*awliyā'*) norms as piercing arrows of opinion towards the necks of its enemies, expending spear-tips in aiding it, lifting its precious light, and wealth without faintheartedness or stinginess, fighting (*mujāhidīn*) its enemies, who Satan has mastered, and who have believed the Devil, having sworn that "God has purchased from the believers their lives and their wealth, with (the price of) the Garden."[156]

So we, whether in mustering troops, the news of whose victory will spread Islam, or whether by preparing a caravan or way to the Sacred House of God, or by building blessed places, are continuing always in various ways to honor this, so among those are reciting the Book of God, praise and raise Him, and the traditions of His prophet, upon whom prayers and peace, and among them are the four rites bestow as imams, raising the flags of knowledge. Among them are seeking medicine and treatment, hoping for healing from illnesses, establishing the light over the religions and bodies, protecting the heath of bodies and religions.

Therefore, the days of our al-Malik al-Manṣūr are the best of days, and our noble period (*dawla*) is the meeting point for creation. These places need imams to be positioned in each one of them [28] to recite its knowledge, and to put its students into circulation according to its wisdom, so that they would be reared according to its mannerisms, and learn from its rite.

We have chosen therefore an imam for every rite, an given precedence to that imam, investing him with laws, and establishing the law of his appointment, so the selected one of the rite of the Imam Mālik is the one who is heir to its precious jewels, and even a possessor (*mālik*), which is the high session of the judge Taqī al-Dīn Abū `Alī al-Ḥasan son of the judge Sharaf al-Dīn Abū al-Faḍl `Abd al-Raḥīm son of the shaykh Jalāl al-Dīn Abū Muḥammad `Abdallāh Ibn Shās al-Sa`dī al-Mālikī.

For that purpose we have issued a command by the highest order that he continue to choose well, that taking appropriate lessons would dominate with good, to delegate to him the lecturing at the Manṣūrī Mālikī College according to the rite of Imam Mālik b. Anas, may God be satisfied with him, as knowledge which is sufficient, not fearing what it contains during the sermon, and noble, who no one will look down upon at the sermon delivery, well-grounded, one who inherits the knowledge the blessed ancestors, permitted, which is uniquely meritorious such that no one contests or partakes of it, unique, which is necessary in our opinion

[156] Q9:111.

for the appointment to this august position, and single, who will aid us in accepting the students in the best possible manner.

So let us praise God Most High for the appropriateness He has given specifically, the priority He gave to him, and bestow this grace with thankfulness that exceeds its merit, and be loyal to Him from its shade, positioning him to recite from his blessed rite, and establish its five foundations.

Let him know that teaching just one man from his students is better than all of that upon which the sun rises, and he should make the signs of his rite manifest, clear, and the circumstances of its performance strong, firm, and let him support his opinion, aid his religion, as the Prophet, may the prayer of God and peace be upon him, said "The people are just about beat camels' livers seeking knowledge, but will not find a learned man more knowledgeable than the learned man of Medina."[157]

Let him receive his students with a cheerful face, and a smiling mouth, and let him apportion among them that which will make them forget Ashhab and Ibn al-Qāsim[158] by guiding them and inspiring them, and let him promise them that he will stay with their studies, guide their past, letting him do well their regurgitation of what they have memorized so as they will get their money's worth.

Let him be fair to their elder ones by urging them on, and aid their younger ones by encouraging them to engross themselves, and let him be good and being gentle and friendly with the students, to use repetition, thinking, and senses in teaching them, and let him endeavor that most of the people understand him to be learned, as there should be no better rumor than it be said concerning a doctor or a legal authority (*mufti*) that he was one of Ibn Shās' students—all this pursuant to the stipulations of the endower, may God make his aid glorious, an endower at his lofty order, may God raise his rule, and the noble signature is raised as a proof in accord.

On Saturday 1 Dhū al-Qaʿda [December 29, 1285] of this year the envoy of the ruler of Yemen arrived, accompanied by presents and gifts. He presented himself before al-Malik al-Manṣūr, with gifts including 13 servants for the [horses'] reins, ten stallions, one elephant, one rhinoceros (*karkand*), eight

[157] Al-Tirmidhī, *Sunan* (Beirut: Dār al-Fikr, n.d.), iv, p. 152 (no. 2821), meaning Mālik b. Anas.

[158] Al-Ashhab (d. 204/819) was a well-known Egyptian Mālikī jurist; ʿAbd al-Raḥmān b. al-Qāsim (d. 191/806) was another.

ewes, eight birds, parrots (or nightingales), three pieces [29] of large wood, each piece of which was carried by two men, and 40 Qanā spears, a camel load, and different types of spices (*bahār*) which was carried on 70 camels, fabrics carried in 100 wicker-baskets, and Yemeni valuables, which were borne on 100 copper trays. He received this from him, and bestowed graciously upon his envoys and him [the Yemeni ruler] as usual.

On 6 Dhū al-Ḥijja [February 2, 1286] there was a fire in the protected Hill Citadel, and Sultanic Treasury as well as the Ṣāliḥī (one) were consumed.

During Dhū al-Ḥijja [February 1286] of this year the shaykh Shams al-Dīn Muḥammad son of the shaykh Jamāl al-Dīn Abū Bakr son of Muḥammad al-Fārisī al-Aykī was appointed to be the senior shaykh in the Saʿīd al-Suʿadā (Felicitous of the Felicitous ones) Hospice (*khānqāh*) in protected Cairo after the death of the shaykh Ṣāʾīn al-Dīn Ḥasan al-Bukhārī, and Ibn al-Mukarram, secretary of the noble roll, wrote him an investiture for that. This is a copy:[159]

> Praise be to God who chose a people for friendship for Him love them and they would love Him, choosing them that alone they would call upon Him, so He would answer them, He would summon them, and they would answer Him, they would be at His service, unveiling the veils of heedlessness to their sight and perceptiveness so they would be able to witness Him during the rest of their states, and draw near to Him in companionship. This is while He would draw them to His holy presence, and seat them by remembrance of Him, when they remembered Him, the secret of their spirits, and the spirit of their secrets, and by permitting them to access His secrets, they attained their goal in the unseen, while he caused them to gnostically know, so they lost [themselves]. He then caused them to gnostically know further, so they did not lose themselves, but He caused them to know what they did not know.
>
> We praise Him and thank Him, for he is the Most High, the most worthy to be thanked by the thankful. They praise Him, devote the beautiful praise to Him of which He is deserved in totality and part, both His disapproval and His aid. We ask of His mercy, and that He would increase His grace, we desire His favor, as we see nothing other than Him.
>
> We testify that there is no God but God alone, who has no associate, a testimony connected to devotion, and we testify that Muḥammad is His servant and Messenger, who completed for us His grace, and made us satisfied with Islam, perfecting for us his clear exposition as his religion. May God

---

[159] Compare partial trans. in Hofer, *The Popularisation of Sufism in Ayyubid and Mamluk Egypt* (Edinburgh: Edinburgh University Press, 2015), pp. 46–8.

pray for him and for his pure family and chosen companions, a prayer that would combine between the nobility of their categories, types and arts.

Afterwards, God Most High when he ennobled Muḥammad by making him the seal of the prophets, he bestowed upon His creation, and had mercy upon them by continuing with his friends (*awlīyā'*). Thus when the earth no longer had prophecy or prophetic miracles (*mu`jizāt*), He did not leave it without the noble of His friends, or the blessings of His giving upon His creation, mercy by which He confers mercy upon them, "a firm handle"[160] which they can grasp. This is so that prayers can be answered through them, disasters can be overcome, those seeking connection [with God] can, and by touching their remains, [miraculous] work can be achieved.

Among them are the replacers (*abdāl*), the noble ones, the pegs, the delegates (*nuqabā'*), and the select ones after the gnostics and the Salvation (*ghawth*),[161] who is unique under the heavens. At every time, it is necessary for God, praised and be raised, to choose from His creation one whom he selects for this type of friendship, causing those who are special to draw near to him by his nobility. Through this inspiring from the first matter, turning the beautiful gaze towards Him, and prophetically inspiring them in the best way to Him, teaching [30] with shaykhs and precedence rising, then taking hold of it with the right hand, making it fair with certainty, then having them take the place of the god-fearers.

Ever since God Most High gave us dominion on the earth, and allowed us to rule with reaching out and taking on the flat land possessed of length and breadth, we have taken as an obligation to treat the subjects' sects well. We know that the actions of this world are a loan of righteousness, which will be collected in the hereafter, so we will do well with the loan, thus God will look upon us and give to us, which will be passed on to the other communities, as a good weal and root to the master of the sword and the pen, of knowledge and flag, in which we specialize, towards the people of Islam and grace, by the nobility of our treatment of the rest of creation.

So let us bind the emirs of the flags and delegate to the learned of the laws, appointing knowledgeable ones, heightening the toilers' levels, and raising the jurisprudents, while giving prominence to the poor (Sufis), giving to each one his due, and fulfilling each obligation to the one obligated.

---

160 Q2:256.

161 All of these are ranks in the Sufi hierarchy.

Since the blessed group of majestic, great, righteous, pious, god-fearing, good shaykhs, who are the friends, the choice, the select of the wool (*ṣūfa*), may God benefit them, who are the company of lights, the troops of the morn, lords of traces, people of preference, inhabitants of loyalty, and brethren of purity. They are the ones who know the portion of the night, masters of the footsteps in which horses are unable to follow, especially as on their faces is the sign of prostration,[162] while their foreheads are lit with the sign of praying at night.

They are the guests of God, who are dedicated to Him, having trust in His generosity, so he tosses their purses to their sagacious ones (?),[163] as they have depended upon Him, having no profession, nor do they possess goods. Their trade is their prostration, their way station is tears, their principal is water and the prayer-niche, their profit is their knowledge, in that earth which is above this earth is preferable.

Even if they are impoverished, and they spread their good works generally, they never deviate with that from the masses to the elites; concentrating upon the devotions, and the larger number, while judging themselves according to their words hour by hour.

Whoever has a shaykh, an example, and an imam who continues to direct their affairs, they will seek to emulate him evening and morning. When they finish their spiritual exercises they will be guided by him to his solitude, when he bestows words concerning the truth and the way, they tend towards his words, when he supplicates to his Lord for salvation, they join with him in his supplication, and when he prays for victory for us over God's enemies and our enemies, we feel secure because of his prayers.

In accord, the noble good opinion is that a shaykh from among them should manage the affairs of their shaykhs, that the one who rises from amongst them should be given precedence to consider their interests, to choose for them the one who is appropriate, the one who when his sign and radiance are seen, it is said "This is the best one!" One who when he is seen among the ranks energetically, his opinion when it is known is not ignorant, one whose asceticism and merit is received from al-Fuḍayl b. `Iyyāḍ,[164] one who when Abū Yazīd [al-Bistamī][165] is mentioned in his session [31], while his righteous actions say "Is there one who can exceed (this)?"

---

[162] The black mark on the forehead which signifies frequent prayer.

[163] The editor notes that this is unvocalized, and offers this as a possibility.

[164] A prominent early `Abbāsid era ascetic warrior.

[165] One of the best-known early Sufis from the `Abbāsid period.

So choose for them one who is in accord with that choice, one whose preferability is correct, one who there is no need to inform him, one when he says "He said that the best saying and related tradition …" and then praises his listener by his knowledge of what he says, rendering his opinion with regard to Sufi teachings and the Law. One who discusses both the bases as well as the branches [of the law], the one who by his exegesis, and his mystical exegesis researches, and reveals the secrets of revelation, speaking with *The Revival of the Religious Sciences*,[166] obtains absolute certainty from it via *The Food of Hearts*,[167] and takes it as an example in jurisprudence and godliness.

He teaches from it what the Chosen One [Muḥammad] laid down religiously, and what he mandated [legally], which is the session of the exalted shaykh Shams al-Dīn, head shaykh of the Sufis. He is inspector over them, and over all of the charitable endowments in al-Ṣalāḥiyya Hospice that is known as The House of Sa`īd al-Su`adā, together with al-Fayyūm Hospice and al-Mashṭūb Hospice in al-Qarāfa, as is usual with those who preceded him.

Placement of his seat is for something in his quarter, and for the good of his family, as well as to gather all of this blessed group, and definitely that appointing him is a personal obligation (*farḍ `ayn*), which does not allow for being deputized, nor to be conjoined, and in assent to what he requested.

All of the majestic number of shaykhs of the wool desired for him, may God benefit them, in that the head shaykhdom should be delegated to him, and the inspection into the matters of the Sufi order, and the hospice charitable endowments. They are satisfied with his administration, his looking over them in the aforementioned manners, and that he would be a shaykh over them.

So let shaykh Shams al-Dīn arise, may God Most High guard him, unroll his prayer-carpet in a place [appropriate] for the likes of him, without hearing a word of opposition behind his back, nor the like because of his merit, and sit in the place in which the head shaykh sits, taking up this august position in which everyone emulates and imitates him, and (his) many injunctions.[168] This is in spite of the fact that they are mandated for others, as he, may God make him mighty, is not in need of them because of the level he has attained in his religion and it's good.

---

166 The great work of al-Ghazālī on Sufism.
167 The work of Abū Ṭālib al-Makkī.
168 Following the editor's suggestion.

So let him treat the all the other shaykhs with kindness, removing the onerous burdens, with friendliness, and let him know that he is head of the Sufi order. Let them follow his Sufi ethics, as he is the one who has realized them by his knowledge that they are precisely those who he needs to reckon, and God forbid that they would not be in need of forbearance.

So let him be gentle with them as long as possible, bringing their hearts by his extra deeds and gifts, and let him treat them affectionately as much in a day as he would others during a full year. Let his heart be a companion to them, for "we exclude gentleness if it detracts from those around,"[169] and let him be assiduous in looking over the affairs of the (charitably) endowed locations from this perspective, to fix what he can, and to renovate what times has destroyed, to shepherd them in the necessary manner. He should build up that which has fallen down, or call attention to it, until its construction starts up again, and its freshness returns to it. He should purify its revenue, and have its abode friendly, while they purify [32] its drink, making its barren land verdant, while they level its heights, so its valleys can flow over obstacles, mending those affairs that have passed.

Let him attain the extra in that which has [...] and position himself to harvest its produce of trustworthy people, and to assign equals for taking it out, and let him spend all of this in accounts following this advice, may God be pleased with him, and the conditions of his (charitable) endower. Let him consider the interests of the Sufi shaykhs, may God benefit them, and what the endowers have stipulated, may God have mercy upon them: food, drink, sweets, clothing, all what they desire, and what souls thirst for, what they might stipulate for them during the days to come, so him establish for them in the aggregate, the months, and the years. Let him bear them forward according to the intention of those who endowed it upon them, and make him one of the charitable in delivering this as a token of respect to them. Let him also be one of those in charge who does well, and acts well, so that the multitude will be happy in the way they are going until they would say, "If only this was numbered as a good deed from us!"

This is with God's praise, the best, and the noble signature is the proof in accord.

[*Obituaries*]

[169] Most probably a Sufi dictum.

Mention of events during the year 685 [1286]

During this year the emir ʿAlam al-Dīn Sanjar al-Dawādārī was returned to the supervision of protected Damascus in place of the emir Shams al-Dīn Sunqur *al-aʿsar* (the left-handed). He commenced working in the chancellery on the morning of Wednesday, 15 Muḥarram [March 13, 1286] of that year.

Mention of the emir Ḥusām al-Dīn Ṭurunṭāy's traveling to Kerak, his taking over it, and the traveling of its ruler, al-Malik al-Masʿūd and his brother Salāmish to Egypt and their dwelling it in

Al-Malik al-Manṣūr Sayf al-Dīn Qalāwūn al-Alfī al-Ṣāliḥī al-Najmī dispatched the emir Ḥusām al-Dīn Ṭurunṭāy al-Manṣūrī, the overlord deputy sultan in the Egyptian homelands, with a large troop from the Egyptian homelands' armies, and commanded him to camp against Kerak and besiege it. So he departed leading the victorious armies on Thursday 2 Muḥarram [February 28, 1286], and traveled on Saturday, the 4th.

He proceeded to Kerak, and the emir Ḥusām al-Dīn Lājīn al-Manṣūrī, the overlord deputy sultan in protected Damascus, dispatched the emir Badr al-Dīn al-Ṣawābī, together with 2000 horse from the Syrian armies to Kerak. The emir Ḥusām al-Dīn Ṭurunṭāy met up with the emir Badr al-Dīn, and they joined forces against Kerak. The emir Ḥusām al-Dīn Ṭurunṭāy had brought siege implements from the Islamic fortresses, and tightened the siege around Kerak, cutting the provisions from it.

The emirs Badr al-Dīn and Ḥusām al-Dīn continued to send back and forth to the supporters of al-Malik al-Masʿūd Najm al-Dīn Khiḍr son of al-Malik al-Ẓāhir Rukn al-Dīn Baybars al-Bunduqdārī al-Ṣāliḥī al-Najmī, the ruler of Kerak, and to make promises to them, until most of them had soured towards the latter.

Then the emir Ḥusām al-Dīn summoned some of the men of Kerak, treating them well, so they joined him against al-Malik al-Masʿūd. When al-Malik al-Masʿūd and his brother al-Malik Badr al-Dīn Salāmish perceived the situation [36] they agreed to hand over Kerak.

Then al-Malik al-Masʿūd sent to the emir Ḥusām al-Dīn Ṭurunṭāy to request a safe-conduct, so he gave him safety from the Sultan al-Malik al-Manṣūr. However, he said, "It is necessary to obtain the Sultan's safe-conduct, and his seal-ring." Therefore, the emir Ḥusām al-Dīn revealed this to the Sultan, whereupon the Sultan sent his safe-conduct, together with the emir Rukn al-Dīn Baybars *al-dawādār* al-Manṣūrī.

He met with al-Malik al-Masʿūd, the ruler of Kerak, and Badr al-Dīn Salāmish, presenting the both of them with the Sultan's safe-conduct, so they descended from Kerak castle to the emir Ḥusām al-Dīn Ṭurunṭāy. This was on Tuesday 5 Ṣafar [April 2, 1286] of this year.

Therefore, the emir Ḥusām al-Dīn Ṭurunṭāy assigned the emir ʿIzz al-Dīn Aybak al-Mawṣilī al-Manṣūrī as the deputy sultan in Kerak. He had been the deputy sultan in Shawbak from the time that it was taken from al-Malik al-Saʿīd son of al-Malik al-Ẓāhir Rukn al-Dīn Baybars. The bearers of tidings about the conquest of Kerak arrived at the sultanic gates at the Hill Citadel in protected Egypt on Friday 8 Ṣafar [April 5, 1286].

Letters from the emir Ḥusām al-Dīn Ṭurunṭāy followed one after the other from when he had been sent to Kerak until the time of its conquest to the Sultan al-Malik al-Manṣūr in protected Egypt. The judge Fatḥ al-Dīn Ibn ʿAbd al-Ẓāhir was appointed to answer them in his own hand. Among the beginnings of the invocations that he wrote to him in his answers and correspondence [are the following]:

> By his sword the most difficult fortresses were conquered by the king, while the spearheads bear fruit with His aid that is more beautiful than that which tender branches put forth. By his determination he guarded Islam in every way, and every guarded place he permitted the vanguard to attack.

From the beginning of the letter he wrote to him, after a number had fled from prison, he wrote to him because of that, and thus every runaway was returned, every rebel was destroyed, while awe of him was impressed upon all who fled as the anger of this dominating state, whether going or returning, and the scope of breathing, so they could not pitch a tent on the earth, so they had to pitch with fetters of chains, using cold iron.

From the beginning of the letter,

> His felicity continues to manifest things hidden, and bring hidden treasures into the open, and it necessitates thanks upon the tongues as long as he has the right disposition, nobility of attainment, and generosity of gift giving. Actions proceeding from his conquering sword set the friends of God apart in nobility of wishes, while the enemies have despicable fates.
>
> Among words there are those that are free from ill omen, hopes of the pure they set out, while the eyes watch over their advance the way a family watches over [a child]. Hearts overflow with its straightforwardness just as the disaster-bearing Pleiades overflow onto the rain-bearing astrals (*anwāʾ*), while the days are counted until the day of its arrival, which is counted as a festival day, and then the scope of its proximity closes in.
>
> If it closes in, then it is distant in terms of desires, and desirous of God, praise and raise Him, in that He encompass him with peace just as He encompassed him with victory, conquering at his hands every refuge at which he arrived in the quickest [37] possible manner.

The emir Ḥusām al-Dīn Ṭuruntāy, al-Malik al-Mas`ūd, ruler of Kerak, and Badr al-Dīn Salāmish, the two sons of al-Malik al-Ẓāhir, traveled together with all who were in Kerak, families, children and the extended Ẓāhirī family. This is what al-Malik al-Ẓāhir had done with the family of al-Malik al-Mughīth, the ruler of Kerak and his family, so may God Most High recompense him with regard to his descendants.

The emir Ḥusām al-Dīn Ṭuruntāy and those who were with him arrived in the Egyptian homelands, and when they were close to the Hill Citadel al-Malik al-Manṣūr rode out to welcome al-Malik al-Mas`ūd and Badr al-Dīn Salāmish, and advanced towards them.

This was on 12 Rabī` al-Awwal [May 8, 1286] of that year, and they both ascended to the Citadel, while he assigned to them both an emirate of 100. They continued to ride together with him in the procession and the square, and he domiciled them together with his own children. Then he heard about things of which he disapproved, so detained the both of them, imprisoned them, and they remained in prison until the days of al-Malik al-Ashraf Ṣalāḥ al-Dīn Khalīl son of al-Malik al-Manṣūr, who sent the both of them to Constantinople, just as we will mention, if God Most High wishes.

Mention of a strange occurrence that happened in Ḥimṣ during this year

On 17 Ṣafar [April 14, 1286] of this year a letter arrived to the emir Ḥusām al-Dīn Lājīn al-Manṣūrī, the deputy sultan in protected Damascus, from the emir Badr al-Dīn Baktūt al-`Alā'ī, who was seconded to Ḥimṣ, accompanied by part of the Damascene army, 2000 horse, from the beginning of this year.

Its contents were, after the *basmala* that he kisses the ground, and finished off by when it was Thursday 14 Ṣafar [April 11, 1286] at the time of the afternoon prayers in al-`Asūla towards `Uyūn al-Qaṣab there was an intensely black cloud, thundering excessively. From the cloud there appeared the likeness of black smoke from the heavens reaching the earth. The form of the cloud was a frightening one, the size of a large column too large for men to embrace.

It was connected to the clouds of the heavens, touching with its tail, then reaching the earth like a frightening tornado (*zaw`ba*), carrying with it rocks of great size, lifting them into the air like shooting arrows and more. Their falling and the crashing of the rocks against each other gave off a fearful sound reaching far places, and this continued in its strength, reaching the victorious army's outskirts. Nothing was encountered but {had been lifted to the air like shooting arrows, and more}[170] and all saddles, [38] armor, provisions, swords,

[170] Although the editor does not note it, this phrase is an exact duplicate of one several lines previously, and appears out of place here. Perhaps a scribal repeat?

mail, arrows, shields, bows, fabrics, muslin (*shāshāt*), scarves (*kulūtāt*), copper or brass kettles (*asṭāl*) encountered had flown into the air just like a bird.

Among all of that there was in Royal Stable, a skin filled with veterinarian horseshoes went out, carried in the air, and atmosphere, just like shooting arrows, and of the total, provisions in their entirety were lifted off the camels for the distance of a spear-throw and more. A number of the army and the youths were also carried and many of the saddles that encountered it were destroyed, as well as the spears.

It ground this area until there was nothing beneficial left, and destroyed a great deal of what it came across on its path, so much of the provisions and the clothes were lost to approximately 200 of the army, and the followers of the emirs, until they had to go without provisions, or clothes.

This snake was concealed from the eye in the sky's clouds, so it headed towards the dry lands from the east. The one from the army who lost his clothes, could only rest under a black cloud. Among them there were those who some of the army took (their things). This occurred even though there was a mamluk who rode by himself and circulated through the victorious army, questioning most people as to what they had lost, and afterwards stated what was previously cited [as to the totals].

This event was unheard of previously, then a rain occurred a short while later, then larger felt tents (*alawāchīq*) were carried away by the wind, even though they were lashed down, but came to be transported in the atmosphere, and God is sufficient for us, and what a Guardian!

Al-Malik al-Manṣūr removed the chief Muḥyī al-Dīn Ibn al-Naḥḥās from the ministry of protected Damascus, and reinstated the chief Taqī al-Dīn Tawba al-Tikriṭī to the ministry in his place. He traveled from the Egyptian homelands to protected Damascus, then arrived in it at the end of Rabī` al-Ākhir [June 24, 1286] of this year. On 2 Jumādā al-Ulā [June 26, 1286] of this year al-Malik al-Manṣūr released the emir Shams al-Dīn Quṭlījā, brother of al-Rūmī.

During this year al-Malik al-Manṣūr issued a decree to destroy the Ẓāhirī cupola in the Hill Citadel by the courtyard, so the initiative to start destroying it began on Sunday 10 Rajab [September 1, 1286] of this year. He ordered the building of a cupola in its place, so it was constructed, and finished in Shawwal [November–December 1286] of this year.

Mention of al-Malik al-Manṣūr's heading to Kerak, and the arrangements he made there

On Thursday 7 Rajab [August 29, 1286] of this year al-Malik al-Manṣūr headed to Gaza, then headed as part of a dispatch unit from it to Kerak, which arrived there in Sha`bān [September 1286] of this year. He ascended to its castle, and arranged its affairs, issuing a command to clean its pool that was filled with clay. Everyone who was there worked in the service of the

Sultan, including mamluks, and the retinue, for a period of seven days, so it was cleaned.

Al-Malik al-Manṣūr asked the emir Rukn al-Dīn Baybars *al-dawādār* al-Manṣūrī to serve as deputy in it. He transferred the emir `Izz al-Dīn Aybak al-Mawṣilī al-Manṣūrī from Kerak to the deputy sultanate in Gaza, and the command of the army there. However, he did not stay long as he was transferred to the deputyship in Safed castle. [39]

On Thursday the 21st [October 12, 1286] the blessed Nile increased two fingers, for a total of two fingers short of 18 cubits, which was the extent of its inundation. Ibn al-Mukarram, the secretary of the noble roll, said on Thursday 18 Ramaḍān [November 5, 1286] of this year which was 11 Hatūr year 1000, the first of the blessed year, 55 according to the sun, may God make its opening and closing good.

Al-Malik al-Manṣūr returned from Kerak, and camped in the Arsūf thicket, staying in it until winter began, being certain of the enemy's movement,[171] and then returning to the Egyptian homelands. His arrival at the Hill Citadel in protected Egypt was on Monday 14 Shawwāl [December 3, 1286] of that year.

During Shawwāl [November–December 1286] al-Malik al-Manṣūr released the emir Badr al-Dīn Baktūt al-Shamsī and the emir Jamāl al-Dīn Aqush al-Fārisī. After the death of the Chief Judge Wajīh al-Dīn al-Bahnasī al-Shāfi`ī for Old Cairo and Upper Egypt {al-Malik al-Manṣūr Sayf al-Dīn Qalāwūn delegated the chief judiciary in Old Cairo and Upper Egypt too}[172] to the Chief Judge Taqī al-Dīn `Abd al-Raḥmān Ibn bint (son of the daughter of) al-A`zz on Wednesday 15 Jumādā al-Awwal [July 9, 1286] of this year.

The Chief Judge in protected Cairo and Lower Egypt was Shihāb al-Dīn al-Khū'ī. After the death of Chief Judge Taqī al-Dīn Ibn Shās al-Judhāmī al-Sa`dī al-Mālikī in the Egyptian homelands, just as is mentioned in his biography, al-Malik al-Manṣūr delegated the chief judiciary according to Imam Mālik b. Anas' rite, may God be pleased with him, to the Chief Judge Zayn al-Dīn Abū al-Ḥasan `Alī son of shaykh Raḍī al-Dīn Abū al-Qāsim Makhlūf son of the shaykh Tāj al-Dīn Abū al-Ma`ālī Nāhiḍ al-Nuwayrī the jurisprudent according to the Mālikī rite, who was at that time Inspector of the Sultanic Treasury.

This was the beginning of the ascent of Chief Judge Zayn al-Dīn Ibn Makhlūf, as he was in charge of al-`Azīz court trust in protected Cairo, when al-Malik al-Manṣūr Sayf al-Dīn Qalāwūn, at the time he was appointed an emir, bought from him the inheritance of one of the emirs—provisions in their totality, which had been intended for orphans. Therefore, the judge Zayn al-Dīn sought him out for the money, so it could be endowed by him, and he intended to return that which he had bought. He talked about that with

[171] That the Mongols would not invade that year.

[172] Addition from the margins according to the editor, which completes the sense.

the judge Zayn al-Dīn, but was prevented from returning it, so the situation ended up that the judge Zayn al-Dīn complained about Qalāwūn to al-Malik al-Nāṣir [sic! = al-Ẓāhir] Rukn al-Dīn Baybars.

Qalāwūn was compelled to produce the sum to be paid, so this remained on Qalāwūn's mind. When he began to rule, the judge Zayn al-Dīn benefited from that very much with al-Malik al-Manṣūr, and he assigned him to the Sultanic Treasury, trusting him, and giving him an incredible amount of authority. Then he delegated the Mālikī chief judiciary in the Egyptian homelands to him, and confirmed him at the Treasury during Dhū [40] al-Qa`da [January–February 1287] of this year, and it is said that his appointment to the Mālikī chief judiciary was during Dhū al-Ḥijja [February 1287] of this year.

During Dhū al-Ḥijja the emir `Alam al-Dīn Sanjar al-Ḥamawī Abū Khurṣ received an investiture to the deputy sultanate in protected Ḥamāh, and the judge Muḥyī al-Dīn Ibn `Abd al-Ẓāhir wrote it for him.

[*Obituaries*]

Mention of the events during the year 686 [1287]

When the report of the death of Chief Judge Bahā' al-Dīn Yūsuf son of Chief Judge Muḥyī al-Dīn Abū al-Faḍl Yaḥyā al-`Uthmānī al-Umawī, known as Ibn al-Zakī, Shāfi`ī Chief Judge in protected Damascus reached al-Malik al-Manṣūr Sayf al-Dīn Qalāwūn al-Alfī al-Ṣāliḥī al-Najmī, ruler of the Egyptian homelands and the Syrian lands, during the previous year as we explained, he issued a command appointing a judge for Damascus. He appointed Chief Judge Shihāb al-Dīn al-Khū'ī, judge for Cairo and Lower Egypt for that, with his deputy in the eastern side judge Sharaf al-Dīn Muḥammad b. `Atīq, and so had him present himself for that purpose.

Chief Judge Taqī al-Dīn Ibn bint al-A`zz hastened to transfer Chief Judge Shihāb al-Dīn al-Khū'ī, so he would be alone in the Cairo judiciary, Lower Egypt, Old Cairo, and Upper Egypt, so this gained him control over both sides.

This was because Chief Judge Shihāb al-Dīn al-Khū'ī on Sunday 15 Muḥarram [March 2, 1287] of this year ascended to the Hill Citadel accompanied by the judge Sharaf al-Dīn Ibn `Atīq, who had appointed him to the Syrian judiciary. Chief Judge Taqī al-Dīn son of the daughter of al-A`zz also attended this council, so the Sultan sought out Chief Judge Burhān al-Dīn al-Khiḍr al-Sinjārī, the jurisprudent, to bestow a robe upon him, and delegated to him the Cairo judiciary and that of Upper Egypt in place of Chief Judge Shihāb al-Dīn al-Khū'ī. He transferred Chief Judge Shihāb al-Dīn al-Khū'ī to the Shāfi`ī chief judiciary in protected Damascus, so he headed there from protected Cairo on 13 Ṣafar [March 30, 1287] of this year, arriving there on Monday 13 Rabī` al-Awwal [April 28, 1287] of this year. That very day he sat to render judgment in al-`Ādiliyya. This was with regard to the matter of Chief Judge Shihāb al-Dīn al-Khū'ī.

As for [49] what was with Chief Judge Burhān al-Dīn al-Sinjārī, he, when the Sultan al-Malik al-Manṣūr bestowed a robe upon him, and delegated the Shāfi`ī chief judiciary in protected Cairo and Upper Egypt to him, just as we previously explained, he sat for judgment in the Manṣūriyya College in protected Cairo, and then moved for sitting to the Justice House opposite Chief Judge Taqī al-Dīn Ibn bint al-A`zz.

However, he suffered for it, and regretted his haste in transferring Chief Judge Shihāb al-Dīn al-Khū'ī to Syria, and tried to appear more in the Justice House. While this was happening the Chief Judge Burhān al-Dīn al-Sinjārī died on 9 Ṣafar [March 26, 1287] of this year, just as is mentioned in his biography. The duration of his appointment to the judiciary was a total of 24 days.

When the Chief Judge Burhān al-Dīn died, the Sultan al-Malik al-Manṣūr delegated the Cairo and Upper Egypt judiciary to Chief Judge Taqī al-Dīn `Abd al-Raḥmān son of the Chief Judge Tāj al-Dīn `Abd al-Wahhāb Ibn bint al-A`zz. Thus, the judiciary of the two cities and the two regions was conjoined, and a robe was bestowed upon him. It was said that he prayed over Chief Judge Burhān al-Dīn al-Sinjārī, while he had the judiciary robe upon him, and praise to the One who does what He wills.

Mention of the emir Ḥusām al-Dīn Ṭurunṭāy's going from Egypt, his taking Ṣahyūn, and Sunqur *al-ashqar*'s return to obedience

When al-Malik al-Manṣūr Sayf al-Dīn Qalāwūn besieged Marqab during the year 684 just as we previously explained, in spite of the fact that Marqab is close to Ṣahyūn the emir Shams al-Dīn Sunqur *al-ashqar* did not present himself to the service of al-Malik al-Manṣūr.

This grated upon him, and he was angered at him as a result, so the emir Shams al-Dīn Sunqur *al-ashqar* sent his son Nāṣir al-Dīn Ṣumghār to the service of the Sultan al-Malik al-Manṣūr, to meet together. However, the Sultan forbade him from returning to his father, and took him to the Egyptian homelands, and continued on until the year [6]86, this year.

The Sultan dispatched his deputy in the Egyptian homelands, Ḥusām al-Dīn Ṭurunṭāy to Ṣahyūn leading a great number of the armies. He camped there, and corresponded with him to hand it over. He reminded him of the Sultan al-Malik al-Manṣūr's promises to him, but he refused that. Then he [Ṭurunṭāy] tightened the cordon around him, placing mangonels, until they were about to take Ṣahyūn fortress by force.

When the emir Shams al-Dīn Sunqur *al-ashqar* saw that he sent asking for a safe conduct, and oaths, so the emir Ḥusām al-Dīn Ṭurunṭāy swore to him that the Sultan would not conceive any evil against him. Then he descended to the emir Ḥusām al-Dīn Ṭurunṭāy, and handed the fortress over to him.

One who described that he witnessed his descent, and how each of them treated the other, told that when the emir Ḥusām al-Dīn was seated in his camp, all of a sudden it was said to him "Here, the emir Shams al-Dīn has come!" so he leaped up, and walked quickly, going out to greet him. The emir Shams al-Dīn alighted, and the emir Ḥusām al-Dīn threw a cloak (*qabā'*) he was wearing down, and extended it to the ground, so that the emir Shams al-Dīn could walk upon it. [50] But the emir Shams al-Dīn lifted it from the ground, kissed it, and wore it, so the emir Ḥusām al-Dīn Ṭurunṭāy was amazed at that.

He treated the emir Shams al-Dīn in the most servile and best possible manner, and assigned a deputy and a governor as well as men to the fortress. He and the emir Shams al-Dīn went to the Egyptian homelands, and when they were close to the Hill Citadel al-Malik al-Manṣūr, and his two sons, al-Malik al-Ṣāliḥ `Alā' al-Dīn `Alī, and al-Malik al-Ashraf Ṣalāḥ al-Dīn Khalīl, rode together with the sons of al-Malik al-Ẓāhir, and the armies.

The Sultan greeted the emir Shams al-Dīn, and they hugged, both ascending to the Hill Citadel. The Sultan brought robes, fabrics and gold ewers, and gifts, leading horses to him, and made him emir of 100, and a command over 1000. He continued in the sultanic service among the senior state emirs, and then there were reports of him that we will mention in their place, if God Most High wishes.

Mention of al-Malik al-Manṣūr heading to Syria

On Sunday 27 Rajab [September 7, 1287] of this year the Sultan al-Malik al-Manṣūr Sayf al-Dīn Qalāwūn departed from the Hill Citadel, and headed to Syria. He arrived in protected Gaza and stayed at Tell al-`Ajūl.

On Thursday 22 Sha`bān [October 2, 1287] of this year a rise in the blessed Nile of two fingers was proclaimed, which completed 23 fingers, plus 18 cubits. This was the end of the inundation for this year.

Nāṣir al-Dīn Muḥammad son of the shaykh `Abd al-Raḥman al-Maqdisī arrived at the sultanic gates from protected Damascus to complain about the Chief Judge Bahā' al-Dīn Ibn al-Zakī, the judge of Damascus, concerning various matters. Then the death of the aforementioned Chief Judge was confirmed just as we previously explained. So what he had intended was cancelled, and he turned away from it.

He met with the emir `Alam al-Dīn Sanjar al-Shujā`ī, the minister of state for the Egyptian homelands, and discussed with him the matter of the daughter of al-Malik al-Ashraf Mūsā son of al-Malik al-`Ādil Sayf al-Dīn Abū Bakr Muḥammad, son of the father of kings Najm al-Dīn Ayyūb b. Shādī b. Marwān, and that she had sold her properties in protected Damascus, but that at the time of sale she was incapable.

Her paternal uncle al-Malik al-Ṣāliḥ `Imād al-Dīn Isma`īl interceded on her behalf,[173] and demanded the return of the properties she had sold, and that

[173] Northrup, pp. 138–9 details this incident.

whatever profits accrued during the interval should be handed over to him. These properties should be purchased for the sultanic private lands (*al-khāṣṣ al-sulṭānī*), so he assented to that, and he wrote seeking Sayf al-Dīn Aḥmad al-Sāmarrī from Damascus, as he was the one who bought Ḥarzamā from her.[174]

He appeared during the month of Ramaḍān [mid-Oct-mid-November] of that year, while the Sultan al-Malik al-Manṣūr was at that time in protected Gaza, so he transported him to the Egyptian homelands. There it was demanded that he sell Ḥarzamā, but he claimed that he had endowed is a charity some time previously, so at that a legal record (*maḥḍar*) was drawn up containing [51] that the daughter of al-Malik al-Ashraf had been incapable during such-and-such a period, and that was the time of selling, and her youth continued until such-and-such a date.

Then it was all straightened out, and the interdict on her behalf was lifted on such-and-such a date, according to clear evidence, which was notarized, and established by one of the chief judges in the Egyptian homelands. When it was established, against the interest of Sayf al-Dīn al-Sāmarrī, the sale was nullified from the very beginning. Then what profits had accrued during the interval were sought for a period of 20 years, which were 210,000 dirhams, after a calculation was equivalent to the price which he paid, so he bought 17 shares of the village of al-Zanbaqiyya[175] from him at the price of 70,000 dirhams, and transported 1,040,000 dirhams. Al-Malik al-Manṣūr then delegated his trusteeship to Nāṣir al-Dīn Ibn al-Maqdisī, and ruled to the detriment of the Damascenes and their notables, just as we will mention, if God Most High wishes.

The Feast of the Breaking [after Ramaḍān] occurred this year on Sunday [November 9, 1287] without seeing the crescent moon, and it was only established with al-Malik al-Ṣāliḥ `Alā' al-Dīn `Alī son of al-Malik al-Manṣūr that his father the Sultan al-Malik al-Manṣūr fasted the month of Ramaḍān from the beginning of Friday by sight [of the moon]. Then this was established by the Mālikīs, and the Feast began on blessed Sunday. Many of the people withheld, and did not break their fast until Monday.

Al-Malik al-Manṣūr then returned from Tell `Ajūl to the Egyptian homelands, and arrived at the Hill Citadel on Monday 23 Shawwāl [December 1, 1287] of this year.

The types[176] [of fabrics] with which the envoys were commanded to travel to Ber Berke were pieces of Alexandrine white cloth with fine embroidery for families/or with a generous cut (*`awwāl*), 200 of them, including gold embroidery honorifics of the sultan, 100 pieces. Among them were silk embroidery

---

[174] Yāqūt, *Mu`jam*, ii, 240 between Mārdīn and Dunyasar.

[175] On the way to Ḥimṣ, where Qalāwūn had camped before the Battle of Ḥimṣ.

[176] This section opens a bit abruptly and appears to be an unconnected fragment.

honorifics as well. The breadth of the embroidery was four fingers, containing 100 pieces, waved-silk (*'uttābī*) pieces, of one color, and those which were similar to one color, the dyeing of which was the work of the house, with gold embroidery honorifics of the sultan 150 pieces, Alexandrine worked pieces its facing side [?][177] white with gold embroidery, and silk embroidery with the honorifics as usual, 100 pieces, Damiettan cheap (*wa-khush*) worked pieces as well, white straps[178] with gold embroidery and silk embroidery, 100 pieces white high sugar, and plants according to what was arranged at the packing, drugs, according to the usual, with extras sent along for the mosque which is being constructed at Qarm, and types of goods, the value of which was 2000 dinars.

Honorifics of the Sultan al-Malik al-Manṣūr were to be written on the mosque, and a fellow, a stonecutter, engraver who would engrave the sultanic honorifics upon the aforementioned mosque would be sent along. Dyes were sent with them for varnishing.

Duplicate of a letter arriving from Medina, which is awe-inspiring for the one who dwells there, our lord and prophet Muḥammad, Messenger of God, the best of prayers and peace [be upon him]. Its content:

> When it was the night of 4 Muḥarram year 686 [February 19, 1287] a fierce rain hit Medina [52] with many floods, and the noble Sanctuary took in, due to this, serious damage. Most of its flat roofs were covered with water, but the worst was the north roof. The rain ran right through the sanctuary and the noble inner sanctum (*ḥujra*),[179] and the water poured into its interior from the cupola openings that are underneath the lead.
>
> There is nothing other than wood under the lead, no plaster or anything else, so the water came through the lead into the wood, and inundated the interior of the sanctum and the cupola up to the height of two rods. Whenever the water touched them, now there is fear that tree-worms will devour them.
>
> This rain harmed people by destroying many houses, plus many palm trees died from the floods that took them, rising to places never previously seen, Salty earth flowed[180] up under the palm trees, so because of that some died, while those which lived fell stunted. Then God sent locust like a cloud, and with it a loud noise like the thunder, so they stayed part

[177] Editor leaving this unpointed *r/z-j/ḥ/kh-s d/dh-w-b/t/n/y-h*, which may be a corruption of the Farsi *rukhsārah.*

[178] Editor leaving this unpointed *d/dh-w-b/t/n/y-a/l-b*, which I am reading as the Farsi *dū bāl.*

[179] Which had been Muḥammad's residence.

[180] Following the editor's proposed reading.

of the night in Medina, then consumed the dates, the palm-boughs, and the green branches.[181]

The outskirts of Medina were verdant, but they consumed the grazing areas, while the rain ruined the running springs and the Blue Spring as well,[182] by which the inhabitants of Medina live, in addition to those who come to it. All of its branch feeders have been destroyed or turned brackish, bitter.

It mentioned that usually the prophetic noble sanctum during the time of the Rightly-guided Caliphs had been covered just once with a covering, until another caliph had been appointed. This included everything other than the pulpit and the garden, as they had been given new coverings each year, without their coverings coming apart. It mentioned that the pulpit and the garden now were in need of a new covering. The date of the letter was during the last tenth of Jumādā al-Ulā year [6]86 [early July 1287] of this year, and God knows best.

Mention of the first raid into Nubia[183]

Al-Malik al-Manṣūr Sayf al-Dīn Qalāwūn, ruler of the Egyptian homelands and the Syrian lands, prepared the emir `Alam al-Dīn Sanjar al-Masrūrī, known as *al-khayyāṭ* (the tailor), who was the appointed governor for protected Cairo, and the emir `Izz al-Dīn al-Kūrānī, and ordered them to go to the land of the Nubians.

So the both of them set out from the sultanic gates in the Egyptian homelands on Monday 6 Dhū al-Ḥijja of the year [6]86 [January 12, 1288] this year. He dispatched a number of the local garrisons from Upper Egypt, and the road guard (*qarāghulāmiyya*), and dispatched the emir `Izz al-Dīn Aydimur al-Sayfī *al-silāḥdār*, who was appointed governor over the Qūṣan districts with his provisions, in addition to the royal mamluks stationed in the Qūṣan districts, the local troops in Qūṣ, and the Bedouin of that region. These are the Awlād Abī Bakr, the Awlād `Umar, the Awlād Sharīf, the Awlād Shaybān, the Awlād al-Kanz, a number of the Bedouin of al-Barlisiyya, and the Banū Hilāl.[184]

---

[181] Ibn al-Mujāwir, *Mustabṣir* (ed. Oscar Lefevrin, Beirut: Manshūrāt al-Madīna, 1986 [reprint]), pp. 257–8 describes a similar locust attack in Medina from this period.

[182] Al-`Ayn al-Azraq, the major spring of Medina, see al-Samhūdī, *Wafā' al-wafā'* (Mecca: Dār al-Kutub al-`Ilmiyya, 1984), iii, p. 985.

[183] Compare Vantini, *Oriental Sources concerning Nubia* (Heidelberg and Warsaw: Polish Academy of Sciences, 1975), pp. 540–2.

[184] Most of these tribes are listed in al-Maqrīzī's treatise on Arab tribes in Egypt, in *Rasā'il* (Eds. Ramaḍān al-Badrī and Aḥmad Muṣṭafā Qāsim, Cairo: Dār al-Ḥadīth, 2006), pp. 134–5, 138; see Sarah Büssow-Schmitz, *Die Beduinen der Mamluken: Beduinen im politischen Leben Agyptens im 8./14. Jahrhundert* (Wiesbaden: Reichert Verlag, 2016), pp. 45–9 for a slightly later period.

The emir `Alam al-Dīn *al-khayyāṭ* headed out leading half of the army on the west bank [of the Nile], while the emir [53] `Izz al-Dīn Aydimur headed out leading the second half on the east bank. This is the bank on which the city of Dongola is located.

The would-be king of Nubia at that time was named Simāmūn, and he was cunning, devious, and bold when compared to his fellows. So when the army arrived at the outskirts of the lands, Simāmūn vacated the lands, and sent to his deputy on the Michael Islands. These were ruled by a duke, who was named Jurays. The one who ruled this state in the eyes of the Nubians was called Master of the Horse. He then ordered the lands controlled by him in front of the army to be vacated, so they would journey from stop to stop in front of the army until they finally reached the would-be king of Nubia in Dongola.

There they stayed until the emir `Izz al-Dīn and those with him arrived, so then they met [in battle], fought, and Simāmūn was defeated. A large number of his followers were killed, while few of the Muslims were martyred. When Simāmūn retreated, the army pursued him to a distance of 15 days from Dongola.

They caught up with Jurays, took him, and took the son of the would-be king of Nubia's maternal aunt. He was one of the nobles among his followers, and among those to whom the kingship could revert.

The emir `Izz al-Dīn assigned the king's nephew to be king, and assigned Jurays as his deputy, then dispatched with them a number of the army, and established for them a tribute which they would bear to the sultanic gates every year. The army then returned after it had taken a good deal of booty: slaves, horses, camels, cattle, and clothes, whereupon what happened we will mention, if God Most High wishes.

[*Obituaries*]

Mention of the events during the year 687 [1288]

During this year Nāṣir al-Dīn Muḥammad son of the shaykh Shams al-Dīn `Abd al-Raḥmān Ibn al-Maqdisī sought to bring a number of inhabitants and nobles of Damascus to the Egyptian homelands, so they were brought. They were the headman `Izz al-Dīn Ḥamza Ibn al-Qalānisī, the headman Naṣīr al-Dīn Ibn Suayd, Shams al-Dīn, son of Jamāl al-Dīn Ibn Yumn, and Jamāl al-Dīn Ibn Ṣaṣrā.

He also sought the Chief Judge Ḥusām al-Dīn al-Ḥanafī, the chief Taqī al-Dīn Tawba, and Shams al-Dīn Ibn Ghānim, so they were all brought to the Egyptian homelands, and their properties were confiscated. 150,000 dirhams was taken from the headman `Izz al-Dīn Ḥamza Ibn al-Qalānisī, 30,000, from the headman Naṣīr al-Dīn Ibn Suayd, from Ibn Yumn, 190,000 dirhams in valued property, from Jamāl al-Dīn Ibn Ṣaṣrā, 300,000 dirhams in valued property, and dirhams [coins], from Chief Judge Ḥusām al-Dīn, 3000 dirhams, and from Shams al-Dīn Ibn Ghānim, 5000 dirhams.

A number of Damascene notables were brought to the Egyptian homelands, so when they were put to the question about transportation of wealth, they proffered excuses, saying that they had been brought [to Egypt] on the post-horses, and that their wealth and belongings were in Damascus. They asked for someone to assess for them what they were transporting, but the emir `Alam al-Dīn Sanjar al-Shujā`ī, the minister for the Egyptian homelands, feared that they, once they headed back to Damascus, would ask for intercession, and it would be granted to them.

Therefore, he sought a number of Kārimī merchants, and ordered them to loan the Damascenes wealth that they could transport, so they did this, and the proofs were written down for them. They were returned to Damascus, and came up with the sums for its owners, because that was their protection money for other than the Islamic Treasury (*bayt al-māl*). When the Damascenes returned to Damascus Jamāl al-Dīn Ibn Ṣaṣrā was appointed to the Chancelleries Inspectorate in protected Damascus, just as we will mention, if God Most High wishes. [63]

Removal of the minister `Alam al-Dīn al-Shujā`ī and the confiscation of his property

During Rabī` al-Awwal [April 1288] of this year the dignitary (*al-najīb*) known as the secretary Bakjarī, one of the state functionaries, was nominated to complain about the emir `Alam al-Dīn Sanjar al-Shujā`ī, minister and administrator for the Egyptian homelands. He came forwards in tandem with the judge Taqī al-Dīn Naṣr Allāh son of Fakhr al-Dīn al-Jawjarī, and with him keeping it private.

He worked to obtain access until he delivered matters to the Sultan al-Malik al-Manṣūr, and verified them before the Sultan. Among the things which he verified and which enraged the Sultan about him were that he said to the sultan with him [al-Shujā`ī] present that he sold a number of spears and weapons from the sultanic storehouses to the Franks. The emir `Alam al-Dīn admitted this, and said:

> Yes, I sold them for a hefty profit and a clear advantage. The profit was that I sold those spears and weapons which were old and falling apart, and were of little benefit. I also sold them at twice their value, and worth, just so the Franks would know that we are selling them weapons out of contempt for them, and taking them lightly, and because we do not care about them.

The Sultan was almost convinced at this, but the dignitary answered him, saying:

> You heap (*mukaththal*)! What is concealed from you is greater than what you let on, so here is an answer: The Franks and the enemies do not allow

> weapons to be sold to them in the manner at which you have hinted. What is common knowledge among them, passed back and forth by the enemies, is that they say that the ruler of the Egyptian homelands and Syrian lands is in such need that he sells his weapons to his enemies. That is about what they say!

At that the Sultan flew into a rage, and his anger was very intense against the emir `Alam al-Dīn. His removal came on Thursday, 12 Rabī` al-Awwal [April 16, 1288], and he ordered for his belongings to be confiscated, and fined him a large amount of gold. He was not allowed to sell any of his horses, his weapons or the provisions or saddles of the emirate. The sum to be paid had to be delivered in cash. He did this after they had fallen upon him, and pressed him with pressers (*ma`āṣīr*) [to torture him].

It reached the Sultan that the emir `Alam al-Dīn had oppressed the people, confiscating from them, and that there were a great many in his private prison who had been there for months and years. Their belongings had been sold, and they were paid a wage of those driven to labor. Some of them were in need of people to ask for papers, so the Sultan issued a command to the emir Bahā' al-Dīn Bughdī *dawādār* to investigate the matter of those who had been confiscated, and to report to the Sultan about it.

So he went out to them, questioned them, so they described the need and destitution in which they existed, whereupon he told the Sultan of what they had said, so he issued a command to his deputy the emir Ḥusām al-Dīn Ṭurunṭāy to investigate them, then released all of them.

On the night before he was to travel, Monday 16 Rabī` al-Awwal [April 20, 1288] a fire broke out in the armory storehouses, and the Ḥusaynī Shrine, inside protected Cairo, but then was put out.

On Tuesday 17 Rabī` al-Awwal [April 21, 1288] al-Malik al-Manṣūr delegated [64] his ministry in the Egyptian homelands to the emir Badr al-Dīn Baydarā in place of the emir `Alam al-Dīn al-Shujā`ī. The judge Taqi al-Dīn Naṣr Allāh son of Fakhr al-Dīn was appointed to the Chancelleries Inspectorate in the Egyptian homelands, and a robe was bestowed upon him, as he took up his duties.

During Rabī` al-Ākhir [May 1288] of this year the headman Jamāl al-Dīn Ibn Ṣaṣrā was appointed to the Chancelleries Inspectorate in protected Syria, and a robe was bestowed upon him, and he went on his way.

In it, the judge Tāj al-Dīn Ibn al-Nuṣayyīnī, a secretary of the roll in protected Aleppo, was released, and he went on his way.

In it the emir Rukn al-Dīn Baybars, *amīr jāndār* (guard) in protected Syria, was given an emirate, and he went on his way.

In it, Shams al-Dīn Ibn Ghānim returned to protected Syria, and was forgiven what was assessed of him. In it he wrote to the emir `Alam al-Dīn al-Dawādārī, the Chancelleries Supervisor in protected Syria, to disapprove of him because of the left-overs, the rude way people spoke of him because of that, and informing him of all of what he was in arrears which was 3,992,700 [dirhams?], and of the stores {its value was 20,000, a third of which was from its store}.[185]

He ordered that he put up 150,000 dirhams of his own wealth, then hunt down the rest of the wealth, and liberate it from those working [officials], and to disburse this wealth in the presence of the emir Ḥusām al-Dīn Lājīn al-Manṣūrī, the deputy of the noble sultanate in protected Syria, and the presence of Taqī al-Dīn Tawba, over the governors, supervisors, the leisured, the employed, the guarantors, those administrators continuing from the regions, and among those who were in it, and it was divided.

The judge Jamāl al-Dīn Muḥammad b. al-Mukarram, secretary of the noble roll, said in his composition *Treasury of the Secretary* what is approximately:

In this year Nāṣir al-Dīn Muḥammad son of Shams al-Dīn `Abd al-Raḥmān son of Badr al-Dīn Abū al-Baqā' Nūḥ al-Maqdisī al-Shāfi`ī was appointed to the trusteeship of the Islamic treasury, and the trusteeship of the sultan's private lands (*khāṣṣ al-sharīf*) in Syria.

Others said in it Nāṣir al-Dīn Muḥammad son of the shaykh Shams al-Dīn `Abd al-Raḥmān al-Maqdisī headed from the sultanic gates to protected Damascus, as al-Malik al-Manṣūr had delegated to him his trusteeship, and the inspectorate of charitable endowments in Damascus and Syria as a whole. This included the inspectorate of the Umayyad Friday Mosque, and the three hospitals, the inspectorate of the nobles, the orphans, the prisoners, the charities, the Sufi hostels, the guardhouses (*rubuṭ*), the walls and other things.

Two supervisors from the sultanic gates headed out with him, who were Shams al-Dīn al-Qushtamarī and Ṣārim al-Dīn Aydimurī. The people went back and forth to his formal session at the time of his arrival in protected Damascus, fearing his evil. All of those with slanderous accusations or judicial complaints thronged at his gate, and so the people began to note the properties they bought for him [65], and his attempt to establish incapacity of those who had sold.

He began to follow the same path as others had with regard to al-Malik al-Ashraf's daughter, so the judges in Damascus forbade assisting him in this, and the emir Ḥusām al-Dīn, the secretary for the sultanate in Damascus, supported them in this. Then Nāṣir al-Dīn Ibn al-Maqdisī forbade the judges from their assigned allowance according to the benefits accrued to the Umayyad Friday Mosque. However, this only increased their boycott of him, so he initiated the construction of the sultanic properties, and rebuilt shops on the Paradise Gate Bridge on both sides, repairing the bridge prior to the

[185] Reconstruction from the editor, who notes that it does not make sense.

construction of the shops. Then he repaired northern Jābiya Gate, which was too low,[186] so he destroyed it, and rebuilt it. However, he did not do anything good other than those two construction jobs and the notaries' bench at the gate of the Friday Mosque.

On Wednesday 9 Rabī` al-Ākhir [May 13, 1288] of this year al-Malik al-Manṣūr released the emir `Alam al-Dīn Sanjar al-Shujā`ī.

On Thursday 19 Rabī` al-Ākhir [May 23, 1288] al-Malik al-Manṣūr removed the emir Badr al-Dīn Baydarā from the ministry in the Egyptian homelands. During it the Sultan sought the Chief Judge Taqī al-Dīn `Abd al-Raḥmān son of the Chief Judge Tāj al-Dīn `Abd al-Wahhāb Ibn bint al-A`zz, and appointed him to the ministry in place of the emir Badr al-Dīn Baydarā, but he asked for this to be rescinded. However, he compelled him, then delegated to him the ministry, and bestowed a robe upon him.

He avoided administration and writing, but only administered specific things in addition to what he already had to do in the chief judiciary and the inspectorate of treasuries. He did not abandon the Treasury Inspectorate, but began for several days sitting for one day in the ministry, the governing council, and the Treasury Chancellery.

This only persisted for a short while, as he did not fulfill the usual task of the ministry, because he held to the literal interpretation of the noble law. Then he had enough of the ministry, so the Sultan delegated his ministry after the Chief Judge to the emir Badr al-Dīn Baydarā al-Manṣūrī, who was the emir of the Sultan's council, then was transferred to being the majordomo, then to the ministry where he stayed until the end of the Manṣūrī period.

During Rabī` al-Ākhir [May 1288] a short note was written to the notables of the lands of Sind, India, China, and Yemen in the form of a safe conduct for those who would choose to come to the Egyptian homelands and the Syrian lands. It was sent with the merchants, and it is the writing of the judge Fatḥ al-Dīn Ibn `Abd al-Ẓāhir. A copy of it:

> The highest God has commanded [66] the high matter: His justice continues to intervene creating safety for the subjects inside a strong fortress, purifying intercessory prayer for his blooming rule (*dawla*) for the inhabitants of east and west. Every one of them is among the saved, dwelling in His pastures for grazers, the Garden of Eden, entering through whichever gate the people wish—from Iraq, from Persia (*`ajam*), from Anatolia (*rūm*), from the Ḥijāz, from the Yemen, from India, from China:
>
> Whoever desires to proceed, of the high-ranking, the nobles, the merchants, those seeking commerce, and those of substance from the regions enumerated, and those which were not enumerated, and those who prefer

[186] Following the editor's suggestion.

to arrive to our realms to stay, or to facilitate transportation back and forth to our wide lands, its overshadowing sides, open spaces, and shaded areas,

So let him determine what God has foreordained for him in that, both in good and in choosing, then present himself to a land whose dwellers are not in need of provisions, nor stores, because it is a Garden of Eden in this world to the one who resides, a means of consolation for those who exchange their birth land, a pleasure of which sight does not weary, nor shun because of the excessive verdancy.

The one who stays there lives in a permanent springtime, good that attends everyone. It suffices that from just one of its descriptions that it is God's beauty spot on His earth, and that blessing is implicit in the saddlebags of one who as part of his profit places the good treatment in it, and a good point as his return. When one descends to it, there is hope as long as he asks [for something] since it has become part of the House of Islam, through swords that were preceded by reproof.

Now its lands are constructed by justice,[187] its inhabitants are many, and its buildings have become vast until they are almost cities. Hardship has become eased in it, so one does not become apprehensive about the way cities look as needs are easily met in it, and it is easy upon the eye. The rest of the people and all the merchants do not fear any wrongdoing in it, as justice has spread.

Whichever merchants staying in Yemen, India, China, Sind or any other place who is informed of our written decree, let them take provision for the journey to it, and arriving there, so as to find the action greater than the written word, to see good treatment in return for keeping these agreements for most, passing from it into a good land, whose lord is forgiving, thankful in the grace of its compensation—who but the most grateful is worthy of compensation—in peace with regard to life and wealth, felicity sweetening the circumstances, and funding hopes.

They will receive from us, every time they prefer some equitable action, its doer will be received favorably, and their livelihood will praise these factors. Their wealth shall remain safe with those to whom it is entrusted, and will save them because they will be shaded by its shade.

Whoever brings goods of spices, or other types [of merchandise] which the noble merchants bring, should not fear for them, nor will anything

[187] Rhyming *`adl* with *`adhl* in the previous line.

go wrong, for justice will be served to them, and whatever is bothering them will be raised away from them. Whoever brings mamluks or slave girls with them shall have their value, above and beyond what he asks, and forbearance to compensate for their value according to what is generally accepted by those who import them from a near land—so how much more from a far land.

This is because our desire is turned to multiplying troops, so whoever imports those, has fulfilled a vital function, so let whoever can bring many, and know that the multiplication of Islam's troops is urgent reason for seeking them, because Islam today is in [67] the glory of its outspread flag and its victorious Sultan.

Whoever of them presents themselves, departs from the darkness to the light; condemnation because of unbelief is his yesterday, while praise in faith is his today. Fighting for Islam is his clan and people, and this our written decree is to all the merchants who are informed of it: their matter is to journey through the earth seeking God's bounty, while others fight in God's path, let them read those of his judgments which are simple, taking guidance from his star being led by his knowledge, riding like people of hope who are being borne into immigration (*hijra*), spreading out their hands in intercessory prayer to those creatures seeking to draw near to their lands, to partake in its goodness, in all verdancy, and all benevolence, and taking times for profit.

The time has come to pluck it, as its rain is about to fall, and these true promises have been sent to them, verifying for them the goodness of hope, establishing for them that the noble signature, may God raise it, raising it, rules that God is in accord with what the pens wrote, and the best trustee.

During Jumādā al-Awwal [June 1288] of this year letters of the emir `Alam al-Dīn Sanjar al-Masrūrī *al-khayyāṭ* arrived from Dongola containing news of its conquest, and the victorious army taking over it, the captivity of its kings, and their relatives, and dependents, the taking of their crowns, and their wives. The emir Rukn al-Dīn Mankūrus al-Fāriqānī arrived with the letters, and a robe was bestowed upon him.

An answer was returned that the emir `Izz al-Dīn Aydimur *al-silaḥdār*, governor of Qūṣ, should stay back in Dongola as deputy sultan, and mamluks, troops and men of his should stay there, but that the emir `Alam al-Dīn and the rest of the victorious army should present themselves [returning].

From the noble gate Sa`d al-Dīn Sa`d son of Dā'ūd's sister was sent to head with the post-courier that there would be a copy with the emir `Izz al-Dīn Aydimur, because he was one of the inhabitants of the country, and an expert on its circumstances and the circumstances of its inhabitants. He set off with the post-courier to Dongola, was given a Mahallā sword, then his movement was slowed, and he stayed in Qūṣ because of what we will mention, if God Most High wishes.

During this month, the judge Zayn al-Dīn Ibn Rushayq was appointed to the judiciary of the border port of protected Alexandria in place of the judge Zayn al-Dīn Ibn al-Munayyar. During it the judge Shihāb al-Dīn Ghāzī Ibn al-Wāsiṭī was sought, and a rescript was written for him to investigate the Syrian lands and the secretaryship of the noble roll, so an allowance was assigned for him, which was 500 dirhams for a month, 10 *ardabb*s (a little under 2000 liters) stores, and he was sent as an investigator to the protected Safedan lands. The emir Sayf al-Dīn Kurd al-Manṣūrī was sent with him as a supervisor, and al-Amjad, close relative of al-As`ad b. al-Sadīd al-Mustawfī, as a collector.

On 5 Jumādā al-Awwal [June 7, 1288] a noble formal command was written in the name of Badr al-Dīn Ṭīmūn b. Rīsha al-Kalbī to be the emir over the Kalbite Bedouin and the Banū Kilāb, both Syrian, [68] who dwell between the Eagle's Pass towards the south, other than the Banū Kilāb and the Syrian and Rūmī Kalbites, who dwell to the north of Eagle's Pass, who are known in the land of Ḥimṣ, Shayzar and Aleppo, and those lands. He guaranteed to gather revenue from the number of their tents in accord with what that number was during the Nāṣirī period. He would be able to levy from that established census a fourth. Whenever as the surplus from the census exceeded the established number of tents then he would be able to levy half.

On Saturday 17 Jumādā al-Awwal, [June 19, 1288] which was 25 Būna year 1004 the level of the blessed Nile was measured, so it was established to be four cubits and 26 fingers.

During Jumādā al-Ākhira [July 1288] of this year Ibn al-Wāsiṭī and Sayf al-Dīn Kurd were summoned to the glorious gate of protected Safed.

On 9 Rajab [August 9, 1288] of this year the emir `Alam al-Dīn Sanjar al-Masrūrī and the army dispatched with him arrived from Dongola at the sultanic gates in the Hill Citadel in protected Egypt. He had the kings of Nubia, their wives, and their crowns with him, and that was a day to remember.

The emir `Alam al-Dīn reported to the Sultan that they ruled the lands of al-Dū and the Nubians, and those places in their totality, having killed its inhabitants, taken them captive, and brought a great many as prisoners. The Sultan sent some of the captives to his courtiers and retinue, and dispersed them among them. The emirs and the army were given the captives to divide among them. Many of them were sold at very discounted prices, and they became common among the people.

The Sultan bestowed a robe upon the emir `Alam al-Dīn Sanjar al-Masrūrī, and appointed him to the Hospitality Bureau (*mihmandāriyya*). The emir

Sharaf al-Dīn al-Jākī *al-mihmandār* had been sent to Alexandria to be involved in the governate in order to inspect the governor there. This appointment was in place of the emir Ḥusām al-Dīn son of the emir Shams al-Dīn Ibn Bākhil, and happened when the latter was detained, his possessions confiscated, and his wives and belongings were brought to him to protected Cairo. This was what was happening with those.

As for what was happening with Simāmūn, king of the Nubians, when the Egyptian army departed Nubia and returned to the Egyptian homelands, just as we previously explained, and he verified their return, he returned to Dongola, fought those in it, defeated them, and returned the lands [to their previous state]. The newly installed king and Jurays presented themselves, with their dispatched army, [69] at the sultanic gates in protected Egypt, delivering (news of) what Simāmūn, king of the Nubians, had done. Therefore, al-Malik al-Manṣūr was angered at that, and ordered the preparations of armies to go as a dispatch force to raid Nubia. What happened then we will mention, if God Most High wishes.

During this year al-Malik al-Manṣūr Sayf al-Dīn Qalāwūn bedded the daughter of the emir Shams al-Dīn Sunqur al-Tikrītī al-Ẓāhirī, and released her father from prison, giving him a command in Syria. Then the Sultan abandoned her.

It was said that the reason for his abandoning her was that her father married her sister to one of his mamluks, and the Sultan disapproved of that, and disliked him, so abandoned her as a result.

It is said that she had acquired a type of haughtiness, and so [bands of] *silāḥdāriyya*, Jamdāriyya, water-carriers, and others connected with the sultanate were made from her servant-girls. Therefore, the Sultan separated himself from her because of that. When her mandatory waiting period was completed, the Sultan ordered her to marry the most contemptible of the emirs' sons, as a way of taking revenge upon her. Then the conduct of the emirs' sons was revealed upon investigation to be extremely bad, so it was agreed that Jamāl al-Dīn Yūsuf son of the emir Shams al-Dīn Sunqur al-Alfi [would marry her] so he married her, and God knows best.

**Mention of the death of al-Malik al-Ṣāliḥ `Alī, son of al-Malik al-Manṣūr Sayf al-Dīn Qalāwūn al-Alfī al-Ṣāliḥī al-Najmī, the heir-apparent**, who had the patronymic of Abū al-Fatḥ, and the honorific of `Alā' al-Dīn, with the regnal title of al-Malik al-Ṣāliḥ. He had high ability, good graces, and was counted among the nobles of the [emirs'] sons, and among the sons' nobles. His father, al-Manṣūr, appointed him heir-apparent, and relied upon him for the administration of the realm. His name was mentioned together after his from the pulpits, and his orders were spoken of by tongues and pens in the mouths and via the inkstands.

We have already related reports which will suffice concerning him, and he continued to be his father's satisfaction and glory until when the Sultan al-Malik al-Manṣūr departed Sunday 15 Rajab [August 15, 1288] of this year, going out to the victorious royal tent outside of protected Cairo traveling to protected Syria, leading his victorious armies.

His son, al-Malik al-Ṣāliḥ, rode with him to the victorious camp, and was present at his board [to eat], staying until the later part of the day, then returning to the victorious Citadel and spending the night sick with severe bloody diarrhea. He lingered for days, being treated by all sorts of treatments, drinking many essences (or jewels) and emeralds belonging to him,[188] having great value.

His father the Sultan rode to him, and ascended the Citadel to visit him on Wednesday 18 Rajab [August 18, 1288], then returned that day to the victorious army. When al-Malik al-Ṣāliḥ's sickness worsened, his father the Sultan returned to the victorious Citadel, climbing the Treasury building on Tuesday 1 Sha`bān [August 31, 1288] of this year, raising the standards and the kettledrums, and then the prayer (*ṭalab*) on Wednesday 2 Sha`bān [September 1, 1288], but al-Malik al-Ṣāliḥ's sickness continued, and his weakness increased until the morning of Friday 4 Sha`bān [September 3, 1288] when he died in the Hill Citadel.

It was said that his illness [70] was liver dysentery. It was said that his brother al-Malik al-Ashraf Ṣalāḥ al-Dīn Khalīl envied him because of his father's favor, so poisoned him and then he died. It is also said differently. Chief Judge Taqī al-Dīn `Abd al-Raḥmān son of Chief Judge Tāj al-Dīn Ibn bint al-A`zz al-Shāfi`ī prayed over al-Malik al-Ṣāliḥ in the Citadel, while his father al-Malik al-Manṣūr and his brother al-Malik al-Ashraf prayed right behind him.

Outside of the protected Citadel Chief Judge Mu`izz al-Dīn Nu`mān son of the Chief Judge Tāj al-Dīn al-Ḥasan b. Yūsuf al-Khaṭībī al-Ḥanafī, Ḥanafī Chief Judge in the Egyptian homelands, also prayed for him. He was buried in the mausoleum of his mother that was built close to the Lady Nafīsa, may God be satisfied with her. He left behind one son from his wife Manakbak, daughter of the emir Sayf al-Dīn Nogai, who was the emir Muẓaffar al-Dīn Mūsā.

Al-Malik al-Manṣūr suffered terribly from the death of his son al-Malik al-Ṣāliḥ, and sat in mourning in the great hall on Sunday the third day from his son's death. All the senior deputies in the lands sent condolences, and he ordered that no one have their hair cut, change their clothing or wear iron. The judge Muḥyī al-Dīn Ibn `Abd al-Ẓāhir said in a summary of a letter he wrote dictated by al-Malik al-Manṣūr to one of the deputies:

> We praise God Most High who compensated us with rewarding inner and outer patience. It was our desire to make him a king in this world (*dunyā*), but God decided to make him a king in the Hereafter.

[188] Note the emerald mine in upper Egypt mentioned by Kāshānī, *`Arā'is al-javāhir*, p. 48, south of Mt. Muqaṭṭam.

Mention of al-Malik al-Manṣūr's delegating the heir-apparency to his son al-Malik al-Ashraf

When al-Malik al-Ṣāliḥ `Alā' al-Dīn `Alī died, as we previously explained, his father al-Malik al-Manṣūr delegated the heir-apparency to his son al-Malik al-Ashraf Ṣalāḥ al-Dīn Khalīl, and he rode with the sultanic insignia on 11 Sha`bān [September 10, 1288] from the protected Hill Citadel. He headed to the Victory Gate, and then through the midst of protected Cairo, exiting from the Zuwayla Gate, and then returning to the protected Citadel, while the emirs, commanders, and armies were in his wake.

The tidings were proclaimed, and al-Malik al-Manṣūr asked of the judges, so they swore all of the emirs, commanders and armies, and he put on the robes as usual, while the preachers mentioned his name as the heir-apparent, and the situation stabilized similarly to that of his brother al-Malik al-Ṣāliḥ.

This was written to Syria and the rest of the lands, and the preachers mentioned his name as the heir-apparent in the rest of the lands, after his father, as had been the case with his brother. An investiture was written but the Sultan was reluctant to sign it, and we will mention the reason for that at the beginning of the reports on the reign of al-Malik al-Ashraf, if God Most High wishes.

During Ramaḍān [October 1288] of this year al-Malik al-Manṣūr delegated [71] the market inspection (*ḥisba*) in protected Damascus to the headman Shams al-Dīn Muḥammad Ibn al-Sal`ūs in place of Sharaf al-Dīn Aḥmad son of `Izz al-Dīn `Īsā Ibn al-Sayrujī. His rescript concerning that arrived at the sultanic gates in the Egyptian homelands.

During it, a Muslim woman was found with the secretary Badr b. Nafīs the Christian in Damascus, together with a number of people, while they were drinking wine. The emir Ḥusām al-Dīn Lājīn, deputy sultan in protected Damascus, was informed of this, so he ordered that the Christian be burnt. He expended most of his money, asking [= bribing] his employer Sayf al-Dīn Kajkan about his case, but the deputy sultan did not agree to let him live. A fire was lit up for him in the Horse Market, so he was thrown into it. As for the woman, part of her nose was cut off, but someone interceded for her, and she was released.

During it after the death of the shaykh Quṭb al-Dīn `Abd al-Mun`im b. Yaḥyā b. Ibrāhīm al-Qurashī al-Qudsī, the preacher for noble Jerusalem, just as it was mentioned in his biography, the judge Badr al-Dīn Muḥammad son of the shaykh Burhān al-Dīn b. Jamā`a al-Kinānī, al-Shāfi`ī by rite, was appointed to the noble Jerusalem judiciary on Monday 11 Shawwāl [November 8, 1288].

After the judge Badr al-Dīn Ibn Jamā`a, the judge `Alā' al-Dīn Aḥmad son of the Chief Judge Tāj al-Dīn Ibn bint al-A`zz was appointed to teach in the Qaymariyya College, and he sat in it for lessons on Sunday 17 Shawwāl [November 14, 1288].

During Dhū al-Ḥijja [January 1289] of this year the emir `Alam al-Dīn Sanjar al-Masrūrī was appointed to the governate of al-Bahnasā and its districts, and with him `Izz al-Dīn Miqdām the brother-in-law of Zayn al-Dīn Ibn al-*m-z/r-i/n/t-h* was appointed to the inspectorate of the districts, so they both set out.

During this year, al-Malik al-Manṣūr delegated the Mālikī chief judiciary in protected Damascus to Chief Judge Jamāl al-Dīn al-Zawāwī, the Mālikī jurisprudent, and God knows best.

[*Obituaries*]

Mention of the events during the year 688 [1289]

The crescent moon was seen the month of Muḥarram during this year on the night of Tuesday [January 25, 1289].

Mention of some reports of Syrian Tripoli from the time when it was conquered during the days of the Commander of the Believers `Uthmān son of `Affān to the time when al-Malik al-Manṣūr conquered it, condensed and abbreviated as its gathered reports.

We had mentioned that during the caliphate of the Commander of the Believers `Uthmān son of `Affān that Mu`āwiya son of Abū Sufyān the Umayyad sent Sufyān b. Mujīb al-Azdī to Syrian Tripoli, which was then three cities joined together. He built a fortress on a field some miles away from it, which was named Sufyān's Fortress.

He cut the provisions from the people of Tripoli, and besieged it, so when the siege grew intense for its people, they gathered in one of the three fortresses, and wrote to the Byzantine king, asking him if he would support them or send to them boats in which they could retreat. He sent many boats, so they sailed in them during a night, and fled.

When Sufyān awoke in the morning, and advanced to fight them as usual, he found the fortress empty, so took possession of it. He wrote to Mu`āwiya with news of the conquest, and Mu`āwiya settled a large group of Jews in it. That is the fortress in which there is the harbor.

The Commander of the Believers, `Abd al-Malik b. Marwān the Umayyad, built it and its fortress. Mu`āwiya used to send a group of troops every year to garrison it, and to appoint as its deputy. When the sea [gate?] was closed (*ghuliqa*), the troops would return, but the deputy would stay commanding a smaller group. Things continued like this until the Commander of the Believers `Abd al-Malik b. Marwān was nominated, whereupon one of the Byzantine patricians [77] (arrived) together with a large number.

He asked for a safe-conduct on the condition that he stay in it, and pay the land (*kharāj*) tax, and this was granted him. But it wasn't long, a little over two years and some months, until at the return of the troops from the city, the gates were closed, while those troops remaining in it [Tripoli] were taken prisoner, together with a number of Jews, and he and his supporters headed towards the Byzantine lands.

God foreordained that the Muslims be victorious over him at sea, while he was leading a number of boats, taken prisoner, and brought to the Commander of the Believers `Abd al-Malik b. Marwān, who killed and crucified him. It is said that his taking over it and killing of those in it was after the death of the Commander of the Believers `Abd al-Malik, and that his son Commander of the Believers al-Walīd b. `Abd al-Malik conquered it.

Tripoli continued to be governed by deputies of the caliphs during the period of the Umayyads and the `Abbāsids, until the Fāṭimids (*`ubaydiyyīn*), kings of Egypt, took over Damascus, just as is mentioned in their histories. They separated Tripoli from Damascus, as previously it was subordinated to it.

They appointed Rayyān the retainer (*al-khādim*) over it on their behalf, then Sanad al-Dawla, then Abū al-Sa`āda, then `Alī b. `Abd al-Raḥmān b. Ḥaydara, then Nazzāl, and then Mukhtār al-Dawla b. Nazzāl. Then its religious judge Amīn al-Dawla Abū Ṭālib al-Ḥasan b. `Ammār took over it, and continued until he died in 464 [1071–2], just as has been mentioned in his biography.

This Ibn `Ammār was an intelligent man, a jurisprudent, with good judgment, although he was a Shi`ite, being one of their jurisprudents. He had a House of Learning in Tripoli in which there were over 100,000 books as an endowment. He himself composed *Kitāb tarwīḥ al-arwāḥ wa-miṣbāḥ al-surūr wa-l-afrāḥ*, and was given the honorific of Jarāb al-Dawla.

When Amīn al-Dawla died, Sadīd al-Mulk b. Munqidh was in Tripoli, fleeing from Maḥmūd b. Ṣāliḥ, so he assisted Jalāl al-Mulk Abū al-Ḥasan `Alī b. Muḥammad b. `Ammār, supporting him with his mamluks, as he had his own supporters with him. So they expelled Amīn al-Dawla's brother from Tripoli, and Jalāl al-Mulk became the ruler.

He continued as governor until he died at the end of Sha`bān 492 [July 22, 1099], just as is mentioned in his biography. His brother Fakhr al-Mulk `Ammār b. Muḥammad b. `Ammār was king over it after him, and stayed in it until [Raymond of] St. Gilles came to fight there, whose name was Raymond (*maymunt*). He was Raymond and St. Gilles is the name of a city from which he originated.

St. Gilles camped there with a company against Tripoli in the month of Rajab 495 [May 1102], besieging it, closing in on it, building a fortress against it, from which to fight its people. It is known by his name until the present day.

Fakhr al-Mulk sent gifts and presents to the kings, asking them for help and aid, but not one of them helped him. When he despaired of them, he offered St. Gilles a large amount of money to depart, and sent him provisions. But he did not respond, so when he was unable to withstand the siege, and incapable of defending it, he left Tripoli after he left his paternal uncle Abū al-Manāqib as deputy in it, and appointed Sa`d al-Dawla Fityān b. al-A`izz with him, paying the army for six months.

He traveled to the Sultan Maḥmūd b. Malikshāh [78] the Seljuq. Abū al-Manāqib sat for some days with the notables and prominent people of Tripoli, and then his speech was mixed up. Sa`d al-Dawla reproved him kindly, but he drew his sword, struck Sa`d al-Dawla, and killed him. Those in the council withdrew, and Abū al-Manāqib climbed the walls, and struck him in his armpits, so the people of the town arrested him, and put him in prison.

They then called out with the insignia of al-Afḍal son of the Commander of the Armies, the associate of the Fāṭimid caliph, ruler of Egypt, and that was in Ramaḍān 500 [May 1107]. Then the accursed St. Gilles died on 28 Ramaḍān [May 23, 1107],[189] and the commander of the Franks, whose name was Cerdagne [*al-sirdānī* = William of Cerdagne] was nominated in his place.

This was what was happening with those; as for what was happening with the people of Tripoli, when they appealed using al-Afḍal's insignia, and this reached him, he prepared for them an army at sea, setting as its commander Tāj al-`Ajam. When it arrived at Tripoli, it seized all the wealth, and everything that the town had stored up.

It reached al-Afḍal that he intended to rebel in Tripoli, so he seized everything he could get his hands on, and appointed Badr al-Dawla as governor. According to some versions, Sharaf al-Dawla was son of Abū al-Ṭayyīb al-Dimashqī, so he arrived at Tripoli. However, its people were weary of the siege, and they saw in his character traits that repelled them from him, so they resolved to expel him.

Then they thought better of it, seeing as they had absolutely no recourse other than with the Egyptians. Boats then arrived from Egypt with foodstuffs and men. They decided together with the commanders of the fleet to arrest the notables of the town, and the supporters of Fakhr al-Mulk b. `Ammār, and his intimate family, to take them and transport them by sea to protected Egypt, and to send the weapons and treasures in Tripoli as well. There was never anything like it among the kings—100,000 dinars in cash money was sent, and when they arrived in Egypt al-Afḍal arrested the family of Ibn `Ammār.

This was what was happening with those; as for what was happening with Fakhr al-Mulk `Ammār b. Muḥammad b. `Ammār, he arrived in Baghdad and met together with the Sultan Maḥmūd. He stayed in Baghdad, but he did not prepare for him what he had requested. When the return of Tripoli to the Egyptians reached him, and that his intimate family, his wealth, treasures, and weapons had all been transferred to Egypt, he returned to Damascus, and entered it on 15 Muḥarram 502 [August 25, 1108]. The king *atābak* Tughtakīn, ruler of Damascus, honored him, asking him to help him to enter Jabala. So he sent an army with him, and entered it.

That was what was happening with those; as to what was happening with the Franks, may God curse them, and defeat those who remain, they had

[189] Raymond of St. Gilles died on February 28, 1105.

persisted in the siege, and hemmed the town in, until they ruled it, killed, took prisoner, pillaged, and took captives, which was on Tuesday 3 Dhū al-Ḥijja 502 [July 4, 1109]. It is said that they took it on Monday, ten nights into Dhū al-Ḥijja 503 [August 31, 1110], and God knows best.

It is said that the reason for the taking of Tripoli was as the Franks had hemmed it in, one in it had written to the Egyptian homelands, seeking aid from its caliph, asking for provisions. So they began to expect the arrival of an answer with supplies and provisions, but while they were in that state, suddenly a boat came [79]. They did not doubt that there was aid in it, but an envoy disembarked from it, saying

> The caliph has learned that there is a beautifully formed girl in Tripoli, and that she is suitable for service, so he has ordered [for you] to send her to him. Send him some apricot wood to make wood musical instruments.

At that they despaired of his help, their resolve weakened, their morale dropped, and they were humiliated. The Franks ruled them from the previously mentioned date; the siege lasted seven years and four months. When [William of] Cerdagne took over Tripoli, he ruled in it, and became independent.

While he was doing this, suddenly a boat arrived there in which was a boy who claimed to be the son of the Frankish king St. Gilles, whose name was Bertrand (*bartān*). With him were elders from his father's supporters, serving him, and managing his affairs, so they went up to [William of] Cerdagne and said "This is the son of St. Gilles, and he wants for you to hand over the city of his father, which his armies captured."

However, Cerdagne refused this, and rose, kicked the boy, and expelled him, so his supporters took him, and began parading him around with the knights, so they had compassion upon him, remembering their oaths to his father. They said, "When it is tomorrow, we will be with him! So attend him and speak with him," and they did this.

The boy son of St. Gilles spoke, whereupon Cerdagne shouted at him, but they knights all rose up against Cerdagne and expelled him from the realm, giving it over to the boy son of St. Gilles. He ruled as king until Bazwāj killed him,[190] which was on Sunday four days into Rajab 531 [March 28, 1137].[191] Most of his supporters were killed, and Peter the Blind was taken prisoner.

The son of the Count Bertrand took his place in Tripoli, but then the *atābak* Zangi took him prisoner when he was in the company of the would-be king of Jerusalem, Fulk son of Fulk. This was close to the castle of Ba`rīn, so the king ascended with a group to Ba`rīn castle, whereupon Zangi besieged

[190] Commander from Damascus.

[191] Conflating Pons of Tripoli with Bertrand.

them, hemming them in, so the king made a truce with him on the condition of handing over Ba`rīn fortress.

The Count, ruler of Tripoli, was freed together with all of the prisoners, and the count returned to Tripoli and stayed there until the Isma`ilis attacked him, killing him. Raymond (*raymund*) ruled after him, who was a boy, and was present at the battle with the Franks over Ḥārim. Al-Malik al-`Ādil Nūr al-Dīn Maḥmūd the martyr son of Zangi crushed them, and slaughtered a great many of them, taking prisoners.

Among his prisoners were the Count Raymond, which was in the year 559 [1163–4]. He stayed in prison until al-Malik al-Nāṣir Ṣalāḥ al-Dīn Yūsuf, son of the father of kings, Najm al-Dīn Ayyūb b. Shādī b. Marwān, ruled, who freed him on 29 Rabī` al-Awwal 590 [March 24, 1194].[192] Rulership remained in his hands and the hands of his children after him until the yeas 688 [1289], this year.[193]

It reached the Sultan al-Malik al-Manṣūr Sayf al-Dīn Qalāwūn al-Alfī, master of the Egyptian homelands [80] and the Syrian lands that the Franks, people of Tripoli, had broken the basis of the peace that was between them and the people of Islam, and violated the conditions of the truce. So he prepared and departed from the hill castle in protected Egypt (Cairo) going towards protected Syria, leading the victorious armies on Thursday 10 Muḥarram [6]88 [February 3, 1289]. He camped outside of protected Cairo, and traveled on Tuesday the 15 of the previously mentioned Muḥarram [February 8, 1289].

Al-Malik al-Ashraf Ṣalāḥ al-Dīn Khalīl, son of al-Malik al-Manṣūr, stayed as his heir-apparent in victorious Cairo, while the emir Badr al-Dīn Baydara al-Manṣūrī was his deputy and minister. At the departure of the Sultan al-Malik al-Manṣūr he wrote to all of the deputies in the Syrian realms and the Islamic fortresses to provision the victorious troops to Tripoli, and to send mangonels and siege implements.

Al-Malik al-Manṣūr arrived leading the Egyptian homelands' armies at protected Damascus on Monday 13 Ṣafar [March 8, 1289] of this year. He departed from it on 22 Ṣafar [March 17, 1289] and surrounded Tripoli with the Islamic armies, besieging it, and initiating a rush, a siege, and bombardment by mangonels. Tunnels were made, and the walls were undermined, so it was taken by force at the 7th hour on Tuesday 4 Rabī` al-Ākhir in the year [6]88 [April 27, 1289].

The duration of the stay, attacking it was 34 days, and the number of mangonels placed against it were 19 in total. Six of these were Frankish, and 13 *qarābughā* ones; the number of miners (*ḥajjārīn*) and firemen (*zarrāqīn*) was

[192] It is difficult to understand this as Count Raymond III died in September–Oct, 1187; perhaps Raymond IV, regent of Antioch is meant.

[193] Raymond III had no children; the county of Tripoli passed into the control of the Princes of Antioch at his death.

1500. When the city was taken many of the Franks fled to an island called Palm Island facing Tripoli in the sea, which it is only reachable by boat. It was to the eternal felicity of the Muslims that the sea at the time of the conquest was at low tide, and had retreated away from Tripoli, revealing to the people places to wade through, so both horsemen and foot soldiers crossed to this island and took prisoner or killed those on it, and pillaged that which they had with them.

A number of the Franks had already boarded a boat, and set off, but the wind blew them to the coast, so the young men (*ghilmān*) and the spear-carriers (*awshāqiyya*) took them, and killed a great number of them. The Muslims pillaged a great deal, and 1200 prisoners arrived at the Sultan's armory-factory (*zardkhāna*).

Among those who were martyred at Tripoli who were known was the emir `Izz al-Dīn Mankūrus al-Fārqānī, and from the freeborn troops (*ḥalqa*) 55 people, may God have mercy on them. When al-Malik al-Manṣūr conquered the city of Tripoli he ordered the city to be rebuilt, and the settling of the army in it, but then it was pointed out to him that destroying it was more of a priority than rebuilding it, so he ordered it to be destroyed, and it was. The breadth of its walls would allow three knights to ride abreast on top of them.

Shaykh Quṭb al-Dīn al-Yūnīnī told in his *History* that when al-Malik al-Manṣūr conquered Tripoli Anafa was handed over, so he ordered [81] for its fortress to be destroyed—it was a powerful fortress. Two of its villages continued to belong to the sister of the Prince. He stated that while the Sultan was outside of Tripoli the son of Sir Guy [Embraico], ruler of Jubayl, presented himself. The ruler of Tripoli had killed his father in the year 681 [1282]. The Sultan honored him, and confirmed Jubayl for him as an *iqṭā`*, but took from him most of its wealth. Al-Malik al-Manṣūr also transferred al-Batrūn and all of the fortresses and towers in that district.

Then the Sultan returned after the victory to protected Damascus, and established the army as usual in Ḥiṣn al-Akrād, when the deputy sultan was the emir Sayf al-Dīn Balabān al-Ṭabbākhī al-Manṣūrī. The garrison would come down to Tripoli from Ḥiṣn al-Akrād, and then the Muslims rebuilt the city adjoining the river, and celebrated in it. Baths, tall structures (*qayāsir*), mosques, schools for learning were built in it, and water flowed in its buildings from its water pipes (*qasāṭil*). The sultan's house was built for the sultan's deputy in the Tripolitean realm to dwell, which was very high overlooking the city.

The emir Sayf al-Dīn al-Ṭabbākhī continued as the deputy until al-Malik al-Ashraf Ṣalāḥ al-Dīn Khalīl, son of al-Malik al-Manṣūr Qalāwūn, had him transferred to Aleppo in the year 691 [1290] as we will mention, if God Most High wills. Tripoli has continued to be governed by deputies from the Egyptian homelands until our own day, and may God make it stay in the hands of the kings of Islam until the Hour arises. We will mentioned some of its governors whose deputyship has reached us if God Most High wishes it. We only digressed at this length so that the reports of Tripoli would be a continuity, even if they were condensed.

When the Sultan was in Tripoli envoys of the ruler of Sīs came to him asking for the sultanic mercies, and seeking his favor. He demanded in return that they hand over the fortress of Mar`ash and Bahasnā, and assess the tribute as usual, He honored them with robes, and returned them. He dispatched Ḥusām al-Dīn Ṭurunṭāy, the Sultan's deputy in the Egyptian homelands, to the Aleppan realm commanding a unit of the army.

Then he traveled from Tripoli, returning to Damascus, as we have previously explained, and stopped at Ḥimṣ, staying there for some days until the envoys of Sīs returned with many gifts, and apologies about handing over Mar`ash and Bahasnā, and expending a large amount of money each year.

So the Sultan traveled from Ḥimṣ, entering Damascus on Monday 15 Jumādā al-Ulā [June 6, 1289] of this year. The Sultan al-Malik al-Manṣūr when he traveled during this year from the Egyptian homelands asked the emir `Alam al-Dīn Sanjar al-Shujā`ī to accompany him, so when the Sultan returned from Tripoli to Damascus, he ordered al-Shujā`ī to renew efforts to obtain wealth in Damascus, so gave him the power [82] to confiscate from people.

Al-Shujā`ī incited the guard to attack the chief Taqī al-Dīn Tawba, whereupon they found much wood, goods and sugar with him, so they offered that to the Damascenes to sell at double price. He would save for one from whom he was confiscating something like a quarter [of its price] or less, so he obtained from this approximately 500,000 dirhams. His goal with regard to this was that the Sultan would be aware of the fact that Taqī al-Dīn Tawba had obtained a great deal of wealth, because of enmity between the two of them.

Then he initiated confiscations from the people, so many of the Damascenes fled to the villages and land plots to conceal themselves from him. He sought out Najm al-Dīn `Abbās al-Jawharī because of a land plot that he had purchased from the daughter of al-Malik al-Ashraf in al-Biqā` al-`Azīzī. He was sought because of the proceeds that he had taken from it, which were 500,000 dirhams. People belonging to him carried jewels worth 80,000 dirhams. The search for him became intense, so he [al-Shujā`ī] came to the school that he had founded in Damascus, and dug in its antechamber (*dihlīz*), and found a tray (*khūnjāh*)[194] of gold, inlayed with jewels, with a inlayed hen (*qurqa*) on top of it, appraised at 400,000 dirhams. There was also a place for casting gold coins, where there were 7000 dinars.

The jewels were taken to the Sultan's Treasury, so then Sultan showed to the emirs that his stay in Damascus was because he expected the emir Ḥusām al-Dīn Ṭurunṭāy, so he arrived on 17 Rajab [August 6, 1289] of this year. The Sultan met him leading the armies, and the Sultan stayed in Damascus until Thursday 2 Sha`bān [August 21, 1289] of this year, whereupon he departed

[194] Probably the Farsi *khwuncha*, "a tray or a small inlayed table."

on that day for the Egyptian homelands after he had acquired a bias against the Damascenes.

He had Taqī al-Dīn Tawba accompany him in fetters. When he arrived at Jamrā Baysān the emir Ḥusām al-Dīn Ṭurunṭāy and the emir Zayn al-Dīn Kitbughā passed him while he was in the armory-factory (*zardkhānāh*), so he [Taqī al-Dīn] cursed the both of them in the coarsest manner. This was usual for him.

It was mentioned what he had done, while the two of them laughed at his cursing them, so the both of them went to the Sultan, and asked him about his order, then they joined him, releasing him, and they took him with them. The emir `Alam al-Dīn al-Shujā`ī was terribly afflicted because of this. He had already written to Nablus, Jerusalem, the land of Hebron, and the coastal lands to seek the governors and administrators (*mubāshirīn*) that they would supply provisions [for the Sultan] to Gaza.

When the release of Taqī al-Dīn Tawba was obtained al-Shujā`ī was enraged, being visibly furious, and stopped talking about confiscations. This was one of God Most High's graces to those who seek, and the Sultan al-Malik al-Manṣūr arrived at his citadel and the seat of his realm safely.

Mention of the dispatch of the army to Nubia a second time[195]

We have already mentioned that the king of Nubia, when the return of the Egyptian army to protected Egypt was certain, returned himself to Dongola, and expelled the king who the emir `Alam al-Dīn *al-khayyāṭ* had set upon the throne, and sought to return the land [to what it had been].

The appointed king presented himself at the sultanic gates, and made known to the Sultan what was agreed. When it was this year [688/1289], al-Malik al-Manṣūr dispatched the emir `Izz al-Dīn Aybak *al-afram*, *amīr jāndār* (guard), to Nubia. Accompanying him from [83] among the emirs were the emir Sayf al-Dīn Qunchaq al-Manṣūrī, the emir Sayf al-Dīn Baktimur *al-jūkandār*, and the emir `Izz al-Dīn Aydimur, in charge of the Qūṣ districts.

He also dispatched also from the junior emirs who were mentioned: junior emir Zayn al-Dīn Kitbughā al-Manṣūrī, junior emir Badr al-Dīn Baydarā al-Manṣūrī, junior emir Sayf al-Dīn Bahādur, the head of al-Jamdāriyya, junior emir `Alā' al-Dīn al-Ṭībursī, and junior emir Shams al-Dīn Sunqur *al-ṭawīl*. The rest were from the central military-districts, and the deputy governors, the Bedouin from the Egyptian homelands, both from south and north. Their number was 40,000 foot soldiers.

The would-be king of Nubia, and his deputy Jurays were provisioned together with them, and the departure of the army from the sultanic gates in the Egyptian homelands was on Tuesday 8 Shawwāl in the year [6]88 [October 18, 1289], this year.

---

[195] Compare Vantini, *Oriental Sources*, pp. 342–4.

More than 500 flame-throwing boats (*ḥarārīq*), in addition to boats both large and small for transporting provisions, armory-factories (*zardkhānāh*) and armor (*athqāl*) accompanied them.

When the army arrived at the border of Aswān, the would-be king of Nubia, whom al-Malik al-Manṣūr had sent with the army, died, and was buried there. The emir `Izz al-Dīn *al-afram* informed the Sultan of that, so he sent a man from among the king Dā'ūd's sister's children, who was at the sultanic gates, and ordered him to be made king in Nubia. So he caught up with them using the post-horses before the army departed from Aswān.

When he arrived to them, the army divided into two halves as usual. The emir `Izz al-Dīn *al-afram* and the emir Sayf al-Dīn Qunchaq with half the army and half the Bedouin on the western bank, while the emir `Izz al-Dīn Aydimur, in charge of the Qūṣ districts, and the emir Sayf al-Dīn Baktimur *al-jūkandār*, with half the army and half the Bedouin on the eastern bank.

They departed and wrote an order for Jurays, the deputy of Nubia, to precede them camp-stop by camp-stop, while the children of al-Kanz, emirs of Aswān, should pacify the country folk, and make them feel secure, as they provisioned the stopping-points of the army.

Usually when the army came to a town, the elders and notables of it would come out, and kiss the ground in front of the emirs, taking a safe-conduct, and that they would continue in their town. This was from Edfo to the Makāyīl Islands, which was the land under the control of Jurays, the master of the horse.

As for the lands beyond that, over which Jurays did not have any control, it was left in the obedience of the would-be king of Nubia. The army looted what it found in those lands, killing its people whoever stayed behind in them, pasturing in their fields, burning their water wheels and homes until they ended up in the city of Dongola. [84]

They found that the king and its people had abandoned it, and they only were able to find an elderly man and an old woman in it. They asked them for news of the king, so they mentioned that he had departed to an island in the midst of the Nile at a distance of 15 days from Dongola. The width of this island is three days [travel] in length.

The emir `Izz al-Dīn, in charge of the Qūṣ districts, pursued them to the previously mentioned island, but the flame-throwing boats did not accompany them, nor any boats on account of the river being impassable with rocks, according to what we will mention further.

[*Obituaries*]

In the year 689 [1290]

In the beginning of this year the emir Ḥusām al-Dīn Ṭurunṭāy, the deputy sultan in the Egyptian homelands, departed together with a number of the emirs and armies to Upper Egypt of protected Egypt. He then came to the stopping-point of Ṭūkh Damnū, opposite the city of Qūṣ, and hunted on this trip. He also pacified the lands, killing a number of Bedouin, and burning some of them with fire, taking their horses and weapons, and their leaders as hostages. He then returned to the hill citadel safely.

During it, al-Malik al-Manṣūr Sayf al-Dīn wa-l-Dunyā Qalāwūn provisioned the emir Sayf al-Dīn al-Taqawī to go to Tripoli, and assigned 600 horsemen to stationed with him in Tripoli. This was the first army stationed in it, as the army previously had been stationed in the fortresses.

In the month of Rabīʿ al-Awwal [March–April 1290] of this year al-Malik al-Manṣūr sought to recall the emir Shams al-Dīn Sunqur *al-aʿsar*, Chancelleries Supervisor in protected Damascus from Damascus on the post-horse. When he arrived at his gate at the Hill Citadel in protected Egypt, he honored him, and said to him,

> Know that the only reason I bought you, made you emir, and appointed you to be supervisor was because I thought that you would give me good advice, obtain funds for me, and take the interests of my rule (*dawla*) into your hands, so stay with collecting revenues.

He bestowed a robe upon him, and delegated the fortresses in the rest of the Syrian realms and the coastland, and the Army Chancellery to him in addition to the Chancelleries Supervision in Syria. So he returned to Syria, and his arrival in Damascus was on Wednesday 20 Rabīʿ al-Ākhir [May 2, 1290] of this year, so he became great in his own mind and waxed arrogant.

In Jumādā al-Ulā of this year al-Malik al-Manṣūr Sayf al-Dīn Qalāwūn ordered the arrest of [91] the emir Sayf al-Dīn Jarmak al-Nāṣirī. In it, after the death of the Chief Judge Najm al-Dīn Aḥmad son of the Chief Judge Shams al-Dīn Abū Muḥammad ʿAbd al-Raḥmān al-Maqdisī al-Dimashqī, the Chief Judge for the Ḥanbalites in protected Damascus, the emir Ḥusām al-Dīn Lājīn, the deputy sultan nominated three men from the Ḥanbalites. They were Shaykh Zayn al-Dīn Manjā, the Shaykh Taqī al-Dīn Sulaymān, and the Shaykh Sharaf al-Dīn al-Ḥasan.

He wrote on behalf of them to al-Malik al-Manṣūr Sayf al-Dīn Qalāwūn, and so the sultanic note (*mithāl*) arrived on the first day of Jumādā al-Ākhira [June 1290] of this year for the emir Ḥusām al-Dīn, the deputy sultan, to entrust the judgeship in Damascus to the judge Sharaf al-Dīn al-Ḥasan son of the preacher Sharaf al-Dīn Abū al-ʿAbbās Aḥmad b. Abū ʿUmar b. Qudāma al-Maqdisī. Therefore, the deputy sultan entrusted the judgeship to him, in accordance with the sultanic order. His investiture was written by the emir Ḥusām al-Dīn Lājīn, the deputy sultan in Damascus, and a robe of honor was bestowed upon him on Monday 9 of the previously mentioned month [June 19, 1290]. He sat in the Great Mosque of Damascus, and judged among the people in accord with the usual manner of judges prior to him.

Mention of what was decided for the Egyptian army in Nubia, and the rule of Dā'ūd's nephew over the realm of Nubia, and what was agreed for him after the return of the Egyptian army[196]

We mentioned previously that the Sultan al-Malik al-Manṣūr dispatched armies to Nubia, and that they ended up in Dongola, where they found Simāmūn the king of Nubia had fled to an island in the middle of the Nile, so they followed him.

When they came opposite the island, they observed a number of Nubian boats, and a great number [of people?]. So they asked about the king and they informed them that he was on the previously mentioned island. They sent to him, and offered him to enter into obedience and to present himself, including the offer of a safe-conduct, but he declined this. The army stayed three days, and gave him to understand that they had sent for the boats and the fireboats, and would be crossing over to him to fight him.

So he retreated from the island in the direction of al-Abwāb, which is at a distance of three days from the island, and is not part of his realm. The *sawākira*—who are the [Nubian] noblemen—with him separated themselves from him, as well as the bishops and the priests, taking with them the silver cross which is held over the head of the king and the crown of the realm. They requested a safe-conduct, and entered into obedience.

So the emir `Izz al-Dīn gave them a safe-conduct, and robes of honor to their notables, and they returned together with him to Dongola leading a great crowd. When they reached it, the emir `Izz al-Dīn *al-afram* and the emir Sayf al-Dīn Qunjaq crossed over to the eastern bank without their army, and conferred with the emirs in Dongola.

The armies wore their battle-gear, and paraded on both sides [of the river], while the fireboats in the river were decorated, and the firemen (*zarrāqūn*) played with the naphtha. The brother emirs prepared a banquet in the Isūs Church, which is [92] the largest church in Dongola.

So when they had eaten, they made the king who had come from the sultanic gates ruler, and crowned him. They had him take an oath to the Sultan al-Malik al-Manṣūr Sayf al-Dīn Qalāwūn al-Alfī al-Ṣāliḥī al-Najmī, the master of the Egyptian homelands and the Syrian lands.

The people of the Nubian lands all swore an oath to him, and renewed the terms of the tribute-compact (*baqt*), which was in force previously, and so the tribute was set. A section from the army was dispatched to be with him [the king], and Rukn al-Dīn Baybars al-`Izzī, one of the mamluks of the emir `Izz al-Dīn, in charge of Qūṣ, commanded them.

The Egyptian army returned, and the period of their being absent from the departing the border of Aswān until returning was six months. They took a

[196] Compare Vantini, *Sources*, pp. 545–7.

great deal of booty, and their arrival at protected Cairo was during Jumādā al-Ulā in the year [6]89 [May 1290].

This was what was happening with them; as for what was happening the ruling king and the deposed king, the deposed king Simāmūn, when the Egyptian army returned from Dongola as we have mentioned, he also returned at night, and began to station himself at the gate of every *sawkirī*—who are the noblemen—by himself, and to call out to him.

When he would come out, then he would kiss the ground in front of him, and swear an oath to him. Only a short time passed until the entire Nubian army was suborned to him, so he marched leading them against the royal palace of the one who ruled the Nubian realm. He sent for Rukn al-Dīn Baybars al-`Izzī to go to the one he served, so that there would be no fighting between them.

So Rukn al-Dīn Baybars and those with him departed for Qūṣ, and king Simāmūn established himself in Dongola. He took the king who the [Egyptian] army had put on the throne, stripped him of his clothes, slaughtered a bull, cut its hide into strips, and wrapped them around him when they were fresh. He then fastened him to a piece of wood, so that they [the strips] dried on him, so he died.

Jurays was also killed, and the king Simāmūn wrote to al-Malik al-Manṣūr Sayf al-Dīn Qalāwūn, seeking friendship, and asking for forgiveness from him. He committed himself to pay the set tribute each year, and even extra, and sent him some slaves, and honorary gifts, a great number.

This arrived at the end of the Manṣūrī period (*dawla*), and the Sultan was preoccupied with what was much more important than Nubia. So Simāmūn stayed [as king] in Nubia until the time of al-Malik al-`Ādil Zayn al-Dīn Kitbughā al-Manṣūrī.

In Jumādā al-Ākhira [July 1290] of this year al-Malik al-Manṣūr Sayf al-Dīn Qalāwūn ordered an investigation of Nāṣir al-Dīn Ibn al-Maqdisī, his trustee (*wakil*) in Syria. The decree arrived in Damascus on the 22nd of the previously mentioned month [July 2, 1290], so he was investigated, and many shameful actions were uncovered. The people were very happy about that, so a petition was circulated about him, and raised to the Sultan concerning what had been uncovered about him.

The answer arrived on Friday 19 Rajab of this year [July 28, 1290], to extract from him what he had found, so he was required to do that, and beaten with whips (*maqāri`*) on the day on which the decree arrived. It was ordered to sell what he had, and to carry away the price.

This continued while he was at the al-`Adhrāwiyya College under proscription until Thursday 2 Sha`bān [August 10, 1290] of this year, whereupon the sultanic decree arrived [93] to bring him to the sultanic gates in protected Egypt. However, when the people gathered on the morning of Friday, they entered into his presence, then found him hung. Those in authority (*awlīyā' al-amr*), the judges and the notary-witnesses were present, and they testified as to the state in which he was found.

They wrote a report on it, he was buried, and the people were at peace from his evil. Al-Malik al-Manṣūr then delegated to the emir `Izz al-Dīn Aybak al-Mawṣilī the command of the army in protected Gaza, and the coastal districts in place of the emir Shams al-Dīn Aqsunqur as an assignment, so the emir `Izz al-Dīn departed on 4 Rajab [July 13, 1290] of this year from protected Damascus for Gaza.

During Sha`bān [689/August–September, 1290] of this year the decree of al-Malik al-Manṣūr went out to Syria that none were to utilize the protected people, the Jews and Christians, in the official communications (*mubāshirāt*), so they were removed from them.

In it, an official note (*mithāl*) arrived to the emir Ḥusām al-Dīn, the governor of Syria, to release the prisoners. In it, the heat increased in Ḥamāh until meat was roasted on the paving stones of the Friday Mosque, according to what the shaykh Shams al-Dīn al-Jazarī told in his *History.* A fire occurred in the house of the ruler of Ḥamāh as he was out hunting. God sent a wind that intensified it, so the fire grew, lasting for two days, into a third. No one could come close to it, so the house burned together with all that was inside of it.

In it, a group of Franks in Acre rose up and killed a number of Muslim merchants in it, who had come for commerce, trusting in the truce that we previously explained. The people of Acre claimed that this was only done by the western Franks, and that it was not at their behest. This was the most significant reason that necessitated the conquest of Acre, as we will mention, if God Most High wills it.

When what the Franks of Acre had done reached al-Malik al-Manṣūr, he issued an order to the emir Ḥusām al-Dīn Lājīn, the Sultan's deputy in protected Damascus, and the emir Shams al-Dīn Sunqar *al-a`sar* to construct mangonels and to prepare armory-factories (*zardkhāna*) for the siege of Acre.

The emir Shams al-Dīn Sunqar *al-a`sar* went to Wādī Murabbīn, which is between the `Akkār Mountains and Ba`lbak. In it there was a great deal of timber and wood for the mangonels, the like of which one would be unable to find any other place. A group reliable in their reports told that there was a tree standing whose height was 21 cubits, using the work cubit, and its base was the same. They verified it by having a man climb to its top and let down a rope from its top to the bottom. Then they wrapped that rope around it, and it was equal, no more and no less. Thus some of the historians have mentioned.

Then the emir Shams al-Dīn Sunqur *al-a`sar* departed for that valley, and levied on the properties of al-Marj, and the Ghūṭa of Damascus a fee of between 500–2000 dirhams, each property in accord with what its revenues earned, to pay for the transportation of the wood for the mangonels. In the same way the properties of Ba`lbak and the Biqā` [were taxed], so the money was raised. The people of Ba`lbak and the Biqā` suffered tremendously from this.

While the emir Shams al-Dīn Sunqur *al-a`sar* was in the previously mentioned valley, engrossed in the cutting of logs and transporting them, there was a heavy snowfall on him, so he rode [94] his horse, and extricated himself from it. The abundant snow caused him to hasten, while doubling the transportation burdens and [difficulties of] his camp, so he abandoned it all.

He saved himself in spite of his recklessness. If he had delayed and attempted in carrying it, he would have perished—him and those with him. His burdens were blocked by the snow, and remained underneath until the advent of summer when most of it had been destroyed.

On Thursday 6 Shawwāl [October 18, 1290] of this year al-Malik al-Manṣūr released the senior emir `Alam al-Dīn Sanjar al-Ḥalabī. He had been imprisoned from Dhū al-Qa`da the year [6]83 [January 1285] until he was released in this year. He was appointed to be the emir of 100 horsemen, as usual, and God knows best.

Mention of some reports of al-Malik al-Manṣūr and his death

Al-Malik al-Manṣūr Sayf al-Dīn Qalāwūn son of `Abdallāh al-Ḥurr al-Alfī al-Ṣāliḥī al-Najmī was among those who avoided the Seven Actions leading to Perdition (*sab` al-mubiqāt*), and had numerous conquests, just as we have mentioned. The conquests, and the defeat of the Tatars in [6]80, and the Franks' leaving because of being in fear of him, was in his 70s.

He had numerous righteous charitable endowments in Cairo, the famous college and the hospital, which is among the most beautiful buildings of the time—needed by kings, and turned to by rich and indigent alike. It is an aid to the poor, a source of pride to the broken. He kept a firm eye upon the lands, length and breadth, and was continually checking documents. There are a number of unusual and strange anecdotes told about him.

One of the unusual things told about him concerning that was that he went out one day to the Victory Cupola, him and a number of the emirs, just for pleasure, so the cloth tents (*ṣawāwīn*)[197] were pitched for him. Then he summoned one of the lambs of the [type which produce] al-Badārī lambskin, so he looked them over, then turned them, choosing from them a lamb with the most healthy limbs, and then divided the rest of the lambs between his emirs. He then said, "Let each one of you rise, slaughter his lamb, and roast it with his own hands, just as we used to do in our lands from before."

Then he rose, slaughtered the lamb he had chosen, roasted it with his own hand, so when he finished he asked the emirs to join him in eating it. When they were present, he took from the shoulder blade, ate it, and the emirs ate from the rest of the lamb, so when he had eaten the meat of this shoulder blade, he cleaned it until he extracted the bone-marrow, then tossed it aside a bit so that it would be dry.

[197] Compare Ibn Iyyās, *Badā'i`*, i:2, pp. 396, 501.

Then he rose and began to wave it above the fire with a rope, then took it out [of the fire], gazed at it, considered it for a long time, then spit upon it, and cursed it, throwing it from his hand. One of the emirs asked him about that, after his anger had subsided, so he said, "By God, he said about this Qipchaq youth, don't send him to Syria! Because if he goes there, he will flee, and make a great dissension."

In his opinion, the Qipchaq [= Sayf al-Dīn Qunjāq] continued to be laggard for that reason, his entire life. When al-Malik al-Manṣūr died, and his son al-Malik al-Ashraf became sultan after him, then was killed, and al-Malik al-Nāṣir Muḥammad son of Qalāwūn became sultan, but then he was removed. Al-Malik al-`Ādil Zayn [95] al-Dīn Kitbughā became sultan, then he was removed, whereupon al-Malik al-Manṣūr Ḥusām al-Dīn Lājīn became sultan, just as we will mention all of that in its place, if God Most High wishes. At that time, he caused the emir Sayf al-Dīn Qunjāq to go to Syria, appointing him to the deputyship of protected Damascus, there was tension between the two of them.

So Sayf al-Dīn Qunjāq fled to the Tatars, and caused a great dissension with the coming of King Ghazan, the king of the Tatars and his armies, doing to the Muslims what we will mention if God Most High wishes, so the matter was just as al-Malik al-Manṣūr, may God Most High have mercy upon him, had predicted.

Among the unusual things is that during the days of al-Malik al-Manṣūr Sayf al-Dīn Qalāwūn it was generally agreed that the emir Sayf al-Dīn Qilīj al-Manṣūrī was among the best, most religious, intelligent and notable among them. He had many good discussions in the secular and religious sciences. He said:

> al-Malik al-Manṣūr Sayf al-Dīn Qalāwūn sent me to a king of the west with a present and a gift,[198] so I stayed with him for a time, then a message came to him from one of the great Frankish kings who was enemies with the Muslims that he requested from him to intercede on his behalf about the marriage of his son to one of the Frankish kings' daughters. Her father was in a state of truce with the king of the west, and there was amity between them, but the king who was asking for the king of the west's intercession was a very fierce enemy to the Muslims and caused them a good deal of harm. However, his son's lust drove him to send to the king of the west to ask for his intercession.
>
> So he said to me "Deal with this issue," but I demurred, so he said, "There is benefit for the Muslims in this, and I think that you should go and deal

[198] If this story has any historical basis, one would assume that the "king of the west" was in Morocco, and probably "one of the great Frankish kings" was Spanish, perhaps Castillian. The inclusion of the apologetic story about the letter from Muḥammad in the latter half of the tale casts doubt upon the veracity of the first part.

with it." He continued being on me until I went and delivered his message to the Frankish king, fulfilling my obligation.

I stayed with the Frankish king for a time, and my situation impressed him, so he began to like me very much, and proposed that I stay with him, being allowed to remain according to my religion, the religion of Islam, but that he would ask al-Malik al-Manṣūr to set me free (*yastaṭliqanī*), but I demurred, and said "There is no way for that to happen ever." He gave me the freedom [of the kingdom] and honored me, so when I wanted to depart from him, he said "I would like to gift you with something incredible, which none of the Muslims at the present time have the like."

I was impressed by this, and I said, "What is it?" He took out a locked box that was of beaten gold, opened it, then took out a pen (*miqlama*) of gold, then took a letter out from it, whose letters had mostly faded. There was a silk covering (*khirqa*) which had been attached to it and other things. He said, "Do you know what this is?" I said "No." He said, "This is a letter from your prophet Muḥammad to my ancestor, Caesar. King after king has continued to pass it down until now. Our kingly ancestors enjoined us that as long as this letter was in our possession, we would have the dominion. This testament was given by Caesar, so we continue to guard this letter closely, and to venerate it extremely, taking blessing from it. None of the Christians know of it other than us. If it was not for your high status with me, your nobility, my trust in your merit and your religion, I would never have shown it to you."

Therefore, I took it, venerated it, took blessing from it, but am not able to read it, because its letters have become disconnected as a result of its dilapidation. Because of this [96] embassy between the king of the west and the Frankish king, who sent to him, there was a truce for a time, and the Muslims were relieved of their evil.

This is one of the strangest and most amazing stories. However, we have described enough reports of al-Malik al-Manṣūr.

The emir `Izz al-Dīn Aybak *al-afram* al-Ṣāliḥī served as deputy sultan over the Egyptian homelands for al-Malik al-Manṣūr at the beginning of his sultanate. Then he asked to be relieved, so the emir Ḥusām [al-Dīn] Ṭurunṭāy al-Manṣūrī was established as the deputy sultan and he continued to be until al-Malik al-Manṣūr died.

The emir Ḥusām al-Dīn Lājīn *al-silaḥdār* al-Manṣūrī, who was known as "Lesser," served as his deputy in protected Damascus after its return from al-Malik al-`Ādil Shams al-Dīn Sunqur *al-ashqar*. During the beginning of his period the emir Jamāl al-Dīn Aqush al-Shamsī served as deputy in the

Aleppan realm until he died, then the emir `Alam al-Dīn Sanjar al-Bāshqirdī until he was removed, then he appointed the emir Shams al-Dīn Qarāsunqur *al-jūkandār* al-Manṣūrī until al-Malik al-Manṣūr died.

The emir Sayf al-Dīn Balabān al-Ṭabbākhī served as deputy in Ḥiṣn al-Akrād, while during the beginning of his period, the emir `Alā' al-Dīn al-Kabakī served as deputy in the Safedan realm, then a number of emirs, and in Kerak the emir `Izz al-Dīn Aybak al-Mawṣilī, then the emir Rukn al-Dīn Baybars *al-dawādār* al-Manṣūrī. In Gaza and Ḥimṣ a number of emirs served as deputies.

His ministers were six people, four from the "pen" bureaucrats, who were the chief Burhān al-Dīn al-Khiḍr al-Sinjārī, time after time, the chief Fakhr al-Dīn Ibrāhīm b. Luqmān, the chief Najm al-Dīn Ḥamza b. Muḥammad al-Uṣfūnī, and Chief Judge Taqī al-Dīn `Abd al-Raḥmān son of the Chief Judge Tāj al-Dīn son of the daughter of al-A`zz. Of the emirs, `Alam al-Dīn Sanjar al-Shujā`ī, who had been appointed to the supervision and administration of the Manṣūrī state. When the ministry was left without a minister, he would sit in the council in place of a minister just as a regular minister—appointing and removing, employing and moving—then he became the minister all alone after the death of the chief Najm al-Dīn Ḥamza al-Uṣfūnī.

In his ministry and his supervision, he used violence and confiscation regularly to gather wealth both legally and illegally. He was harsh upon those working with him, and they were terrified of him, until finally both the elite and the commoners disliked him, and even desired for al-Malik al-Manṣūr's regime to be removed because of him. He continued in the ministry until the Sultan removed him and appointed the emir Badr al-Dīn Baydarā al-Manṣūrī, and he continued in the ministry until al-Malik al-Manṣūr died.

It reached the Sultan al-Malik al-Manṣūr that some of the Muslim merchants had mamluks, who were being taken to the gate of al-Malik al-Manṣūr, so when they arrived at the port of Acre, the Franks killed them [the merchants] and took the mamluks that they had with the goods. He was enraged to hear that, and in pain, but then it reached him that the inhabitants of Acre had taken vengeance upon a number of Muslim merchants [97] killing them, so he resolved to go towards them to break the truce which had been established because of the occurrence of this event on their part.

They sent to him begging forgiveness, but he did not receive them, and sent to Syria to prepare mangonels because of the upcoming siege, just as we previously explained. He prepared, and was determined to set out to Acre, but took ill while he was in the Hill Citadel. This did not deter him from departing to where he was going, and rode from the Hill Citadel, staying at his camp at the Straw Mosque outside of protected Cairo. This was the first stop, and it was during the last tenth of Shawwāl in the year [6]89 [late October early November 1290].

His illness continued until he died in the camp, at the Straw Mosque stop, in the outskirts of protected Cairo on the day of 6 Dhū al-Qa`da [November 10, 1290] of this year, and he was carried to the Hill Citadel at night, and stayed until the end of Thursday 1 Muḥarram year 690 [January 11, 1291].

On that day, al-Malik al-Ashraf Ṣalāḥ al-Dīn Khalīl sent an amount of money to the Manṣūriyya gravesite in Cairo to give as charity there. When it was the night of Friday 2 Muḥarram [January 12, 1291], the corpse of al-Malik al-Manṣūr was transported from the Citadel to its grave which had been constructed at the Manṣūriyya College inside protected Cairo.

It was said that his son al-Malik al-Ashraf Ṣalāḥ al-Dīn Khalīl had caused him to drink poison, so he died in the morning of Friday 10 Muḥarram year 690 [January 20, 1291] in the camp, and was carried to the Hill Citadel at night, then carried to his grave at the Manṣūriyya Cupola between the palaces in protected Cairo.[199] He was brought in through the Barqiyya Gate, and they prayed over him at the al-Azhar Mosque.

Then he was born to the grave. The emir Badr al-Dīn Baydarā and the emir `Alam al-Dīn Sanjar al-Shujā`ī stayed by his tomb, while al-Malik al-Ashraf dispensed an amount of gold on the morning of his interment to the [Qur'ān] reciters. God knows best what in this happened.

The period of al-Malik al-Manṣūr's sultanate was eleven years two months and 14 days, but it is said eleven years five months and 17 days. He left behind as an inheritance for his five children, who were al-Malik al-Ashraf Ṣalāḥ al-Dīn Khalīl, the one who ruled after him, al-Malik al-Nāṣir Nāṣir al-Dīn Muḥammad, the emir Aḥmad, who died during the sultanate of his brother [al-Ashraf], and two daughters, who were Dār al-Mukhtār al-Jawharī, whose name was Iltamish, and Dār `Anbar al-Kamālī, whose husband was the son of al-Malik al-Nāṣir.

al-Malik al-Manṣūr ruled mamluks, Turks, Mongols (*mughal*), and others never ruled by any king in the Egyptian homelands previously during the time of Islam. It is said that their number reached 12,000, and many of them were mastered during the Manṣūrī period or by those deputized from the noble sultanate in the Syrian lands and the Egyptian homelands as we have previously explained. There were also those that became autonomous from the sultanate, in which the Friday sermon was given, and the mint was struck in their name, as we will mention in its appropriate place, if God Most High wills.

The rest of the Manṣūrī mamluks continued to be the senior emirs through most of the period of al-Malik al-Nāṣir [98] Nāṣir al-Dīn Muḥammad son of al-Malik al-Manṣūr Sayf al-Dīn Qalāwūn al-Alfī al-Ṣāliḥī al-Najmī, may God Most High have mercy on both of them.

---

[199] This is an odd report, inconsistent with all of the other accounts of Qalāwūn's death. Perhaps it gained currency because there was such a significant delay between his death and his burial.

Mention of the sultanate of al-Malik al-Ashraf Ṣalāḥ al-Dīn Khalīl son of al-Malik al-Manṣūr Sayf al-Dīn Qalāwūn son of `Abdallāh al-Ḥurr al-Alfī al-Ṣāliḥī al-Najmī in the Egyptian homelands and the Islamic realms that were attached to it

Al-Malik al-Ashraf Ṣalāḥ al-Dīn Khalīl son of al-Malik al-Manṣūr Sayf al-Dīn Qalāwūn al-Alfī al-Ṣāliḥī al-Najmī was the eighth of the Turkish dynasty to rule in the Egyptian homelands, the Syrian lands and the Ḥijāzi quarters, and those Islamic realms that were added after the death of his father al-Malik al-Manṣūr, may God Most High have mercy on him.

His enthronement upon the Sultanic throne in the protected Hill Citadel was on Sunday 7 Dhū al-Qa`da year 689 [November 11, 1290] this year. Absolutely no one opposed him, because the emirs, the ones possessing the right to appoint and to remove (*al-ḥall wa-l-`aqd*), and the sultan's deputies among the rest of the Egyptian and Syrian *mamluk*s were *mamluk*s of his father.

All the rest of the *mamluk* emirs from the Ṣāliḥiyya Najmiyya [regiment] manifested agreement, obedience, and willingness to follow and haste to swear allegiance. It was said that he was enthroned on the sultanic throne on Monday 8 Dhū al-Qa`da [November 12, 1290], and all the emirs, commanders, dignitaries of the state, notables, lords, judges and secretaries swore allegiance to him as usual, and the preachers preached on his behalf on Friday 12 Dhū al-Qa`da [November 16, 1290].

It was said that everything was settled for al-Malik al-Ashraf by 10 Muḥarram year 690 [January 13, 1291] by the emirs' agreement about him, and we have already mentioned that al-Malik al-Manṣūr had already obtained for al-Malik al-Ashraf the title of heir-apparent after the death of his brother al-Malik al-Ṣāliḥ `Alā' al-Dīn `Alī, and fitted him with the sultanic insignia. However, the writing of his appointment was delayed, although al-Ashraf had requested this time after time, while his father al-Malik al-Manṣūr delayed giving his permission to write the appointment.

Then he discussed it with the Sultan, who decreed that it be written, so it was. When it was brought before al-Malik al-Manṣūr for him to sign it, he delayed again, and returned it to the Judge Fatḥ al-Dīn Ibn `Abd al-Ẓāhir, the head of the Chancellery Department. He did not sign it, but al-Malik al-Ashraf sent to the judge Fatḥ al-Dīn requesting the appointment.

He apologized that he had not presented it for signature, and it was presented a second time to al-Malik al-Manṣūr, but he refused it, saying, "O Fatḥ al-Dīn, I will not have Khalīl rule over the Muslims." Then al-Malik al-Ashraf sent requesting the appointment, but Fatḥ al-Dīn was afraid to say that the Sultan had refused to sign it, and apologized again.

He addressed al-Malik al-Manṣūr about its contents, and presented it to him, but he threw it out, and said, "I have already said to you that I will not have Khalīl ruling over the Muslims!" Therefore, he took the appointment without a signature, and departed. During this it was decided that the Sultan would depart, going to Acre, and his death [occurred].

So when al-Malik al-Ashraf became sultan he requested the Judge Fatḥ al-Dīn Ibn `Abd al-Ẓāhir, and said, "Where is my appointment?" so he rose and brought it to him [99], even though it was without al-Malik al-Manṣūr's signature. He then apologized that the Sultan al-Malik al-Manṣūr had been distracted from signing it by the hustle and bustle about the enemy, so al-Malik al-Ashraf said to him "O Fatḥ al-Dīn, the Sultan refused to give it (the sultanate) to me, so instead God gave it to me." Then he threw the appointment at him, so it remained without a signature. After that, it was with his son the judge `Alā' al-Dīn until he died, may God Most High have mercy upon him.

When al-Malik al-Ashraf sat as Sultan some of the poets said, praising him:

Your cry, O just one, giver of justice, giving hope for the relief described,
Render Gods servants unneedful, as your generosity is a sea which is known,
The people obey you out of choice, no spear or blade humiliates them,
How many kings have ruled Egypt, how they were generous, but yet not acting immoderately,
Until the Victorious One (al-Manṣūr) came, causing the populace to forget those previously by his actions,
They never put forth his godfearingness, nor left the like of what he left behind,
So be proud of the acquisitions boastfully; you have gained (them), as you are al-Malik al-Ashraf!

Al-Malik al-Ashraf bestowed robes of honor up the rest of the emirs, the commanders, the lords, the judges, the secretaries, dignitaries of the state, and possessors of positions, as usually happened, and then al-Malik al-Ashaf rode with the sultanic insignia on Friday after the prayers 12 Dhū al-Qa`da year 689 [November 16, 1290]. It was said that his riding was on Saturday 13 Dhū al-Qa`da [November 17, 1290].

He went through the Lions Square, which is under the Hill Citadel close to the Horse Market, on the outskirts of protected Cairo, while the emirs and all the armies were in his service. He ascended to the Hill Citadel before the afternoon calling to prayer, and we will mention the reason for his returning to the Citadel hastily, if God Most High wills it.

Mention of Ḥusām al-Dīn Ṭurunṭāy's detention, and his execution, as well as Zayn al-Dīn Kitbughā and his imprisonment

Al-Malik al-Ashraf Ṣalāḥ al-Dīn Khalīl son of al-Malik al-Manṣūr used to dislike the emir Ḥusām al-Dīn Ṭurunṭāy, the deputy sultan in the Egyptian homelands, very much for the following reasons. Among them were the public rejection he used to demonstrate towards him, the denigration from him, snubbing[200] his deputies, and harming those connected with him.

Other issues were his favoritism towards his brother al-Malik al-Ṣāliḥ `Alā' al-Dīn `Alī, and his tending towards the latter. When al-Malik al-Ṣāliḥ died, the position of heir-apparent passed after him to al-Malik al-Ashraf, most of those who had tended away from him tended towards him, and those who had despised him sought to be close to his heart.

However, the emir Ḥusām al-Dīn only increased his aversion towards him, and continued as usual to harm those connected with him [al-Ashraf]. He incited al-Malik al-Manṣūr against the Chancellery Inspector of al-Malik [100] al-Ashraf, the judge Shams al-Dīn Ibn Sal`ūs, until he was beaten, and removed from his responsibilities, as was mentioned in another place. He treated him in this manner, from which al-Malik al-Ashraf was unable to defend him because of the emir Ḥusām al-Dīn's power over al-Malik al-Manṣūr. Nevertheless, he concealed what he felt, was patient in a way that no other would have been able to be.

When al-Malik al-Ashraf became ruler, and he was firm in his position, the emir Ḥusām al-Dīn Ṭurunṭāy stood before him as deputy sultan, as usual with the Sultan al-Malik al-Manṣūr his father, and made it clear that he hated his actions, and his mind was turned against him. He secretly mandated destruction of his [al-Ashraf's] administration, removing the command from him, while al-Malik al-Ashraf verified all that. Some of his inner circle also made false accusations against him as well.

When al-Malik al-Ashraf had ridden to the Square, just as we have previously explained, the emir Ḥusām al-Dīn Ṭurunṭāy, the deputy sultan, decided to assassinate al-Malik al-Ashraf while he was riding, resolving to kill him before he finished his rounds.

When he came close to the stable, al-Malik al-Ashraf became aware of this, so when al-Malik al-Ashraf had gone through four squares, the emir Ḥusām al-Dīn Ṭurunṭāy and those who conspired with him were at the Raiding Gate. Therefore, when the sultan finished off at the head of the square, and came close to the Stable Gate, most people thought that he would turn towards the Raiding Gate to complete the round as usual.

Instead he turned towards the Citadel, rushed, crossing towards the Stable Gate. When al-Malik al-Ashraf turned the emir Ḥusām al-Dīn Ṭurunṭāy and those with him galloped forward, trying to catch him. By the time they reached the Stable Gate al-Malik al-Ashraf had already entered, and his mamluks and courtiers had surrounded him, so what Ṭurunṭāy had planned came to naught.

al-Malik al-Ashraf made haste, dismounted, summoned the emir Ḥusām al-Dīn Ṭurunṭāy, but the emir Zayn al-Dīn Kitbughā al-Manṣūrī forbade the

---

200 Reading *i-h-n-at* as *ihāna.*

latter from entering into al-Malik al-Ashraf's presence, warning him of that. He said, "By God, I am afraid for you from him so do not go into his presence without a band or a group who you know will protect you. If something happens, then he won't go back on his word."

However, he believed that no one would dare to approach him because of the terror he inspired in people, his position in the state, and he thought that the Sultan al-Malik al-Ashraf would not make haste to detain him. So he said to the emir Zayn al-Dīn Kitbughā in response to what he had told him "By God, even if I were asleep Khalīl wouldn't dare to wake me up!" and rose and entered into the presence of al-Malik al-Ashraf. The emir Zayn al-Dīn Kitbughā continued to stand guard over him as he entered with him.

When the emir Ḥusām al-Dīn Ṭurunṭāy was before al-Malik al-Ashraf, he had already decided with the emirs of his personal guard (*khāṣakiyya*) that he would be detained, so they made haste to do that, and detained him, taking his sword, whereupon Kitbughā began to scream, saying "What (*ayish*) is he doing? What is he doing?" repeating it over and over, so al-Malik al-Ashraf ordered for the emir Zayn al-Dīn Kitbughā to be detained also, so he was. He was imprisoned until al-Malik al-Ashraf ordered for the emir Ḥusām [101] al-Dīn Ṭurunṭāy to be killed.

He was killed on Monday 15 Dhū al-Qa`da year [6]89 [November 19, 1290]. It was said that he was tortured in front of al-Malik al-Ashraf until he died. It was said that al-Malik al-Ashraf beat him with his hand until he died that very hour. It was commonly believed that he found him when he had entered into his presence, wearing chain mail under his [garments of] deputyship. It was said that his death was on Thursday 18 Dhū al-Qa`da [November 22, 1290] in the Hill Citadel, and that he remained for eight days having been cast into the citadel prison. Then he was taken out Friday night 26 Dhū al-Qa`da after he had been wrapped cloth, then carried on a regular shield (*janawiyya*)[201] to the small mosque (*zāwiya*) of shaykh Abū al-Su`ūd in Qarāfa of protected Old Cairo.

The shaykh `Umar al-Su`ūdī, the small mosque's shaykh, washed him, wrapped him (in cloths) from his own wealth, and buried him outside of the small mosque a bit to the south of it at night. It stayed like that until the time when the emir Zayn al-Dīn Kitbughā al-Manṣūrī ruled, who we have mentioned that al-Malik al-Ashraf detained him, and then he ruled the Egyptian homelands, as we will mention if God Most High wishes. He ordered that the corpse of Ḥusām al-Dīn Ṭurunṭāy be transferred to his mausoleum, which he built in his college known as al-Ḥusāmiyya, which is close, by his house on

[201] David Nicolle, *Arms & Armour of the Crusading Era 1050–1350: Islam, Eastern Europe and Asia.* (London: Greenhill, 1999), glossary, s.v., called that way because they were modeled upon Genoese shields.

Rolling-pin Line, which today is towards the Neighborhood Market inside protected Cairo.

When al-Malik al-Ashraf detained the emir Ḥusām al-Dīn Ṭurunṭāy he deputized the emir `Alam al-Dīn Sanjar al-Shujā`ī to post a guard around his belongings, and to sort out his wealth, because of the well-known enmity that was between the two of them. Al-Shujā`ī went down to the house of the emir Ḥusām al-Dīn Ṭurunṭāy which is in Cairo, and carried away its treasures and stores, seeking his secret deposits, and digging up places in his house, looking for everything.

He took away a massive amount to the treasuries and the Islamic Treasury (*bayt al-māl*). It is said that the total of what he took from his wealth in gold coinage was 600,000 Egyptian dinars, and of the dirhams was 17,100 Egyptian *raṭl*s [= 7,637.76 kg]. There was no counting the value of the provisions, the fabrics, the horses, and the mamluks because of the amount. It is said that he had amassed all of that and stored it away because he was seeking the sultanate for himself, but he did not attain his wish.

Al-Jazarī tells in his *History*, saying: One of the older emirs told me that the total of what was taken from the house of the emir Ḥusām al-Dīn Ṭurunṭāy and carried to the Citadel, and spent upon the emirs during the first part of the Ashrafī period was in gold coinage 600,000 Egyptian dinars, and of dirhams, 170 Egyptian *qinṭār*s [= 7,638.1 kg]. This is not to speak of the stores, the horses, the mules, the camels, the implements, the properties, which were not counted because of their number, and of the provisions, the copper smelting house, the refectory, the armory, the saddles, the bridles, the factory for making riding clothes, the pantry (*ṭashtkhānāh*), and the factory for making sleeping-mats, and sewing—what no other emir or king had.

This is also not including the trade goods, wealth for traveling in his name, the loans, deposits, types of sugar-candies (*qunūd*), honeys, cattle, sheep and goats, and slaves, for all of this was not counted due to its number, nor is its value known in the Egyptian homelands other than [102] what his scriveners and deputies concealed in Egypt and Syria. As for his mamluks, al-Malik al-Ashraf reviewed them, and took those he chose, and dispersed the rest among the emirs.

Days after the emir Ḥusām al-Dīn Ṭurunṭāy was killed, the son of the emir Ḥusām al-Dīn, who was blind, asked to be admitted into the presence of al-Malik al-Ashraf, so he permitted him. When he stood before him, he placed a kerchief (*mandīl*) upon his face, wept, and stretched out his hand, said, "Something, for God's sake!" He said that his family had days in which there was not anything to eat, so he [al-Ashraf] had compassion upon him, and released some of Ṭurunṭāy's properties [to him]. He said, "Use the extra, then praise the One who neither the days nor the epochs change. Nothing interferes, removes or distracts Him; every day He is involved."

Al-Malik al-Ashraf released the emir Zayn al-Dīn Kitbughā and returned him to the position he had held.

Mention of the delegation of the deputy sultanate in the Egyptian homelands to the emir Badr al-Dīn Baydarā al-Manṣūrī

When al-Malik al-Ashraf detained the emir Ḥusām al-Dīn Ṭurunṭāy just as we have previously explained, the emir `Alam al-Dīn Sanjar al-Shujā`ī took over the deputyship for some few days, without having the deputy's robe bestowed upon him, or having an investiture written for him. This was not publicized, but then al-Malik al-Ashraf delegated his deputyship in the Egyptian homelands to the emir Badr al-Dīn Baydarā al-Manṣūrī, bestowing a robe upon him, as usual for deputy sultans, and gave over to him the *iqṭā`* fiefs which had been made over to the emir Ḥusām al-Dīn Ṭurunṭāy, and other things.

On 19 Dhū al-Qa`da [November 23, 1290] of this year the post arrived at protected Damascus telling of the death of al-Malik al-Manṣūr, and the accession of al-Malik al-Ashraf, so the deputy in Damascus swore in the emirs, the commanders, the armies and the bureaucrats as usual. Al-Malik al-Ashraf ordered for the emir Shams al-Dīn Sunqur *al-a`sar* al-Manṣūrī, the Chancelleries Supervisor in Syria, to be sought, so the post arrived in protected Damascus to seek him out on 4 Dhū al-Ḥijja [December 8, 1290] of this year.

So he was headed to the sultanic gates on the 8th, and when he arrived in front of al-Malik al-Ashraf, he ordered him to be beaten, so he was time and again. He stayed on at the official command (*tarsīm*) until the chief Shams al-Dīn Ibn al-Sal`ūs arrived from the noble Ḥijāz, as he was on pilgrimage during this year. When he presented himself during the year [6]90 [1291] the Sultan handed Shams al-Dīn Sunqur *al-a`sar* over to him.

When al-Malik al-Ashraf removed the emir Shams al-Dīn Sunqur from the Chancelleries Supervision in protected Damascus, he appointed the emir Sayf al-Dīn Ṭūghān al-Manṣūrī in his place, and al-Malik [103] al-Ashraf reinstated the chief Taqī al-Dīn Tawba al-Tikrītī to the ministry in protected Damascus. He arrived there on 5 Muḥarram of the year [6]90 [January 8, 1291]. A guard was placed around the belongings of the emir Shams al-Dīn Sunqur *al-a`sar* in accord with the sultanic decree.

In Dhū al-Ḥijja of the year [6]89 [December 1290] Malik al-Ashraf issued a decree to have the emir Badr al-Dīn Baktūt al-`Alā'ī present himself from protected Ḥimṣ to the sultanic gate, and so he did.

In Dhū al-Ḥijja the previously mentioned month, al-Malik al-Ashraf issued a decree to renew the appointment of the emir Ḥusām al-Dīn Lājīn al-Manṣūrī the Lesser, the deputy sultan in protected Damascus by his deputyship of Damascus. It was written and his *iqṭā`* fiefs which were established to the end of the Manṣūrī period were expanded in Ḥarastā, and this was sent at the hand of the emir Shams al-Dīn Aqsunqur al-Ḥusāmī. This Aqsunqur, who had been a mamluk of the emir Ḥusām al-Dīn, was given command of ten. So the emir Shams al-Dīn Aqsunqur al-Ḥusāmī arrived in protected Damascus with that on 18 Dhū al-Ḥijja [December 22, 1290].

[*Obituaries*]

Mention of the events of the year 690 [1291]

On 6 Muḥarram of this year [January 9, 1291] al-Malik al-Ashraf Ṣalāḥ al-Dīn Khalīl son of al-Malik al-Manṣūr Qalāwūn al-Alfī al-Ṣāliḥī al-Najmī, master of the Egyptian homelands and the Syrian lands, released al-Malik al-`Azīz Fakhr al-Dīn `Uthmān son of al-Malik al-Mughīth Fatḥ al-Dīn `Umar son of al-Malik al-`Ādil Sayf al-Dīn Abū Bakr son of al-Malik al-Kāmil Nāṣir al-Dīn Muḥammad son of al-Malik al-`Ādil Sayf al-Dīn Abū Bakr Muḥammad son of Najm al-Dīn Ayyūb son of Shādī son of Marwān al-Ayyūbī, the ruler of Karak, of his father.

Al-Malik al-`Azīz had been imprisoned by al-Malik al-Ẓāhir Rukn al-Dīn Baybars on 14 Rabī` al-Awwal year 669 [October 31, 1270]—the total of his imprisonment had been 20 years, nine months and 22 days. When al-Malik al-Ashraf released al-Malik al-`Azīz he gave him a good pension, but kept him under house arrest. He occupied himself with investigation, copying texts, and was not allowed to go out other than for Friday prayers or to the baths or for an absolute necessity.

Mention of some reports of Shams al-Dīn Ibn al-Sal`ūs, the ministership being entrusted to him, and his haughtiness over the emirs and others

The chief Shams al-Dīn Muḥammad son of Fakhr al-Dīn `Uthmān son of Abū al-Rajā' Ibn Sal`ūs al-Dimashqī was in the beginning a merchant from the people of Damascus, but was not from the wealthy merchants. He used to take the role of formal sessions and leadership upon himself until the merchants among themselves used to describe him as "chief" mockingly.

Then he attached himself to the retainers and became connected to the master Taqī al-Dīn Tawba al-Tikrītī, the minister of protected Damascus [107] during the Manṣūrī period. So he began to be employed in several ways, and was transferred to being in charge of the noble market inspection (*ḥisba*) in Damascus during the month of Ramaḍān 687 [October 1288], as we have previously explained.

Then he was appointed to the Chancellery Inspectorate for al-Malik al-Ashraf in Syria, and demonstrated initiative, and let properties in Syria for al-Malik al-Ashraf, engaged in business for him, and obtained wealth because of that. So he was brought before al-Malik al-Ashraf, who liked him, and was presented at the gate of al-Malik al-Ashraf in Ṣafar year 688 [March 1289], and appointed a deputy in the Market Inspectorate in Damascus when the chancellor was the judge Tāj al-Dīn Aḥmad son of the judge `Imād al-Dīn Muḥammad Ibn al-Shīrāzī.

When Ibn Sal`ūs presented himself to the gate of al-Malik al-Ashraf he transferred him to his Chancellery Inspectorate at his gate in the Egyptian homelands in place of the judge Tāj al-Dīn son of *al-a`mā* (the blind man), and ennobled him with the ministership. He continued in the chancellery of al-Malik al-Ashraf and his trusteeship (*wikāla*) until Jumādā al-Ulā year 689 [May--June 1290]—the previous year.

It was accepted that al-Malik al-Ashraf ennobled him with a yearly honorary robe similar to the robe of ministership. Then al-Malik al-Manṣūr saw him while he was wearing this robe, and disapproved of his appearance. He asked the emir Ḥusām al-Dīn Ṭurunṭāy, the deputy Sultan in the Egyptian homelands, and he said, "This is the minister of al-Malik al-Ashraf," and mentioned his negative points to the Sultan al-Malik al-Manṣūr.

Therefore, the Sultan was angered at that, and disapproved, ordering him to be summoned. The latter was brought before him (the sultan), whereupon he denied his being in the service of his son without his permission or the permission of his deputy or his minister. The Sultan ordered the robe he was wearing to be torn off, and it was, and to hand him over to the Chancelleries Supervisor on that day, who was the emir Zayn al-Dīn Aḥmad al-Ṣawābī, and ordered the confiscation of his things, and for him to be disgraced,[202] and be beaten.

He sent the emir Ḥusām al-Dīn Ṭurunṭāy to him to humiliate, disgrace, and to hasten beating him, but al-Malik al-Ashraf sent to the Chancelleries Supervisor to stop him from that, and to threaten him if something bad happened to him. The supervisor was afraid of al-Malik al-Ashraf's vengeance (*ghā'ila*), so he held off on disgracing him. He issued a command to him in a hall in which the supervisor was sitting, during the time of his taking rest, but then al-Malik al-Ashraf managed to intercede with the emir Ḥusām al-Dīn Ṭurunṭāy with regard to him. He corresponded with him, and sent a number of letters to him, and to others with the same content, until al-Malik al-Manṣūr responded to this intercession, so liberated him. He ordered him to go, so he went, and stayed in his house.

This event was the most harmful event against the emir Ḥusām al-Dīn Ṭurunṭāy, the deputy sultan, and was the principal reason for his being detained and killed, as we previously explained. Ibn al-Sal`ūs continued to be in his house until the time of the pilgrimage during the following year, so then headed to the noble Ḥijāz.

Just then the death of al-Malik al-Manṣūr occurred, with the sultanate of al-Malik al-Ashraf, just as we have also previously explained, and it was said that when the wealth of the emir Ḥusām al-Dīn Ṭurunṭāy was carried to al-Malik al-Ashraf, and it was placed before him, he began to fondle it, saying:

Whoever lives a day after his enemy, has defeated fate. [108]

---

[202] Or have his robe torn off.

Then he would say "Where are you, Ibn al-Sal`ūs?" and he wrote to Ibn al-Sal`ūs with that, and it is said that al-Malik al-Ashraf wrote him in his own hand between the lines, approximately the following:

O Reddy (shuqayr), O face of good, hurry up! We are now king.

When al-Malik al-Ashraf's letter arrived to Ibn al-Sal`ūs while he was on the road, he had returned from the noble Ḥijāz, and he told him that he had become king, and urged him to hurry up and return to him, he [Ibn al-Sal`ūs] gathered those notables and secretaries in the caravan, and brought them over to his side, and they rode in his service. They were obedient to him, treated him politely just as one treats ministers, and were in awe of him.

It was like that until he arrived at the Hill Citadel in protected Egypt. The emir `Alam al-Dīn Sanjar al-Shujā`ī had been acting as the minister from the time that al-Malik al-Ashraf began to rule until the time when Ibn al-Sal`ūs came without an investiture or a proclamation. So when Ibn al-Sal`ūs arrived on Tuesday 20 Muḥarram year [6]90 [January 23, 1291] from the noble Ḥijāz to the Hill Citadel, he met with the Sultan al-Malik al-Ashraf, gave him the peace greeting and he congratulated each one on what God Most High had given them.

When it was Thursday 22 Muḥarram [January 25, 1291] al-Malik al-Ashraf delegated the ministry in the Egyptian homelands to the chief Ibn al-Sal`ūs, and bestowed a robe upon him, giving him full power over the state which no minister during the Turkish rule previous to him had ever had. He dispatched a number of royal mamluks to serve him, and to ride in his service, to serve as foot in his train, to stand before him, and to carry out his commands.

When he wanted to ride to the Citadel the inspectors' inspector and the Chancelleries Supervisor would meet at his gate, together with the governor of Old Cairo, and the state collectors, the regional inspectors, the supervisors of business dealings, and other notables of this type.

Then the four Chief Judges and those following them would be present. When all of these had gathered together at his gate, his chamberlain would inform him that the procession was complete. Completeness of the procession means in their view the presents of the four Chief Judges. So then the chief would depart at that, and ride, while the people went before him according to their classes.

The closest to him would be the Shāfi`ī Chief Judge and the Mālikī Chief Judge would be before him, while the Ḥanafī Chief Judge and the Ḥanbalī Chief Judge would be before them, with the inspectors' inspector, the notables, the state collectors, the regional inspectors in accord with their rank.

The judges would continue with him until he had sat in the council, whereupon they would depart, then return in the evening of that day to the Citadel, and ride in his procession in front of him until he reached his house, even if he was delayed at night in the Citadel until the time of the later evening prayers. Then the Citadel gates would be locked, and the chief's [109] procession would return back to the Stable Gate.

The judges would come and stay upon their mules outside of the sultanic Stable Gate, and would not depart until he had departed and ridden. They would follow in his wake to his house as usual, not leaving it alone. He never rose to stand for one of their greats. This was not the arrangement for the ministers previous to him.

As his procession grew, and the greats stayed thronging in the streets of Cairo, while it was tight for them, because of the numbers of people with him, as the male slaves would crowd around the way to al-Qarāfa and its dwellers because of that, he became very prominent, and puffed up, disdaining people. He came to abandon the ministers' manner, until the senior emirs would enter his sessions, but he would not even rise completely for them, or for some of them even turn towards them.

Sometimes he would summon the *amīr jāndār* or the majordomo in spite of their high-ranking positions. When he would summon someone, he would say "Find so-and-so *amīr jāndār* or so-and-so majordomo," calling each of them by their given names, not by their titles. Beyond that, he would also belittle the deputy sultan the emir Badr al-Dīn Baydarā. He would not turn towards him, nor share in his duties, and even act arrogantly towards him and oppose him in those things he intended to do, or cancel his pet projects.

All the while, the emir Badr al-Dīn Baydarā suffered his rudeness in silence, nor could he take him by surprise because of al-Malik al-Ashraf's favor towards him, which he could see. It is told on the authority of Shihāb al-Dīn b. 'Ubāda, who said:

> I saw the chief Shams al-Dīn on one of the procession days, after he had risen from the ministers' council, wanting to enter the Treasury, but the emirs who wanted to render obeisance to him encountered him, they and the deputy sultan, the emir Badr al-Dīn Baydarā. All of the senior emirs would hasten to his service—among them were those who would kiss his hand—and all would give him the right-of-way, or make signals to get out from in front of him.
>
> When he trod upon the top stair-rung with his leg, the both of them were there, him and the emir Badr al-Dīn Baydarā, deputy sultan, at the same time. Each of them said the peace greeting, and he motioned to make obeisance, but the deputy made much more obeisance to the minister than the minister did to him.
>
> He said: I saw him as he returned with the chief, but he did not walk opposite him. On the contrary, the deputy would go ahead of him slightly, incline his head towards that of the chief, and talk with him. They were like that until they reached the bench (*masṭaba*) upon which

> the majordomo and the Housing Inspector would sit, which is inside the second door from the stair door in the direction of the Treasury, close by the Upholsters Gate previously.[203] This place is not one of the mosque doors, which was constructed during the days of al-Malik al-Nāṣir Nāṣir al-Dīn Muḥammad son of al-Malik al-Manṣūr Qalāwūn al-Alfī al-Ṣāliḥī al-Najmī.
>
> He said: When they both reached that place, the chief grasped a hold of the hand of the emir Badr al-Dīn Baydarā, the deputy sultan, and motioned to him to go back.
>
> He said: I heard the chief said to him, "In the name of God, O emir Badr al-Dīn!" and he didn't say more, but never was the like heard from him.

Then there happened what we shall mention in its place, if God Most High wishes. [110]

On Friday 7 Ṣafar of the year [6]90 [February 9, 1291] al-Malik al-Ashraf ordered for the emir Shams al-Dīn Sunqur *al-ashqar*, who had pretended to be sultan in Syria, and taken the regnal name of al-Malik al-`Ādil,[204] to be detained, together with the emir Sayf al-Dīn Jarmak al-Nāṣirī and a number who had various trespasses (*dhunūb*).

Among those which were numbered against the emir Shams al-Dīn Sunqur *al-ashqar* were that he had said that no one had ever treated him as well as Ḥusām al-Dīn Ṭurunṭāy. Al-Malik al-Manṣūr had always protected him, and forbade detaining him when he [al-Ashraf?] had wanted it, saying, "By God, no one will detain him until they detain me first." Ṭurunṭāy was also loyal to him in accord with what he had concluded with him when he had asked him to descend from Ṣahyūn.

However, he did not reciprocate this immense good treatment, and this protection of him. This was one of the major reasons for his being detained, as he spread his secrets.

On this day al-Malik al-Ashraf released the emir Zayn al-Dīn Kitbughā al-Manṣūrī. He had been detained when he had sought to defend the emir Ḥusām al-Dīn Ṭurunṭāy, the deputy sultan in the Egyptian homelands, just as we previously explained. When al-Malik al-Ashraf released the emir Zayn al-Dīn Kitbughā, he also returned his command to him, and favored him greatly.

---

[203] See Rabbat, *The Citadel of Cairo: A New Interpretation of Royal Mamluk Architecture* (Leiden: E.J. Brill, 1995), pp. 146f, on the Citadel during the reign of al-Ashraf.

[204] Appears to be a mistake, as *al-ashqar* took the regnal name of al-Malik al-Kāmil.

Mention of al-Malik al-Ashraf's going to Syria, conquest of Acre and other Frankish places, and the poems about that

Acre stayed in the hand of the Franks, may God Most High curse those from the past and defeat those who remain, from the time that they took it back during the days of the Sultan al-Malik al-Nāṣir Ṣalāḥ al-Dīn Yūsuf son of Najm al-Dīn Ayyūb son of Shādī son of Marwān al-Ayyūbī, master of the Egyptian homelands and the Syrian lands. This was in the year 587 [1191] just as we have previously mentioned, until al-Malik al-Ashraf Ṣalāḥ al-Dīn Khalīl son of al-Malik al-Manṣūr Sayf al-Dīn Qalāwūn al-Alfī al-Ṣāliḥī al-Najmī conquered in the year 690, as we will describe, if God Most High wishes.

Their staying was a total of 103 years, and the reason for its reconquest, as we have previously mentioned, was the breaking of the treaty by killing the merchants at the end of al-Malik al-Manṣūr's, the father of al-Malik al-Ashraf, days. Al-Malik al-Manṣūr had been concerned with Acre's inhabitants' issues, and had prepared for raiding them. He had departed for that, but fate overtook him without mercy as we have previously explained.

When the issue of al-Malik al-Ashraf had stabilized, and other issues had been dealt with, he turned his attention to Acre and raiding it. He deputized the armies from the Egyptian homelands and the rest of the Syrian realms and fortresses, and ordered the Sultan's deputies in the Syrian and coastal realms as well as the deputies in the castles and fortresses to prepare chainmail production and wood for mangonels, miners (*ḥajjārīn*) and others.

He deputized the emir `Izz al-Dīn Aybak *al-afram, amīr jāndār*, for that purpose, so he departed from the Egyptian homelands, and arrived in Damascus [111] at the end of Ṣafar this year [March 10, 1291]. He prepared wood for the mangonels from protected Damascus, and he emerged on its outskirts at the beginning of Rabī` al-Awwal of the previously mentioned year [March 11, 1291].

All of that was completed on 12 Rabī` al-Awwal [March 22, 1291], and the emir `Alam al-Dīn Sanjar al-Dawādārī, one of the emirs in Syria, took it, and divided it among the emirs who were commanders of 1000s. Each emir and those attached to him took the load that they were ordered to transport, then the emir Ḥusām al-Dīn Lājīn, the Sultan's deputy in protected Damascus, departed leading the last of the troops with the rest of the army on 20 Rabī` al-Awwal [March 30, 1291].

This is what was agreed with regard to protected Damascus, and al-Malik al-Ashraf also deputized the emir Sayf al-Dīn Ṭughrīl al-Ighānī to the fortresses and the realms urging them to hastily prepare mangonels and war implements. So the deputies quickly turned towards that, and al-Malik al-Muẓaffar, the ruler of Ḥamāh, arrived in Damascus on 23 Rabī` al-Awwal [April 2, 1291] leading the army of Ḥamāh, accompanied by mangonels and chainmail.

The emir Sayf al-Dīn Balabān al-Ṭabbākhī, the sultanic deputy for the conquests, leading the fortresses' and Tripoli's armies, arrived with the mangonels and chainmail they had on 24 Rabī' al-Awwal [April 3, 1291], and the rest of the deputies arrived leading the Syrian mamluks and their armies at Acre. This was what happened with regard to the deputies of protected Syria.

As for what happened with regard to al-Malik al-Ashraf, he, when he had determined to go to Acre, ordered a gathering of all the learned, the judges, the notables and the Qur'ānic readers at the grave of his father al-Malik al-Manṣūr in the Manṣūrī Cupola inside protected Cairo. They gathered on Friday 28 Ṣafar [March 9, 1291], and stayed the night reciting the glorious Qur'ān, and performing deeds of great importance—donation of a large amount of money.

Al-Malik al-Ashraf was present at the gravesite on the morning of Friday, and gave a large amount of wealth and clothing to charity, and dispersed a large amount of wealth among the Qur'ān reciters and the poor (Sufis). He also dispensed dirhams and a massive amount of garments to the schools, the watchtowers (*rubuṭ*), the small worship-places (*zawāyā*) the Sufi hospices (*khawāniq*). This was a way to bid farewell to his father al-Malik al-Manṣūr as he was determined to depart raiding Acre.

Then he returned from the gravesite of his father to his Citadel safely, and when it was Tuesday 3 Rabī' al-Awwal of this year [March 13, 1291] the Sultan al-Malik al-Ashraf descended from the protected Citadel, and departed leading the victorious armies in the direction of Syria. He had already sent his high helmet crest (*adira*) to protected Damascus, so then they arrived at its citadel on Monday 7 Rabī' al-Ākhir [April 16, 1291] of this year.

On Thursday 3 Rabī' al-Ākhir [April 12, 1291] the Sultan al-Malik al-Ashraf arrived at the camp near Acre at the 3rd hour of the day [about 9am]. The mangonels arrived at Acre the day after the arrival of the Sultan, which were 92 mangonels. They were set up, their preparation was completed in [112] four days, and the screens were in place.

The Franks, may God Most High curse those of them in the past, and defeat those remaining of them, when they were aware of the interest and determination of the Sultan al-Malik al-Ashraf, wrote to the Frankish sea-kings, asking them for aid, and they came to them from every place, gathering in Acre. Among them were a large number, and they strengthened themselves, not even locking the gates of their town.

Al-Jazarī tells in his *History*, on the authority of the emir Sayf al-Dīn son of al-Jamaqdār, that al-Malik al-Ashraf camped up against Acre on Thursday 4 Rabī' al-Ākhir, and on the day after his arrival the mangonels, and the war implements and siege implements for castles and fortresses arrived from the city of Damascus.

These were a total of 92 mangonels, among them were Frankish, *qarābughā* and satanic ones. He said: We assembled the mangonels in four days from the date of their arrival, and began the siege and the tunneling on 16 Jumādā al-Ulā [May 24, 1291] of this year. When it was Friday 17 Jumādā al-Ulā [May 25, 1291] al-Malik al-Ashraf determined to do a rush, so he ordered for there to be 300 camel-skin drums organized, and for them to be beaten at once.

When they were beaten, the people of Acre were terrified at what they heard from that, and al-Malik al-Ashraf rushed leading the armies before the sun's rising on that day. The sun rose when the Sultanic standard and the Islamic troop (*`iṣāba*) was on the walls, and the Franks, may God Most High curse and defeat them, turned fleeing, boarding boards, and abandoned the dwellings after a large number of them had been killed during their stampede to the boats.

The Muslims also killed, took prisoners and looted, and killed an innumerable number of Franks, taking women and boys who cannot be described or counted. God, mighty and majestic, exchanged unbelief for belief, and the church-bell for the call to prayer, so praise to the One who is not distracted by anything over another.

It was said that when the Muslims were about to conquer Acre, and those inside of it realized that fact, around 10,000 men of them departed requesting safe-conduct. However, al-Malik al-Ashraf dispersed them among the emirs, then they killed all of them down to the last man. The Sultan sent a large number of the prisoners to the Islamic fortresses, and the Sultan ordered the destruction of Acre. They initiated razing its walls, and burning it [beginning] from Saturday 18 Jumādā al-Ulā [May 26, 1291].

The length of the siege of Acre from the time when al-Malik al-Ashraf let go of his reins to when it was conquered was 44 days. The following emirs were martyred during the siege of Acre: `Alā' al-Dīn Kushtghadī al-Shamsī, who was transported to Juljūliyya and buried there, `Izz al-Dīn Aybak al-`Izzī, *naqīb* of the victorious armies, Sayf al-Dīn Āqush al-Ghutamī, Badr al-Dīn Bīlīk al-Mas`ūdī, and Sharaf al-Dīn Qayrān al-Sakzī—those were the emirs. Among the commanders of the freeborn troops, four [113] men, and a small number of the army.

God Most High conquered by the hand of al-Malik al-Ashraf, and during his days, the famous coastal cities Tyre, part of Sidon, Haifa, and `Athlīth without fighting, and that was because God Most High had caused fear to fall upon the hearts of its people after Acre had been conquered, and because they knew that they could not hold it. So they departed from it, and saved themselves. The Sultan al-Malik al-Ashraf ruled it from the rest of Jumādā al-Ulā [June 1291].

On Sunday 19 Jumādā al-Ulā [May 27, 1291] the news of the city of Tyre being handed over came to the Sultan.

In addition, on 20 of it [May 28, 1291] the news of the handing over of Sidon and the flight of part of its people came to the Sultan. Part of them rebelled in a tower in it, so when the Sultan possessed Tyre and part of Sidon, Haifa and `Athlīth he ordered them to be razed totally, and they were. Then the rest of

Sidon was conquered and Beirut at the hand of the emir `Alam al-Dīn al-Shujā`ī, as we will describe if God Most High wishes, in another place.

Al-Jazarī said in on 21 Jumādā al-Ulā [May 29, 1291] of this year al-Malik al-Ashraf dispatched the emir Shams al-Dīn Nabā known as Ibn al-Jamaqdār, *amīr jāndār*, to raze the city of Tyre, so he traveled from Acre with the decree to raze it.

He said: Among the related marvels of its conquest and destruction was what was described by the Shaykh `Imād al-Dīn al-Iṣbahānī in his *History*. He said during the year 518 [1124–5] al-Bursiqī ruled Aleppo, and a wind blew that carried the sand of al-Ruṣāfa into the castle of Ja`bar, and during it Tyre was conquered. Its governor was `Izz al-Dīn Nabā, minister of Egypt, who sold it for a substantial amount of money to the Franks. He feared the Egyptian caliph, so he fled from him to Damascus, and it continued under Frankish rule until al-Malik al-Ashraf Ṣalāḥ al-Dīn Khalīl son of al-Malik al-Manṣūr Sayf al-Dīn Qalāwūn conquered it in the year 690 [1291]. It was razed at the hand of the emir Shams al-Dīn Nabā, *amīr jāndār*, so this coincidence is amazing. The Franks gained Tyre by purchase from a man named Nabā, and continued to rule it until it was destroyed by a man named Nabā as well.

Another strange coincidence in the conquest of Acre was what the Judge Muḥyī al-Dīn Ibn `Abd al-Ẓāhir told. He said: The Shaykh, jurisprudent and knowledgeable one, Sharaf al-Dīn al-Būṣīrī saw in his dream before the going of al-Malik al-Ashraf to the siege of Acre someone declaiming:

The Muslims have already taken Acre, and made the unbelievers be satisfied with an agreement,
Our Sultan has led horses to them who will trample the mountains completely,
The Turks have vowed since they left they will not leave the Franks in control. [114]

When al-Būṣīrī woke he told this to a number of people, then al-Malik al-Ashraf went in the midst of that. God Most High conquered it at his hand, and the matter was just as al-Būṣīrī said—nothing was left for them or of them in the coastlands just as we will describe if God Most High wills. This has continued to our very day, praise be to God Most High.

Concerning this the judge Muḥyī al-Dīn Ibn `Abd al-Ẓāhir, may God Most High have mercy upon him, said:

O Sons of al-Aṣfar,[205] *God's vengeance that is not to be denied has taken hold of you,*
al-Ashraf has camped upon your coastlands, so rejoice in continuous unease.

[205] Classical reference to the Byzantine Christians, whose ultimate reference is unclear ("Sons of the Yellow [one]).

Many poets described this conquest in their poems, so among those who praised the Sultan al-Malik al-Ashraf and mentioned this conquest was the meritorious shaykh Badr al-Dīn Muḥammad b. Aḥmad b. ʿUmar al-Manbijī, who was a merchant living in Cairo. He said:

You have reached the outer limits of hope, leaving behind all the kings of yore,
You attained with generosity alone what the earth's kings were not able to even with tricks among the people,
So let its bird anoint your favored dynasty, as it is a gleam on the faces of (all) the dynasties,
Be happy with your high countenance, felicity has come to you with an unsnapable rope,
For you are the Righteous One of the religion and this world; in them bearing unbearable hardships,
How many desires have you fulfilled, spending the nights considering with your sharp-cutting resolution, naked unnotched,
How many fortresses you have conquered, from which for so long kings have returned in frustration,
You are the one who did not leave unbelief a city in which to take refuge, nor any hope for its religion,
You protected bright-shining Acre in a way kings were unable to do with unchecked resolution,
The best-warded city it was yesterday in its fortification and strength; a stronghold for timeless nights,
How many of the earth's kings called upon her desirous, but it rejected them haughtily, from distraction,
You turned aside from hunting, not wasting time, nor allowing imaginations to wonder,
Whether they have a filial woman—how many suitors other than you desired to marry her, but did not say so or achieve it,
Until you ordered it, then touched her, while she was obedient after refusing, conforming to your command,
Others desire her, but at your hands was the conquest (predestined) from all eternity,
A conquest too lengthy for prose to encompass it descriptively, or for composing poetry which has time to ripen,
You attacked it, and it was struck after its inhabitants were surprised by blackest treachery in return for treachery, [115]
Among a clanging army whose stars are like the night, appearing to the seer to be of swords and spears,
The army covered both abyss and hillock, overspreading plains and mountains,
You would imagine them and the noble horses under them to lions dressed in majesty upon the summits,

The eye does not apprehend from them other than their eyeballs that they are wearing their war apparatus by day,
Against it you had armies confront, which had you confronted the hard mountains with them, they would have disappeared and ceased to exist,
So it (Acre) became after the glory of dominion tractable because of humiliation, dominion age-long in shambles,
Becoming a ruin, its inhabitants with nothing, the hand of the days writing it as a proverb,
Its weapons carried off, (once) pleasurable for entertainment because of decoration and dress, now laid waste,
Its remains wiped out, more pleasing to the soul than a lush garden, now destroyed,
The Trinity has been removed from us by al-Ashraf, the lord, the Sultan, and the Oneness of God is overjoyed,
An administration possessed of wisdom, in vengeful glory, renewed age in mature opinion,
Their spirits carried off by the edge of Indian (swords), their possessions by the attack of spoils,
Razed, never to be built, dispersed what was gathered, cut short what was continuous, without celebrating,
When their cities on the coast became wilderness after the inhabitants no longer work them,
How much of an army you caused to stay there due to fear of your might when you traveled from it?
You continue to be possessed of a rank in heavenly glory, and rulership, grasping the shooting stars' forelocks!

The judge Shihāb al-Dīn Abū al-Thanā' Maḥmūd al-Ḥalabī, a Correspondence secretary, said, when he saw the fires blazing in the midst of Acre, after its foundations had collapsed, and its walls fallen:

I passed by Acre after its walls had been razed, a flint kindling fire was prepared in its midst,
After it had become Christian, to my eyes it was now Zoroastrian, with its towers prostrating to the fire.

He said also:

Praise be to God, the state of the crosses is humiliated, while the Arab Chosen One's religion by the Turks is glorified,
This is that to which hopes aspired—were the vision of it to have been sought in sleep, one would have been ashamed to ask for it,
After Acre, when its sea-foundations were shaken, polytheism on land has no further foothold, [116]

Secluded (woman) who has been kept from marriage for a long time, while the ravishing hand was harsh upon it,

Unbelief after it has no further place to flee on land or sea after its destruction,

Our hopes imagined it, so we see when considering it that its reality is even more wondrous,

As for wars, how many have grown as tribulations; the one born is terrified, and does not become a youth,

Walls surrounding it on land and sea; around its central square houses higher than poles,

A foolish place, whose walls are forbidding and strong in guard, fortifying against being overwhelmed by brave (attackers),

Plated with flat surfaces, all around it battlements (protecting) from the spears, and towers of leather shields (yalab),

Just as clouds guide from their lightning bolts, clouds with arrows are double without being guided,

It is as if every zodiac sign/tower around him is a constellation of mangonels, striking the earth with meteors,

Armies of God beating them to it with their advance, enraged for the sake of God, not for possession or property,

A lion, refusing to turn its face away from the nations, calling the Highest Lord, praise Him, father,

How much kings before him desired it and cast at it, collecting armies, but not being victorious or even positioning themselves,

His kingdom had barely begun; it was in its beginning, when he gained that which people (previously) had not within a year,[206]

His ambition was not sated other than with that which had incapacitated both Persian and Arab kings,

So she became, while tending towards the two seas, both kindled in flame and in an uproar,

An army of Turks abandoned (taraka) the war with them—a shame; their inaction was a type of illness,

They plunged their garment into the sea, so that the two men were alike, even though they differed in situation and genealogy,

They mounted it, so their firmness left no tower unturned in the horizon,

They handed it over, so no vengeance-seeker left a neck unbloodied in it or a hand without plundering,

Coming to its pasture, it was not defended, as its mangonels stood down, and no longer shot,

O Day of Acre, you have forgotten the previous conquests, and what were written in the books,

[206] Within a year of his taking power.

Eloquence after gratitude did not reach your mouth; almost those possessed of poetry and speech did not undertake it,
(Battle) Days longed for you for people's sake, so praise God, we have seen with our own eyes up close,
You have enraged the worshipers of Jesus (`Īsā) when you destroyed them, but there is satisfaction for God in that rage, [117]
God caused the Army of Victory to rise, so make haste with the omens of conquest among the spears and sharp (swords),
And the Chosen One, the Guide, the Proclaimer oversees closely what al-Ashraf the Sultan has leveled out,
He was pleasured by this victory, and the shining Ka`ba was happy at its news in its veil,
Its fame roams the earth like the wind, with the dry land in delight, and the sea at war,
The white (swords) waded through the bloody sea; nothing of the white showed other than a colored side,
Shining spears sunk into their blue eyes,[207] *as if they were rope seeking the heart,*
Blazing up while it overflows their necks; then the overflow increases in shining and flame,
A sea of their blood has been added to the sea, gone like a dewdrop enveloped by the sea,
While their iron defended them from its heat, then fear's hand chained them to it in terror,
Passing judgment, so our (sharp) swords trampled them killing, but preserving their possessions for plunder,
How many champions have gone forward like unfeeling mountains, so tomorrow are like ruined campsites,
As if while the spear-tip seeks him, a tower is hurled down—beyond it is the star with a tail (a comet),
Glad tidings, O King of this World, for the realms have been made noble by you, and raised in level,
What will happen after Acre, since climbing its hump was easy for you?
Rise to the earth, for this world in its totality without a sign extends its forelocks to you,[208]
How it has cried out, while it was in the enemy's captivity for a time, but the kings' hunt neither listened nor responded,
You came to it, O Ṣalāḥ al-Dīn, fulfilling a promise, that believed Ṣalāḥ al-Dīn has not disappeared,

[207] Cf Q.
[208] The taking of the forelock is usually seen as a symbol of submission from pre-Islamic Arabia.

Just as their blood flowed of old protected by the sea from going, so you (once again) caused it to flow,
You took vengeance (tha'r) for Ṣalāḥ al-Dīn when it was enraged at him for concealing God in the title,
However, you brought armies like flooding, against their opponents' (sharp) swords among them,
Surrounding it with mangonels which stood before its walls with a clashing numerous (army),
Raised, every positioners position double, so that each is ready for cutting and breaking,
You bored it with tunnels bringing high mountains down, and its shame was revealed unveiled,
After rushing it in the morning, so it was filled with terror, its two cheeks fell towards the dirt,
(White) swords sang on necks, as its towers sank to the ground, jousting one against the other,
Leaving the walls covering in blood, so it is decorated in perfume—were it not for the people's blood, it would not be perfumed, [118]
Each helmet stands out like a full-bosomed woman, with heads scattered around, having been led (as a bride) without merriment,
She has left, having been disobedient around us, but returned in the morning obedient, in the hands of her close neighbors,
They thought the houses' proud towers would guard them, but instead they bound them, so they could not leave and flee,
So protecting them, but for the swords, in order that none of them would take refuge in fleeing,
Fires rose in among them, and raged, putting out the disasters implicit in the religion,
Those towers came to be Abū Lahab, while the "carrier of firewood" was suspended from them,[209]
You cleared the sea of them, so who will tell the one he meets from his people of woe and war?
The greatest blessing has been perfected, which was completed by Tyre's conquest without siege or positioning (mangonels),
Two sisters in that unbelief's cross conjoined each one of them, not sisters in genealogy,
If the sea color is not dyed there because of what is upon it, tongues are aflame!
So God has given you the sea realm, so watch as the felicity of the land realm is made clear for you,

[209] Ref. to Q111, which is a curse against the Prophet Muḥammad's uncle Abū Lahab, and his wife "carrier of firewood."

For the one whose starting point was Acre and Tyre together, China is closer to his hand than Aleppo!
The realm is raised through you, until its cupola has its pegs extended towards the Pleiades,
You continue to be the Glorious One of Victory, made splendorous by every victory, receiving the gift, vigilant.

Mention of his detaining the governor of Damascus, the Sultan's return and entrance to it, and the removal from office and governorships he decided there, and his return to the Egyptian homelands

When al-Malik al-Ashraf was preoccupied with the siege of Acre the emir `Alam al-Dīn Sanjar al-Ḥamawī, known as Abū Khurṣ, hastened to al-Malik al-Ashraf leading the emir Ḥusām al-Dīn Lājīn al-Manṣūrī the Lesser the sultan's deputy [119] in protected Damascus. Then this emir Ḥusām al-Dīn developed a fear concerning al-Malik al-Ashraf, and he said [to himself]: he is determined to arrest you.

Fear drove him to ride from the royal pavilion (*wiṭāq*) at Acre during the night, fleeing, so the emir `Alam al-Dīn Sanjar al-Dawādārī rode and followed after him, then caught up with him. He said to him

> By God, do not be the cause of this troop's perishing. This land, the people (Mamluks) are about to conquer it. When the Franks learn of your flight they will be heartened by it. The army rode behind you, but you have distracted the Sultan's firm resolution from the siege of Acre towards you.

Therefore, he placated him, and he returned to his camp thinking that this would be concealed, and that al-Malik al-Ashraf did not know about it. This was on 8 Jumādā al-Ulā [May 9, 1291] of this year, so when it was the day after this event al-Malik al-Ashraf bestowed a robe of honor upon the emir Ḥusām al-Dīn Lājīn, so his heart was eased, then arrested him on the day after, and sent him to the citadel of Safed under guard. Then he was sent from it to the Hill Citadel in the Egyptian homelands.

The short missives (*batā'iq*) came to protected Damascus after Friday prayers 17 Jumādā al-Ulā [May 25, 1291] the day of the conquest of Acre, in which it was mentioned that the Muslims conquered Acre by force with the sword, so protected Damascus and its outskirts was decorated for that occasion, and the proclamations were sounded out.

When al-Malik al-Ashraf completed his desire to conquer Acre and what was around it, he returned from it in the direction of Damascus. His arrival there was in the third hour on Monday 12 Jumādā al-Ākhira [June 12, 1291] of that year. He entered it in a way that no king had previously entered. With him was his minister the master Shams al-Dīn Ibn Sal`ūs, and there was great joy at their entrance. It was decked out even more beautifully than before, and al-Malik al-Ashraf stayed in the Damascus Citadel.

On the day of al-Malik al-Ashraf's entrance to protected Damascus he delegated the deputy sultanship in Damascus to the emir `Alam al-Dīn Sanjar al-Shujā`ī al-Manṣūrī in place of the emir Ḥusām al-Dīn Lājīn, so the junior officers of al-Shujā`ī entered the same day al-Malik al-Ashraf entered. Al-Malik al-Ashraf increased the *iqṭā`* holdings of the emir `Alam al-Dīn al-Shujā`ī, and assigned for him that which had never been assigned to any of the deputies or anyone else. He decreed that he could use whatever he wanted from the treasuries without previous consultation.

On that day al-Malik al-Ashraf delegated the deputy sultanate of Kerak to the emir Jamāl al-Dīn Aqush al-Ashrafī in place of the emir Rukn al-Dīn Baybars *al-dawādār* al-Manṣūrī in accord with his asking to be relieved of the deputyship. Al-Malik al-Ashraf confirmed him among the number of emirs in the Egyptian homelands.

In addition, on this day after al-Malik al-Ashraf settled in at Damascus citadel, the august emir `Alam al-Dīn Sanjar Arjawāsh al-Manṣūrī, the deputy in Damascus Citadel, stood before the Sultan. The emir Sharaf al-Dīn Ibn al-Khaṭīr al-Rūmī was much given to jesting in front of al-Malik al-Ashraf at the expense of the emirs and others, and intended [120] by this to open the Sultan al-Malik al-Ashraf's mind, and to amuse him.

Sometimes al-Malik al-Ashraf would give him a look that indicated that he understood the purpose of his jesting about those he singled out. When it was this day, and the emir `Alam al-Dīn Arjawāsh stood before al-Malik al-Ashraf, just as we previously mentioned, the Sultan looked at the emir Sharaf al-Dīn Ibn al-Khaṭīr, and signed to him to jest about Arjawāsh. Ibn al-Khaṭīr looked at Arjawāsh, then turned to the Sultan and said "The mamluk's father in [Anatolian] Rūm has a gray donkey, blind in one eye, who looks exactly like this emir `Alam al-Dīn Arjawāsh," so the Sultan laughed.

Arjawāsh did not get the jest, nor was it to his taste, but he continued forward, so when he heard Ibn al-Khaṭīr's words, and the Sultan laughing at him, he was angered, and said, "This is childish!" When the Sultan heard him he was angered because of that, and he ordered him to be detained, so he was, and was beaten painfully a number of times in front of the Sultan. Then he ordered him to be fettered, for him to wear a cloak, and for him to be worked with the prisoners, so this was done. This was a great bewilderment to him, and a deep humiliation.

The guard fell upon his belongings, and took most of his earnings, which included a large amount of wealth, and he was imprisoned in the citadel. Then the Sultan ordered for him to be borne on the post horses to the Egyptian homelands in fetters, so the master of the post had him sent [thus]. Intercession was made for him, so he was returned midway, then the Sultan released him, and returned him to the Citadel deputyship, after the Sultan had returned to the Egyptian homelands in the month of Ramaḍān [September 1291] of this year. He continued in that post until he died.

On Sunday 18 Jumādā al-Ākhira [June 18, 1291] of this year al-Malik al-Ashraf removed the emir Sayf al-Dīn Tūghān from the Chancellery Supervision in protected Damascus, and returned him to the governate of the hinterland, where he had been previously.

On this day al-Malik al-Ashraf delegated the Chancellery Supervision to the emir Shams al-Dīn Sunqur *al-a`sar*, where he had been previously. He had been released prior to this time.

On Wednesday 12 Rajab [July 11, 1291] of this year al-Malik al-Ashraf removed the chief Taqī al-Dīn Tawba from the Damascus ministry, and cancelled the office in Damascus. He appointed the judge Muḥyī al-Dīn Ibn al-Naḥḥās in place of Taqī al-Dīn, except that he was called inspector of Syria.

On 18 Rajab [July 17, 1291] al-Malik al-Ashraf delegated to the judge Sharaf al-Dīn Aḥmad son of `Izz al-Dīn `Īsā Ibn al-Sayrajī the inspectorate of the noble market (*ḥisba*) in protected Damascus in place of the judge Tāj al-Dīn Ibn al-Shīrāzī.

On Wednesday 19 Rajab [July 18, 1291] the Sultan al-Malik al-Ashraf traveled from the Damascus Citadel, and headed returning to the Egyptian homelands. When it was the time for [121] dawn prayers on Monday 9 Sha`bān [August 7, 1291] of this years' months, al-Malik al-Ashraf arrived in protected Cairo, and entered through the Victory Gate and went through Cairo, exiting through the Zuwayla Gate, and then ascended to the Hill Citadel, victorious, happy, and joyful. His entrance into Cairo was a day to remember. Cairo was decorated prior to his arrival spectacularly, the likes of which had never been seen nor heard of during previous days. After his arrival if anything the decoration became more amazing, and the happiness increased because of this tremendous victory which al-Malik al-Ashraf had accomplished, and because of his safe return to his citadel and the seat of his realm, filled with spoils, and God knows best.

In Sidon there remained a rebellious tower, so al-Malik al-Ashraf deputized the emir `Alam al-Dīn Sanjar al-Shujā`ī, the deputy sultan in protected Damascus, to besiege it. He went to it on Tuesday 4 Rajab [July 3, 1291], arriving in Sidon and besieged the tower, taking it on Saturday 15 Rajab [July 14, 1291]. The emir `Alam al-Dīn then returned to Damascus after conquering it on the post-horses, so arrived in it when al-Malik al-Ashraf was departing for the Egyptian homelands on Wednesday 19 Rajab [July 18, 1291], so he met with him and saw him off.

Mention of the conquest of Beirut

When al-Malik al-Ashraf had departed to the Egyptian homelands he ordered the emir `Alam al-Dīn al-Shujā`ī, the deputy sultan in protected Damascus, to go to Beirut and to conquer it. So the emir `Alam al-Dīn went to it, while its Frankish people had entered into obedience.

When the emir `Alam al-Dīn arrived there, its people came to meet him, and settled him in its castle. Therefore, when he had established himself there, he ordered them to transfer their children, their wives and their moveable things to its castle, so they did that. They thought that he had done this out of concern for them, so when they moved to the castle, he arrested the men, bound them, and threw them in the moat (*khandaq*). So rule of the lands and conquering them was on Sunday 23 Rajab [July 22, 1291].

Then the emir `Alam al-Dīn returned to protected Damascus and arrived there on Friday 27 Ramaḍān [September 23, 1291]. No further grouping of Franks remained on the coastlands, so the entire coastland was empty of them—to God be praise and grace, and may it stay that way until the Day of Resurrection. None remained behind in the Syrian lands other than its Christian peasants, as they were included in the protection (*dhimma*) paying the poll-tax, and God knows best.

When al-Malik al-Ashraf conquered these conquests, he bestowed some of them as charitable endowment properties for the benefit of his father al-Malik al-Manṣūr's mausoleum (*turba*). These were al-Kābira close to Acre, Tel al-Mafshūkh close to it as well, Kardāna and its mills, also close, and from the Tyrian coast, Ma`raka, and Ṣiddīqīn.

He bestowed properties as charitable endowments upon the Ashrafī Mausoleum [122] which were Qariyat al-Faraḥ/Faraj close to Acre, Qariyat Shafr`amr close to it, Qariyat al-Ḥamrā' close to it, and from the Tyrian coast Qariyat Ṭibr Daba,[210] and God knows best.

Mention of the emir Baysarā's release and his connection to al-Ashraf

On Wednesday 18 Sha`bān [August 16, 1291] of the months of this year, al-Malik al-Ashraf ordered the release of the emir Badr al-Dīn Baysarā al-Shamsī al-Ṣāliḥī al-Najmī. Al-Malik al-Manṣūr had imprisoned the emir Baysarā at the beginning of his rule. A noble sultanic release was written for the emir Badr al-Dīn Baysarā, a copy of which, after the noble *basmala* is the following:

> Praise be to God for His complete grace, His all-encompassing mercies, and his gifts that began in the houses of Islam as an unsetting star, and his bounties, which travel and are generous, reviving destroyed hopes in a day, after they had been buried in the tightest of graves by its very touch, with every denier acknowledging its merit.
>
> I praise with a praise causing previous blessings to return, and benefiting the source of nobility that is specific and general. In addition, we testify

[210] Following the editor's suggestion.

that there is no god other than God, alone, without any associate, a testimony whose dues we pay, and whose disobedience we avoid. We testify that Muḥammad is His servant and Messenger, described by the noble qualities, characterized by knowledge and forbearance, for expressing prayer, the following of which causes continuous virtues—and abundant peace (upon him).

Afterwards, the worthiest of those who are treated well, and receive the good qualities of this dominating dynasty are hope and the giving of hope to one who if the champions of Islam are enumerated, he would be first mentioned, and if bravery were described, he would be at the head of the line of every well-known brave man.

If the heavens of the dominion were decorated with stars, he would be its shining new moon, if those possessed of exemplary opinions were assembled his would be the best, the most interesting, if the qualities of those "possessed of authority"[211] were numbered he would be the greatest commander (*amīr*) of those commanded—beautifying the processions by his presence with the highest stature, decorating the ranks with the most resplendent moon.

He is the one who acknowledges al-Ashraf (the most noble), the highest, the lordly, and the senior; when his honorifics are mentioned, they are al-Badrī, Baysarā al-Shamī, al-Ṣāliḥī al-Najmī al-Malikī al-Ashrafī: Thus, he is the one described in this manner, with the praise, and goodness, having these good qualities and benefits.

For this reason, the Malikī al-Ashrafī al-Ṣalāḥī, Sultanic, lordly, high noble good opinion necessitates that the disaster of his days be uncovered, and that in his honor the moons (*budūr*) be clothed not eclipsed during his dazzling reign, so that he be released this very hour without delay, and that he make obeisance before the most magnificent sultanic place. This will be without having to ask permission from a deputy, nor a minister, if God wishes.

This release was placed in a grey-yellowish purse, sealed upon it with the Sultan's [123] seal. It was conveyed by the emir Badr al-Dīn Baydarā, the deputy sultan in the Egyptian homelands, to the Gate of the Pit, together with the emir Zayn al-Dīn Kitbughā, and a number of senior emirs.

The emir Badr al-Dīn Baysarā was brought out from the pit that is in the Hill Citadel, the release was read to him, the order given to strike off his fetters, and a sultanic honorary gift was brought to him.

---

211 Cf. Q4:59.

However, Baysarā said, "Do not break the fetters from my legs, nor will I don the honorary gift until after I make obeisance before the Sultan" and he was resolved upon that. The Sultan was informed, so he commanded to break his fetters, and have him brought before the Sultan. When he [al-Ashraf] saw him, he rose to honor him, greeted him, honored him, clothed him with the honorary gift, sat him at his side, bestowed wealth upon him, and fabrics, and immediately made him commander over 100 horsemen, giving him numerous *iqṭā`* fiefs.

Among these were Munyat Banī Khaṣīb, Darsittā in al-Jawālī (tributes), and the Ḥasharī inheritances. The Sultan brought him close, and made him intimate, being alone with him, being personable with him, respecting him, and doubling his favors, such that the emir Badr al-Dīn Baysarā was ascribed to the Ashrafiyya [regiment], whereas during the previous part of his life he had been ascribed to the Ẓāhiriyya and others. He would be written down [previously] as Baysarā al-Shamsī, but now was written down as Baysarā al-Ashrafī.

On Friday 4 Ramaḍān [August 31, 1291] of the months of this year, al-Malik al-Ashraf released the emir Shams [al-Dīn] Sunqur *al-ashqar*, who had pretended to be sultan in Syria, and had taken the regnal name of al-Malik al-`Ādil. He also released the emir Ḥusām al-Dīn Lājīn "the Lesser" al-Manṣūrī who had been deputy sultan in protected Damascus, the emir Rukn al-Dīn Baybars Taqṣū, and the emir Shams al-Dīn Sunqur *al-ṭawīl* from imprisonment, and ordered them as usual.

Al-Malik al-Ashraf ordered the emir `Alam al-Dīn Sanjar al-Dawādārī to be detained, so he was detained in protected Damascus. The deputy sultan in Damascus sent him to the sultanic gates in protected Egypt in fetters. His arrival at the Hill Citadel was on Thursday 17 Ramaḍān [September 13, 1291].

During this year al-Malik al-Ashraf removed the Chief Judge Taqī al-Dīn `Abd al-Raḥmān son of the Chief Judge Tāj al-Dīn `Abd al-Wahhāb son of the daughter of al-A`zz al-Shāfi`ī from the position of the Shāfi`ī chief judiciary in the Egyptian homelands, and from all religious responsibilities. This was because of matters for which he hated him dating from his father al-Malik al-Manṣūr's time.

Among these were that the Chief Judge Taqī al-Dīn, may God Most High have mercy upon him, used during the Manṣūrī period, to cultivate the mind of al-Malik al-Ṣāliḥ `Alā' al-Dīn `Alī son of al-Malik al-Manṣūr, and to promote him over al-Malik al-Ashraf.

Among these were what was in the chief Shams al-Dīn Ibn al-Sal`ūs' heart against him. Among them were the prayer of a righteous man who he accused, but did not find guilty, which we will describe the reason for that, if God Most High wishes, and other things.

My master [124] and my shaykh Ḥanafī Chief Judge in the Egyptian homelands the following of which it is a summary:

It reached me that among the totality of the reasons for Chief Judge Taqī al-Dīn son of the daughter of al-A`zz, the Shāfi`ī Chief Judge in the Egyptian homelands, being removed, and his tribulation, was the prayer of a righteous man. I said, "Master, who is this righteous man?" He said "Shaykh Shams al-Dīn Muḥammad son of Shaykh Jamāl al-Dīn Abū Bakr son of Muḥammad al-Fārisī al-Aykī, the senior shaykh in the Sa`īd al-Su`adā' (Felicitous of the Felicitous) hospice (*khānqāh*) in protected Cairo."

I said, "Master, what was the reason for his prayer?" He said, "The shaykh was a man of noble proportions, and it was his habit, when he sat in the shaykhly sessions at the hospice, and opened the codex [Qur'ān], engrossing himself in recitation, that he would not rise for anyone or be distracted by anything until he finished with his recitation."

When Chief Judge Taqī al-Dīn was appointed to the ministry in the Egyptian homelands, it was usual for whoever was appointed to the ministry from the turbaned (religious) to supply him with a prayer-carpet at the Sa`īd al-Su`adā' hospice. The senior shaykh there was a partner to its shaykh, so when the Chief Judge Taqī al-Dīn was appointed to the ministry, he sent a prayer-carpet to the hospice for him to use in the afternoon prayer as was usual.

So it was furnished for him as usual at the time of the hospice denizens' being present after the afternoon prayer, and the shaykh Shams al-Dīn al-Aykī, shaykh of the hospice, and a number of Sufis prepared to greet the Chief Judge Taqī al-Dīn. However, he was delayed, and the shaykh Shams al-Dīn feared that the time during which it was his wont to sit was running out, so he sat, and the Sufis sat as usual, and the quarters' parts dispersed as usual, each one engrossed in the glorious Qur'ān recitation.

While they were in this situation, all of a sudden Chief Judge Taqī al-Dīn arrived, so the Sufis in the hospice rose for him, greeted him, and wished him peace, while the shaykh Shams al-Dīn did not rise, nor change his demeanor in the slightest, but continues his recitation, while he was sitting as was his wont.

The Chief Judge felt slighted by this, so when the shaykh finished with his recitation while the Sufis were performing their remembrance [of God] and intercessory prayer as was the usual, the shaykh Shams al-Dīn rose and wished the Chief Judge Taqī al-Dīn peace, and then sat.

One of the Sufis who had evil, envy and ambition with regard to him [Shams al-Dīn] became aware that the Chief Judge felt slighted by the shaykh, so he arose from his place, and sat in front of the Chief Judge, saying "O our master, I have some complaints against this shaykh." The Chief Judge said to the shaykh "Rise, and face your opponent, and listen to his complaint."

However, the shaykh said, "I do not have any disagreement with him, nor does he have any complaint against me." However, the judge merely became more angry at this, and drove him back, saying to all of those present "Hold him, and use him as an example," so they held him, and threw away his turban. He said to the judge "You have inflicted an arbitrary punishment upon me, so may God inflict the same upon you!" At that, the judge flew into a rage at him, ripped off his garment, and things happened to him that we will have to summarize.

When al-Malik al-Manṣūr Sayf al-Dīn Qalāwūn died and his son al-Malik al-Ashraf Ṣalāḥ al-Dīn Khalīl was appointed sultan after him, and he appointed the chief Shams al-Dīn Ibn al-Sal`ūs to his ministry, the chief mentioned to the Sultan what the Chief Judge Taqī al-Dīn had done, [125] some of which we have mentioned previously. At that time al-Malik al-Ashraf was reminded of what the chief had told him of this matter, to assemble the senior Shāfi`ī jurisprudents from the inhabitants of Cairo and Old Cairo of those who would be appropriate for the chief judiciary. He would then put each of them on the spot, without the others knowing about it.

Therefore, the chief did as the Sultan ordered him to do, and had a number present themselves, doing what the Sultan ordered him to do, not informing them of anything. Then he informed the Sultan of their being assembled, so he became to summon them one by one, asking each one of them about his fellow. He would say, "I intend to appoint him to the chief judiciary in the Egyptian homelands," so then he would mention some of his bad qualities.

When all of them had presented themselves in front of the Sultan, and he had asked them, and they had informed him of their situation, but not a single one of them thanked his fellow, but rather condemned him and mentioned his bad qualities, the Sultan ordered the chief to have them go home.

So when they had gone, the Sultan said to the chief "There is not one of these that is worthy of the judiciary. Look into who I should appoint who is unknown to them, and who does not know them." So he prompted him to delegate the judiciary to the judge Badr al-Dīn Muḥammad [son of] the shaykh Burhān al-Dīn Abū Isḥāq Ibrāhīm son of Abū al-Faḍl Sa`d Allāh b. Jamā`a b. `Alī b. Jamā`a b. Ḥāzim b. Ṣakhr b. `Abdallāh al-Kinānī al-Shāfi`ī al-Ḥamawī, who was the preacher and judge of noble Jerusalem.

He said "This one does not know them, nor do they know him, nor are any bad qualities to be found in him. He is among the best of people, and the most thankful"—there was an old connection between the two of them—so when the Sultan heard his minister's words, and what he was proposing, he ordered him to summon the judge Badr al-Dīn Ibn Jamā`a from noble Jerusalem. The chief carried out his order, and sent the post courier to him on Wednesday 9 Ramaḍān [September 5, 1291] of the months of this year, so had him presented.

The arrival of Chief Judge Badr al-Dīn, may God Most High have mercy upon him, to Cairo was on Monday 14 Ramaḍān [September 10, 1291] and he met with the chief Shams al-Dīn Ibn al-Sal`ūs, and broke his fast with him on the night of Thursday, the 17th [September 13, 1291]. He received complete honor, so when it was the morrow, which was Thursday the chief met with al-Malik al-Ashraf concerning the matter of the Chief Judge Badr al-Dīn, and he ordered him to present himself.

When he was presented before him, he [al-Ashraf] removed Chief Judge Taqī al-Dīn son of the daughter of al-A`zz from the chief judiciary in the Egyptian homelands, and delegated the chief judiciary in the Egyptian homelands in his place to the Chief Judge Badr al-Dīn Muḥammad Ibn Jamā`a. He also delegated the instruction in the Ṣāliḥiyya Najmiyya College to him, together with the judiciary, as well as the preaching in the al-Azhar Friday Mosque, and other functions.

This was the first appointment of Chief Judge Badr al-Dīn Ibn Jamā`a. Then Chief Judge Badr al-Dīn descended from the Hill Citadel, and kept his appointment concealed, not revealing it that day. When it was at meal-time on Friday evening he ate with the chief Shams al-Dīn Ibn al-Sal`ūs, so then the chief addressed him as Chief Judge in the presence of the people, and was open about his appointment, and the removal of Chief Judge Taqī al-Dīn son of the daughter of al-A`zz, and he sought [126] the senior officials.

When they presented themselves, he informed them of the appointment of Chief Judge Badr al-Dīn, so they congratulated him, and the matter became public knowledge. When Chief Judge Badr al-Dīn Ibn Jamā`a departed from the session of the chief Shams al-Dīn the investiture arrived accompanied by the son of the judge `Izz al-Dīn al-Ḥanbalī.

When it was the morning of Friday 18 Ramaḍān [September 14, 1291] the Chief Judge Badr al-Dīn wore the robe, and ordered the notaries to attend his formal session. The chief sent to him informing him that he had issued a written command for him to give the sermon at al-Azhar Friday Mosque in addition to his judiciary functions and instruction at the Ṣāliḥiyya College.

So he rode wearing his robe to the chief's house, then returned to his home, then rode to the al-Azhar Friday Mosque to deliver the sermon, while the robe was on him. There was a written order for him and the rest of the chief judges to wear a head-cloth (*ṭaraḥāt*),[212] so each judge wore the head-cloth, and had to ride with it on for a time. When the Chief Judge Badr al-Dīn completed the sermon, and led the Friday prayers, he returned to his home, then moved over to the Ṣāliḥiyya College on the next Friday, teaching there Sunday 12 Shawwāl [October 8, 1291] of the months of this year. It was a celebrated lesion, and a day to remember. This was what happened with regard to the Chief Judge Badr al-Dīn Ibn Jamā`a, may God Most High have mercy upon him.

As for what happened with Chief Judge Taqī al-Dīn son of the daughter of al-A`zz, may God Most High have mercy upon him, after the appointment of Chief Judge Badr al-Dīn Ibn Jamā`a he experienced a trial (*miḥna*) because of the chief Shams al-Dīn Ibn Sal`ūs. A number accused him before the Chief Judge, and others bore false testimony against him for matters of which God Most High had exonerated him.

[212] See Dozy, *Dictionnaire*, pp. 254–62.

They said very negative things against him, accusing him of terrible things. He was snared by them, and had to defend himself against being made an example. Among them was that they testified that he would fasten the waist-belt (*zunnār*)[213] underneath his clothing.

My shaykh and master Chief Judge Zayn al-Dīn Ibn al-Bisṭāmī, may God Most High have mercy upon him, told me that it reached him that Chief Judge Taqī al-Dīn son of the daughter of al-A`zz, may God Most High have mercy upon him, when it was said to him he was in his trial that

> Many bore witness against you that you would fasten the *zunnār* belt under your clothing.

He said:

> There is no god but God—how would that be?? Or how would an intelligent person imagine when the Christians do not do such a thing willingly, nor is this a sacrifice that is demanded in their religion—but the rulers demand this of them in order to differentiate them from the people of Islam (that a Muslim would do it willingly?). This was because their head-garments at that time were white and some think that they did this as a great humiliation to them, and so they would have to bear this on top of their clothing.
>
> So why would I then wear it below my clothing, when we belong to God, and to Him we are returning, and we take refuge in God from the souls' portions!

It is said that when the chief Shams al-Dīn Ibn al-Sal`ūs ordered the confiscation of Chief Judge Taqī al-Dīn son of the daughter of al-A`zz, may God Most High have mercy upon him, he punished him, issued a written order against him, demanding wealth from him openly, and a number of horrible things happened with regard to him.

The situation only got worse for him, as his intention was to rip him to pieces by beating, but God Most High protected him from him, and his finale was for the good,[214] just we will mention [127] if God Most High wishes.

The Chief Judge Taqī al-Dīn continued to endure humiliation and being ripped apart, until it was decided that he ascend one day in the direction of the Hill Citadel. He was walking, while those envoys guarding over him were riding.[215] Three emirs from al-Malik al-Ashraf's *khāṣakiyya* were descending from the Citadel then. So the Chief Judge said to them "O emirs, won't you look into my situation, the humiliation I am in, with these envoys?"

---

[213] One of the identifying pieces of clothing for Christians and Jews.

When the emirs heard his words, they took out their maces (*dabābīs*) from their places, turned them upside down, and went at the envoys, beating them, and saying, "The Chief Judge walks, while you ride?" They said, "The chief ordered us to do this; we have no blame, nor do we even want to do this."

At that, the emirs returned, ascending towards the Hill Citadel and met with al-Malik al-Ashraf. Each of them threw his sword before the Sultan and said "O lord (*khavand*), the matter of the Chief Judge has reached such an extent that he walks while the envoys ride," and they described his humiliation. He said to them "He deserves worse than that! Because they said about him that he is an unbeliever, who wears the *zunnār* belt beneath his clothing."

However, they said, "O lord, if the Muslims' judge is an unbeliever then Ibn al-Sal`ūs is a Muslim, but won't you give him to us, or else we will get Ibn al-Sal`ūs and take vengeance upon him?" The Sultan said, "I give him to you," and ordered him to be released.

It is said that the emir Badr al-Dīn Baktāsh al-Fakhrī, *amīr silāḥ*, took care of the Chief Judge Taqī al-Dīn, so when he was tormented in this manner, and the order given to confiscate from him, and he learned of what had been decided about him, he took him under his wing. He resolved to question al-Malik al-Ashraf concerning him, and to intercede on his behalf.

The Sultan had already detained the emir `Alam al-Dīn Sanjar al-Ḥamawī, known as Abū Khurṣ, even though the emir Badr al-Dīn Baydarā, the deputy sultan in the Egyptian homelands, had taken care of him. The emir Badr al-Dīn Baydarā had discussed with the emir Badr al-Dīn *amīr silāḥ* that he would intercede on his behalf, but he ducked out of it, as he wanted to intercede on behalf of the Chief Judge, and it was not possible for him to intercede on behalf of two at the same time.

Therefore, they then agreed that the emir Baydarā would intercede on behalf of the Chief Judge, while the *amīr silāḥ* would intercede on behalf of Abū Khurṣ. The both of them interceded for the both of them, in spite of the deep hatred that existed between the emir Baydarā and the Chief Judge, so the Sultan released both of them at the same time.

Chief Judge Taqī al-Dīn stayed permanently in al-Qarāfa after his removal from the rest of his positions. Absolutely nothing was left of them for him. He had previously had a total of 17 high positions, among the Cairo and Old Cairo judiciary, and the rest of the Egyptian homelands' districts, the preaching at the al-Azhar Friday Mosque, the Treasury Inspectorate, the Endowments Inspectorate, being the senior shaykh in the Egyptian homelands, inspecting the Ẓāhirī inheritance, with his children, his properties and his endowments, together with other high positions.

---

214 Cf. Q7:128.

215 Implying that he was not a Muslim.

It is said that the total of what was conveyed from him was 38,000 [dirhams?], not including the riding beasts, which were three, together with the expenses and the debt. In spite of all of this, he was firm in the face of all these terrible trials that continued. No submissiveness was ever seen from him, nor any humility towards any other than God, mighty and majestic.

This continued until the chief Shams al-Dīn Ibn al-Sal`ūs [128] approached him personally, and appointed to instruct at the Imam al-Shāfi`ī College, may God be satisfied with him, in al-Qarāfa al-Ṣughrā "the Lesser," so he taught there, and what happened to him we will mention if God Most High wishes.

On Friday 25 Ramaḍān [September 21, 1291] al-Malik al-Ashraf ordered that the caliph al-Ḥākim bi-amr-llāh Aḥmad son of the emir Abū `Alī al-Fatā son of the emir Abū Bakr son of the Imam al-Mustarshid bi-llāh, the `Abbāsid Commander of the Believers, would come out and deliver the Friday sermon personally to the people at the Citadel mosque, to mention al-Malik al-Ashraf, and his being appointed in charge of the Muslims' affairs in his sermon.[216]

So he came out, while he had the insignia of the `Abbāsids, a black gown, with an embellished sword, and delivered a sermon which he would have preached during the days of al-Malik al-Ẓāhir Rukn al-Dīn Baybars al-Bunduqdārī al-Ṣāliḥī al-Najmī, but merely changed the name of al-Ẓāhir and inserted the name of al-Ashraf. There were 30 years, nine months and 13 days between the sermon he preached for al-Malik al-Ẓāhir and the one he preached that day for al-Malik al-Ashraf.

It is said that sermon was delivered on Friday 24 Shawwāl [October 20, 1291], so when the caliph completed his sermon, he did not lead the people in prayer, but the Chief Judge Badr al-Dīn Ibn Jamā`a came forward, and led the people for the Friday prayers, continuing to preach in the Citadel. The judge Ṣadr al-Dīn `Abd al-Barr son of the Chief Judge Taqī al-Dīn Ibn Razīn filled in for him at the al-Azhar Friday Mosque.

On 2 Shawwāl [September 28, 1291] the emir `Alam al-Dīn al-Shujā`ī, the deputy sultan in protected Damascus, ordered the razing of all the shops (*ḥawānīt*) on al-Zalābiyya Bridge in Damascus, as well as clear away all the buildings on the Baniyās River, and al-Majdūl River under the protected Damascus Citadel as far as the Green Square Gate and to the hospice. So the places for travelers (*masā'iḥ*), and the factory, the houses, the dwellings, the hostels (*khānāt*), the guesthouse, and bathhouse which al-Malik al-Sa`īd son of al-Malik al-Ẓāhir had constructed were destroyed, together with the places for travelers which were on the Baradā River, the drinking-place known as al-`Ajamī, Arjawāsh drinking-place, and nothing but the mosques remained.

On 9 Shawwāl [October 5, 1291] al-Malik al-Ashraf ordered for the two emirs Sayf al-Dīn Qarā Ruslān al-Manṣūrī and Jamāl al-Dīn Aqūsh *al-afram* al-Manṣūrī. So the emir `Alam al-Dīn al-Shujā`ī, the deputy sultan

---

[216] See al-Bayhaqi, *Faḍā'il al-awqāt*, p. 52 for the spiritual significance of this time.

in Damascus, detained them, imprisoning the both of them in the citadel. Al-Malik al-Ashraf reassigned their *iqṭā`* fiefs to the emirs `Izz al-Dīn Izdimur al-`Alā'ī and Shams al-Dīn Sunqur *al-masāḥ*.

During Shawwāl [October 1291] the emir `Alam al-Dīn al-Shujā`ī, the deputy sultan [129] Damascus initiated the construction of the Damascus Citadel, which al-Malik al-Ashraf had assigned for him. He involved himself in this, and sought marble from all directions.

On the night of Monday 4 Dhū al-Qa`da [October 29, 1291] of this year al-Malik al-Ashraf ordered a gathering of the judges, the jurisprudents, the notables, and the Qur'ān readers in the Manṣūrī Cupola, the mausoleum of his father al-Malik al-Manṣūr. An impressive ceremony, at the one year anniversary of his father['s death].

The emir Badr al-Dīn Baydarā, the deputy sultan in the Egyptian homelands, and the chief Shams al-Dīn Ibn al-Sal`ūs spent the night in the Manṣūrī Cupola on this night, so when it was daybreak, al-Malik al-Ashraf and the caliph al-Ḥākim bi-amr-llāh presented themselves at the Manṣūrī Mausoleum, while the caliph was wearing black.

The caliph then delivered an eloquent sermon in which he encouraged the taking of Iraq. This was a day to remember! Moreover, al-Malik al-Ashraf donated copious amounts of charity, and he together with the caliph returned to the Hill Citadel.

Al-Malik al-Ashraf wrote to the emir `Alam al-Dīn al-Shujā`ī, deputy sultan in Damascus, to perform a ceremony like the one that was held in the Manṣūrī Cupola, so the post arrived with that to the deputy of Damascus on Saturday, 9 Dhū al-Qa`da [November 3, 1291]. So the deputy sultan in protected Damascus held a ceremony for that, and the people gathered for it on Monday night 11 Dhū al-Qa`da [November 5, 1291] at the Green Square in front of al-Ablaq Palace. People gathered for recitation of the mighty Qur'ān from the afternoon of Sunday until midnight of Monday night. Then the preachers spoke, and the people departed at daybreak.

On Thursday 13 Dhū al-Ḥijja [December 7, 1291] of this year's months, the emir `Alam al-Dīn al-Shujā`ī, deputy sultan in protected Damascus increased the size of the smaller Green Square in which al-Ablaq Palace is located by a sixth towards the north, close to the river. This was until between the square's wall and the river was the space of a cubit and a half for work. He allocated the walls among the emirs the troops and some of the populace. He personally together with his mamluks worked, and no one shirked from the work, so the construction was completed in two days.

During the final tenth of Dhū al-Ḥijja [last part December 1291] the shaykh Sayf al-Dīn al-Rujayḥī was detained. He was among the progeny of the shaykh Yūnus, and he was sent from Damascus to the sultanic gate in protected Egypt on the post horse.

During the first part of this year, the construction of protected Aleppo Citadel was completed. The emir Shams al-Dīn Qarāsunqur al-Manṣūrī, deputy sultan in Aleppo, had initiated its reconstruction during the Manṣūrī period, but it was only completed [130] at this time. The name of al-Malik al-Ashraf was written upon it, and it had been Hűlegű, the king of the Tatars, who had razed it, just as we have previously explained.

During this year al-Malik al-Ashraf ordered the expulsion of the two sons of al-Malik al-Ẓāhir Rukn al-Dīn Baybars al-Bunduqdārī al-Ṣāliḥī al-Najmī, who were al-Malik al-Mas`ūd Najm al-Dīn Khiḍr, the ruler of Kerak, and al-Malik al-`Ādil Badr al-Dīn Salāmish, the king of the Egyptian homelands in the past. Al-Malik al-Manṣūr removed them from imprisonment, and had them transported to the land of the Lascarid (Byzantium), king of the Franks.

When the both of them were expelled, he sent them together with their mother to the border-port of Alexandria accompanied by the emir `Izz al-Dīn Aybak al-Mawṣilī, the majordomo of the *`āliyya.* He headed with them, and transported them from it via the Mediterranean Sea (*al-baḥr al-māliḥ*) to Constantinople. When they arrived, the Lascarid treated them well, arranging a livelihood for them and those with them.

The death of al-Malik al-`Ādil Badr al-Dīn Salāmish occurred there, so his mother endured this patiently, placing him in a coffin, but not burying him until she returned with him to the Egyptian homelands just as we will mention if God wishes.

[*Obituaries*]

Mention of the events of the year 691 [1292]

On Friday 14 Ṣafar [February 5, 1292] of this year there was a terrible fire in the Hill Citadel in the Egyptian homelands in one of the treasuries. A great part of the treasures, precious objects and books were destroyed.

On Thursday 11 Rabī` al-Awwal [March 2, 1292] of this year al-Malik al-Ashraf ordered that the Qur'ān readers, scholars and senior officials be gathered at the Manṣūrī Cupola for a final noble recitation. Therefore, the people assembled for that, and the Sultan al-Ashraf descended on the morrow to visit the tomb of his father, and to bestow copious charity.

On Friday 29 Rabī` al-Awwal [March 20, 1292] the caliph al-Ḥākim bi-amr-llāh the `Abbāsid delivered a sermon in the Hill Citadel mosque in protected Cairo—an eloquent sermon in which he urged sacral warfare, and commanded a general muster, then leading the people in prayer.

Mention of al-Malik al-Ashraf heading to Syria

We have previously mentioned that the caliph delivered a sermon and urged sacral warfare, ordering the general muster, so when it was the 8th hour on Saturday 8 Rabī` al-Ākhir [March 29, 1292] of the months of this year al-Malik al-Ashraf headed from protected Cairo in the direction of Syria leading the Egyptian armies.

During the last part of Rabī` al-Ākhir [end March 1292] the post arrived from al-Raḥba to protected Damascus, informing that a group of the Tatars raided the outskirts of al-Raḥba, and made off with numerous quadrupeds. So the emir `Alam al-Dīn al-Shujā`ī, the deputy sultan in protected Damascus, dispatched a number of the Damascus army to it on 28 Rabī` al-Ākhir [March 19, 1292]. [136]

On Saturday 6 Jumādā al-Ulā [April 25, 1292] of this year the Sultan al-Ashraf arrived in protected Damascus, accompanied by his minister the chief Shams al-Dīn Ibn Sal`ūs. Al-Malik al-Ashraf ordered a disbursement upon all of the Egyptian and Syrian armies, and this was done on Monday 8 Jumādā al-Ulā [April 27, 1292].

During the middle tenth of Jumādā al-Ulā [beg. May 1292] the emir Shams al-Dīn Sunqur *al-a`sar* married the daughter of the chief Shams al-Dīn Ibn al-Sal`ūs with a dowry whose amount was 1500 dinars cash, with a down payment of 500 dinars.

Al-Malik al-Muẓaffar, the ruler of Ḥamāh, arrived to greet al-Malik al-Ashraf, and then al-Malik al-Ashraf reviewed the troops, and placed the Syrian army before his train until protected Aleppo. At the 5th hour on Monday 16 Jumādā al-Ulā [May 5, 1292] the Sultan al-Ashraf headed out, leading the Egyptian army from Damascus, and arrived in Aleppo, and entered it on 28 Jumādā al-Ulā [May 17, 1292]

Conquest of the Qal`at al-Rūm castle, and its being renamed Qal`at al-Muslimīn

On Friday 4 Jumādā al-Ākhira [May 23, 1292] of the months of this year the Sultan al-Ashraf traveled from Aleppo leading the rest of the Islamic armies: Egyptian, Syrian, Aleppan, and coastal, in the direction of Qal`at al-Rūm and camped against it on Tuesday 8 Jumādā al-Ākhira [May 27, 1292], besieging it, tightening around it, and placing 20 mangonels against it. Five of these were Frankish, while 15 were *qarābughā* and satanic. The mangonels cast, and tunnels were made.

After al-Malik al-Ashraf had headed towards Qal`at al-Rūm by a few days a black slave climbed the walls to the rooftops of the sultanic harem's quarters in the Damascus citadel. He was detained, put to the question, and then mentioned that one of the prayer-criers in the citadel mosque had placed a ladder for him, so he had climbed it to that level. The Sultan was kept appraised of this, so the written order arrived the both of them should have their limbs cut off, and they should be nailed up, so this was done to the both of them.

The emir `Alam al-Dīn al-Shujā`ī, deputy of Damascus, had a major role in the conquest of Qal`at al-Rūm, as it was he who came up with the stratagem of making a chain close to the castle battlements, with part of it fixed to the ground, while the army took hold of it, and ascended to the castle.

Among those who ascended to the castle were Sayf al-Dīn Aqjabā, one of the mamluks of the emir Badr al-Dīn Baktāsh al-Fakhrī, *amīr silāḥ*. He was not among his notable mamluks, but was in the service of his son, Ṣalāḥ al-Dīn Khalīl. He worked out a stratagem, and ascended to the castle walls, then fought fiercely, and was wounded. Then the Sultan began to watch him, and asked about him, so he came to be aware of it, then sent a robe to him and gifted him with wealth, and promised him an *iqṭā`* fief. He ordered his owner (*ustādh*) Badr al-Dīn to remind the Sultan of him when he returned to Aleppo, but he did not do this. Afterwards he was among the [137] commanders of the freeborn troops, and was made into an emir of a marching-band in the year 719 [1319–20] and then was a governor of the Fayyūm district in the Egyptian homelands.

Qal`at al-Rūm was conquered, with the assistance of God Most High, on Saturday 11 Rajab [June 28, 1292] of the months of the year 691, this year, by force, and the fighters in it were killed, while the women and progeny were taken captive. The Catholicos of the Armenians was found in it, and he was taken prisoner.

The duration of the stay against it until it was conquered was 33 days. Al-Malik al-Ashraf erased the name of this castle from being al-Rūm [Byzantines' Castle], and named it Qal`at al-Muslimīn [Muslims' Castle]. 1200 prisoners from among this castle's prisoners arrived at the sultanic factory. From the emirs, the emir Sharaf al-Dīn Ibn al-Khaṭīr and the emir Shihāb al-Dīn son of the emir Rukn al-Dīn, *amīr jāndār*, were martyred.

On Monday 13 Rajab [June 30, 1292] a short missive arrived in protected Damascus with the news of Qal`at al-Rūm's conquest, so Damascus was decorated, and the tidings were proclaimed of that. When this incredible conquest was completed, letters of good tidings were composed to the Islamic realms. Among those written to Damascus was a letter from al-Malik al-Ashraf to the Chief Judge Shihāb [al-Dīn] al-Khū'ī. A copy of it is:[217]

In the name of God, the Merciful, the Compassionate

> (From) his brother Khalīl son of Qalāwūn, this correspondence is to the judge's high council, the majestic, the great, the Imam, the learned one, the generous, the influential, the perfect, the unique, the chief, the ascetic Shihāb al-Dīn. He is the beauty of Islam, pride of creatures, nobility of the learning, glory of the chiefs, pride of the notables, sun of the *sharī`a*, the chosen one of kings and sultans, who God made special through types of greetings, and presented him with enjoyable things that return to "the seven oft-repeated (stories)."[218]

---

[217] Compare with the text in Anonymous, ed. Zettersteén, *Beiträge zur Geschichte der Mamlūkensultane in den Jahren 690–741: Nach arabische Handschriften* (Leiden: E.J. Brill, 1919), pp. 10–2.

[218] Q 15:87.

Some news of our victory and triumph has come to his hearing, containing in which its description, praise words and meanings, that proclaim to him the conquest of what pens have written proclaiming to the various climate-regions (*aqālīm*). Neither the robes of those telling of happy news traveling in their best attire, nor this age's preachers' tongues upon the pulpits have been more eloquent in content than those preceding them–namely the good news of the conquest of Qal`at al-Rūm.

This is the congratulation for every victory desired for Islam in the attainment of what was desired, and among the best narratives of this clear victory, and bestowal that should be communicated to the rest of the believers. Both far and near can be equally pleased in the proclamation and information, especially in the telling of happy news traveling to the rulers, to make the joyous proclamation public to the people, and to obligate each one possessing rank to take part in the merriment, both in different types and kinds.

This was that we rode to raid it from Egypt—there were kings previous to us who had put off going to it, and have called to it, without receiving a positive answer, asking the breeze about its mountains, but receiving tell of its big-headed vultures, seeking counsel from those with judgment concerning besieging it, but hearing nothing but colorful words and disparaging opinions—but we continued to travel, sending the reins [138] to similar locations, and extending the necks of noble horses towards it, in order that their power and his power be sufficient to carry out the journey.

We approached its difficult and forbidding mountains, rugged in places, with towering heights without a pathway or a meeting point, but the noble resolution continued to ease its difficulties; intractable (rivers) forded by placing small boats over the stones amidst their eddies, while big noble horses ascended up, their girths laden with heavy armor.

When the most noble (*ashraf*) Sultan overlooked it (*ashrafa `alayhā*) making its mountains open (road), besieging it in a way similar to that of Acre and its sister (cities). This was even though it was more fortified than Acre, we placed a number of mangonels against it, so that stones fell upon it like vultures, hunting spirits from their bodies. Even if walls were placed between them, they [the mangonels] would have preyed upon its towers with its hard stones, just as a lion preys upon its prey.

This, together with the tunnels that were dug in its curtain-wall (*badana*) at the speed of imagination, in spite of its vigilant eyelids, its outstretched columns, and its marshalled guard, while it was firmly rooted in Euphrates mountains, having dug a moat around it through which the Euphrates flowed on one side, while the Marzubān River on the other. Its designer had placed it upon a mountaintop that approaches the Gemini in its elevated points, and the foot of its "polished palace."[219] It is as if it was a throne on water,[220] so when the viewer eyes it, it seems to him to be like a star in the heavens.

This hemming in continued to bite at the sides of the mountain, squeezing its udders by its rope, cutting by riverbeds of fighting with its picks, and breaking down all opposition. Therefore, we arrived at it, in spite of its arrows, with a will that would not bend without it surrendering, and we rendered every judgment against it—unwilling to accept its houses without arbitration.

When God permitted it to be conquered, the doors of right were closed upon the Armenians and Tatars, as well as the bestowal that purifies the garments of recompense for the fighters (*mujāhidīn*) from the people of belief. This citadel was conquered by God's power and His aid, on Saturday 11 Rajab [July 5, 1292]. Praise be the One who eased its difficulties, hastened gaining it, enabled taking it and its inhabitants, and gathered it into the totality of the Islamic realms.

Therefore, the high session should take its portion from this glad proclamation, which the angels of heaven proclaim, to the king of the outstretched (land), the Sultan of the earth. Everyone whose obedience has pleased God resounds in thanks, while those deniers of the truth unpleasing (to God) are angered, and those who God opposed have been opposed.

Whoever expects from this accomplishment that the promise has been made good, neither going to exile nor distance will save him, for by the conquest of this citadel and ascending on top of it, the taking of this border fortress and refuge, Sayḥūn and Jayḥūn [Rivers] will be realized [= conquered].[221]

After the conquest of the Euphrates Gates by breaking its locks, they can no longer hope to save themselves through locking that citadel. After this conquest, if God Most High wills, will be nothing less than the conquest of the east, [Seljuq] Rūm and Iraq, and the dominion of the lands from the sun's setting to the sun's rising. God Most High will support us as a

[219] Cf. Q27:44.

[220] Satan's throne is said to be on the water.

[221] Two rivers usually associated with Anatolia.

result of our righteous entreaties that which will start the realization of good hopes to come, if God Most High wills.

Written on the day of the blessed conquest in the month of Rajab, year 691 [June 1292], according to the noble written command. [139]

Also letters from the emir `Alam al-Dīn al-Shujā`ī, the deputy sultan in protected Damascus, to the Chief Judge Shihāb al-Dīn al-Khū'ī as well, which was the work of the meritorious Sharaf al-Dīn al-Qudsī, a duplicate of which following the *basmala* is:[222]

May God redouble the happiness of his Excellency, the high, lordly, judge, Shihāb [al-Dīn],

And then mentioned his titles and descriptions,

… as the delegations' proclamations continue to him one after the other, the strings of congratulations both in prose and poetry overflow with him, and the opening verses of (*sūrat*) al-Fatḥ are recited with every verse of victory the pen on paper prostrates itself in gratitude. This includes the secrets of victory, so let the ears listen to its unusualness with that which will not be written as a report, treasuring this up as the manifestation of playing to win, so be guided thereby in happiness and reward.

The owned one (*mamlūk*) seeks to open by praising God for the favor He has bestowed, and opened to His friends (*awlīyā'*), giving from the enemies in accord with their enmity, making happy with the victory which He aided by His help, supported with His heavens' angels, as long as the aid continues with His might, seeking thereby to increase it through His bounty.

This is followed by prayers upon our *sayyid* Muḥammad, may the prayers and peace of God be upon him, causing the udders of conquest to stream forth milk, seeking to whet by his auspiciousness the blades which are against those who disbelieve in God, and in accord with the prayer of His messenger Noah,[223] guiding by the proclamations to the proximity of pulpits those to be honored in happiness.

Inkstands' mouths are gaping with ink in mention of him, while ears drink in the latest news coming in, which constitutes a fire in the enemies'

[222] Compare Anonymous, ed. Zetterstéen, pp. 14–7 (full text).

[223] Q71:26–7 where Noah asks God not to leave any unbelievers alive after the Flood.

hearts, while a light in those of (God's) friends (*awlīyā'*). Let the one present make haste to take part in his listening, so that he had return to his family happy, as it ended up that he has sent it forth while the victory's flags were waving, and his promises were fulfilled.

Proclamations have gone out in every direction with its post, and the sultanic noble announcements have emanated from Qal`at al-Rūm on the backs of beasts never before broken for a rider, leaving from its hilltop and summit among the native-born and the foreigner, while the spearheads are still dripping with their blood, so that the Euphrates is not fit for drinking.

Belief by this (conquest) has extended its tents, so the victorious swords have beaten polytheism to add rewards to its journey, and have established once and for all Islam's precedence, the Friday peoples' swords killing with their sides until the Saturday people [Jews] felt compassion for the Sunday people [Christians]. God has caused the signs of the Trinity to go until the very number three almost has vanished from the numbers, and has disassociated from them those who would have aided them by His aid until the Euphrates preferred the dry up around them lest its overflow be seen as an aid [to the Armenians].

The muezzin is sounded, while the bells are dumb, the word of faith is raised, so it became a sign of guard after it had been changed, and the call of truth is sounded around it from the mountains, which have heard even though they are deaf. The caller with an echoing tongue continues speaking from the high rising peaks.

This citadel had been on the Islamic borderlands as a bone in the gullet or a heartburn in the chest, like the sudden eclipse at the rising of the full moon, not free from hidden hatred, while manifesting softness, all the while concealing treachery, while proffering apologies. Its inhabitants were comfortable betraying [140] the neighbor, and making peace with the Tatars, supplying them with people and wealth against Islam, and being equal to them even in dress and in situation, helping them with gifts and kindnesses, while guiding them to sensitive locations.

They relied upon avoiding conflict, claiming that their citadel had always been protected from catastrophes, being deceived by it—and were it not for the noble assaults they would have been proved right—relying upon its fortifications, as long as the flashing lightning of its border fortress glanced through the clouds.

It is a fortress on a steep slope, with its roundness jutting out; the only path to it is through uninhabited rocky areas. Eyes cannot see it until the hearts reach the throat; it is as if it is a concealed object waiting to kill in imagination's capacity, while it lies in wait, turning away that which is apparent, while it lies hidden.

Towering mountains anchor it with their tails, extending the tents and canopies of clouds over it, while the firmly rooted mountains quarrel over it, concealing some of it from the other and dividing its sections. It is for terrorizing, loftiness, and establishing, next to the Euphrates, conjoining fire, air, water, and earth.

The Euphrates extends around it from its east like a sword in the hand of a vengeance-seeker, while another river encompasses it from the west, like a covering, winding with it like walls. On its highest peak the gaze makes out with difficulty, alighting upon what you imagine to be its apex, even though one can only have it pointed out by a guide.

It is the same from its east and its west, as the sun never looks upon it, nor the moon at the time of rising, nor sees it during the evening time. Around it, there are deep valleys like moats, which never will know the crescent moon except by someone describing it, nor more than half the sun. As for the road to it, a grain would slip from its back, and the range of one's glance dims from traveling its easier parts, not to speak of its harder ones.

In there are Armenians gathered by al-Takfūr [Leon III] and Tatars above their maximum for the purpose of raiding. They sacrificed many below it, having put on armor to defend it, having made haste to drink death's cup, fearing that Takfūr would deny (*yukaffir*) them, or their caliph who rules from it, the Catholicos, would reject them. "Satan made their deeds appear enticing to them."[224]

Their hopes were delivered to the field of error, so "when the two cohorts saw each other, he turned on his heels,"[225] leaving the both of them biting their hands with regret. When our master the Sultan, may God make his dominion eternal, ordered the victorious armies to besiege it, to assault it from behind, and in front, their horses' steps were brought down from the mountain-backs, as they surrounded it [Qal`at al-Rūm] from every side just as a halo surrounds the crescent moon, and these pointing swords made their way to it.

Terror preceded them as a guide, as they advanced over these ways and realms with wealth and people, trusting that they expended neither small

224 Q8:48.
225 Ibid. Citations of this verse hark back to the Battle of Badr (624).

amounts nor large, nor crossed valleys without being faster than pigeons in their advance, on the wings of arrows. Rocks of this virginal young woman[226] dripped with blood of necessity—and for necessity, there are laws. Whorish [141] behavior removed her covering of shame, as it crept through her joints like a sickness in her bones, in spite of the fact that it was established upon a rock, which did not permit [the use of] iron.[227]

However, God made our Sultan glorious by victory, so the circumstances of conquest cam according to what he desired. The victorious mangonels were erected in front of it, so they were certain of a painful punishment. They came to expect death's lightning from a hail of stones, which made everything they hit decayed. They took part in the war prayer, as its arrows were the bending (*rukū`*), their towers were the prostration, and their citadel had a handing over (*taslīm*).[228]

We continued to launch attacks upon them, raid after raid, giving them because of their thirst to drink the stones' hits, which even if they were from stone demonstrated hardness and seriousness. It was angered like a prisoner against the whip, seeking to conceal the pains it was enduring, complaining a wounded person's complaint for an end and sympathy with the tongue.

This was until they lost what they had been hoping for, as our mangonels trampled their mangonels, and "so the truth came to pass, and what they were doing was invalidated."[229] When its walls fell, and its secrets were violated by the tunnels' hand, the onlooker would imagine that it had been humbled, but the one up close would see that it was still in a stronger state, and protected from shooting and being shot, glorying over those "able to seek out an opening in the earth, or a ladder into the sky …"[230] dispensing with the walls' place, as its stones broke over the lions of war like vultures raining down.

This blessed conquest was on the morning of Saturday 11 Rajab year 691 [June 28, 1292] by the sword, violently, so the blades separated unbelief's diseased filth by suppressing enmity and its source through the (Muslim) community's army (*khamīs*) on Saturday against the Sunday people [Christians], so may God bless the community's army on its Saturday.

---

[226] Qal`at al-Rūm in the previous circular was likened to a virginal young woman.

[227] Presumably this metaphor refers to the tunneling that was going on.

[228] Also referring to the ritual blessing of peace upon Muḥammad that is part of the prayer.

[229] Q7:118.

[230] Q6:35.

> Let us take the opportunity of these glad tidings by which the religion has become elevated to the height of a lighthouse, manifesting light, pitching the tent of its proclamation throughout the four corners, remembering in love of conquests the first days with the Emigrants and the Helpers. So let us publicize this from the heads of truthful witnesses, and write it in the codices of the first conquests on the level of one who is tormented by a doppelganger (*qarīna*)[231] or an example of martyrdom-seeking, and give support to the army in its mission, which overtops all others, its prayers which strengthen the strong, supporting the hand and putting the foot forward, and participate in this sacral warfare (*jihād*) until our terror of far enemies be equivalent to what has happened, and they get what they gave.
>
> More proclamations will come after this one, as a title precedes a letter, as one begins calculation, as the superogatory bending (*rak`a*) is to the five (mandatory prayers), and as the false dawn is to the true rising of the sun. God Most High will make His shooting-star flash brilliantly, the light of His knowledge shine brightly in the horizons, treasuring up final congratulations altogether in accord with all that has come because of happiness being complete—if God Most High wills—and written on the aforementioned day of conquest, praise be to God, Lord of the Worlds.

A number of other letters proclaiming good tidings were written but we have sufficed with those we have mentioned fearing excessive length.

Al-Malik al-Ashraf assigned the emir `Alam al-Dīn al-Shujā`ī, the deputy sultan in Damascus, [142] to reconstruct Qal`at al-Muslimīn, and what the mangonels and tunneling destroyed. He ordered him to raze its suburbs and to move them further away, so al-Shujā`ī stayed back doing that, accompanied by the Syrian army.

A-Malik al-Ashraf traveled from Qal`at al-Muslimīn on Saturday 18 Rajab [July 5, 1292] and returned to Aleppo, staying there for the rest of Rajab and for half of Sha`bān [July-mid-August 1292]. Al-Malik al-Ashraf removed the emir Shams al-Dīn Qarā Sunqur al-Manṣūrī from being deputy sultan in Aleppo, and assigned in his place the emir Sayf al-Dīn Balabān al-Ṭabbākhī al-Manṣūrī. He made the emir Izz al-Dīn Aybak al-Mawṣilī Chancellery Inspector in protected Aleppo.

It is said that he appointed him to Qal`at al-Muslimīn, and what he had added to it, but he refused to accept the appointment, so the Sultan was angered at him, and ordered that he be detained. This was delegated to the emir Jamāl al-Dīn Aqush al-Fārisī, so he stayed (in that position)

[231] One's evil shadow-twin, in the Qur'ān (4:38, 43:26) masculine, but in later popular Islam transposed to feminine.

for some days, but then died, so the Sultan returned the emir `Izz al-Dīn Aybak al-Mawṣilī.

The Sultan al-Malik al-Ashraf traveled from Aleppo to Damascus, so his arrival there, and his entrance into it was at the 8th hour of Tuesday 20 Sha`bān [August 6, 1292] of this year. In front of him there were the prisoners, and among them was the Armenian Patriarch, the Catholicos (*katāghīkūs*), ruler of Qal`at al-Rūm,[232] and it was a day to remember.

During Sha`bān [July 1292] al-Malik al-Muẓaffar, ruler of Ḥamāh, divorced his wife, daughter of his maternal uncle al-Malik al-Nāṣir Ṣalāḥ al-Dīn Yūsuf son of al-Malik al-`Azīz Muḥammad son of al-Malik al-Ẓāhir Ghāzī son of al-Malik al-Nāṣir Ṣalāḥ al-Dīn Yūsuf son of Najm al-Dīn Ayyūb son of Shādhī son of Marwān the Ayyūbid, so the people found fault with him on this, and thought him rotten for doing it. She personally headed from Ḥamāh to the Egyptian homelands, and died there 20 days after her arrival.

During Sha`bān al-Malik al-Ashraf ordered the emir Badr al-Dīn Baydarā, deputy sultan in the Egyptian homelands, to head out to the al-Kasrawān Mountains,[233] so the emir Badr al-Dīn Baydarā took himself there at the head of most of the Egyptian armies, accompanied by the emir Shams al-Dīn Sunqur *al-ashqar*, Shams al-Dīn Qarāsunqur al-Manṣūrī, the emir Badr al-Dīn Baktūt al-Atābakī, the emir Badr al-Dīn Baktūt al-`Alā'ī, and others among the senior emirs.

He went towards the Kasrawān Mountains, while the emir Rukn al-Dīn Baybars Ṭaqṣū, the emir `Izz al-Dīn Aybak al-Ḥamawī and others came to them from the coast, meeting at the mountain. Those summoned praised the emir Badr al-Dīn Baydarā's resolution and the sharpness of his intelligence. He gave them a reprieve in their affairs, which they used to gain the mastery over some of the army in these rugged areas, and mountain passes.

They were able to get the better of them, so the army returned half-defeated. The inhabitants of those mountains wanted to get at them, so the army was very disturbed. The emir Badr al-Dīn had to soften the hearts of al-Kasrawān, and to treat them well. He bestowed robes upon a number of their notables, [143] so they went overboard in their demands, but he assented to what they sought.

He granted the release of a number of them who were imprisoned in Damascus for crimes and offenses they had done. Killings, pillage and victory for [the inhabitants of] al-Kasrawān the like of which they had never had before occurred because of this. The emirs and the army were in pain from this episode, which necessitated some of them being open about the emir

[232] Stephen IV (d. 1293).

[233] The region to the northeast of Beirut, abutting Mt. Lebanon. See Usāma Qablān, *Shī`at Kasrawān wa-l-ḥamalāt al-Mamlūkiyya: Dirāsat fī rasā'il Ibn Taymiyya* (Beirut: Dār al-Wafā', 2018), pp. 67–74.

Baydarā's bad administration. They accused him of being lenient with them, and taking a break from fighting with them, until they had gotten the better of him, because of his greed. They also said that he had received a bribe from them (*tabarṭala*), taking a large amount.

The people were worked up about this, and the emir Badr al-Dīn Baydarā headed with the armies to Damascus, where al-Malik al-Ashraf greeted him, approaching him, and alighting at his alighting, to give the peace greeting. However, when he was alone, he disapproved of his bad conduct, and his neglect of the army. He became sick because of that, until it was widely suspected among the people that he had been poisoned, but then he became better during the first tenth of Ramaḍān [mid-August 1292] of this year's months.

Then the Sultan gave a great deal of charity thanking God Most High for his improved health, and freed a large number of those who were in the prisons, and then gave charity, and also refrained from a large number of confiscations that were in the works, which were contrary to the Law.

The religious leadership, the judges, the Qur'ān readers and the shaykhs gathered during 10 Ramaḍān [August 25, 1292] in the Damascus Mosque to do the final recitation, and the mosque was on fire during the night, just as it had been for the midmonth of Sha`bān.[234] The army's camels sickened, which spread until all the pavilions were removed away from them. Even the emirs could hardly find camels to bear their heavy armor, so they had to suffice with mules and half-breed horses (*akādīsh*).

On Wednesday 20 Ramaḍān [September 4, 1292] al-Malik al-Ashraf ordered the disabled from the Egyptian army to return to the Egyptian homelands, so they left on the next day, Thursday 21 Ramaḍān.

On Friday 22 Ramaḍān [September 6, 1292] al-Malik al-Ashraf prayed the Friday prayer in the Damascus Mosque, and attended listening to the sermon. After the return of al-Malik al-Ashraf from Qal`at al-Rūm he released the emir `Alam al-Dīn Sanjar al-Dawādārī, and ordered for him to be brought from the Egyptian homelands to protected Damascus, so he was, then the Sultan bestowed a robe upon him, asked him to accompany him to the Egyptian homelands, and made him a commander.

On the night of the Festival [September 14–15, 1292] during this year the emir Ḥusām al-Dīn Lājīn "the Lesser" al-Manṣūrī from his house in Damascus. It had been related to him that al-Malik al-Ashraf wanted to detain him. When it reached al-Malik al-Ashraf that the emir Ḥusām al-Dīn had fled, he ordered for it to be proclaimed in Damascus about that whoever brought him in would receive 1000 dinars, while whoever concealed him would be hung.

Then the Sultan rode with his personal guard and a number of the emirs, abandoning the Festival repast in favor of searching for the emir Ḥusām al-Dīn. The emirs dispersed right and left in search of him, and they returned

[234] An important optional fasting period for Muslims.

[144] after the late afternoon (prayers) in the worst state of being exhausted, but did not find a trace of him, nor was there any news of him, and a complete absence of victory over him.

The people were praying the Festival prayer on that day in the Green Square, and when al-Malik al-Ashraf returned, having not been victorious over the emir Ḥusām al-Dīn, he felt anxiety. What happened was that the emir Ḥusām al-Dīn, when he fled from his house, took refuge with a group of the Arabs (Bedouin) who he trusted. But they instead detained him, and brought him to al-Malik al-Ashraf, who imprisoned him.

The emir Rukn al-Dīn Baybars Ṭuqṣū had already spoken against the emir Badr al-Dīn Baydarā, saying that he had received bribes for [the operation against] al-Kasrawān. Baydarā was angered at him, and kept it secret inside, waiting for a turn in fortune.

When the Sultan detained the emir Ḥusām al-Dīn, the emir Baydarā addressed the Sultan concerning detaining the emir Ṭuqṣū, because the emir Lājīn had married his daughter. Therefore, he detained him, and sent him and Lājīn to the Hill Citadel in the Egyptian homelands.

It is said that al-Malik al-Ashraf detained the emir Ṭuqṣū and the emir Shams al-Dīn Sunqur *al-ashqar* on Friday 22 Ramaḍān [September 6, 1292] of this year. He wanted to detain the emir Lājīn, but he fled, just as we previously explained. The most likely account is that the Sultan did not detain the emir Shams al-Dīn Sunqur *al-ashqar* in Damascus on that date, but only detained him in the Egyptian homelands after the Sultan's return to it, just as we will mention, if God Most High wills.

In the middle of Ramaḍān [August 30, 1292] after the death of the judge Fatḥ al-Dīn Muḥammad son of the judge Muḥyī al-Dīn `Abdallāh son of the shaykh Rashīd al-Dīn `Abd al-Ẓāhir, chief of the Correspondence Chancellery in the Egyptian homelands, in protected Damascus, because he had been accompanying the Sultan, the Sultan al-Malik al-Ashraf bestowed his allowances and salary, and assigned them to his son the judge `Alā' al-Dīn `Alī. He was young, but was established in all of the Correspondence bureaus.

Al-Malik al-Ashraf, after the death of the judge Fatḥ al-Dīn, appointed to the chiefship of the Correspondence Chancellery: the judge Tāj al-Dīn Abū al-Ẓāhir Aḥmad son of the judge Sharaf al-Dīn Abū al-Barakāt Sa`īd son of Shams al-Dīn Abū Ja`far Muḥammad Ibn al-Athīr al-Tanūkhī al-Ḥalabī. However, he only lasted a month, or almost a month, then was collected to the mercy of God Most High on Thursday 19 Shawwāl [October 3, 1292] of this year, on the outskirts of protected Gaza, as he was returning to protected Cairo. He was buried there, as is mentioned in his biography.

Al-Malik al-Ashraf then appointed to the chiefship of the Correspondence Chancellery his son the judge `Imād al-Dīn Isma`īl, and he continued until the end of the year 692 [December 2, 1293].

On 6 Shawwāl [September 20, 1292] the Sultan delegated the deputy sultanate in protected Damascus to the emir `Izz al-Dīn Aybak al-Ḥamawī in place of the emir `Alam al-Dīn Sanjar al-Shujā`ī. He delegated the deputy sultanate in the conquered regions to the emir Sayf al-Dīn Ṭughrīl al-Ighānī in place of the emir [145] Sayf al-Dīn Balabān al-Ṭabbākhī because of his being transferred to the deputy sultanate in the Aleppan realm, just as we previously explained.

On Saturday 6 Shawwāl [September 20, 1292] the emir `Alam al-Dīn al-Shujā`ī arrived at Damascus with the Syrian armies after he had reconstructed the sections of Qal`at al-Rūm which had been destroyed. Then it reached him that al-Malik al-Ashraf had removed him from being deputy in Damascus.

On the night of Tuesday 9 Shawwāl [September 23, 1292] during the last third al-Malik al-Ashraf traveled from protected Damascus returning to the Egyptian homelands. He had issued a written command to the inhabitants of the Damascus marketplaces that each one of them was to come out with a lit candle in his hand at the time of the Sultan's riding. Therefore, they came out altogether, and were arranged from the Victory Gate, one of the Damascus gates, to the Mosque of the Footprint.[235] When the Sultan rode, these candles were lit up, and he left, but it stayed like that until the end of the gathering.

After the Sultan had headed from Damascus to the Egyptian homelands the judge Muḥyī al-Dīn Ibn al-Naḥḥās asked to be relieved of the duties of Chancellery Inspector in Syria, so he was relieved. He was assigned to the Treasury Inspectorate in place of the judge Amīn al-Dīn Ibn Hilāl.

The judge Jamāl al-Dīn Ibn Ṣaṣrā was assigned to the Chancellery Inspectorate, while the Sultan al-Ashraf assigned the emir Shams al-Dīn Qarāsunqur *al-jūkandār* al-Manṣūrī to command the royal mamluks.

The Sultan al-Malik al-Ashraf arrived in the Egyptian homelands and entered protected Cairo through the Victory Gate, and transversed it, departing through the Zuwayla Gate, and then ascending to the Hill Citadel safely on Wednesday 2 Dhū al-Qa`da [October 15, 1292] from the months of this year.

The decoration, the banners, the congratulations and the candles that were done passed all boundaries, and were above and beyond what the inhabitants of Syria and Damascus had done. The people celebrated hugely, while they were pleased and happy, and God knows best.

Mention of the killing of a number of emirs, and the release of the emir Ḥusām al-Dīn Lājīn, deputy of Damascus

It was said that when al-Malik al-Ashraf Ṣalāḥ al-Dīn Khalīl returned to the Egyptian homelands, just as we previously explained, he detained the emir Shams al-Dīn Sunqur *al-ashqar*, the emir Sayf al-Dīn Jarmak al-Nāṣirī, and

---

[235] See Ibn Mibrad, *Thimār*, p. 244. Al-`Aynī, *`Iqd*, iii, p. 166 says that the candle-lighting was for al-Ashraf's wife, who was pregnant and about to give birth.

others, and ordered them to be imprisoned, so they were. Then he ordered for them to be brought out, together with the other emirs who were in prison, and that they be strangled in front of him. Therefore, they were brought out and strangled in front of him.

They were the emir Sayf al-Dīn al-Hārūnī, the emir Badr al-Dīn Baktūt, the emir Sayf al-Dīn Jarmak, the emir Shams al-Dīn Sunqur *al-ashqar*, the emir Rukn al-Dīn Baybars Ṭuqṣū al-Nāṣirī, and a number besides them.

They brought the emir Ḥusām al-Dīn Lājīn "the Lesser," who had been deputy of Damascus as the last of the lot. When the bowstring was placed upon his neck, and they wanted to garrote him, the string broke [146] because of God Most High's foreordination.

It is said that he mumbled to justify himself "O lord, I have no fault (*dhanb*), other than Ḥamawī Ṭuqṣū, and he has perished, so I divorce his daughter!" The emirs felt compassion for him, and interceded for him, guaranteeing him, so the Sultan pardoned him, bestowed a robe upon him, and placed him in his armory just as he had been during the days of his father al-Malik al-Manṣūr, giving him a good *iqṭā* fief. Praise to the One who does as He wills!

It is said that the one who had been designated to garrote the emir Ḥusām al-Dīn Lājīn, the emir Shams al-Dīn Qarāsunqur al-Manṣūrī, had mercy upon him, and expected that there would be intercession for him, so the emir Badr al-Dīn Baydarā, the deputy sultan in the Egyptian homelands, interceded for him, so the Sultan ordered him to be released, while he was thinking that he was as good as dead. But God Most High kept him safe because of the fact that he would one day become the Sultan in the Egyptian homelands and the Syrian lands, just as we will mention if God Most High wishes.

It is said that the killing of those aforementioned emirs and the release of the emir Ḥusām al-Dīn Lājīn was on the first day of Muḥarram, at the beginning of 692 [December 12, 1292] and God knows best which of these it was.

[*Obituaries*]

Mention of the events of the year 692 [1293–4]

At the beginning of this year al-Malik al-Ashraf Ṣalāḥ al-Dīn Khalīl son of al-Malik al-Manṣūr Sayf al-Dīn Qalāwūn al-Alfī al-Ṣāliḥī al-Najmī, ruler of the Egyptian homelands and the Syrian lands, delegated the deputyship in the Tripolitan realm and the fortresses to the emir `Izz al-Dīn Aybak *al-khazindār* al-Manṣūrī in place of the emir Sayf al-Dīn Ṭughrīl al-Ighānī as he had asked to be relieved from the deputyship and requested that. He arrived in Damascus on 27 Muḥarram [January 7, 1293] of this year, accompanied by five emirs of marching bands, and headed in its direction.

During Muḥarram the house of Najm al-Dīn Qabaq was sold to the sultanic Ashrafi lands (*al-khāṣṣ al-sharīf*). Its letters arrived in the wrapping of a noble note (*mithāl*), and the letters were handed over to Majd al-Dīn Ibn al-Khashshāb in the august governing council.

The judge Jamāl al-Dīn Muḥammad Ibn al-Mukarram in his composition *The Secretary's Treasury*. He said: A note arrived, whose date was 5 Muḥarram [December 16, 1292] that Sayf al-Dīn Timur should complete this by the end of the month, collecting for him the usual amounts from the judges and the well-respected (*mu`tabirīn*).

Mention of al-Malik al-Ashraf's heading towards Upper Egypt, and his safe return to his Citadel

On 4 Muḥarram [December 15, 1292] of this year al-Malik al-Ashraf headed in the direction of Upper Egypt among the districts of the Egyptian homelands to hunt. He asked his minister Shams al-Dīn Ibn al-Sal`ūs to accompany him, and left the emir Badr al-Dīn Baydarā as deputy in the Hill Citadel, while he was weak.

The Sultan ended up at the city of [154] Qūṣ and used it as a base for hunting. He ordered the chamberlains and officials to call out among the army that they should prepare themselves to raid Yemen. The chief Shams al-Dīn Ibn al-Sal`ūs investigated Upper Egypt, then found those regions under the chancellery of the emir Badr al-Dīn Baydarā there were *iqṭā`* fiefs, purchased properties and protected properties which were worth more than the sultanic private lands (*al-khāṣṣ al-sultānī*).

He also found that the sultanic purse in the districts of Upper Egypt was empty of any stores or revenues, while the purse of the emir Badr al-Dīn Baydarā was full. Therefore, he presented all of this to the Sultan al-Ashraf, and informed him of it, so the Sultan turned against the emir Badr al-Dīn Baydarā.

This information came to the emir Badr al-Dīn Baydarā, so he intended to mend relations with him, so he prepared for the Sultan an impressive gift. Part of it was a tent of a blackish-red substance,[236] with tent-ropes of silk (*ibrīsim*), tent-pillars of sandal-wood, adorned with silver inlayed with gold, and carpeted with a silk carpet, plus those gifts which would be appropriate for a tent such as this.

He pitched the tent at al-`Adawiyya, so when the Sultan returned from Upper Egypt, he stayed in the pitched tent for an hour of the day, but did not manifest outwardly any cheerfulness at the gift, nor did he find it to be impressive. Then he rode and ascended to his Citadel, and his realm's seat (*kursī*) safely, and expropriated some of the emir Badr al-Dīn Baydarā's regions for the private sultanic purse.

On Thursday 21 Muḥarram [January 1, 1293] of this year after the death of the emir `Alam al-Dīn Sanjar al-Ḥalabī "the greater" his livelihood was sealed

[236] Al-Qalqashandī, *Ṣubḥ*, iv, p. 41 states that al-Ashraf changed the Mamluk uniform colors from yellow to red. This could also explain why the Sri Lankan ruler was offering red dye above.

off, and the Sultan al-Ashraf was informed while he was traveling in Upper Egypt of his order. He left behind two daughters and four wives. The answer came back on 4 Ṣafar [January 14, 1293] of this year, containing the release from his livelihood, and its being handed over to his deputies, and if he died, to his creditors. This should be mentioned at his command upon the sultanic noble riders being presented at his Citadel safely.

During Ṣafar [January 1293] there was a terrible earthquake in the lands of Gaza, al-Ramla, Lydda and Kerak, but the worst of it was in Kerak. Three towers from its castle were destroyed.[237]

A letter from al-Ghars son of Shāwar, governor of al-Ramla, arrived, detailing in it rains falling, and the continual storms night and day, as many of the houses and vaults in al-Ramla had been destroyed. The torrent cut its bridges, its curved mills were destroyed, while its stones and implements were broken. Twelve lions were found dead in the floodwaters, having drowned in the torrent.

Shortly after the flooding a terrible earthquake followed, which was strong throughout the coastal lands. Many places were destroyed, and the minaret of al-Ramla Friday Mosque split, and it fell. He wrote to him to make an inventory report, as the minaret of Gaza Friday Mosque also fell. An order was issued that a report be made for it, so the emir `Alā' al-Dīn Aydughdī al-Shujā`ī was deputized from Damascus to reconstruct what was destroyed in Kerak, accompanied by construction engineers, and God knows best.

The letter of the emir `Izz al-Dīn Aybak al-Rūmī, [155] deputy for the Ashrafī [conquest] Qal`at al-Muslimīn, whose name had been Qal`at al-Rūm, arrived, requesting 30 head-gear[238] so that he could investigate the reports of the abandoned [Mongols]—dressing his soldiers so that when they were in their lands, no one would immediately identify them so that they could intermingle.

During this year al-Fidāwiyya [Assassins] fell upon *ḥ/j-n-s-a-i* [=Naqājū][239] the police chief (*shiḥna*) of `Āna, in the Baghdad market close to the Ḥārūq House Gate, then killed him. [The assassin] fled, and hid in the ruin of Baghdad, while Baghdad was in turmoil, and an uproar that lasted for days.

---

[237] See Ambraseys, *Earthquakes in the Mediterranean and Middle East: A Multidisciplinary Study of Seismicity up to 1900* (Cambridge: Cambridge University Press, 2009), p. 353 (mentioning Ibn al-Furāt).

[238] From the Farsi *sarāqūch(ā)*; see al-`Aynī, *`Iqd*, iii, p. 115 where the Mongols are said to ride with it.

[239] Probably Naqājū, the emir of the armories, see ps.-Ibn al-Fuwaṭī, *Ḥawādith*, p. 514, where the attacker is said to have been a *bāṭinī* (Assassin). According to this account, the assassin as he was being arrested called out for al-Malik al-Ashraf to redeem him. The implication appears to be that he was sent by al-Ashraf, and that may be the reason for Ibn al-Furāt including the notice in his text. The assassin was tortured to death.

A pack-load was prepared for the emir Ḥusām al-Dīn Muhannā son of `Īsā, king of the Bedouin, because of his marriage of a daughter who was marrying him—a total of 25 loads, while the pack-load for his mother was a tent from the treasury, as usual, and so this was handed over to his chamberlain complete (or Kāmil).

A written order was issued to the emir `Alā' al-Dīn Tambakī al-Wazīrī to build a well, and an irrigation system in al-`Arīsh, and so Yaḥyā b. Aḥmad, Ismā`īl b. Ḥusayn and Aḥmad b. Khalīf from the divers (well-borers) were sent to him.

During this year the report that the emir `Alā' al-Dīn al-Barīdī, governor of al-Ashmūnayn, killed himself, arrived. Then Sayf al-Dīn Baktimur al-Mūsikī was appointed in his place. In it the Sultan al-Ashraf ordered for the emir `Izz al-Dīn Izdimur al-`Alā'ī, one of the emirs in protected Damascus, to be detained, so he was, then sent to the sultanic gates in protected Egypt through Gaza during the month of Rabī` al-Awwal [February 1293] of this year.

Mention of al-Malik al-Ashraf heading towards Syria

After the return of al-Malik al-Ashraf from the region of Upper Egypt (*al-sa`īd*) just as we previously explained, he prepared and ordered the armies to be prepared to go to Syria. He ordered the emir Badr al-Dīn Baydarā, the deputy sultan in the Egyptian homelands, to lead the armies to Damascus on the main road, while the chief Shams al-Dīn Ibn al-Sal`ūs, was headed on it with the sultanic treasury.

The Sultan al-Ashraf, however, rode on fast camels, while a number of the emirs and al-Khāṣakiyya rode in his wake. He headed to Kerak, and personally inspected its fortress, and put its affairs in order. Then he headed from it to protected Damascus. His arrival there was on 9 Jumādā al-Ākhira [May 17, 1293] of the months of this year. The emir Badr al-Dīn Baydarā and the chief Shams al-Dīn arrived after him by three days.

Mention of the conquest of Bahsanā, Mar`ash and Tell Ḥamdūn, and taking them from the Armenians, and adding them to the Islamic realms

Bahsanā was among the greatest of the castles, and the strongest, and it had many properties. It was located in the mouth of the Darband, and was in the hand of the kings of Islam at Aleppo until the cursed Hülegű, king of the Tatars, ruled Aleppo. The [156] deputy of Bahnasā then was the emir Sayf al-Dīn al-`Aqrab, on behalf of al-Malik al-Nāṣir Ṣalāḥ al-Dīn Yūsuf al-Ayyūbī, the ruler of Aleppo and Damascus. The former sold it to the [Armenian] ruler of Sīs for 100,000 dirhams, of which he gave him [the latter] 60,000 dirhams, and handed it over to the Armenians, the inhabitants of Sīs.

It remained in their hands until the riders of the Sultan al-Malik al-Ashraf, son of al-Malik al-Manṣūr appeared in Damascus during this year, whereupon he ordered the armies to be prepared to go to the lands of Sīs. Envoys of the ruler of Sīs arrived at the noble sultanic gates in protected Damascus, asking for the mercies and consideration of the Sultan, and they expended substantial gifts.

The issue was resolved in that they would hand over Bahnasā, Mar`ash and Tell Ḥamdūn to the Sultan, so the Sultan had them return accompanied by the emir Sayf al-Dīn Ṭūghān, the governor of the Damascus region. They were handed over, together with their lands, and the post arrived with the [news] of that during the first tenth of the month of Rajab [June 6–16, 1293] of this year.

The tidings were sounded for that, and the Sultan al-Malik al-Ashraf assigned the emir Badr al-Dīn Baktāsh *al-zardkāsh* to be the deputy sultan for Bahnasā, and appointed a judge and a preacher for it, assigning men and guards for it. Then the emir Sayf al-Dīn Ṭūghān arrived accompanied by envoys from the ruler of Sīs with loads and honorary gifts. Their arrival in Damascus was on 28 Rajab [July 4, 1293] after al-Malik al-Ashraf had headed from Damascus to the Egyptian homelands. So they headed in his wake to the Egyptian homelands.

On 2 Rajab [June 8, 1293] al-Malik al-Ashraf headed from Damascus to Ḥimṣ leading a number of the armies, but sent the unfit of the army to the Egyptian homelands in return. Then the Sultan headed from Ḥimṣ to Salamiyya as a guest of the emir Ḥusām al-Dīn Muhannā son of `Īsā, king of the Bedouin. However, when he extended his hospitality to the Sultan, he [al-Ashraf] ordered him to be detained, together with his brothers, so they were, while they were at a meal.[240]

He sent him under guard accompanied by the emir Ḥusām al-Dīn Lājīn, so they arrived in Damascus on Sunday 7 Rajab [June 13, 1293], while the Sultan arrived in Damascus during the afternoon of that day. The Sultan al-Ashraf gave the emirate over the Bedouin after the emir Ḥusām al-Dīn Muhannā and his brothers were detained to their paternal cousin the emir Shams al-Dīn Muḥammad b. Abū Bakr b. `Alī b. Ḥudhayfa.

During the month of Rajab [June 1293] al-Malik al-Ashraf ordered the emir `Izz al-Dīn Aybak *al-afram*, the *amīr jāndār*, to head to Shawbak Castle, and to destroy it. This was at the time when the Sultan headed from Damascus to Ḥimṣ, so he conferred with him about that, and clarified for him that this was a bad decision.

However, he upbraided him, so he headed towards it, razed it, but left a small bit of it. Its being razed was a mistake, and bad administration. Castles and fortresses are the refuges of Islam, the treasures of the Muslims, and it is

[240] A violation of classical laws of hospitality.

in them that they take refuge during difficult times, sieges, and when enemies appear, so this was an unbelievable matter.

During the month of Rajab a letter from the deputy sultan in Ba`lbak arrived informing that [157] heavy rains and very heavy snow had fallen in the city of Ba`lbak. The rain would fall as if it were mixed with clay, and that the torrent had come up to the gate of Ba`lbak named the Damascus Gate, and had overtopped it, and had even reached the walls' battlements, then it had receded.

However, it is uprooted many orchards, moving rocks and stones, and that the roads had been swallowed up. He enumerated the damages in Ba`l-bak, so its cost was more than 150,000 dinars. The Sultan ordered the emir Badr al-Dīn Baydarā to head leading the armies to the Egyptian homelands: him, the chief Shams [al-Dīn] Ibn al-Sal`ūs and the treasury, just as they had returned from Ḥimṣ, so they both headed from Damascus on Thursday 11 Rajab [June 17, 1293].

The Sultan headed after them from Damascus leading some of the emirs and the Khāṣakiyya. He rode from Damascus at the 7th hour on Saturday 13 Rajab [June 19, 1293]. This was so he could be alone with his cronies for hunting, and not have to worry about the armies. He arrived in Gaza on the morning of Wednesday 17 Rajab.

Alter the return of the Sultan al-Malik al-Ashraf to the Egyptian homelands he ordered the emir Sayf al-Dīn Ṭūghān, governor of the Damascus region, to head to the deputy sultanate of Qal`at al-Muslimīn which had been named Qal`at al-Rūm in place of the emir `Izz al-Dīn Aybak al-Mawṣilī al-Manṣūrī. He appointed the emir Sayf al-Dīn Asandimur Kurjī to be the governor of the Damascus region in place of the emir Sayf al-Dīn Ṭūghān.

During Shawwāl [September 1293] of this year al-Malik al-Ashraf ordered the emir `Izz al-Dīn Aybak *al-afram*, *amīr jāndār*, to be detained, so he was during Shawwāl. A guard was set around his livelihood and the revenues he obtained in both the Egyptian homelands and Syria.

After the death of the Chief Judge Mu`izz al-Dīn Nu`mān son of the Chief Judge Tāj al-Dīn al-Ḥasan son of Yūsuf al-Khaṭībī al-Urzanjānī, Ḥanafī Chief Judge in the Egyptian homelands, al-Malik al-Ashraf appointed the Chief Judge Shams al-Dīn Aḥmad known as al-Surūjī al-Ḥanafī in his place in the Ḥanafī chief judiciary during Sha`bān [July 1293] of this year.

During Dhū al-Ḥijja [November 1293] of the months of this year al-Malik al-Ashraf ordered a ceremony for the circumcision of his brother al-Malik al-Nāṣir Muḥammad son of al-Malik al-Manṣūr Sayf al-Dīn Qalāwūn. In his honor there should be *qabaq* games held under the Hill Citadel close to the Victory Gate. The *qabaq* was held on 20 Dhū al-Ḥijja [November 21, 1293], and the emirs, senior [officers] and those who were usually involved threw it.

The Sultan al-Ashraf disbursed money [158] and robes to whoever caught it. The one who caught it was the emir Badr al-Dīn Baysarā al-Shamsī al-Ṣāliḥī al-Najmī who was related to al-Ashraf, so he threw it in a way no one else ever had previously. This was that he had made a special saddle, and fastened very firmly around the rump.

When the Sultan saw him, he said to him "You have excelled, O emir Badr al-Dīn! Since you have made that special saddle to ease riding for you!" He said, "If this mamluk has excelled, then I have had six sons, and they are all at the service of the Sultan. I only made this saddle specifically for the *qabaq*."

Then the emir Badr al-Dīn Baysarā rode hard towards the *qabaq* goalpost (*ṣārī*). Usually, the thrower would not cast until he had gone towards the goalpost, but Badr al-Dīn rode until he had passed the goalpost, so people did not doubt that he had missed the throw. Then he went down upon his back on the horse's back until his head was on the horse's buttocks, then he threw while he was in that position after he had passed it.

Moreover, he hit the gourd (*qar`a*) and broke it![241] The people shouted at that, and acclaimed him. The utility of the saddle became apparent to the Sultan, so the Sultan ordered that the rest of the prize left at that point be given to the emir Badr al-Dīn Baysarā, and it was. This was 35,000 dirhams, and a robe was bestowed upon him, as he was acclaimed a hero in peoples' hearts even more than previously.

Others knew that they were unable to duplicate this feat, so then there was the blessed circumcision on Monday 22 Dhū al-Ḥijja [November 23, 1293]. A great deal of gold was scattered upon the emirs in washbasins, until they were filled to overflowing.

At the end of this year [December 1, 1293] after the judge `Imād al-Dīn Isma`īl son of the judge Tāj al-Dīn Abū al-Ẓāhir Aḥmad son of the judge Sharaf al-Dīn Abū al-Barakāt Sa`īd son of Shams al-Dīn Abū Ja`far Muḥammad Ibn al-Athīr al-Ḥalabī al-Tanūkhī had been appointed as chief of the Correspondence Chancellery in the Egyptian homelands the judge Sharaf al-Dīn Ibn Faḍl Allāh al-`Umarī joined him in the Correspondence Chancellery.

[*Obituaries*]

Mention of the events of the year 693 [1293–4]

1 Muḥarram 693 [December 2, 1293] was Thursday.

Mention of some of al-Malik al-Ashraf son of al-Malik al-Manṣūr's news, his conduct, and his going to al-Buḥayra to hunt and his murder

We have previously mentioned some of the reports of al-Malik al-Ashraf Ṣalāḥ al-Dīn Khalīl son of al-Malik al-Manṣūr Sayf al-Dīn Qalāwūn al-Alfī, ruler

[241] Li Guo, *Sports as performance: the Qabaq-game and celebratory rites in Mamluk Cairo* (Berlin: EB Verlag, 2013), pp. 13–6 gives a detailed account of this game, summarizing the other sources.

of the Egyptian homelands and the Syrian lands, the lands he conquered, and what he did to the Franks, the people of unbelief and stubbornness.

We will now mention some of his conduct, and the report of his murder. He was, may God be clement towards him, a generous, brave, courageous king, riding lightly, victorious in his battles. Just as some of his depicters have said, he was a lion, determined, a champion, a Leo (*dirghām*), who conquered his realm through sacral fighting (*jihād*), and overrunning lands. He cleansed the coastland, cutting the approach from its inhabitants, hunting by the snare of his mangonels both Acre and Sidon, fulfilling a promise to their waterways and filled land-ways—a promise kept—he overtopped the walls of the inhabitants of Tyre, and stormed the houses of the people of Beirut.[242]

He achieved the greatest goal against the inhabitants of Bahsanā, and strengthened it against the door of evil when it was conquered, ascending afterwards to Qal`at al-Rūm—was it not conquered?[243] Its times have perished in wars, and vengeance has been taken for Ibn Ayyūb,[244] especially when he conquered Acre. Its land was pounded by his horses' hoofs, its walls were razed, its virgins taken captive, while its uncouth (men) killed, and its fields shepherded. Therefore, the Muslims were happy, and gained the victory, but the unbelievers were exterminated.

In spite of his impulsiveness, may God Most High have mercy upon him, he had a rare sense of humor. He loved strangers, and would discourse with literati. He had a clear mind, and was very perceptive.

One of the stranger (anecdotes) that it is told about him in [166], that he was sitting one of the days in the square, while the reciters were reciting the mighty Qur'ān before him. His father, al-Malik al-Manṣūr was on that day besieging Syrian Tripoli, so al-Malik al-Ashraf "May God aid him! During this year Tripoli was taken." This became well known about him, and mouths and ears were filled with it.

Only a short time elapsed until the reports came with the conquest of Tripoli at the aforementioned hour, and the matter was just as he said it. This was because of a matter that God Most High revealed to his mind, and informed him that kings have unblemished minds.

The judge Muḥyī al-Dīn Ibn `Abd al-Ẓāhir said while describing al-Malik al-Ashraf and his resplendent merit:

> I never saw nor heard of a quicker mind to understand than his, nor more of an ability to comprehend what the imagination reveals. I have written

---

[242] Each of these characterizations is a pun on the name of the captured city, irregardless of the historical fact (Tyre was not taken by its walls being climbed for example).

[243] More puns, the one on Qal`at al-Rūm referring to Q30:1 "The Romans [*rūm*] have been conquered."

[244] Saladin.

> on his behalf, and had been asked to write, and he read every single written letter, and understood its written bases and ramifications. Indeed, he was more perceptive than I and the other secretaries. He corrected many things, and this was because of good intuition, and empathy, that God's grace bestows upon those whom He wishes.[245]

Al-Malik al-Ashraf became so great in his own mind that towards the end he would write in place of the seal-signature "kh" to represent the first letter of his name.[246] He forbade the Correspondence secretaries from writing to any of the emirs or deputies (using) *al-za`īm*,[247] as he used to say, "There is no leader for the army other than me."

They used to levy a toll at the Jābiya Gate in Damascus upon every camel bearing wheat five dirhams, but when al-Malik al-Ashraf was appointed in the Egyptian homelands a dispensation arrived from him that this toll was abolished. Among the lines of the written command were his handwriting with the signature-pen:

> … to remove this injustice from our subjects, and to encourage both nobles and commoners to pray for us …

So when it was 3 Muḥarram of the year 693 [December 4, 1293] the Sultan al-Malik al-Ashraf rode from the protected Hill Citadel, and crossed over to the Giza bank [of the Nile], heading towards hunting in the al-Buḥayra region. He was intending to go after wild pigeons.

He was accompanied by the emir Badr al-Dīn Baydarā, the deputy sultan in the Egyptian homelands, and the chief Shams al-Dīn Ibn al-Sal`ūs, and most of the emirs. However, when the Sultan arrived at al-Ṭarāna, the chief Ibn al-Sal`ūs separated from him, and headed towards the border-port of Alexandria to gather revenues, and to send gifts of fabrics.

When he entered Alexandria, he found the emir Badr al-Dīn Baydarā's deputy in Alexandria had taken over the merchandise goods, the collection of taxes, and other things. So he wrote to the Sultan with that information, notifying him that he did not find the expected tax-revenues (*iṭlāqāt*) in the border-port.[248]

The Sultan was enraged at this, and summoned the emir Badr al-Dīn Baydarā in the presence of the emirs, and spoke to him harshly, insulting him, and threatening him. Therefore, Baydarā tried to sweet-talk him in answer so that

---

245 This selection does not appear in Ibn `Abd al-Ẓāhir's panegyric concerning al-Ashraf as it now stands. The above statement seems more like a eulogy, and as such, seems difficult to ascribe to Ibn `Abd al-Ẓāhir, who died a year before al-Ashraf (and was probably not close to the circles of power during al-Ashraf's reign).

246 Khalīl.

247 "Leader."

he left the presence of the Sultan safely. He then assembled the senior emirs from his coterie, who were [167] the emir Ḥusām al-Dīn Lājīn "the Lesser," who had been deputy of Damascus, and who he [al-Ashraf] had wanted to kill, but God Most High saved him, the emir Shams al-Dīn Qarāsunqur, both Manṣūrīs, and others. They conspired to fall upon al-Malik al-Ashraf and to kill him.

Al-Malik al-Ashraf had given his senior emirs permission to head to their *iqṭā`* fiefs, and had gone alone with his Khāṣakiyya. During the course of that, the Sultan rode with a small number of his mamluks to hunt close to the royal tent, at the Tarūja campsite.

The emir Sayf al-Dīn Ibn al-Jamaqdār, *amīr jāndār*, told, saying:[249]

> al-Malik al-Ashraf used to order me to say to the emir Badr al-Dīn Baydarā that the Sultan has ordered you to go in this region under the banners leading the emirs, and army. However, when I said that to him, he demonstrated aversion to my face, and then after that said, "Hearing is obeying," while I would see the marks of anger and rage on his face. He said, "Why are you nagging me?" He would give off signs that I could not trust him.
>
> Then I left him, and headed to the armory factory (*zardkhānāh*) then bore it as usual. I went together with my two companions the emir Ṣārim al-Dīn al-Fakhrī and the emir Rukn al-Dīn Baybars, *amīr jāndār*, and we proceeded onwards.

He said:

> I asked the emir Shihāb al-Dīn Aḥmad b. al-Ashall, *amīr shikār*, concerning how the Sultan al-Ashraf was killed at the time when we met after our journey. He said to me: When the royal tent and the army traveled, the news came to the Sultan that there were many birds in Tarūja, so he drove on, and ordered me to ride hard in his wake. He said, "Hurry up! So we can beat the *khāṣakiyya*!"
>
> So I rode hard with him, and we indeed saw many birds, so he dropped many of them with the crossbow (*bunduq*). Then he turned to me saying, "I'm hungry, do you have something I can eat?" I said, "By God, I don't have anything other than a loaf (*raghīf*) and some chicken in my

---

[248] Ibn Ṭūlūn, *Inbā' al-umarā' bi-anbā' al-wuzarā'* (ed. Muḥṣinnā Ḥamd Muḥṣinnā, Beirut: Dār al-Bashā'ir al-Islāmiyya, 1998), pp. 84–6 details how Ibn Sal`ūs was tortured to death after al-Ashraf's assassination.

[249] Compare the account in al-Ṣafadī, *al-Wāfī bi-l-wafayāt* (Beirut: Dār Iḥya al-Turāth al-`Arabī, n.d.), xiii, pp. 250–1.

knapsack (*ṣūlaq*)[250] which I was saving for myself." He said, "Give it to me," so I did, whereupon he ate it all.

Then he said to me "Hold my horse, so I can dismount to piss, because I have been stretched out with him." I said, "This isn't a sultan's trick! He is riding a stallion while I am riding a nag (*ḥujra*), so the two are not compatible!" He said to me "Then you get down, and ride behind me until I get down."

He said:

Therefore, I got down, and gave him the reins of my horse, and then I held him, and rode him [the horse] behind him. Then he got down, sat on his haunches and pissed. He stayed fiddling with his penis, and joking with me, then rose, rode his stallion, holding on to my horse, so that I rode too. While he and I were conversing, all of a sudden there was dust rising, coming towards us.

The Sultan said, "Find out for me what is the meaning of that dust, what is it? Therefore, I rode hard—and all of a sudden, I met the emir Badr al-Dīn Baydarā and the emirs. So I asked them about the reason for their coming, but they did not speak to me, nor answered me at all or even turned to me. They continued riding hard until they came close to the Sultan, and the emir Badr al-Dīn Baydarā was the first to strike, cutting his hand off with a sword.

Then he struck him a second time on the shoulder blade. The emir Ḥusām al-Dīn Lājīn came after him, and said "O Baydarā, whoever wants the rule of Egypt and Syria, let him strike like this!" Then he struck the Sultan on his shoulder, so it severed it, and he fell to the ground.

Bahādur, head of the guard, came, and hating what he did, pierced his buttocks with his sword, and leaned on it until it cut up to [168] his gullet. The rest of the emirs, such as Qarāsunqur, Aqsunqur al-Ḥusāmī, Nogai, Muḥammad Khawājā, Ṭurunṭāy *al-sāqī*, Alṭinbughā, head of the guard, and those emirs who joined in with them, attended him, each one after the other doing an evil action.

Thus, they revealed what was in their hearts. This tale proves that the Sultan had separated himself from his mamluks, and none other than Shihāb al-Dīn *amīr shikār* al-Jākī were with him.

[250] The sense seems to indicate this meaning—described as one of the mamluk's implements, worn dangling from the sword-belt on the right side: al-Qalqashandī, *Ṣubḥ*, iv, pp. 41–2.

It is said that the emir Badr al-Dīn Baydarā and those emirs who were with him, when they assembled to kill al-Malik al-Ashraf, the Sultan headed off leading a small group of his Khāṣakiyya mamluks. So then the emir Badr al-Dīn Baydarā seized the opportunity, and rode, accompanied by the emir Ḥusām al-Dīn Lājīn, the emir Qarāsunqur, the emir Bahādur, head of the guard, the emir Aqsunqur al-Ḥusāmī, the emir Nogai, the emir Muḥammad Khawājā, the emir Ṭurunṭāy *al-sāqī*, the emir Alṭinbughā, and those who joined in with them.

They headed towards the Sultan; there was a ford between then, so they crossed it, whereupon when al-Malik al-Ashraf saw them, he said to one of his mamluks "Ride, and find out what is going on with those! If it is good, then you come back, with them a few a time; if it is bad, then you ride, leave them, and tell me what they are up to." When the mamluk rode to them, he turned out to be one of those who had conspired with them from the royal mamluks.

Therefore, he told them what the Sultan said to him, and he said, "You won't find a better time than this!" So he escorted them a few at a time. When they had neared him [the Sultan], and eye met eye, the emir Badr al-Dīn Baydarā approached him. Then the Sultan said to him "Is it good, Baydarā?" However, he said, "No, we are up to no good," and then unsheathed his sword, and struck him, but he warded it off with his hand, so it just struck a glancing blow.

It is said that his hand flew aside because of this back thrust, so the emir Ḥusām al-Dīn Lājīn cursed him, and struck the Sultan with a blow that severed his shoulder. Then swords took him from every angle, cutting him up, until he became a pile of meat.

The Sultan al-Malik al-Ashraf Ṣalāḥ al-Dīn Khalīl, may God Most High have mercy upon him, was killed Saturday 10 Muḥarram of the year 693 [December 11, 1293] this year. It is also said that he was killed on 12 Muḥarram [December 13, 1293].

When he was killed, he remained laying in the place in which he was killed for two days, then the emir `Izz al-Dīn Aydimur al-`Ajamī, the governor of Tarūja, came together with its people, and bore al-Malik al-Ashraf from the place in which he was killed to Tarūja. They washed him in the baths, then wrapped him, placed him in a coffin, and put him in the Islamic Treasury (*bayt al-māl*) at the governor's residence in Tarūja.

This was until the emir Sa`d al-Dīn Kajbā al-Nāṣirī came from protected Cairo, then transported him in his coffin to his mausoleum, which he had begun constructing outside of protected Cairo close to the Shrine of Lady Nafīsa, may God be pleased with her, known as al-Ashrafiyya. So he was buried there, and that was at dawn on Friday [169] 22 Ṣafar [January 22, 1294] of the months of this year.

The period of his sultanate was three years, two months and four days. Al-Malik al-Ashraf left no male child; but left two daughters. His wife, their mother, was Ardakīn, daughter of the emir Sayf al-Dīn Nogai, and his brother the Sultan al-Malik al-Nāṣir Muḥammad son of Qalāwūn inherited from him together with them, and Dār Mukhtār al-Jawharī, al-Malik al-Ashraf's guardian. The hall in the Hill Citadel known as al-Ashrafiyya is ascribed to him, and God knows best.

[*Baydarā became Sultan, but only lasted for one day before he himself was killed.*]

GLOSSARY

afram toothless.
amīr/emir one who has command over a set number of troops.
amīr akhūr armour bearer to the Sultan, in charge of the Sultan's horses.
amīr jāndār commander of the guard.
amīr majlis in charge of medical affairs and appointments.
amīr shikār in charge of hunting, especially birds.
amīr silāh armorer, in charge of the weaponry.
ashqar ruddy, most probably referring to Central Asian complexion.
atābak/atabeg senior figure in the army, sometimes an emeritus, a mentor or a patron.
a`sar=aysar left-handed (also unlucky).
basmala the formula "There is no god but God, and Muḥammad is God's Messenger," which precedes any action or writing that a Muslim does.
bayn al-qaṣrayn "between the two palaces" a location in Cairo.
bunduq/dār probably in charge of crossbows and heavy weaponry.[1]
dawla period, dynasty, rule.
dihlīz lit. a vestibule, but used for the royal tent when the Sultan was traveling.
firmān a royal edict.
ghulām/ghilmān lit. youths, but used for young or junior soldiers, and for male slaves.
al-ḥājj one who has performed the mandated Muslim pilgrimage to Mecca.
ḥalqa free-born troops (as opposed to mamluks).
ḥarbdār presumably in charge of spears.
hijra the immigration of Muḥammad and the Muslims from Mecca to Medina, the starting point for the Muslim (lunar) calendar.
Ilchiyya Mongol ambassadors.
iqṭā` fiefs given out on a temporary basis.
jāndār the guard.
jāshnakīr the taster.
jeter the royal umbrella shading Mongol dignitaries.

1 See Nicholle, glossary; also al-Qalqashandī, *Ṣubḥ*, v, 431, vii, 142.

jūkandār batman for the popular game, similar to polo.
khāṣakiyya the personal guard of an emir.
al-khayyāṭ the tailor.
khazindār/khāzindār the treasurer.
mafārida uncertain, perhaps the single volunteers in the Mamluk army.
maḥmal the camel-borne palanquin that was the center of the pilgrimage journey.
mamlūk/mamālīk lit. owned; military slaves from a range of ethnicities, but usually during the thirteenth century from Central Asia.
masāḥ *mihmandār* in charge of hospitality.
naqīb a title below that of deputy or governor.
qarāghūl the road guard.
quriltāy the Mongol general council.
sāqī cup bearer.
shadd al-dawāwīn Chancelleries Supervisor, in charge of the finances.
silāḥdār armor-bearer.
sūra a chapter of the Qur'ān.
tamaghāt the red seals which verified a Mongol official document.
ṭawīl tall.
tawqī` a rescript.
al-ṭayyār the flyer (it is not clear why Badr al-Dīn Bīlīk acquired this nickname).
zardkāsh armory engineer.

BIBLIOGRAPHY

Primary sources

al-`Aynī, Badr al-Dīn Maḥmūd (d. 855/1451), *`Iqd al-jumān fi tā'rīkh ahl al-zamān*. Ed. Muḥammad Muḥammad Amīn, Cairo: al-Ha'ya al-`Āmma li-l-Kitāb, 1988 (3 vols).

al-Bayhaqī, Aḥmad b. al-Ḥusayn (d. 458/1066), *Faḍā'il al-awqāt*. Ed. Khilāf Maḥmūd `Abd al-Samī`, Beirut: Dār al-Kutub al-`Ilmiyya, 1997.

al-Dārimī, `Abdallāh b. `Abd al-Raḥmān (d. 255/869), *Sunan al-Dārimī.* Ed. Muṣṭafā Dīb al-Baghā, Damascus: Dār al-Qalam, 1996 (2 vols).

al-Dawādār, Baybars al-Mansuri (d. 725/1325), *Zubdat al-fikra fi tā'rīkh al-hijra*. Ed. D.S. Richards, Berlin: Orient Institute, 1998.

Droge, A.J. (trans.), *The Qur'ān: A New Annotated Translation*. Sheffield: Equinox, 2013.

Ibn `Abd al-Ẓāhir, `Alī b. Muḥammad b. `Abdallāh (d. 691/1292), *Tashrīf al-ayyām wa-l-`uṣūr fi sīrat al-malik al-Manṣūr*. Ed. Murād Kāmil and `Alī al-Naggār, Cairo: Wizārat al-Thaqāfa, 1961.

Ibn al-Furāt, Muḥammad b. `Abd al-Raḥīm (d. 808/1405), *Tā'rīkh al-duwwal wa-l-mulūk*. Ed. Constantine Zurayk, Baṣra: Dār al-Ṭibā`a al-Ḥadītha, 1939. (vols. 7–8). Part. trans. M.C. and U. Lyons, *Ayyubids, Mamluks and Crusaders: Selections from the* Tā'rīkh al-duwal wa-l-mulūk *of Ibn al-Furāt*. Cambridge: Heffer, 1971 (2 vols).

Ps.-Ibn al-Fuwaṭī, *Kitāb al-ḥawādith*. Ed. Bashshār `Awwāḍ Ma`rūf and `Imād `Abd al-Salām Rā'ūf, Beirut: Dār al-Gharb al-Islāmī, 1997.

Ibn Ḥajar al-`Asqalānī, Aḥmad b. `Alī (d. 852/1448–9), *Inbā' al-ghumar bi-abnā' al-`umar fī al-tā'rīkh*. Ed. Muḥammad `Abd al-Mu`īd Khān, Beirut: Dār al-Kutub al-`Ilmiyya, 1986 (reprint: Hyderabad ed.) (5 vols).

_______, *Raf` al-iṣr `an quḍāt Miṣr*. Ed. `Alī Muḥammad `Umar, Cairo: Khānjī, 1998.

Ibn Ḥajar al-Haytamī (d. 973/1565), *al-Iḍāḥ wa-l-bayān li-mā jā' fi laylatay al-raghā'ib wa-l-nisf min Sha`bān*. Damascus: Dār al-Hudā, 2010.

Ibn Iyyās, Muḥammad b. Aḥmad (d. 931/1524), *Badā'i` al-zuhūr fī waqā'i` al-duhūr*. Ed. Muḥammad Muṣṭafā, Beirut: Franz Steiner, 1960–74 (8 vols).

Ibn al-Jazarī, Muḥammad b. Ibrāhīm b. Abī Bakr (d. 738/1337–8), *Tā'rīkh ḥawādith al-zamān wa-anbā'hi wa-wafayāt al-akābir al-a`yān min abnā'ihi*. Ed. `Umar `Abd al-Salām Tadmurī, Beirut: al-Maktaba al-`Aṣriyya, 1998 (3 vols).

Ibn al-Mibrad al-Maqdisī, Jamāl al-Dīn Yūsuf b. Ḥasan Ibn `Abd al-Hādī, (d. 909/1503–4), *Thimār al-maqāṣid fī dhikr al-masājid. Les Mosquées de Damas*. Ed. As`ad Talas, Damascus: Institut Français de Damas, 1943.

Ibn al-Mujāwir, Yūsuf b. Ya`qūb (d. 691/1291–2), *Tā'rīkh al-mustabṣir: Ṣifat bilād al-Yaman wa-Makka wa-ba`ḍ al-Ḥijāz*. Ed. Oscar Lefevrin, Beirut: Manshūrāt al-Madina, 1986 (reprint).

Ibn Ṭūlūn, Muḥammad b. `Alī (d. 952/1545–6), *Inbā' al-umarā' bi-anbā' al-wuzarā'*. Ed. Muḥṣinnā Ḥamd Muḥṣinnā, Beirut: Dār al-Bashā'ir al-Islāmiyya, 1998.

Kāshānī, Abū al-Qāsim `Abdallāh (fl. *ca.* 700/1300), *`Arā'is al-javāhir ve-nafā'is al-aṭā'yib*. Ed. Iraj Afshar, Tehran: Mā`ī, 2007.

Kartlis Tskhovreba: History of Georgia. Ed. Roin Metroveli, trans. Stephen Jones, Tbilisi: Artanuji, 2014.

al-Maqrīzī, Aḥmad b. `Alī b. `Abd al-Qādir (d. 845/1441–2), *al-Mawā`iẓ wa-l-i`tibār fi dhikr al-khiṭāṭ wa-l-āthar*. Ed. Aymān Fū'ād Sayyid, London: Mu'assasat al-Furqān, 2013 (7 vols).

_______, *al-Muqaffā al-kabīr*. Ed. Muḥammad `Uthmān, Beirut: Dār al-Kutub al-`Ilmiyya, 2010 (6 vols).

_______, *Rasā'il al-Maqrīzī*. Eds. Ramaḍān al-Badrī and Aḥmad Muṣṭafā Qāsim, Cairo: Dār al-Ḥadīth, 2006.

_______, *al-Sulūk li-ma`rifat duwwal al-mulūk*. Ed. Muḥammad `Abd al-Qādir `Aṭā', Beirut: Dār al-Kutub al-`Ilmiyya, 1997 (8 vols).

Nemoy, Leon (trans.), *Karaite Anthology*. New Haven: Yale University Press, 1952.

al-Nuwayrī, Shihāb al-Dīn Aḥmad b. `Abd al-Wahhāb (d. 723/1323–4), *Nihāyat al-arab fi funūn al-adab*. Eds. Mufīd Qāmiḥa and Ḥasan Nūr al-Dīn, Beirut: Dār al-Kutub al-`Ilmiyya, 2004 (31 vols).

Pachymeres, Gregorios (d. *ca.* 1310), *Relations Historiques*. Ed. Albert Failler, Paris: Institut Français d'Etudes Byzantines, 1984 (Vols I–II).

al-Qalqashandī, Aḥmad b. `Alī (d. 821/1418), *Ṣubḥ al-a`shā fi ṣinā`at al-inshā'*. Ed. Muḥammad Ḥusayn Shams al-Dīn, Beirut: Dār al-Kutub al-`Ilmiyya, 2012 (15 vols).

al-Ṣafadī, Ṣalāḥ al-Dīn Khalīl b. Aybak (d. 764/1363), *al-Wāfī bi-l-wafayāt*. Eds. Aḥmad al-Arnawā'ūṭ and Turkī Muṣṭafā, Beirut: Dār Iḥya al-Turāth al-`Arabī, n.d. (29 vols).

al-Sakhāwī, Muḥammad b. `Abd al-Raḥmān (d. d. 902/1496–7), *al-Ḍaw' al-lāmi` li-ahl al-qarn al-tāsi`*. Beirut: Dār al-Jīl, 1992 (6 vols).

al-Samhūdī, `Alī b. Abdallāh (d. 911/1506), *Wafā' al-wafā' bi-aḥwāl dār al-muṣṭafā*. Ed. Muḥammad Muḥyī al-Dīn `Abd al-Majīd, Mecca: Dār al-Kutub al-`Ilmiyya, 1984 (3 vols).

al-Shīrāzī, Quṭb al-Dīn Maḥmūd (d. 710/1310–11), *Akhbār-i Mughulān dar anbāneh-yi Quṭb*. Ed. Iraj Afshar, Qum: Maktabat Ayatullāh al-`Uẓmā al-Mar`ashī, 2010. Trans. George Lane, *The Mongols in Iran: Qutb al-Din Shirazi's* Akhbar-i Moghulan. London: Routledge, 2018.

al-Tirmidhī, Muḥammad b. `Īsā (d. 279/892), *al-Jāmi` al-ṣaḥīḥ*. Ed. `Abd al-Wahhāb `Abd al-Laṭīf, Beirut: Dār al-Fikr, n.d. (5 vols).

al-`Ulaymī al-Maqdisī, Mujīr al-Dīn `Abd al-Raḥmān b. Muḥammad b. `Abd al-Raḥmān al-Ḥanbalī (d. 928/1522), *al-Uns al-jalil fi tā'rikh al-Quds wa-l-Khalil*. `Amman: Muhtasib, 1973.

Vantini, Giovanni (trans.), *Oriental Sources Concerning Nubia*. Heidelberg and Warsaw: Polish Academy of Sciences, 1975.

Yāqūt b. `Abdallāh al-Ḥamāwī (d. 628/1229), *Mu`jam al-buldān*. Beirut: Dār Ṣādir, n.d. (6 vols).

al-Yūnīnī, Quṭb al-Dīn Mūsā b. Muḥammad (d. 726/1326), *Dhayl Mira'at al-zamān*. Ed. Ḥamza `Abbās, Abu Dhabi: Abu Dhabi Center for Heritage and Culture, 2007. Trans. Antranig Melkonian, *Die Jahre 1287–1291 in der Chronik Yūnīnīs*. Freiburg im Breisgau: Becksman, 1978.

Zettersteen, K. (Ed.), *Beiträge zur Geschichte der Mamlūkensultane in den Jahre 690–741: Nach arabische Handschriften*. Leiden: E.J. Brill, 1919 (= Anonymous).

Secondary sources

Agius, Dionisius, *Classic Ships of Islam: From Mesopotamia to the Indian Ocean*. Leiden: E.J. Brill, 2008.

Ambraseys, Nicholas, *Earthquakes in the Mediterranean and Middle East: A Multidisciplinary Study of Seismicity up to 1900*. Cambridge: Cambridge University Press, 2009.

Amitai, Reuven, "Foot Soldiers, Militiamen and Volunteers in Mamluk Syria," in Chase Robinson (Ed.), *Texts, Documents and Artefacts: Islamic Studies in Honour of D.S. Richards*. Leiden: E.J. Brill, 2003, pp. 233–249.

________ (Ed.), *Holy War and Rapproachment: Studies in the Relations between the Mamluk Sultanate and the Mongol Ilkhanate (1260–1335)*. Turnhout: Brepols, 2013.

Behrens-Abouseif, Doris, *The Book in Mamluk Egypt and Syria (1250–1517)*. Leiden: E.J. Brill, 2018.

Bűssow-Schmitz, Sarah, *Die Beduinen der Mamluken: Beduinen in politischen Leben Agyptens im 8./14. Jahrhundert*. Wiesbaden: Dr. Ludwig Reichart Verlag, 2016.

Dozy, Reinhart, *Dictionnaire détaillé des noms des vêtements chez les Arabes*. Beirut: Librarie du Liban, 1843 (reprint).

*Encyclopaedia Islamica*². Eds. C.E. Bosworth, *et alia*. Leiden: E.J. Brill, 1960–2000.

Guo, Li, *Sports as Performance: The Qabaq-game and Celebratory Rites in Mamluk Cairo*. Berlin: EB Verlag, 2013.

Hofer, Nathan, *The Popularisation of Sufism in Ayyubid and Mamluk Egypt 1173–1325*. Edinburgh: Edinburgh University Press, 2015.

Holt, P.M., *Early Mamluk Diplomacy (1260–1290): Treaties of Baybars and Qalawun with Christian Rulers*. Leiden: E.J. Brill, 1995.

Humphreys, R. Stephen, *From Saladin to the Mongols*. Albany: SUNY Press, 1977.

Irwin, Robert, "Tribal Feuding and Mamluk Factions in Medieval Syria," in Chase Robinson (Ed.), *Texts, Documents and Artefacts: Islamic Studies in Honour of D.S. Richards*. Leiden: E.J. Brill, 2003, pp. 251–264.

Jackson, Peter, *The Mongols and the Islamic World: From Conquest to Conversion*. New Haven: Yale University Press, 2017.

James, David, *Manuscripts of the Holy Qur'ān from the Mamlūk Era*. London: Alexandria Press, 1999/Riyāḍ: King Feisal Center for Research and Islamic Studies, n.d.

Mazor, Amir, *The Rise and Fall of a Muslim Regiment: The Mansuriyya in the first Mamluk Sultanate*. Bonn: Bonn University Press, 2015.

al-Nāyil, `Abdallāh b. Muḥammad, *Ṣinā`at al-asilaḥa al-thaqīla wa-l-nāriyya fī al-dawla al-Mamlūkiyya (648–923/1250–1517)*. Riyad: al-Jami`a al-Tā'rīkhiyya al-Sa`ūdiyya, 2006.

Nicolle, David, *Arms & Armour of the Crusading Era 1050–1350: Islam, Eastern Europe and Asia*. London: Greenhill, 1999.

Northrup, Linda, *From Slave to Sultan: The Career of al-Manṣūr Qalāwūn and the Consolidation of Mamluk Rule in Egypt and Syria (678–689 A.H./1279–1290 A.D.)*. Stuttgart: Franz Steiner, 1998.

Qablān, Usāma, *Shī`at Kasrawān wa-l-ḥamalāt al-Mamlūkiyya: Dirāsa fī rasā'il Ibn Taymiyya*. Beirut: Dār al-Wafā', 2018.

Rabbat, Nasser, *The Citadel of Cairo: A New Interpretation of Royal Mamluk Architecture*. Leiden: E.J. Brill, 1995.

Trapp, Erich, *Prosopographisches Lexikon der Palaiologen Zeit*. Vienna: Verlag der Österreichischen Akademie der Wissenschaften, 1976–96. (CD-Rom version).

Vallet, Éric, "Diplomatic Networks of Rasulid Yemenin Egypt (seventh/thirteenth to Early Ninth/Fifteenth Centuries)," in Bauden Frédéric and Malika Dekkiche (Eds.), *Mamluk Cairo, a Crossroads for Embassies*. Leiden: E.J. Brill, 2019, pp. 581–603.

Ziadeh, Nicola, *Damascus under the Mamluks*. Norman: University of Oklahoma Press, 1964.

INDEX

Emirs' names are arranged according to their honorific, as this element of their name is the one that is the most consistently given in the sources. In a number of cases it is not known what their personal names were, and some names with the same honorifics whose personal names are unknown may overlap. Checking other sources such as al-Ṣafadī and al-Maqrīzī has clarified some ambiguities, but others remain. Ruling monarchs have been placed in **bold** to highlight their significance, as sometimes the name under which they are listed is not the one by which they were popularly known.

For Product Safety Concerns and Information please contact our EU
representative GPSR@taylorandfrancis.com
Taylor & Francis Verlag GmbH, Kaufingerstraße 24, 80331 München, Germany

www.ingramcontent.com/pod-product-compliance
Lightning Source LLC
Chambersburg PA
CBHW071449110726
47908CB00003B/566
* 9 7 8 1 0 3 2 2 3 7 5 6 5 *